Schilder's Struggle for the Unity of the Church

Schilder's Struggle for the Unity of the Church

by

Rudolf van Reest

Translated by Theodore Plantinga

INHERITANCE PUBLICATIONS
NEERLANDIA, ALBERTA, CANADA
PELLA, IOWA, U.S.A.

Library and Archives Canada Cataloguing in Publication
  Reest, Rudolf van, 1897-1979
    Schilder's struggle for the unity of the church / by Rudolf van Reest ; translated by Theodore Plantinga.
  Translation of: Opdat zij allen een zijn.
  Includes bibliographical references and index.
  ISBN 1-894666-79-8
    1. Schilder, K. (Klaas), 1890-1952. 2. Gereformeerde Kerken in Nederland—History. 3. Reformed Church—Netherlands—History—20th century. I. Plantinga, Theodore, 1947- II. Title.
  BX9479.S3R413   2006   284'.2'092   C2006-900761-6

Library of Congress Cataloging-in-Publication Data
Reest, Rudolf van, 1897-1979.
  [Opdat zij allen een zijn. English] Schilder's struggle for the unity of the church / by Rudolf van Reest; translated by Theodore Plantinga.
      p. cm.
  Includes bibliographical references and index.
  ISBN 1-894666-79-8 (pbk.)
    1. Schilder, K. (Klaas), 1890-1952. 2. Reformed Church—Netherlands—History—20th century. 3. World War, 1939-1945—Religious aspects—Reformed Church. 4. Gereformeerde Kerken in Nederland (Vrijgemaakt)—History—20th century. 5. Reformed Church—United States—History—20th century. I. Title.
  BX9479.S35R44 2006
  284'.2092—dc22
  [B]
                                                              2005037053

Translated by Theodore Plantinga
Original published in Dutch as *Opdat zij allen één zijn 1 & 2*, (1962-1963) by Oosterbaan & Le Cointre, Goes, The Netherlands.

2nd Printing (paperback) 2006

All rights reserved © 1990, 2006, by Inheritance Publications
Box 154, Neerlandia, Alberta Canada T0G 1R0
Tel. (780) 674 3949
Web site: http://www.telusplanet.net/public/inhpubl/webip/ip.htm
E-Mail inhpubl@telusplanet.net

Published simultaneously in U.S.A. by Inheritance Publications
Box 366, Pella, Iowa 50219

Available in Australia from Inheritance Publications
Box 1122, Kelmscott, W.A. 6111 Tel. & Fax (089) 390 4940

Printed in Canada

Contents

Translator's Preface 7

Introduction 13

Chapter 1 Davidic or Solomonic? 19

Chapter 2 Woe to You, My People! 85

Chapter 3 Occupied Possession 213

Chapter 4 That They May All Be One 314

Appendix I: North American Developments 375
    by Theodore Plantinga

Appendix II: The Stocking is Finished 395
    by Klaas Schilder
    Response by Herman Hoeksema 401

Appendix III: Your Ecumenical Task 404
    by Klaas Schilder

Appendix IV: Church Polity in 1886 and 1944 415
    by C. Veenhof

Index 420

Translator's Preface

When Rudolf van Reest wrote his account of the upheaval in the Reformed Churches of the Netherlands, he still felt very close to his dear friend Klaas Schilder (who had died some years before) and to the battles of the 1930s and 1940s. As we read his account today, it is important to remember that its author was essentially a journalist and literary man who also offered his reading public a number of novels, biographies, books of commentary on the contemporary scene, and even a multi-volume survey of Dutch literature. His love of literature and poetry comes through in his Schilder book, for he wrote it suggestively, injecting into his text more in the way of feelings, allusions, and a personal slant than we generally expect to find in books about church matters.

Because of these features in his writing style, it is not always easy to discern what he is driving at. In connection with specific episodes he deals with, I had to seek additional information about the circumstances. In many cases, I have added material I deemed helpful for understanding the text: in a few cases I placed it directly in the text, but in most cases I relegated it to a translator's footnote. One helpful piece of information which readers should have available right from the outset is that "Rudolf van Reest" is a pen name. The author's real name is K. C. van Spronsen (1897-1979).

In my efforts to get behind suggestive (and sometimes incomplete) comments in order to flesh them out and make the text accessible to readers who are far removed from the events in both space and time, I was assisted especially by two people who deserve hearty thanks for their fine contribution to this project — Dr. Karel Deddens (formerly of the Theological College of the Canadian Reformed Churches) and Dr. Harry Van Dyke (Redeemer College). They both worked through the entire translation carefully, made numerous useful suggestions, and contributed material to be included in the translator's notes. Several other people also read early drafts and/or made helpful suggestions regarding English wording and translator's notes: Dr. Jacobus De Jong (the Theological College), Dr. Jelle Faber (former principal of the Theological College), Roelof Janssen (the publisher), and Harry Zekveld (one of my students at Redeemer College).

The book abounds in references to persons, places, churches, organizations, and so forth. Many of those references have been made more complete than they are in the Dutch original, e.g. by adding a first name or initial not present in the Dutch. In some cases I have supplemented the original text by providing a slightly amplified account of the matter being discussed, an account drawn from another book by Van Reest[1] or some standard treatment of the events of 1944.[2] Although I was not able to consult the author himself regarding such supplementation, I did discuss the subject matter of the book with various people who know much more about it than I do and could therefore advise me on such matters.

The text contains numerous references to publications written in Dutch periodicals, books, and brochures. Those that function in the story have been given an English name to make the text easy to read for those who know no Dutch. I do not mean to create the impression that such publications were either written in English or translated into English. In the notes I have made some additional references to works available only in Dutch. Such titles could be left untranslated since those who do not read Dutch will not be able to look up these references anyway.

In one area I found the book incomplete, namely, the impact of Schilder and the church struggle of the 1940s on the North American church scene. Some material could be added in translator's footnotes, of course, but when it came to the question of the relationship between Schilder and the Protestant Reformed Churches (a matter of considerable interest to Van Reest), something more substantial than a footnote was needed. Therefore I have added an appendix on the North American developments, which is followed by a second appendix containing Schilder's final statement on this matter, together with a brief response to Schilder by Herman Hoeksema. A third appendix is Schilder's speech "Your Ecumenical Task," which was translated into English some time ago but is not readily available. A final appen-

---

[1] He wrote quite a number of books. The ones on which I have drawn are *De braambos,* two volumes (Goes: Oosterbaan & Le Cointre, 1969-70); *Van kust tot kust* (Oosterbaan, 1948); and *Terugzien na vijfentwintig jaren* (Oosterbaan, 1972).

[2] A helpful source for the wartime period is *K. Schilder als gevangene en onderduiker,* by W. G. de Vries (Groningen: De Vuurbaak, 1977), which presents selections from letters Schilder wrote while in prison and in hiding, along with some explanation and commentary. I have also drawn on *Gedenkt uw voorgangeren,* by C. Veenhof *et al.,* a memorial volume published by Oosterbaan shortly after Schilder's death in 1952.

dix, drawn from a brochure by Rev. C. Veenhof, deals with church-order parallels between 1886 and 1944.

In writing the appendix on North American developments, I not only undertook substantial reading (and rereading) of relevant works but also talked with a number of people who participated in those events or could draw on non-published knowledge. Therefore I would like to thank the following individuals for sharing their recollections and impressions with me: Rev. Henry R. De Bolster, Dr. Jelle Faber, Rev. Jerome Julien, Rev. Edward Knott, Dr. Remkes Kooistra, Rev. John H. Piersma, Rev. Lubbertus Selles, Mr. William Smouter (a nephew of Van Reest), Rev. Gijsbertus van Dooren, Rev. James Van Weelden, and Dr. Henry Zwaanstra.

To make the book more usable, I have also added an index — but one that is restricted to main themes and to people, organizations and periodicals that played a role in the story. The index is not intended to be exhaustive: for example, no attempt has been made to index the various phases through which the church struggle moved. The sequence in which the story is told is roughly chronological.

At various points the author makes comments to the effect that we *now* see that such-and-such is the case. Readers should bear in mind that *his* "now" refers to the time when the book was being written (it came out in two volumes in 1962 and 1963). When there are temporal references to the current situation in *translator's notes,* they refer to the time of translation, i.e. 1989-90.

This difference in temporal reference is a good reason for carefully distinguishing the input of the translator (and the people mentioned above who assisted and advised him) from the comments of the author. The translator's notes are intended to be factual and informational. As one born *after* the deplorable events of 1944, I do not feel I am in a position to correct Van Reest except on occasional matters of fact, where I have made small changes without announcement. Only in the appendix on North American developments have I taken the liberty of disagreeing openly with Van Reest regarding certain points in the main story he tells.

The feeling that pervades his account has been left undisturbed as much as possible. In other words, I have resisted the impulse to moderate the book in terms of the feelings that come through, even though I realized that some people might be offended. I believe Van Reest has told his story honestly; yet I'm sure no careful reader will deny that it is also one-sided in some respects. The author himself was well aware of how much an author's artistry contributes to the shaping of his story. In the introduction to his survey of Dutch literature he affirms that a poet is not like a mirror, reflecting in a neutral way what stands before it. "There are no neutral or objective poets or writers," he tells us. "Behind every work of art stands the *person*." Moreover, every poet and writer reflects his own time.[3] When Van Reest utters these statements, he does not make an exception for his own writings.

Readers of this book who have no personal recollections dating back to the 1940s should bear in mind that for Schilder and many others, the struggle against illegitimate Nazi authority in the occupied Netherlands could not be entirely separated from the struggle against illegitimate authority in an increasingly synodocratic church. The articles Schilder published in *The Reformation* after the German takeover in May of 1940 have been reprinted in a book entitled *Occupied Possession* (Dutch: *Bezet bezit*). The country was under an illegal and illegitimate occupation, and her lawful sovereign (Queen Wilhelmina, who spent the occupation years in England) was unable to exercise her lawful rights.

It is significant that Schilder also used the phrase "occupied possession" in relation to the Theological School in Kampen (Oudestraat), from which he had been banished in 1944 by the same synod that deposed him as a minister. The liberated Reformed Churches soon established their own Theological School in Kampen (on the Broederweg), which they regarded as a legitimate continuation of the School on the Oudestraat. The casual observer might sum up the situation by saying that the liberated churches had established a new seminary, which happened also to be located in Kampen (on the Broederweg), but Schilder and company maintained that they were continuing the original seminary, just as they continued the original churches. The School on the Oudestraat was "bezet bezit" (an occupied possession). The School on the Broederweg celebrated its hundredth anniversary in 1954 as the legitimate continuation of the School established by the Secession churches back in 1854!

Once we see this connection between the different contexts in which the term "occupied possession" is used, we begin to understand why so much of Van Reest's story revolves around World War II and the occupation of the Netherlands. Schilder, as a theologian

---

[3] See *Dichterschap en Profetie*, Vol. 1 (Oosterbaan, 1953), pp. 5-6.

and church leader deeply committed to *Reformed* thinking, did not regard divine authority as limited to church life: it also extended to government and public affairs. Therefore it was incumbent upon believers to stand up for what God demanded not just in the church but also in relation to the state, so that the rights of the Lord would be respected in both domains. To be liberated (in both church and state) would mean that one was free to obey and serve the Lord. But many had to pay a high price as they sought liberation.

The recognition of this larger canvas on which Schilder (his name means painter) exercised his talents leads me to a second observation which, I hope, will be of some help to those who know him only from afar. Schilder is sometimes dismissed as a man entangled in small quarrels, a man who wasted enormous talents on relatively trivial matters. But Van Reest's book demonstrates the truth of what Prof. J. Kamphuis once said about Schilder, namely, that he concentrated on what for him was the main issue *(hoofdzaak)*. Kamphuis continued: "In Schilder, therefore, we often find a deliberate disregard of certain matters in order to be able to focus on the main issue. His objectives were very broad, but he concentrated on the points that were threatened."[4]

And so there are two elements to be kept in mind as we see Schilder repeatedly taking a stand. First, there is "the main issue" (Schilder did not have time for trivialities). Second, there is the concrete, specific set of circumstances in the context of which something fundamental was at stake. Those circumstances may be hard to reconstruct and understand today, many decades later; this is the reason why a treatment of Schilder needs a historical setting. The reader who succeeds in holding these two (the set of circumstances and the main issue) in his mind as he works through this book (and perhaps through some of Schilder's own writings as well) will surely be enriched in his own Reformed understanding of our task in this world.

Theodore Plantinga
Redeemer College
Ancaster, Ontario

---

[4] In an interview with G. Puchinger, published in the latter's *Is de gereformeerde wereld veranderd?* (Delft: W. D. Meinema, 1966), p. 218. Kamphuis has also dealt with this theme in "Concentratie op wat hoofdzaak is," in *Verkenningen,* Vol. 2: *Opstellen over de Kerk en haar geschiedenis* (Oosterbaan, 1964), pp. 169-189.

20e JAARGANG   No. 46   6 JULI 1945

DE REFORMATIE
WEEKBLAD TOT ONTWIKKELING VAN HET GEREFORMEERDE LEVEN

DIE UWE JEUGD VERNIEUWT ALS EENS AARENDS   PSALM 103:5

Onder redactie van Prof. Dr K. SCHILDER

Alle stukken bestemd voor de Redactie zende men aan: Prof. Dr K. SCHILDER, Vloeddijk 14, Kampen	Uitgevers: OOSTERBAAN & LE COINTRE N.V., Goes Telef. No. 2424 — Postrekening No. 58000	Abonnement: ƒ 4.— per half jaar bij vooruitbetaling. Voor het Buitenland en Ned. Indië ƒ 10.— per jaar. Advertentiën: 40 ct. p. regel. Losse nummers 20 ct.

INHOUD: Weerkeer — Hoofdartikel: Woordgezag of Wetenschapsdwang I — Uit de Schrift: Het apotheotisch draven en thuiles — Kerkelijk leven: De dolemtie moreel veroordeeld — Gelezen/Hoorend — Een zuivere gebod — Brieven aan een jongeren tijdgenoot — Parnchoure — Kerknieuws — Aan onze lezers.

WEERKEER

Toen met behulp van verraad van N.S.B.-ers, onder wie zes niet geschorst voormalig gereformeerd Haagsch predikant, duitsche hand de perssen van "De Reformatie" stil legde na een nummer van 16 Augustus 1940, den uitgever beroofde van zijn ns 10 Mei 1940 merkwaardig snel uitgedijde abonnementslijsten, en den redacteur achter en celdeur stopte, die met de letter „P" voorzien was, en derhalve hem als „passant", waarschijnlijk naar een concentratiekamp, bleek aan te merken, ontbrak aan eerstgenoemde de gelegenheid, de lezers in te lichten over de oorzaak van het verdwijnen van ons blad, en over onze overtuiging, dat het te eeniger tijd in eenigen vorm zou wederkeeren.

Die tijd is langer uitgebleven, dan wij dachten. Maar door de groote genade Gods is hij er eindelijk. Wij zeggen Hem daarvoor van harte dank.

Die dank wordt niet verminderd door het feit, dat in de bijkans vijf jaren, die ons van uitgever en lezers verre hebben gehouden, de noodzaak is ontstaan, den „vorm", waarin ons blad thans opnieuw verschijnt, heel anders te doen zijn dan daar achter die deur met de letter P ooit is gedroomd. Op het verrand, waarop zooeven werd gedoeld, is een ander gevolgd. — en dat lag op het terrein der kerk. De Haagsche predikanten, bij den stadgenoot-verrader van Koningin en volk niet schorsten, hebben wij alarm geroepen tegen den niet-stadgenoot, die van synodale besluiten van 1944 zich op een honderdmaal korter afstand verwijderd had op ten aanzien van de synodale besluiten van 1936 — inzake de N.S.B. De afstand was honderdmaal korter, de actieradius ook. Want de man, tegen wien de Haagsche predikanten — vas „succes" verzekerd, naar uit de naïeven mond van den hunner bleek — alarm riepen, had geen blad meer; zijn blad, het was het onze, was door duitsche revolutionairen „stilgelegd"; hij had slechts de synode zelf over zijn distancieering van één van haar besluiten ingelicht; en daarna, toen zij werkeloos bleef, de raden der gereformeerde kerken, die er recht op hadden dit te weten. Maar de ex-predikant, tegen wien de Haagsche bedienaren van het Woord geen publiek alarm sloegen, schoon hij de besluiten van 1936 inzake N.S.B. met voeten trad, schreef in schier alle bladen. En schreef reeds eerder aan hen. En liet in die alle aan ieder weten, dat en hoe hij zich van het gereformeerde leven had gedistancieerd.

De situatieteekening is kort en onvolledig, maar het vervolg is toch wel min of meer bekend. Er kwam een schorsing, er kwam een afzetting, en een aantal andere ambtsdragers, dat in de honderden reeds loopt, deelde in hetzelfde lot. De scheur was

daarmee getrokken in het eens zoo bloeiende gereformeerde kerkelijke leven in Nederland.

Het eerste gevolg voor ons blad is uiteraard, dat zonder meer van de medewerking van velen, wier naam op 18 Aug. 1940 nog in den kop van ons blad vermeld stond, wordt afgezien. Ons nummer geeft geen lijst van medewerkers nog. Ze zijn er wel: reeds zijn nieuwe, hechte banden gelegd, versterkt door de groote vreugde, die het her-ademen in een gezuiverde kerkelijke atmosfeer begeleidde. Het kerkverband is onder wie aan het kerkverband zijn trouw gebleven, geord. — en uit een zóó versterkt kerkverband groeit het medewerkerschap in een gemeenschappelijken voorlichtings- en samenhin-

> O levende oirsprong ....
>
> O levende oirsprong aller gaeven,
> Die 't al knut koesteren, en loeven.
> En in woestijnen droogh en naer
> Ons noodruft schafte veertigh jaer:
> Hier water uit de hardste steenen;
> Daer Manne, oon hut en tenten henen,
> In 't krieicken van den dageraed.
> Gespreit, als koriandersaed:
> Als dauw, en rijp, verzamt in krinicken,
> Tot troost der hongerige buicken:
> O grondelooze waterwel.
> Ontsluit uw wateraders snel.
> Verquick ons met een zee van boven,
> Op dat u vee en menschen loven.
>
> Joost v. d. Vondel, Gebroeders, 575—588.

dingsdienst snel en vlot. Dat we nog geen namen publiceerden, ligt niet aan het ontbreken ervan, doch aan de onmogelijkheid van contact met alle, die tot medewerking bereid zullen blijken. We hopen spoedig hun namen te kunnen melden.

Het tweede gevolg is, dat ons blad zijn naaste werkprogram zich vanzelf ziet aangegeven. Niet alleen brengt de desolate toestand, waarin land en volk verkeeren na de aanvankelijke bevrijding van een deel van 't rijksgebied, de roeping mede, om te pogen het licht van Gods Woord daarover te doen schijnen. Maar ook plaatsen de voorgenaamde kerkelijke procedure ons voor den noodzank, de droeve rechtskrenking, daarin aan den dag getreden, bloot te leggen, de voosheid der dienaangaande verscheen synodale rapporten aan te wijzen, en het aanwoord op een ingebrachte beschuldiging, voor welk antwoord een synode in haar officieelen handel geen plaats wilde inruimen, niettemin hier te geven. Voorts is de opbouw van ons blad synodale misgrepen verscheurd kerkelijk leven naaste en blijvende roeping.

Noch door de nationale, noch door de kerkelijke ellende is ons blad uit zijn koers gebracht. Deze volzin is geen bijdrage tot de kennis van onze zelf-

analyse, doch bedoelt de richting, waarin ons blad zich de laatste jaren bevoeg, als onveranderd aan te wijzen. Mede om daarvan uitdrukking te geven hebben wij, uitgever en redacteur, besloten, de nummering van jaargang en nummer te vervolgen als ware er geen hiaat van bijkans vijf jaren. Het zijn de heeren, komen immers niet met een nieuw orgaan, doch met het oude. Gebrekkige postverbindingen zullen in den eersten tijd velerlei ongerief mogen verantschuldigen. Evenals het nog even uitblijven van onze wekelijksche Catechismus-bijlage. Schoon het vijf-jaren-intermezzo een pijnlijk duidelijke streep gehaald heeft door de „berekeningen", die de redacteur voor zijn levenswerk gemaakt had, wij hopen toch den draad van deze bijlage op te nemen, daar, waar de duitscher hem ons uit de handen rukte.

In diepe smart, doch met dankbare verwondering over wat Gods genade vermocht heeft in hun korstondig leven, gedenken wij die medewerkers, die in ons laatst verschenen nummer nog aan ons blad verbonden waren, doch sinds geleden hebben, dan wel bezweken zijn onder de wreede hand van den overweldiger van Mei 1940. Het zijn de heeren, neven de broeders: Dr R. J. Dam, Ds J. Kapteyn, Dr M. B. v. 't Veer. Zij hebben evenals ouderling A. Scholtens, die ook nauw met ons blad meeleefde, hun levend geloof doen werken door de liefde. De liefde bracht het voorlaatste offer, dat van de vrijheid, of ook het laatste, dat van het leven. In dat offer bleken zij getrouw aan wat ons blad heeft gepredikt en getuigd in de bewogen jaren, die vóór 10 Mei 1940 den inhoud van ons orgaan zich veelszins hebben weerspiegeld. En hoe verheugd het ons, te weten, dat zij allen zonder uitzondering, met ons gekozen hebben wel zouden gekozen hebben te gaan langs het pad, dat ook onze redacteur gemeend heeft te moeten volgen. Met Ds Kapteyn en ouderling Scholtens is in dezen niet kunnen gesproken worden. — maar hun houding was geen oogenblik onreker geweest. Met Dr R. J. Dam, die zonder gerucht zich schaarde onder de drie Kamper docenten, die de traditie van het verleden slechts in vrijmaking van ongoddelijke synodale besluiten wisten te kunnen bewaren, en met Dr M. B. van 't Veer, dien velen reeds als dies vierde zich dachten, kon wel worden gesproken. Hun taal was duidelijk als hun daad.

In een samenvattende beschouwing over het tijdsgewricht, waarin we ons bevinden en onze positiekeuze dienaangaande treden wij thans niet: ons blad zal vanzelf zijn aandacht hieraan geven.

Met de bede, dat de herwonnen vrijheid moge dienstbaar gesteld worden, ook door onzen zwakken, en thans misschien nog meer dan vroeger door anderen arbeid te vaak belemmerden arbeid, aan de doorwerking der beginselen, die onze universiteitsbezoekende inzichtveerde aandacht hebben, leggen wij de nooden van ons blad neer voor Hem die de eeuwen regeert, de volken der wereld naar de voleinding stuwt, maar altijd „de volken" Israëls „bemint". (Deut. 33 : 3).   K. S.

It was Schilder's wish that because the last number of
De Reformatie *published before it was shut down was*
Volume 20, Number 45, the first issue published again after the
five-year gap should be Volume 20, Number 46. And it was done!

Introduction
by Jacobus De Jong

When I was asked to write an introduction for this book, I agreed readily, for I know that the English translation represents a very valuable addition to the literature dealing with the events of 1944 and the history of the liberated Reformed Churches. I first read Van Reest's book on Schilder during the initial year of my theological studies, and I still remember the impression it made on me. Van Reest has an honest and straightforward style; he writes in a way that is simple, direct, and ideally suited for young people. A number of years later I met him when I "preached" as a candidate in the small church of Maartensdijk, where he was then a member. Although many years had passed since Schilder's death, he still spoke about him with a fresh enthusiasm and maintained that Herman Hoeksema really had not understood him! Little did he realize that his book would one day appear in English! If what he said about Hoeksema was true, this book may help a number of people gain a fuller and more accurate understanding of the many-sided work of Schilder.

As I read through the book again in English translation, it became clear that Van Reest paints a somewhat flattering picture of Schilder. Through his eyes we encounter a man who appears well-nigh faultless, almost superhuman. Not only does Schilder become a heroic figure, Van Reest also accents the elements in Schilder that appealed particularly to him — the artist, the musician, the journalist. Those were the same qualities he loved in Bilderdijk, of whom he also presented a somewhat skewed picture![1] Indeed, one gets the impression that if Bilderdijk had lived in Van Reest's time, he would have joined the liberated churches!

Yet one should not overlook the positive value of this book, especially from the viewpoint of church history. The book is essentially accurate on historical details. (Some small corrections have been incorporated into the translation.) Besides — and this is even more important — it is also accurate in its assessment of the issues involved in the ecclesiastical struggle that marked the later part of Schilder's life. Those events, of course, will always be interpreted in different ways by different people. However, in Van Reest's book we have a forthright view of the events as seen by a brother who regarded it as his duty to liberate himself from a

---

[1] See '*n Onbegriepelijk mensch: Het leven van Mr. W. Bilderdijk* (Goes: Oosterbaan & Le Cointre, no date).

synodical hierarchy that sought nothing but increasing the turmoil in the churches.

As for Van Reest's description of Schilder as a person, the reader will have to make up his own mind. People affect each other in different ways, and those who are especially gifted (as Schilder was) are not always easy to get along with. Yet it is not the person of Schilder that should dominate the reader's interest as he works through this book. Schilder himself would hardly have approved of a Schilder school or a following that idolized him as a person without any regard to his thought. He was not a theologian looking for epigones. Indeed, he was instrumental in leading many students — and even ministers who had never been students of his in formal respects — back to the source, namely, Scripture and its exegesis. His later writings are marked by a much deeper and more thorough exegetical style than his earlier works. His particular style of writing and working did bring him a following; yet the very nature of that style, as *prophetic,* should prevent anyone from stopping with Schilder. In effect, his writings function as a window or instrument through which one is enabled to see deeper treasures in the Scriptures, and so be strengthened in faith and in the union with Christ.

Who was Klaas Schilder, and how did he come to have so much influence on a large group of people? He was born on December 10, 1890, in the Dutch city of Kampen. His mother became a widow early in life, and as a young boy Schilder had to spend many hours helping at home. Yet his exceptional gifts were recognized early, and his mother was advised to enrol him in the local *gymnasium* for an academic education on the secondary level. He completed his studies there in 1908 and enrolled at the Theological School (seminary) of the Reformed *(Gereformeerd)* Churches in Kampen in 1909. He graduated on January 14, 1914, receiving the Candidate's degree *cum laude.* After taking the necessary ecclesiastical examinations, he was ordained in his first congregation in Ambt-Vollenhove on June 21, 1914. Shortly before that he had married Anna Johanna Walter, who remained a faithful support and companion to him throughout his life. They had two daughters (Johanna Gretha, who married a lawyer named H. de Wilde, and Eppie Jansje Huberta Maria, who married W. G. de Vries) and two sons (Petrus Antonius Catharinus, who became a lawyer, and Johannes, who became a medical doctor). Schilder went on to serve the churches of Vlaardingen (1916-19), Gorcum (1919-22), Delft (1922-25), Oegstgeest (1925-28), and Rotterdam-Delfshaven (1928-33).

Schilder's unique gifts became increasingly apparent during his student years. He wrote poems in both Greek and Latin and contributed articles to the Student Almanac. From an early stage, his writings were characterized by a sense of urgency and movement. Some commentators have pointed to the influence of Nietzsche on his style, while other note strong affinities to Kierkegaard. Little is known of his life during this period, but it seems to have been marked by some struggle and turmoil. However, the difficulties were short-lived, and in his first congregation we find him channeling his gifts for the upbuilding of the churches. From the outset he was a regular contributor to various church papers.

Schilder's early writings are marked by certain recurring characteristics: insightful analysis, a pointed style, and an exceptional command of language. Sometimes his sentences were long, but he was never verbose. Especially in these early works, we find a sense of effortless expression.

His best-known work of this early period is his well-known trilogy *Christus in Zijn Lijden.*[2] This work has been taken as a prose response to Bach's *St. Matthew Passion,* and there are certainly some structural elements in the work that lend support to this conclusion. In addition to many articles published in *The Reformation,* a weekly paper. Schilder also brought out a number of books. At one point he took a study leave to work on a doctoral dissertation in philosophy[3] at the Friedrich Alexander University in Erlangen, a school with a strong confessional Lutheran background.

In 1934 Schilder was appointed as successor to Prof. A. G. Honig as Professor of Dogmatics at the Theological School in Kampen. Honig was thankful that such a gifted writer and scholar was to continue in his chair. At about the same time he became the editor-in-chief of *The Reformation,* the weekly church paper which occupies a place of considerable importance in the story Van Reest tells in this book.

Van Reest deals extensively and fairly accurately with Schilder's life as a professor in Kampen. The first five years of his work there were marked by increasing polemical discussions on crucial issues in church life. Then came the dark years of the war and the deepening ecclesiastical crisis. For a number of years there is a gap in his publishing: letters, sermons, and brochures are the extent of his published work in this pe-

---

[2] Published in an English translation by Henry Zylstra under the title *Christ in His Suffering* (1938).

[3] The dissertation dealt with the history of the concept of paradox and was entitled *Zur Begriffsgeschichte des "Paradoxon": Mit besonderer Berücksichtigung Calvins und des nach-Kierkegaardschen "Paradoxon"* (Kampen: Kok, 1933). This dissertation is available in German only, although some of the same themes were dealt with by Schilder in two books written in Dutch, entitled *Bij Dichters en Schriftgeleerden: Verzamelde Opstellen* (Amsterdam: Uitgeversmaatschappij Holland, 1927) and *Tusschen "Ja" en "Neen": Verzamelde Opstellen* (Kampen: Kok, 1929).

riod. During the last three and a half years before his suspension and deposition in 1944, he was under orders of the Nazi occupation authorities, whose ideology and authority he had challenged in published writings *after* the German takeover, not to write and publish anything. This decree was issued when the Nazis released Schilder in December of 1940 after his imprisonment; later a second arrest was attempted, but Schilder escaped and went into hiding.

The liberation took place almost a year before Allied troops drove the last of the Germans out of the Netherlands. After the war the liberation in the church spread and took root. For Schilder there followed a period of seven years of relative peace and quiet, during which he wrote and published at an intense rate — perhaps too intense, when we consider the toll taken on his well-being by the war. His life ended on March 23, 1952, when he was 61 years old. He was not seriously ill during the last weeks of his life, but he had been warned by his doctor that his health was in great danger.

I will refrain from passing any judgment on Van Reest's description of Schilder as a person, beyond what I have already said. During this anniversary year, a great deal is being written in the Netherlands about Schilder as a person, and much of it is also interesting and enjoyable to read. But the *person* should not stand in the foreground. The way to do justice to Schilder is to focus on what he *taught,* about which too little has appeared in English. Two dissertations have been devoted to Schilder: one, written in Afrikaans, deals with his doctrine of the covenant, while my own highlights many aspects of his thought from the perspective of his view of revelation.[4]

With respect to the way Schilder fulfilled his office, I also leave the reader to judge for himself. But there is one point in the book on which I feel some comment is required. Van Reest states that Schilder rejected applications in his sermons since he recognized their uselessness (see p. 119). Such a statement about applications is not only highly questionable from the standpoint of homiletics, it does not square with the facts either. A cursory reading of sermons by Schilder (many have been published in his "Verzamelde werken") reveals that they include many imperatives, exhortations and applications to the situation of the churches of his day. Indeed, Van Reest seems to contradict himself, for he later quotes the words of Rev. John D. De Jong about Schilder, who stated that in his preaching Schilder placed a great deal of emphasis on responsibility (see p. 338). This comment is more accurate than what Van Reest

---

[4] My dissertation is entitled *Accommodatio Dei: A Theme in K. Schilder's Theology of Revelation,* (Kampen: Mondiss, 1990).

himself said. It is possible that Van Reest was not distinguishing clearly enough between application as such and *moralistic* application (which is generally contrasted with redemptive-historical preaching).

There are a number of other reasons why I am thankful for the publication of this book. First, it will give people outside the Canadian Reformed Churches some insight into the *raison d'être* of these churches. Second, it will prove an asset to the younger generation in these churches, for the book also shows that the struggle for the unity of the church did not end with the liberation in 1944. Indeed, Van Reest notes how Schilder later had to oppose tendencies toward independentism which had manifested themselves among liberated people and churches in the Netherlands (see pp. 352-353 below). Like Luther, Schilder had to turn against many of those who had followed him in the liberation because the essential motives for liberation were not the same for them.

History has proven that Schilder was only too correct. The 1960s brought about an ecclesiastical crisis in the liberated Reformed churches in the Netherlands, a struggle that concerned the basic attitude to be taken toward the liberation.[5] Many who had liberated themselves regarded the liberation as acceptable for the church but not as something of such magnitude that its principles had to be applied to all areas of life. It was indeed a step for justice in the church, but it was not a reformation to be compared to what had happened in 1834 (the Secession) or 1886 (the Doleantie). People of this persuasion promoted cooperation for social and political matters and so forth with synodical organizations and with Christians in other churches.

Like the liberation itself, the ecclesiastical struggle of the 1960s brought much grief to families, some of which were divided, with strong personalities at odds with each other on fundamental issues. Yet this struggle was unavoidable, for it concerned many of the things Schilder

---

[5] At the end of the 1960s, a schism developed in the liberated Reformed churches in the Netherlands. The direct occasion of the schism was the so-called "Open Letter" of October 31, 1966, in which a number of ministers proposed to re-evaluate the entire history of the liberation and to undertake a critical examination of the relationship of the liberated churches to the other churches in the Reformed world. However, the letter questioned the basis of the church in that it proposed to open up that basis for discussion. In addition to this incident, there were a number of doctrinal controversies in local situations. Finally, some churches left the federation, and others were placed outside it because of their refusal to affirm their allegiance to the basis of the church. Between 1967 and 1969, about 20,000 people left; after a period of informal association, these unaffiliated congregations ("Buiten-Verband") formed a new denomination, which is now known as the Dutch Reformed Churches *(Nederlands Gereformeerde Kerken)*. These churches have chosen a path that deviates markedly from the unity of faith as found in our confessions.

had always fought for. At stake was the heritage of the Reformation as it is reflected in the order of the church.

Therefore this book can also serve to warn a new generation against complicity and complacence in faith and its struggles. Members of the Canadian Reformed Churches can surely be thankful for their heritage and take pride in what the Lord has given them, and continues to give them in the possibilities open to them. But let no one fall into a false pride, as though we have now "arrived" and can be sure that all struggle for the sanctity and unity of the church and its growth is now behind us. Indeed, we must be intent on maintaining the reality and application of the antithesis in all areas of life without any exception.

This book appears after the synodical churches of the Netherlands issued their 1988 declaration of regret regarding the events of 1944 (see the note on p 370). This is but one of a number of statements and declarations which, while expressing a measure of regret about the events that took place, do little to repair the actual damage. Any serious Reformed Christian who knows about the developments in the Netherlands since 1944 will see that there is little salt left in the synodical churches. It is increasingly clear that we can have no genuine or lasting fellowship with those who continue to seek fellowship with these church groups.

At the same time, this book will also be of value for a wider audience. Schilder is a theologian many have heard about but few really know. In the course of my intensive study of Schilder, I became aware that there is quite some interest in Schilder and his thought in North America. And despite the conflict in which he was embroiled for a good part of his life, it can be said that Schilder was a truly ecumenical theologian: hence it is fitting that this book should include his speech "Your Ecumenical Task" (see Appendix III below). He sought and worked for a true unity of faith with all true believers. In this regard, the quotation of the prayer of Christ on his tomb ("That they may all be one," John 17:21a) is a fitting description of his life's work.

Allow me a word of congratulation to Theodore Plantinga on his translation. Plantinga has managed to capture the popular flavor of Van Reest's style and carry this over into English, even while he chooses expressions and terms unique to himself. All in all, a job well done! It is certainly my hope that these labors will be rewarded and will be used by God for the purpose originally intended — the unity of the church of God.

Chapter 1

Davidic or Solomonic?

The way things were

In the year 1927, the well-known writer Seerp Anema issued a brochure entitled *Davidic or Solomonic?*,[1] Although this brochure did not become widely known among our people, they would have done well to spend some time on it.

The purpose of the brochure was to seek a reorientation on behalf of the Reformed sector of the population. And it was not the first such attempt. Back in 1921, Prof. Anne Anema had written a brochure entitled *Our Time and Our Calling: A Word Addressed to Our Reformed People*. His brochure also sought a reorientation. Was there any reason for these efforts?

Indeed there was. When Dr. Abraham Kuyper died in 1920, an important period in the life of our Reformed people came to an end. To many people he was "Abraham the Mighty" *(de Geweldige)*, which was how the well-known caricaturist Hahn had drawn him in jest; Hahn's famous drawing was even used on the cover of a book made up of caricatures of Kuyper.[2] Around the same time, a whole generation of spiritual leaders who, for many years, had set their stamp on the Reformed sector of our population began to fade away. I need not mention their names.

As our people stood by the graves of those leaders, they could not help feeling a little like orphans. After all, they had been raised on *The Herald* and *The Standard*. In these papers they had found a faithful exposition of what they themselves thought but often were not able to express. Problems were formulated in crystal-clear fashion and then the solutions were given. The spirit of the times was sketched and combatted on a principial basis. The trumpet had never given

---

[1] This title, along with many others below, is presented in English translation. The inclusion of an English title is not meant to suggest that the work is available in English but is only intended to make the subject matter dealt with in the book more accessible to those who know no Dutch. On occasions when the actual Dutch title might be of interest to readers who know some Dutch, I will include it (in whole or in part) in parentheses. —TRANS.

[2] *Dr. A. Kuyper in de caricatuur* (Amsterdam: Van Holkema & Warendorf, 1909).

forth an uncertain sound. The course to be followed was always laid out clearly. The helm was in firm and experienced hands, and so the "little people" *(kleyne luyden)* were faithful to their leaders.

But what now? And there is something else of importance to be considered. In this period after the great world war of 1914-18, there were shifts underway, also in the life of our Reformed people. How peaceful it had been before that catastrophic year 1914! Those who still had some recollections of that time could hardly find any points of comparison with what we are experiencing today.

The Boer War at the beginning of this century had been a very important event in our lives. At the time it seemed to be the only thing to talk about. The war in the Balkans which took place not long afterwards seemed far away by comparison: we hardly paid any attention to it.

How peaceful it was in our fields and on our roads, for there were almost no automobiles or motorbikes. A rented coach pulled by a horse still cut a fine figure in our quiet cities and towns. We didn't talk about driving on the right-hand side of the road. What self-enclosed peace people could enjoy during a long winter evening as they sat in a room in their home, undisturbed by radio or television, with the quiet sound of a gas lamp in the background. It was still a completely self-contained world, in which Father and Mother stood wonderfully central. The family was still an oasis; it was an arsenal for strengthening one's resolve and gaining the spiritual equilibrium that equipped one for life outside the enclosed family circle. How well *The Standard* provided people every day — and *The Herald* every week — with ammunition for their arsenal. Moreover, back in those days, we as young men also had our young men's societies under the leadership of Vonkenberg. Yes, it was really something!

Kuyper and Vonkenberg

In those days I was living in Kralingen (a suburb of Rotterdam), where we had no fewer than *three* young men's societies in our congregation. I was a member of "The Sower," which had fifty-three members in all. In addition to the usual members' meetings every Sunday evening (we took no vacations!), we had six divisions or groups which met on Sunday morning right after the first worship service and again on Sunday afternoon before the second service. Those divisions or groups specialized in the following subject areas: Bible Study, Doctrine, Society, Church History, Calvinism, and National (i.e. Dutch)

History, and Literature. When I look through the anniversary booklet that was put out in 1915 to commemorate our society's twenty-fifth anniversary, I keep coming across the same names in certain of these divisions. One name comes up in five of them.

The subjects that were to be discussed in the members' meetings were first taken up in the divisional meetings and clarified there, so that the person introducing the subject was well prepared and able to stand up to criticism, which often was far from mild. What preparations we undertook! We had a large library, of which we made heavy use. Two subjects were taken up in a single evening meeting, and often we barely had time for a break between them. How we talked on and on, with more than a little nonsense mixed in!

I remember that Kuyper was then writing his long series of articles in *The Herald* about the consummation of all things.[3] In those articles he talked about the intermediate state of the soul, and about the realm of the dead, and Sheol and Gehenna. The result was that we became thoroughly confused. What on earth was Kuyper trying to teach us now? There were heated debates at our members' meetings, and finally we accepted a proposal made by our president, namely, that we set up a committee to study these matters further and make a presentation to us at a future meeting. The committee carried out its assignment willingly — even valiantly. When it came forward with the results of its study, the title was "The Solution of Some Difficult Questions." Now, we may smile at such a title, for genuine solutions to problems were rarely hit upon at such meetings. Yet it must be admitted that the young man's society did help us understand what the problems were. There are so many young people nowadays who don't get even that far.

Our trust in Kuyper remained unshaken. That's how things went in those days. And that trust simply *had* to remain unshaken, for he was our "Bible." *E Voto* (his commentary on the Heidelberg Catechism) and *De Gemeene Gratie* (about common grace) and *Pro Rege* (dealing with the kingship of Christ) and *Ons Program* (politics) — those were our sources. Geesink's four volumes entitled *On God's Ordinances* were also used when it came to ethical questions. And it was all so easy and convenient: those books contained indexes arranged

---

[3] Published in book form as *Van de voleinding,* four volumes (Kampen: Kok, 1929-31). Most of the fourth volume was translated into English and published as *The Revelation of St. John,* tr. John Hendrik De Vries (Grand Rapids: Eerdmans, 1935, reprinted in 1963). —TRANS.

by names and topics and Scripture passages. Once Kuyper had spoken on a subject, that was the end of the matter!

"The Sower" surely hit a high point in October of 1915, at its silver anniversary feast, when the aged Kuyper himself attended our festivities as our guest speaker. To be able to meet this 78-year-old leader with his magisterial head, to greet him on behalf of our young men's society, to shake his hand and look him in the eye — what a thrill!

I remember quite well why he made an exception for us and accepted our invitation. (He normally declined such invitations because of his age.) It had to do with the city of Rotterdam, which began to devour everything around it: Katendrecht, Hillegersberg, Charlois, Delfshaven. Yet Kralingen, that is, the *church* of Kralingen, said boldly: "We shall remain the *local* church." Kralingen refused to go along with the centralization and did not want to become part of the Rotterdam church. Kuyper was rewarding Kralingen by speaking to its young people. The *local* church — Kuyper had made so much of this as part of the conception of the church underlying the Doleantie. And that unforgettable evening in October, while the first world war raged in other countries of Europe, he illustrated anew the importance of this notion.

And next to Kuyper — or rather, right behind him — stood Rev. J. E. Vonkenberg. He was a man of steel, but he had a heart as gentle and tender as a mother. How eagerly we looked forward each Friday to his Reformed young men's magazine! His articles and features and scattered observations were Kuyperian through and through. Yet he did not follow Kuyper slavishly, and he could certainly not be called an epigone![4] When we faced the issue of being pro-German (as opposed to pro-English) during the first world war, he took a stand in direct opposition to his elderly teacher. He argued that Kuyper had taught us that Calvinism had taken root not in Lutheran Germany but in Scotland and America. Why, then, should our sympathies now turn to the east in this conflict? He abhorred the traitorous German invasion of Belgium, a neutral country. And I believe that although almost everyone was pro-German back in those days, Vonkenberg was right — not because of the course Calvinism had taken in history but simply because of the facts.

---

[4] The term "epigone," which the author uses often, especially in Chapter 2, is not as familiar in English as in Dutch. It stands for someone of a later generation who is less accomplished or distinguished than his forebear or predecessor. —TRANS.

What a teacher Vonkenberg was for us! How inspiring his League Days for us as young men were! Lying before me as I write is a report on such a rally held in Haarlem in 1922. Vonkenberg turned his attention that day to the rising Ethical-Irenic spirit in our churches. More specifically, he made some charges against the Dutch Christian Student Union: "In opposition to the spirit that speaks to us from this movement, the leadership of our League let its powerful NEVER be heard. And today the League leadership, speaking as one man, with no dissent in its ranks, reiterates its emphatic stand: NEVER." At the bottom of the page is a note: "Of great interest for the meeting was the fact that at the very moment following upon these words, the entire leadership of the League stood up and repeated his assurance: NEVER." Vonkenberg went on: "And I know that you, my esteemed hearers, would be willing, if asked, to rise from your seats and underscore the declaration of your leaders by saying: NEVER." At this point we have another note: "Overwhelming enthusiasm in the meeting. With great excitement people stood up from their seats and, with a passion that is rather unusual among people of our calm national disposition, repeated tumultuously: NEVER."

That was the kind of excitement living among many thousands of our Reformed young men under the unforgettable leadership of Vonkenberg. Did he inflame them only for as long as his meetings lasted? Not at all: on his recruits he made an impression that lasted all their lives. In the magazine he published and the study material he made available, he overwhelmed us with guiding principles. I still remember clearly reading a chapter on "Calvin in Geneva" under the general heading of "Calvinism." It was a revelation for me, as a young fellow of only sixteen years of age, how much this reformer had managed to accomplish in Geneva.

We had no problem finding things to do with our "free time." We had to work hard: many of us worked from seven in the morning until six at night, and on Saturdays until five o'clock. If you had an office job, you were a bit better off, but then you would have to use your free time to work hard for diplomas. We had great respect for our teachers, those learned people of privilege who saw to it that the Literature division of our young men's society came fully into its own.

Movies? In those days they could easily enough be found on the Coolsingel (a street in Rotterdam), with all its alluring advertisements. But I am convinced that not one of us even came close to considering movie attendance. The movies were part of "the world," and thus contraband. We still lived in a time when Father and Mother would simply not have allowed it, and if the minister had any reason to suspect that one of his catechism pupils was going to the movies, he would wait for him at the entrance to the cinema and march him off. In those days there was still a sharp antithesis between the world's young people and the young people of the church.

Am I implying that the young people then were more pious and virtuous than they are today? Not at all. Our Reformed young people back in 1915 were also included under what Lord's Day 3 of the Heidelberg Catechism says about man's corruption and his inability to do any good and his inclination toward all evil.

But we should remember that *families* were different in those days. Father and Mother were not like so many parents today. Their life was sober and simple; they asked little for themselves and sacrificed everything for their children. They lived close to the Lord. Their *example* made such an impression on us. If you had gone to a movie, you would never have managed to keep it to yourself while your father was praying at the table. That's just how things were.

Am I suggesting that all the activity at the young men's society meetings was intellectual only? That it was dogmatic instruction which left our hearts cold? That it was form without spirit? That it was confession which bore no fruit in experience? Well, I cannot recall a single occasion when we as young people talking together touched personally on our relationship to God. We would simply not have dared to mention something like that. We chattered on about problems, about guiding principles, about our young men's magazine, about the people in our own circles, our division, the leadership of the young men's society, and so forth. But that's about as far as it went.

Yet I do recall one special occasion when I was all worked up about a debate in our meetings and was talking about it at home with my mother. She ran her hand over my head and said quietly, "Will you please make sure that you do not leave your heart entirely out of this matter, Son?" It was the sort of thing you never forget, and it makes your remembrance of your mother even more precious when you have grown old yourself.

And since I am now drifting off in the direction of personal recollections, let me tell you about one more episode. When I was eighteen years old, I became very sick and sought medical help far away from home. While I was away, some faithful friends from "The Sower" looked me up, even though it cost them quite a bit of time and money.

As they stood by my sickbed, they talked about the work of the young men's society and passed on bits of news. But when it came time to say goodbye, there were also a few who blushed and quietly whispered, "I'll pray for you." And today I still treasure letters, which by now are more than 45 years old, from those young fellows, for in their letters they dared to reveal something of what lay deep within them: they told me about their spiritual relationship to God and pointed to the Source of comfort and strength.

Ah, we were so timid when it came to sacred things! Various of those young fellows, whose robust health I had envied, are already with their heavenly Father, to whose service they had dedicated their youthful energy. I also bless their memory.

The change

That's the way things were in those days, but then came the change. Because of the war, many of the young men wound up far from home. Even though they were fortunate in being spared the horrors of war itself, they did have to do without the familiar shelter of their parental home. Many were lodged in barracks, camps, and school buildings in modern areas or in Brabant and Limburg, where one found both light-hearted frivolity and dark superstition. Vonkenberg saw the great dangers in this, and with his warm fatherly heart he labored mightily to get Christian military homes established everywhere. How he struggled to keep our young men together!

And then came the "peace." I put this word in quotation marks because it was the "peace of Versailles," which was no real peace at all. The humanism of Woodrow Wilson, the American president with his "fourteen points," foundered in the face of English and French hatred, and it cost Wilson his life.

But the Netherlands had made profits during the war years; we had become wealthy in material respects. We had hundreds of war profiteers. And so we had the "nouveaux riches" among us, and people who had once been poor engaged in the craziest financial capers you can imagine. The "hard" Dutch guilder was soon worth millions of marks in Germany. Our people, who formerly had never been away from home for more than a day or so at Scheveningen (a seaside resort near The Hague) or at Artis (the Amsterdam zoo), made journeys outside the country and profited from the strength of our guilder in comparison with worthless foreign currencies. People began to tell each other fantastic stories about experiences in Brussels, Paris, and Berlin.

A different spirit came over our people, especially the younger generation. The simplicity, the sober outlook, the intimate sense of community — all of this began to disappear. The boundaries began to blur,[5] and for many the antithesis moved to the background. Instead people opened themselves to the prospect of synthesis, to a broad and open outlook, for what we had called "the world" turned out to be an exciting and entertaining place that now appealed to us.

There is another factor to be mentioned, and it is just as important. Even "the world" appeared to be undergoing a change. The "modernists" of the 1920s seemed entirely different from the modernists who were around when Kuyper was a young man. The nineteenth century, which was the age of pure materialism, of the deification of matter and energy, and of hatred against all that called itself Christian, was over. There didn't seem to be any hatred left against the "narrow-minded" people who took religion too seriously.[6] The time was past in which a man like Kappeyne would declare that he could only overcome his inclination not to accept a cabinet post when he remembered that being in the cabinet would afford him opportunity to beat down the hated Christian opposition to the liberal enlightenment.[7]

At the beginning of our century Herman Bavinck had said that "the soul" would triumph, and it appeared that he was right. Liberals and modernists began to talk "religious" language. Bavinck wrote: "In broader circles we see a dawning awareness of human dependence and misery, along with a conviction about the seriousness of sin and the need for a Redeemer, and also an awareness of the necessity of atonement and regeneration, a belief in the mystery of the world, and a thirst for communion with the living God. Doctrines that had long been regarded as antiquated and irrelevant, such as the doctrines of the fall into sin, of miracles, of Christ, of regeneration, and of heaven

---

[5] The author uses the Dutch phrase "verflauwing der grenzen" here, which was also the name of a famous rectoral address by Kuyper. The dangers against which Kuyper had warned in that address of 1892 were the very dangers faced by the Reformed young people in particular. Kuyper's address was published in English translation as "Pantheism's Destruction of Boundaries," in *The Methodist Review*, July and September, 1893. —TRANS.

[6] The author speaks of hatred "tegen de 'fijnen,' tegen de lieden van de 'nachtschuit' en van de 'nachtschool.' " This is a literary allusion to people who are backward, behind the times, obscurantists, and lovers of ignorance, enemies of true enlightenment. —TRANS.

[7] Johannes Kappeyne van de Copello (1822-95) was the minister responsible for interior affairs in a Liberal cabinet in the 1870s. He was remembered for his opposition to Christian education, especially as expressed in his proposal for a revision of the 1857 law governing schools, which had the unintended effect of galvanizing Calvinist forces that were trying to make room for Christian schools. —TRANS.

and hell, came up for fresh discussion. People became jealous of the riches contained in the religious language used in Christian circles, and many showed greater appreciation for the ancient Christian confession."[8] Perhaps Bavinck was being somewhat too optimistic here, but there was indeed a change in the spirit of the times. In the place of materialism came religiosity; rationalism gave way to neo-romanticism; mysticism took the place of the deification of matter. In broader circles, a theosophical mysticism, in particular, won many adherents.

These developments are somewhat understandable. During the nineteenth century many people had lived in a foolish cultural optimism, believing that it was within man's power to secure happiness for himself; they believed that if people would only live by faith in the power of materialism, linked with a Humanistic rationalism, they would be able to create a paradise on earth. Hence we can understand their hatred of people who opposed this philosophy of cultural optimism, people who pointed to the Bible instead and refused to join in with this human foolishness. From the standpoint of the freethinking liberals, it was not all that strange that such people should be called "dead flies" that "make the perfumer's oil stink" (see Ecclesiastes 10:1) — those people with their Bible texts, wanting to spoil the beautiful policies of the liberal government.[9]

But just when the Peace Palace in The Hague was finally finished, World War I broke out and the cultural optimism was shattered. Those who know history well can see how people in the first two decades of our century came to repudiate the optimism of the nineteenth century. And so a different spiritual posture was adopted in the camp of the leftists.[10]

Also relevant to the changing situation were the social circumstances in which the Reformed segment of the population lived. When Kuyper undertook his battle against the reigning liberalism, the Reformed people consisted largely of what he liked to call "kleyne luyden" (little people). They were mainly lower middle class people who had to work very hard to keep their heads above water economically. There may have been a few hundred, at most, who possessed a bit more by way of property. Because our people did not have the funds needed to give their children a higher education, the "intellectual"

---

[8] "Modernisme en Orthodoxie," published in 1911.

[9] This allusion to a Bible text is at the same time an allusion to a famous speech of 1875 made by Kappeyne. —TRANS.

[10] The author refers here to secularists of all persuasions — free-enterprise conservatives as well as radical socialists. —TRANS.

segment among them was miniscule when compared to what one found among the propertied classes of the wealthy liberals.

Now, through the growth in material prosperity around the turn of the century, our people became able to give their own children a better education than they themselves had received. And we began to establish our own institutions for education beyond the primary level. In greater numbers than earlier, our Reformed young people studied at the Free University of Amsterdam. It was now possible for them to get Christian education leading toward careers as lawyers, government officials of various sorts, teachers in secondary schools, doctors, and so forth.

An intellectual middle class began to form, and it sprang up from the ranks of the "little people." But this led to changes in the structure of society and social life, and also to some differences in spiritual outlook. Our young people in the higher schools came into contact with the classics, with theater, with the literature of ancient Greece and Rome, and also with the literature of England, France, and Germany. In many of these younger people there was already a tendency to break — in whole or in part — with the traditions of earlier Reformed people, in which the conservative element remained very strong.

Settling accounts with Kuyper

In the ranks of our Reformed people, then, a split developed. The older ones still hung on to "Kuyper," whereas many of the younger ones had settled accounts with "Abraham the Mighty." I remember well a conversation in the early 1920s with a theological student at the Free University, who assured me that no student there studied Kuyper anymore. Instead they studied the powerful work of the rising Swiss theologian Karl Barth, who, as he explained it, had subjected the last elements of a fossilized Kuyperianism for "state, church, and society" to a sharp, unmerciful and devastating critique. Remember that he was talking at the very institution which Kuyper, only a few decades earlier, had founded as an act of faith.

Anxiety and uncertainty crept over a good portion of the Reformed populace that had grown up under Kuyper and still continued to revere him after his death as the great leader for Reformed life. And things didn't get any better when the Netelenbos case came along. Rev. J. B. Netelenbos, who was a Reformed *(Gereformeerd)* minister in Middelburg, preached in the National Reformed *(Hervormd)* church[11] at The Hague, in the pulpit of Dr. J. A. Cramer, who was one of the Ethicals.[12] This had happened in 1917. When Netelenbos was dealt with by the church authorities, it became apparent that on various points he had departed from the confessions. The result was that he was deposed in November of 1919. There were certain passages of Scripture (Genesis 2 and 3, Numbers 22:28) which he could not accept as written. Moreover, he wished to ground faith not in Scripture but in *experience,* and he declared that he viewed Scripture as infallible in its *ideas* but not in the *form* in which it had come to us.

The position of Netelenbos represented the thinking of the Ethicals and was not Reformed at all. And it soon became apparent that he was not the only one in the Reformed *(Gereformeerd)* churches who thought along such lines. For example, two ministers named J. C. Brussaard and J. G. Geelkerken brought requests for revisions to the Synod of Leeuwarden in 1920.

The Dutch Christian Student Union

The Synod of Leeuwarden upheld the decision to depose Netelenbos and also pointed to the great danger to Reformed life posed by the Dutch Christian Student Union. Many Reformed students were members of this organization. The Synod declared: "The dominant current in this Union represents a great danger for someone who hopes to become a minister of the Word, for the standpoint of the Dutch Christian Student Union is ill-defined and subjective. It does not appear that the Christ of the Scriptures is confessed, and the conduct of a great many of its members is unchurchly."

Now, this organization, which exercised a great deal of influence in student circles, does appear to have been moving more and more in the direction of the Ethicals. At the time it was established, the Apostles' Creed could still be used as a basis, but it soon fell away. Even a

---

[11] Dutch has two words for Reformed: *Hervormd* and *Gereformeerd.* The national church which dates back to the Reformation and from which the Secession *(Afscheiding)* churches withdrew, beginning in 1834, is called *Hervormd,* whereas the churches which trace their history back to this secession call themselves *Gereformeerd.* I will insert these Dutch terms in parenthesis wherever necessary to avoid confusion. —TRANS.

[12] The Ethicals represented an effort to mediate between theological liberalism, on the one hand, and the warm piety of the orthodox, on the other. They stressed the consciousness of the Christian congregation as a source of truth, as opposed to the "legalism" of creedal orthodoxy. These Ethicals, who were already a force on the scene throughout the careers of Kuyper and Bavinck, are discussed by Jan Veenhof in *Revelatie en inspiratie: De Openbaring- en Schriftbeschouwing van Herman Bavinck in vergelijking met die der ethische theologie* (Amsterdam: Buijten & Schipperheijn, 1968). —TRANS.

statement of purpose that mentioned the triune God appeared to be too much, and in 1918 the purpose was reformulated as follows: "to introduce and build up the Christian life- and world-view, which is grounded in the Bible and which, linking up with the historical development of Christianity, takes account of the needs and demands of the present time." On this vague basis people proposed to unite with everything and everybody, provided the names "Christian" and "Christianity" were used. This student union was indeed a great danger for the Reformed churches and Reformed life, and it had a greater influence than many people realized.

Earlier I mentioned that the Synod of Leeuwarden (1920) warned against this organization and membership in it. But not all who were members of the Reformed churches agreed with this warning. Prof. Anne Anema saw nothing of the danger. In his brochure *Our Time and Our Calling,* which I mentioned earlier, he maintained that the Netelenbos case was not a symptom of anything but only an incident. He wrote: "What became clear to me from repeated personal discussions is that we have no reason to believe that the direction [taken by the younger men] represents a movement that wishes to depart from the principle of Calvinism." In this comment we have a striking reminder of the fact that those who are well educated do not always possess the gifts needed to test the spirits and to recognize intellectual currents for what they are.

It is rather naive to take one's point of departure in the declarations of the younger men themselves when they claimed they wanted to remain Reformed and Calvinistic, and then to conclude that there is no danger whatever and that everything is in order. Because of his total failure to understand what was going on around him, Prof. Anema could not have any appreciation for the decision made by the Synod of Leeuwarden. He said the following about it: "I have the impression that our Synod, as an ecclesiastical assembly, has looked at the whole matter too exclusively through ecclesiastical glasses."

This is a questionable sentence, the kind of sentence we sometimes hear nowadays in our own liberated Reformed churches[13] from the mouths of those whom people sometimes call our "intelligentsia." We are given to understand that beyond churches and ecclesiastical meetings, there are also "non-ecclesiastical" zones of life.

---

[13] The Reformed churches that originated in the schism of 1944, in which Schilder was involved, are sometimes referred to unofficially as "liberated" *(vrijgemaakt).* —TRANS.

There is nothing new under the sun. Forty years ago people reasoned in exactly the same way when they wanted to be "broader" or "more ecumenical," and as a result they became blind to the dangers looming ahead. Anema claimed to see not just "church life" but something else in addition, namely, a "kingdom of God," and when one sees things in this broad perspective, he reasoned, "and then draws up the balance, the result is a hefty balance on the credit side for the kingdom of God." What he was referring to was how one ought to assess the Dutch Christian Student Union. Thus he placed himself in opposition to the decision of the Synod of Leeuwarden, and in his brochure he declared: "For my part, I believe that an organization like the Dutch Christian Student Union deserves our help and support."

A man like Vonkenberg would draw an entirely different conclusion, of course. He whole-heartedly applauded the decision made by the Synod of Leeuwarden. In his magazine for Reformed young men, he warned repeatedly against the Dutch Christian Student Union. Once when he was preaching in the small vacant church of Kralingsche Veer, there were visitors at the home of the family with whom he lodged, which was not unusual. The discussion that Sunday evening was about calling a minister for the congregation. When he asked how the calling process was coming along, Vonkenberg was told that it was not a simple matter to find the right man for the right place. He then offered a reaction that was typical for him: "When you are thinking of calling someone, do you ask him whether he has ever been a member of the Dutch Christian Student Union?" The answer was no. Vonkenberg immediately declared: "That should be your very first question. And if he says, 'Yes,' you should ask him whether he regrets having been a member. If he answers, 'No,' you must not call him."

Fortunately, there were more ministers who saw the great danger this movement posed to our churches. J. C. Sikkel, B. van Schelven, P. J. W. Klaarhamer, and others raised their voices against it. Prof. D. P. D. Fabius also recognized the danger, and Rev. O. Boersma put out a brochure in which he warned earnestly against the danger of belonging to it. Another strong opponent of the Dutch Christian Student Movement was Prof. Lucas Lindeboom, who declared that an organization which allowed the person and work of Christ to be defamed and which maintained good relations with modernist students could not be evaluated positively. Membership in such an organization would have to be forbidden.

Yet there were many who were completely blind to the danger. The 1916-17 annual report of the Dutch Christian Student Union indicated that almost all the students at the theological seminary of the Reformed *(Gereformeerd)* churches in Kampen were members and that the Kampen students attended the conferences faithfully. There were 130 Reformed members in all,[14] and five of them served on the national board. According to the 1919 yearbook, thirty-three theological students at the Free University were members, and twenty-four theological students at the seminary in Kampen.[15] Listed among the former members who continued to contribute to the organization were twenty-five Reformed *(Gereformeerd)* ministers, two professors at the Free University, and one at the seminary in Kampen.

The spirit of the Ethical and Irenic theologians rapidly penetrated our churches. First Netelenbos and then Geelkerken (1926) were the deadly fruits of this spirit. If you would like to see what spirit those developments awakened among the Reformed young people, you should read a book published by Dr. J. J. Buskes in 1959 entitled *Hurray for Life*. Buskes was a member of the Dutch Christian Student Union from 1917, when he entered university, until 1924, and he soon found himself serving on the board of this organization as a representative of its Free University chapter. He reports that not a single professor at the Free University ever advised him against membership in this organization, and that men like Herman Bavinck and C. van Gelderen never stopped giving their support to the Dutch Christian Student Union. Buskes admits: "In my own life and in the lives of many others, the Dutch Christian Student Union relativized a great deal that I had accepted as absolute from my own Reformed circles. For this I can only be thankful to this orginazation."[16]

---

[14] It should be borne in mind that higher education was a comparative rarity in those days, and also that even today there are proportionally fewer young people attending university-level institutions in the Netherlands than in North America. The figure of 130 students does *not* mean that comparatively few Reformed young people studying on the university level were members. —TRANS.

[15] The seminary in Kampen was established in 1854 by Reformed churches stemming from the Secession of 1834. The Free University (founded in 1880) included a theological faculty which trained ministers for the Reformed churches. After the union of the Secession churches with Kuyper's Doleantie churches in 1892, the Reformed churches drew ministers from both institutions. —TRANS.

[16] *Hoera voor het leven* (Amsterdam: W. ten Have, 1963), pp. 63, 64. The Prof. Bavinck whom Buskes knew stood at the end of his professorial career. He had begun teaching at the Theological School of the Secession churches in Kampen in 1882, and it was while he was there that he wrote his four volumes of dogmatics (entitled *Gereformeerde dogmatiek*). In 1902 he became a professor at the Free University. The elderly Bavinck is summed up as

Chapter 1 — Davidic or Solomonic?

Just how much was "relativized" in the life of Buskes is abundantly clear from his book: he developed into a Barthian through and through, and he became anti-militarist, a member of the Labor Party, and a staunch opponent of all that is Reformed. Yet Buskes was among the students who served as pall-bearers at the funerals of Kuyper and Bavinck. At Kuyper's grave he joined in singing: "Thou art their strength and glory; all their foes they scorn, for Thou hast favored us: exalted is our horn" (Psalm 89, stanza 8) and "Blest are the people who acclaim Thee as their King, who know the festal shout and of Thy mercies sing" (stanza 7). And at Bavinck's grave: "The LORD His goodness has revealed: He is to us a sun and shield" (Psalm 86, stanza 6).[17]

But Buskes was also among the victims of the Dutch Christian Student Union who buried Kuyper and Bavinck *spiritually*. Van Randwijk's later Barthian novel entitled *A Son Buries His Father* could have been the life story of Buskes.[18] But it wasn't only *his* story. The group that finally left our churches with Geelkerken was fairly small. But some seventy ministers or so who had supported him backed down and stayed quietly in their parsonages once they saw that his position had no support among the ordinary people. Back in the 1920s we were thankful that the group that had actually left was small, but we have good reason to wonder whether the Reformed churches really were better off because of the decision made by the seventy ministers. The result was that the spirit of the Dutch Christian Student Union continued to work in our churches.

---

follows by Buskes: "His entire life was a continual struggle for harmony, for synthesis, a struggle which engaged him with head and heart, with intellect and mind, with his feelings and his imagination, and which involved the entire cosmos, both material and spiritual things, both nature and history, both the world and the kingdom of God . . . He was very much aware of the opposition between modern culture and Christian faith — no less than Kuyper was. But unlike Kuyper, he was always looking beyond the antithesis for a way — if only the narrowest footpath — by which these two could encounter each other. He was not quick to use such words as "paganism" and "antithesis." He spoke repeatedly of synthesis, humanity, catholicity, and the universal. He was as opposed to absolutism as to relativism, and it was hard for him to find the positive solution. He devoted his entire life to the solution of the problem of Christianity and culture. He did not find the solution, but he did wrestle with the problem and had a difficult life" (p. 34). —TRANS.

[17] The singing at these funerals was in Dutch, of course. Here and in some other places in the text, I have quoted parallel English wording as we find it in the *Book of Praise: Anglo-Genevan Psalter,* which is the hymnal of the Canadian Reformed Churches. —TRANS.

[18] In this novel set in the depression, the son kicks over the narrow traces of the church and opts for the social welfare programs instead, calling the Christian organizations bourgeois and "establishment-affirming." —TRANS.

After the church reformation of 1944, when the group that truly loved the Reformed confessions was chased out in a blind spirit of self-assertion, that spirit led the churches to an accelerated decline: under the influence of the Ethical-Irenic younger element of the 1920s, which was at home in the Dutch Christian Student Union, the churches sailed off in a deadly direction. By 1944, however, changes were no longer being made in the name of Ethical-Irenic Christianity; instead the innovators sailed under the flag of Barthian dialectical theology. Thus they bowed anew before dogma, which they had earlier abhorred so completely and had shaken off with the slogan "Not form but spirit, not confession but experience."[19] But now it was *Barthian* dogma, and it seemed to suit them, for it rejected the antithesis, emptied the church's confession of any meaning, and interpreted the Word of God apart from the Spirit of God on the basis of human will and desires. Even more intensively than in the 1920s, the innovators hungered for an "ecumenical" Christianity with a basis that any heretic could find agreeable.

But the roots of this growth that was deadening our Reformed life were to be found in the 1920s. Buskes was not the only one who came from a Kuyperian Reformed home, became a student at the Free University and a minister in the Reformed churches, and then was spiritually devastated by Barthianism by way of the Dutch Christian Student Union, only to tell people at the end of his life that he was happy and thankful to be in the procession that rode through The Hague as part of the ceremony for the unveiling of Troelstra's statue.[20] He was also pleased to be part of a committee that raised the money to make the statue possible. In addition there was Stufkens, another Free University product, of whom Buskes says that dozens of members of the Dutch Christian Student Union found their way into the Labor Party through his influence.

Barend Schuurman was also fully at home in the Dutch Christian Student Union. In his essay on Schuurman, Prof. Hendrik Kraemer speaks of the "tensions" in his life and calls them "fields of force" in which and between which Schuurman had to find his way. Among those "tensions" were his parental home (he came from a solid, genuine Reformed family), the Free University, and the Dutch Christian

---

[19] These slogans are parallel in sentiment to some we have heard in English-speaking countries, such as "No creed but Christ" and "Doctrine divides, service unites." —TRANS.

[20] Pieter Jelles Troelstra was a prominent socialist politician who announced in 1918 that the time had come for revolution in the Netherlands. —TRANS.

Student Union. And when you read the moving letter from Barend Schuurman to his Reformed father, which Buskes quotes, you think of the novel *A Son Buries His Father:* "Certainly, I believe the intentions of the Reformed churches are upright when they repeatedly say they want to go back to the Bible, but I do not see them giving up everything else; I do not see them daring to go by Christ and His Word and Spirit alone or facing the waves of indeterminacy, of dangerous incalculability, on the basis of His fixed command. What I see instead is that they cross the abyss of Scripture by means of the bridge of the confessions, and that a great many points of disagreement in our time are simply dealt with on the basis of formulations of 1619 and get solved using the intellectual tools of 1619." He goes on to say that he has set aside "the norms of 1619." Buskes also says of him: "In this letter Barend Schuurman speaks representatively: his voice is the voice of many."

This is a serious warning that applies to our time as well; it applies to people in our own churches who do not want to hear anything about our confessions having a normative character. Anyone who lets go of the confessions of the churches is liable to wind up anywhere and renders himself vulnerable, just as a fortress without walls lies open before any enemy who may attack. History is very instructive here.

When the first issue of *Word and Spirit* appeared on October 2, 1925, it was apparent that various people influenced by the Dutch Christian Student Union had gathered around this periodical: H. C. van den Brink, J. C. Brussaard, G. Brillenburg Wurth, the two Wiersingas, Prof. F. J. J. Buytendijk, Prof. H. J. Pos, and Dr. L. van der Horst. After the Synod of Assen, this periodical became the publication of the so-called Church in Restored Federation (the churches which followed Geelkerken). Four professors and a lecturer at the Free University joined this "Restored Federation": Buytendijk, P. A. Diepenhorst, Pos, R. H. Woltjer, and W. Zevenbergen. For twenty years this small group maintained an independent existence. In 1946 it was made up of seventeen ministers and some 7000 souls, divided over a number of small congregations.

When this group allowed itself to be absorbed into the National Reformed *(Hervormd)* churches in 1946, it denied the Secession of 1834 and the Doleantie of 1886 and wound up in an agglomeration of religions. Perhaps these people thought they were living out Christ's prayer in John 17, but the real unity of those who are in Christ was totally lacking, for the simple reason that our Savior only prayed — indeed, only *could* pray — for the unity of those who *keep His Word* (John 17:6). No such assurance could be given for the fellowship of the National Reformed *(Hervormd)* churches, where the Christ of the *Scriptures* did not find obedience but where Karl Barth, with his theology that strayed away, dominated the ruling party of the "middle orthodox" and was regarded as a church father.

The younger generation

Earlier I noted that not all the people in the Reformed *(Gereformeerd)* churches who found it too narrow there and asked for "open windows" and "open doors," who wanted a broadening of the confessions, who pleaded for more "spirit" and less "form," and so forth — not all of these joined the "Restored Federation." On the contrary, most of them stayed where they were once they realized that the ordinary people in the church would not go along with them. They did not want to wind up in a "miniature congregation," to use a phrase of Buskes. The ministers on whom Dr. Geelkerken had counted for support simply decided to make do. Whether they liked the decision of Assen or not, they accepted it, and one after the other they withdrew from *Word and Spirit*. I know of one who emulated King William II: before the constitutional revision of 1848, when things got tense in Europe, this king was converted overnight from an extremely conservative position to a liberal one. This minister, likewise, was converted in a single night from an outspoken anti-Assen position to a pro-Assen stand. Later he became a staunch opponent of Schilder.

There were also some who had objections to Assen not on doctrinal grounds but because of church polity. Today there are probably not very many people outside the synodocratic churches[21] who would defend the so-called "new church law" that was hastily created at that time. I don't propose to talk about such people. But it remains a catastrophe for the formerly Reformed *(Gereformeerd)* churches that many who agreed with Geelkerken in terms of substance found one reason or another to leave him in the lurch, reasons which did not testify to much stability and integrity on their part. And their weakness turned out to be a channel which today allows free flow for the

---

[21] The people of the liberated Reformed churches object to the hierarchical approach adopted by the synods of the federation of churches by which they were expelled in 1944. The author characterizes those churches as "synodocratic," making use of a term which Schilder also employed. —TRANS.

Chapter 1 — Davidic or Solomonic?

stream that shows more and more willingness to follow the example of the "Restored Federation" in 1946 by fraternizing with the National Reformed *(Hervormd)* churches. That stream has been around since the 1920s and must take the responsibility for much of the ecclesiastical misery we suffered in the 1930s and 1940s.

The church weekly called *The Militant Church,* which was established at the time of the liberation for the express purpose of combatting the liberation,[22] continues to serve as a mouthpiece for this group. And it has prepared the way for the contacts between the National Reformed churches and the synodocratic churches.[23] History does not *always* repeat itself, but on occasion we do encounter repetitions that surprise us.

This group within the synodocratic churches, which keeps growing and getting stronger, shows that it is ready to follow the example set by the "Restored Federation" back in 1946. Buskes used the following image when speaking of this union: "In 1946, the small ship of the Restored Federation sailed into the harbor for the last time. It did not sail away again. Its crew went over to a bigger ship." Indeed, those who were left subordinated themselves to the regulations of a hierarchy. At the helm was Karl Barth, and the course he steered was dialectical theology, which involved a strict separation between the officers, on the one hand, and the ordinary crew members along with the passengers, on the other hand, who didn't concern themselves with the direction and scarcely knew where the ship was taking them. Just as in the case of Rome, it was a matter of being led by the "clergy," from whom the "laity" then felt ever more estranged; indeed, the distance between clergy and laity began to look more and more like a vacuum. (This is a complaint that stems from a Barthian theologian!) And it could hardly be otherwise.

A National Reformed minister named W. A. Zeydner used a still different image at the time of the union: he expressed the hope that the Restored Federation would be like the Moselle River, which flows into the Rhine but can still be seen in the Rhine for a long time.[24] I'm

---

[22] The liberation referred to here is not the expulsion of German troops from Dutch soil in 1945 but the church struggle of 1944 which ended in the expulsion of Schilder and many others. —TRANS.

[23] By the time this translation was undertaken, these two church bodies, the *Hervormd* and the *Gereformeerd,* had indeed moved a long way together down the road to reunification ("Samen op weg"). —TRANS.

[24] The Rhine is well known for its pollution. After the waters of the Moselle join the Rhine, they are still recognizable in terms of their source. —TRANS.

afraid this hope is without any ground, for in this case both the Rhine and Moselle find their origin in the same Swiss mountain — Karl Barth.

What motivated them?

It is very much to be regretted that things had to turn out this way. And when we look ahead to the coming takeover by the younger generation in the synodocratic churches, the generation that is coming into its own more and more now that the older generation oriented toward Kuyperianism is fading away, we have even more reason for regret. We should remember that they were students produced by the schools of the Secession (the seminary in Kampen) and the Doleantie (the Free University).

It is not enough simply to note that such-and-such events took place in the 1920s and 1930s. There must be *reasons* for the things that happened; we need to look into the background. Why did it all turn out the way it did?

We must do justice to these men who are our brothers, even if we regard them as wayward brothers. Why did they come under the influence of the Dutch Christian Student Union? Why did so many of them break with an old and trusted tradition? Why did they repudiate their father and bury him spiritually?

To take one example, it is very moving to see what a struggle of heart and mind Barend Schuurman underwent. This young man, who registered as a theological student at the Free University in 1909, wrote to his father as follows about his struggle: "It is the gravity of the time and the seriousness with which I approach my Christian faith that has brought me to this decision . . . ." Also: "There have been moments recently when I felt not only the necessity but also the joy of the step that I have taken, that I have been allowed to take, as a privilege to which I have been called and by which I am allowed to do something special for God's kingdom. I have no desire, now that I am freed from human authority, to go my own way; what I want and pray for is to be nothing more than a slave of Jesus Christ . . . ." Remember what Buskes said: the voice of Barend Schuurman was representative — it was the voice of many.

The question keeps coming up: What moved these young men in the 1920s to give up the precious Reformed confessions, the rich treasure of the church, so full of comfort, which so many thousands had sealed with their own blood and passed on to their children as the most precious inheritance possible? How is it possible that someone like Schilder, with all his digging into the treasures of the Church, could be so moved by what he found, while others who grew up in the same spiritual home did not love the inheritance they had received and could cast away the treasures as worthless?[25] And when they cast the treasures aside, it was not in a spirit of indifference; indeed, Schuurman testified that he wished to serve Christ and be His slave!

We must not dispose of this question in a cheap way (as people sometimes try to do) by saying: "It all goes back to divine election. God gave it to the one and withheld it from the other." I will stay away from the deepest ground, which belongs to the hidden things of God, and limit myself to what we can see. We must bear in mind that when God carries out His hidden counsels, nothing drops down from heaven; rather, it is all realized via intermediaries, by way of cause and effect. And so I repeat my question: How did all of this come about?

In the *Reformed Weekly* of February 17, 1961, I read an article by Prof. G. Brillenburg Wurth entitled "The Reformed and the Ethicals." The article was part of a series in which he dealt with the younger generation of the 1920s and the influence of the Dutch Christian Student Union upon them. In his student years Brillenburg Wurth had also experienced this movement. He participated in the publication of the periodical *Word and Spirit* before it went over to the cause of the "Restored Federation," and thus he was drawing on his own experience as well.

He points out that from three angles, in particular, the direction which had taken by the Ethicals and by the kind of theology they praised was of great importance for him and for the other members of the younger generation of those days. In the first place, he and the others were deeply interested in the question of Christianity and culture, and this was one of the things that excited them about the Ethical theology, which they came to know via the Dutch Christian Student Union. This theology seemed to combine an earnest desire to be Christian with a complete openness to the needs and aspirations of modern man and of modern life. Although they were not blind to the dangers

---

[25] In the conclusion to his treatment of Question 6 (Lord's Day 3) of the Heidelberg Catechism, Schilder writes: "It is a great blessing to be Reformed, and thus to think in a Reformed way, even when we think about a world which did not yet need the great reformation."

involved in the openness, the mentality behind it had an abiding impact on their Reformed mission.

What excited them in the second place was that this Ethical theology was Christocentric. Among the Ethicals not much was said about dogmatic principles, but there was a great deal of talk about *Christ*. For the Ethical theology, Christ was the great Principle — almost the only Principle. They did not want to hear about truths (plural), for Christ Himself was *the* Truth. Their testimony addressed itself to the heart and the conscience, and in this latter respect they helped pave the way for what later came to be called "existential theology." This strong emphasis on "experience" also led them to turn away from definiteness in confessional matters.

To this second aspect Brillenburg Wurth adds a third, writing:

> Their emphasis on "the Christ of experience" had another consequence. Their faith in Christ was ultimately grounded in what they had been able to experience of Him personally. This meant that they came to take a much freer stand in relation to the Bible and were much less apprehensive than the Reformed were when it came to Biblical criticism, which was always advancing in their time ... Now, no one has suggested that they, like so many modernists, built up their theology on the basis of their own reason. They regarded faith as inconceivable apart from the Word of God. But for them that Word of God did not coincide with the Bible; ultimately, the Word of God was Christ Himself. Therefore they often reduced the Scriptures to the testimony they contained concerning Christ. Moreover, that Scriptural testimony had to reverberate in the hearts and consciences of the believers. As for the rest of the Bible's contents, they had no great objection to historical-critical investigation of them, even if such investigation ended in far-reaching negative results.

Naturally, these were the very matters that constituted the order of the day in the Dutch Christian Student Union. Brillenburg Wurth reports that in the Reformed younger generation of that time, there were some who could no longer resist the suggestions of the Ethicals on these points and were drawn along under their influence in the direction of the kind of Biblical criticism that undermines Biblical authority. This helps us understand the Netelenbos case, and here we also find the origins of what later became the Geelkerken case.

The way of thinking represented by the Ethicals, which was later transposed into dialectical theology, won out so fully in the synodocratic churches that a second "Assen" would not be possible among them any more. Geelkerken and others of his ilk would be able to operate undisturbed in that fellowship of churches.

But now we must try to answer the question: To what extent was the younger generation correct in its criticism of the Reformed life from which it had sprung? There are two aspects to be considered in answering this question.

Kuyperianism

In the first place, Kuyperianism must take some of the blame. We continue to honor Kuyper as a church reformer, a man who, through God's providential ordering, was able to accomplish great things by way of reformation. If we are to assess Kuyper fairly, we must always place him in his historical context, in the time in which he lived and worked. His weak side was not very apparent in the days when he first appeared on the public stage; at that time he was still completely immersed in the work of church reformation. Only later, when he became more and more of a political figure and left his home in Amsterdam on the Prins Hendrikkade for the Kanaalstraat in The Hague, did his weak side become more apparent. His scholastic tendencies then came to stronger expression. And his weaknesses put quite a stamp on our Reformed people. Earlier I pointed to his tremendous influence on our young people, through writings of his which they heard read aloud week by week from *The Herald,* and daily from his asterisked editorials in *The Standard,* which shone before our eyes like glittering stars.

Was there anyone in those days who saw the dangers of "scholasticism"? I still remember how the simple people (Kuyper's "kleyne luyden") used to say, "We want *dogmatic* sermons." What they meant were sermons built up out of Kuyper's writings — *E Voto* and *De Gemeene Gratie* and *Pro Rege*. They wanted sermons that dealt with the covenant, baptism, the church, and so forth, with all the divisions and distinctions which the ingenious Kuyper, with his irresistible style and wealth of imagery, impressed on our people.

Are we now to blame Kuyper because of this influence? If we answer yes, we should also ask: Was there anyone in those days who did *not* fall under his spell? Even Schilder's early career had a Kuyperian stamp: when he prepared the second edition of his great work *Christ in His Suffering,* he had to revise it considerably to free it of Kuyperian scholasticism.

And what about Kuyper himself? I repeat: we must view him as a child of his times. He had grown up in a time of rationalism, when people everywhere were demanding that attention be paid to the claims of reason. That was the "spirit of the times" in those days, and not even the greatest genius could escape it.

But his scholasticism had terrible consequences — not only for Kuyper himself, and not even in his own case first of all. The consequences were very grave among his followers, and they were most serious of all among the epigones who wanted to canonize him after his death.

Scholasticism

The fatal danger here is that scholastic thinking can lead to the loss of the Bible. When one approaches the Bible with *a priori* constructions in mind, it cannot help but remain closed. As an example of how this comes about, let us consider baptism. If we adopt a certain premise as logically supreme and do not *constantly* consult the Word as our norm, we will be forced to draw some logical conclusions. The premise, in this case, is that baptism is for *believers,* for it is a sacrament. The conclusion then drawn is that when our children are baptized, we must assume that they are believers. Yet practice makes it clear that not all children of believing parents are believers once they have grown up. Yet they were baptized. What are we to make of this? We are then told that we must baptize on the presumption that the child at the baptismal font already has regeneration in its heart or will receive regeneration, whether before, during, or after baptism. But the train of logical reasoning also demands some further consequences, for we still have to face the question what we are to make of baptism when it is administered to babies who later turn out not to be saved, not to be regenerated, contrary to what we had presumed at the time of baptism. There is only one conclusion that could be drawn: their baptism was not a genuine baptism at all. In scholastic terms it all fits neatly together; the logic seems impeccable.

Chapter 1 — Davidic or Solomonic?

Now, if you have once accepted this *a priori* train of reasoning, you will also want your conclusions to fit in with what we read in the Bible about these matters. You are then asking the Bible to prove what you had already figured out in advance. This is the fatal danger in an *a priori* approach to the Bible, for when you adopt such an approach, you are no longer listening objectively and willingly to what the Bible actually says; instead, you are reading your own train of thought into the Bible. The result is a Bible — or better, a book — that is no longer the Word of God but a product of human thought processes.

Once you are caught up in this dangerous net, the one evil will beget the other. Closely bound up with the scholastic view of baptism is the scholastic understanding of self-examination. If you have wrestled all your life with "presumptive regeneration,"[26] if you are told that no one knows whether his baptism was genuine or only apparent, it becomes very important to ascertain how your spiritual standing can be determined. The standard answer is that you must embark on the path of self-examination. The object is to find out whether you are a genuine believer or not. How is this self-examination to be carried out? The answer given by this scholasticism is that you must look for the distinguishing marks of faith in your own spiritual life.

How, then, can you be assured of being a believer? When I was young, we heard all sorts of distinguishing marks mentioned in sermons, in catechism instruction, at home visitation, and in the visits we received when we fell ill. Do you love the Lord? Do you love the believers? Can you get along without the Church? Can you get along without the Bible? Do you pray faithfully? Are you sorry for your sins? Do you fight against your sinfulness? Do you freely accept the path along which the Lord is leading you? And there were more such questions — there was almost no end to them.

Thousands and thousands of people wrestled with those questions — and still struggle with them. (The "distinguishing marks" theory is just as much alive today as it was fifty years ago.) But who has ever gotten anywhere with those questions? Yes, you can soothe your conscience and give a positive answer to all the questions and then declare that everything must be in order as far as your salvation is concerned. And you can get along for a while that way, but what

---

[26] *Veronderstelde wedergeboorte* in Dutch, i.e. the regeneration which, according to this theory, is presupposed or presumed or assumed to have taken place prior to baptism. — TRANS.

happens when there is a crisis in your life, or when you fall a long way into sin, or when you are no longer of one mind with the Lord? What is striking about the distinguishing marks theory is that each mark had to be backed up by a further distinguishing mark which would guarantee its authenticity.

Let's take an example. Suppose that when you are asked whether you love the Lord and whether you can get along without the Church and the Bible, you give the right answer in each case. Even then you face a further question: *Why* do you love God's people? *Why* can't you get along without the Church or the Bible? Is your *heart* speaking in the answers you give — or just your *head?* After all, you might answer as you do simply because you want to go to heaven when you die. Are those distinguishing marks genuine, then? Have you perhaps deceived yourself? In times of darkness, when you face a crisis, it is quite well possible that all those distinguishing marks will collapse like a house of cards, and that you will then face a frightening question: Could it be that I was baptized on the basis of a presumption that turns out not to be true in my case, and that my baptism is therefore not genuine?

And these are not just academic or theoretical questions. I know of many people who lived in continual anxiety about these matters — and still do. We have heard many complaints about people lacking the assurance of faith or of the joy of faith; people talk about dullness, despondency and doubt.[27] All of this is a consequence of this scholastic way of thinking under which so many of us sighed and struggled and plodded along during the first decades of our century. A. Janse

---

[27] The issues at stake here are hard to understand today because the doctrinal declarations that were being enforced in the many suspensions and depositions in 1944 and thereafter have since been repudiated in virtually all Reformed churches that held or considered them — including the churches that deposed Schilder. Yet, to follow the story, it is helpful to understand the disputed doctrines and the effect they could have on ordinary church life, especially in relation to the promises connected with baptism, self-examination, and preparation for the Lord's supper. These matters are explained at some length — in English! — by Rev. Gijsbertus van Dooren in *And We Escaped* (Burlington: Golden Jubilee Committee, 1986), which is his personal account of what he and the congregation he served went through by way of church struggles on a local level during the years of German occupation. The sections most relevant to the disputed doctrines are pp. 10-11, 18-19, 32-40, 85-90, 96-97, 130-134, 156, 210-217. Also helpful on the theological questions — for those who read Dutch — is C. Veenhof, *Om de "Unica Catholica": Een beschouwing over de positie van de bezwaarden onder en over de synodocratie* (Goes: Oosterbaan & Le Cointre, 1949). The doctrinal issues have also been dealt with at length by E. Smilde in *Een eeuw van strijd over verbond en doop* (Kampen: Kok, 1946). —TRANS.

writes: "I heard about a minister who said, after the sacrament of baptism was administered, 'And let's hope it was a true baptism.'" '[28]

Preaching

And there is something else to be mentioned. If the question was whether or not one possessed faith and if the demand for self-examination with regard to one's state — I did not say standing! — was so pressing, and if most churchgoers wrestled with this matter, naturally all of this had an effect on the preaching. And so we wound up listening to the infamous "exemplary" preaching. It almost seemed that the Church would be presented as a "grace shop," for it was by the Church that you had to get into heaven. The Church could show you the way and, indeed, had the obligation to do so. The question of *personal* salvation was the one posed primarily: even though we had begun with Calvin, we wound up with Luther.

What poverty this exemplary preaching represented! One Sunday the people of the church would have Abraham held before them as a hero of faith and would be asked in conclusion: Do you also have faith? The idea was that you had to look a little like Abraham, even if only from a distance. If you did, all was well. The next Sunday the people would be told that they, like Jacob, had to have their own "Jabbok," or at least their own "Peniel." What these men, and many others in the Old Testament, meant in terms of God's plan of salvation for His Church, how the line of redemptive history had to lead to the birth of Christ — of these things we heard nothing. The preachers just didn't get around to these matters because they were so busy with the spiritual adventures and conversion stories of Abraham, Jacob, and so forth, whom they held up as examples before the individual believers. After all, weren't they presented to us in Hebrews 11 as a "cloud of witnesses"?

Through such preaching, the redemptive historical meaning of the Bible was not opened up for the Church of the Lord. In fact, Christ was absent. What did we get to hear about Christ in such preaching? When it came to His suffering, the exemplary approach plodded along down the same old path. And then one could talk about the soul of Peter, or of Judas, or of Pilate, or of various of the figures around the cross. But what about the Savior Himself, who was nailed to that cross?

---

[28] *Around the Reformation*, p. 132.

It was all so sad and impoverished and empty and dry! And yet the tendencies in this type of preaching were entirely the result of the dominance of scholasticism.

This evil had not *begun* with Kuyper. At the Synod of Dort, Maccovius, who was a professor at Franeker, had to be admonished and told to be more restrained in speaking about the hidden things of God. This man had become notorious for his many scholastic distinctions. Voetius was also a lover of scholasticism. And when you read the sermons that were preached in the closing years of the seventeenth century and throughout the eighteenth century (to the extent that they are available in printed form), you have to ask yourself repeatedly how it was possible for our church people to continue to swallow this stuff. Consider the evaluation which the Calvinist poet Constantyn Huygens gave of the preaching of his time, which was only a little while after the Synod of Dort. Scholasticism was the order of the day, and Huygens was moved to complain: "Oh, what sort of revival will be needed to bring the world men like *Paul* and *Peter* again?"[29]

When we look at the sermons, or fragments of sermons, that stem from this period, we are not surprised at the complaint of Huygens. Almost nothing was done in the way of Scriptural exegesis; instead the ministers were busy with scholasticism. Moreover, the exemplary method was used much of the time. Moral lessons — which were by no means superfluous in that era — made up the substantial content of much of the preaching. There was no shortage of moral theology.

I regard the improper proclamation of the Word of God — or perhaps the failure to proclaim the Word at all because the ministers were too busy laying out their own ideas and constructions — as one of the chief causes of the ecclesiastical decline that led to such terrible deformation at the end of the eighteenth century. In all times and seasons we must ask: How shall they believe if they have not a preacher? It pleased God to tie the well-being of His Church directly to the proclamation of His Word. Whenever a lid is placed on the proclamation, we get deformation instead of reformation.

We should also draw the lesson of history in our liberated Reformed churches. Scholasticism crouches outside our door too, and it is eager to devour us. All too easily we begin to cherish ideas of our

---

[29] I have written more about this matter elsewhere: see Vol. 3 of *Dichterschap en Profetie* (Goes: Oosterbaan & Le Cointre, 1957), pp. 92-93.

own, which we then love to see authorized in Biblical terms and decked out with Scripture references. I believe that Rev. B. Telder did not pay sufficient heed to this great danger when he wrote his book about what happens after death.[30]

Mysticism

Another danger of scholasticism is that it is defenseless against mysticism. It was the great tragedy of Kuyper's work that although he recognized the dangers of mysticism so clearly and tried to pull our people away from it during the last decades of the nineteenth century and succeeded insofar as he largely overcame their passivity in political and social matters, he was not able to strike a deadly blow at the very root of subjectivism. This failure resulted from his scholastic constructions about the covenant, baptism, self-examination, the concept of the church, and so forth.

People are sometimes inclined to think of scholasticism and mysticism as opposites, but I have seen them walking hand in hand. During the course of my life I have run into a good deal of mysticism, some of it in extreme forms. But nowhere have I heard more scholastic reasoning than among mystics, who talk about levels, distinctions, states, standings, the internal and the external, and so forth. There is no end to their labyrinthine reasoning with its zigs and zags. And none of it has anything to do with the Word of God; it has sprung from the muddy stream of their own false ingenuity.

In the preaching methods used at the beginning of our century, there was no adequate weapon against mysticism. In most places in the Netherlands such mysticism did not make as much headway as on the islands of South Holland, along the rivers, in the coastal areas, and on the Veluwe, but we must nevertheless recognize that mysticism, along with scholasticism, is something our people have in their blood. And Kuyper did not give us much resistance against it. Thus this stream continued to dominate our churches until the 1920s and 1930s.

Anxiety and complaints

Such was the situation among us when, after the first world war, a rising younger generation in the Reformed world began to make its

---

[30] *Sterven en dan?* (Kampen: Kok, 1960). In this book he twists all kinds of Bible texts in an effort to get the Bible to prove that his own ideas about soul sleep are correct.

voice heard and thought it could find a home in the Dutch Christian Student Union — at least, those who were students themselves. When we now read what Brillenburg Wurth tells us about his own experiences and place his observations against this background, we begin to understand what was going on. *Something* had to give way after Kuyper's death. Church life, preaching, and the general rigidification (also confusion) which took the form of a sterile dogmatics simply *had* to leave various people unsatisfied.

The anxiety was almost universal. Not only were there complaints about the younger generation, who wanted to go in the Ethical direction of the Dutch Christian Student Union, but there were also well-grounded complaints about superficiality and worldliness on the part of our church people. It seemed that everyone could sense that something was in the process of changing; people realized that the ground was shifting and that things were going wrong somehow. Yet they did not know how to arrive at a pure diagnosis — to say nothing of prescribing the right therapy.

There is more to be said about these complaints. Men like Fabius, Sikkel, and De Moor had already seen the symptoms of decline and raised their voices against it. At the Synod of 1914, held in The Hague, Dr. J. C. de Moor complained about a laxity which left people "more eager for the favor of men than the good pleasure of the Lord. There are two things we need desperately: more depth and more unity."

Dr. de Moor was always a remarkable figure in our churches. He was a very gifted and earnest theologian, a shepherd of the flock entrusted to him, with which he dealt without respect of persons, and to which he could speak very sharply when the occasion demanded. He was one of the founders of the periodical *The Reformation* (1920), and it was especially because of his influence that Dr. H. W. van der Vaart Smit, an unstable man, was not able to put his dangerous stamp on this periodical right from the beginning.

Dr. de Moor looked after the book review section of *The Herald,* which was one of the most attractive features of that paper while he was in charge of it. In his book reviews he did not mince words: when it proved necessary, he could roundly criticize a cheap conversion story or a book written by following some formula. His own three-volume work on the opening of the heavens *(De Hemel Geopend)* was read with great appreciation.

Chapter 1 — Davidic or Solomonic?

At the famous Synod of Assen (1926), where Dr. J. G. Geelkerken was repudiated,[31] Dr. de Moor offered the following words in a sermon at the prayer service held before the synod began its work: "We can do nothing *against* the Truth but only *for* the Truth." How he viewed the situation is quite clear from the following words, which also formed part of his remarks:

> It is painful that our Synod has to meet on this occasion under such circumstances. Since 1892 we have had various difficulties to deal with at our synods, but never did the waters of worldly thinking, passion, and enmity against others rise so high as they do now, and never did the church of Christ become an object of mockery as much as it is now. It is just the way Bilderdijk sketched it in his "Decline *(Ondergang)* of the First World," when he describes what one of the devils has thought up to defeat mankind: "It was the fire of contention, the most destructive of all catastrophes; that crept around in the army, hidden in the smoke; and promised victory for the enemy without a battle." Unless God prevents it, the outcome could be what Bilderdijk goes on to describe: "There was no powerful army anymore; there was no band left; only three hundred fighters, separated from each other by corpses, soldiered on in the face of death, when once there were thirty times three hundred; exhausted, they raised a weary arm and nodding head on heaps of dead."

A little farther on Dr. de Moor said:

> When we removed a straying brother in 1920, we did not purge the evil, nor did the drive toward reformation that manifested itself at this synod [Leeuwarden] appear to

---

[31] It is worth noting that Prof. S. Greijdanus raised certain objections to the way Geelkerken was dealt with: he agreed that Geelkerken's position was untenable but maintained that the *general synod* did not have the authority to depose him. Greijdanus also dealt with this matter in articles in *The Reformation* of 1939, when he discussed Dr. M. Bouwman's dissertation *Voetius over het gezag der synoden* (Amsterdam: S. J. P. Bakker, 1937). The Geelkerken case functioned as a precedent for the deposition of Schilder as a minister by a general synod. Reformed church order stipulates that if a minister is to be deposed, both his consistory and the local classis must be involved. The deputies of the (particular) synod are also consulted, but the general synod plays no role in the matter. —TRANS.

possess enough inward power to renew our church life in its totality. Let us, I beg you, not reproach and blame each other, but let us instead humble ourselves together. For God opposes the proud but gives grace to the humble (I Peter 5:5).

De Moor did not restrict himself to these words of admonition; he also showed himself to be a man of prophetic vision who saw the dangers of his time and armed his people against them. In the same sermon he declared: "In their confessions and in the defense against erroneous teachings which the confessions include, the Reformed churches possess a most precious treasure. They must always be careful to guard this treasure, and they will always have to exert themselves to unmask the lie." These were precious words, and they retain their value today — also for our liberated Reformed churches.

The words of this sermon were his last words, for during the Synod of Assen he died of a heart attack, when he was only forty-eight years old. Could it be that his faithful heart, like the heart of many a faithful servant in the Kingdom of God, had broken under the pressure of the suffering it had to bear because of the decline and falling away within the churches?

How earnestly this man lived, and how much propriety he manifested in his relations with his brothers! For example, in this sermon, which later appeared in print, he made a reference to something Schilder had written in *The Trumpet*. But first he sent a copy of the entire address to Schilder so that the latter would be aware that De Moor was appealing to his words. And what a humble spirit in a man of so much knowledge and so many gifts! Fourteen days before he gave the sermon, he sent a copy to a reporter writing for one of our papers and asked him if he would print it as a pull-out section. What is noteworthy is not just that this request was immediately granted but that Dr. de Moor also said to this reporter: "And if you find anything in the tone of the address or in some other aspect of it that can better be left out or changed, just say so."

Symptoms of decline

Figures of such eminence are rare, and as we survey the 1920s we do not come across a lot of them. If there was anyone who saw the decline underway in our churches, surely it was Dr. de Moor. But he was not the only one.

Chapter 1 — Davidic or Solomonic?

The church reformation of 1886 was a good thirty years behind us when complaints began to be voiced everywhere to the effect that church awareness was fading away. It seemed that people did not know any longer why they had been "liberated" from the yoke of the hierarchy. At the Synod of Rotterdam in 1917, Rev. J. H. Landwehr stated: "Twenty-five years ago, not many people would have thought that our church awareness would be weakened to such an extent as we see in our time. What I am referring to is the undeniable fact that among old and young there is too much ignorance and even indifference about our own ecclesiastical position."

Rev. C. L. F. van Schelven also appealed to the people not to give up the Calvinism to which the Doleantie had called them back: "All the more so when we see that we are not living in a time of *transition* but in a time when our principles are being weakened, a time when the boundaries are being blurred, when our birthright is being sold, when we are imitating what this person or that, after a short stay in England or America or Germany or Switzerland, has discovered — or *thinks* he has discovered. Methodism and pragmatism are idolized so much that people shrug their shoulders and ask you, in a tone of pity: 'Why are you getting so worked up about *Reformed principles?*' " He also wrote: "The eighty-sixers are becoming few — indeed, scarce. This is to the delight of some of the members of the younger generation; they probably regard the eighty-sixers as a nuisance." Rev. J. C. Sikkel recently said that many of the younger ones are "decorators and plasterers" more than they are openers of God's Word. The eighty-sixers were the generation that would soon be buried. The complainers were dying out, people assured each other. All there was left to do was to rejoice — in the modern style.

In his book *Antithesis or Synthesis?* Dr. Cornelis van der Waal appeals to a brochure entitled *In Holy Calling,* which Sikkel published in 1916.[32] Sikkel saw the decline in the Reformed *(Gereformeerd)* churches very clearly and wrote about it as follows:

> Once in my youth, a contemporary of mine who was an enemy of the Calvinists made a comment that cut right through to my soul. With a nice smile he said: "We'll cut the Reformed back down to size — but not by burning

---

[32] Van der Waal's book is still highly relevant for us today. It has not been read as much as it should have been, and in the camp of the synodocratic churches it was entirely ignored and rendered ineffective by silence.

them at the stake. We'll use champagne instead! We'll let them drink our most exquisite wine from our finest glasses." Since then we have seen hundreds of our young people fall away — sons and daughters of Reformed homes. They may still call themselves Reformed, but *in principle* they are lost to us. They are now right at home in higher business circles, in professions, in higher studies. They have become accomplished and practical in a world of thought and life in which *no* Reformed principle is recognized. They have drunk that champagne and are still drinking it.

Dr. van der Waal adds:

These moving prophetic words clearly outline the extent of the externalization. The Reformed people were in the process of moving away from their foundation. The doctrines of "common grace" and "sphere sovereignty" were used to rob the antithesis of its power. Outside the "church-as-institute," the Word no longer had a firm grip on us. The beautifully integrated Reformed "organism" neglected to live out of its *own* principle. Sikkel's complaint of 1916 corresponds to the one Groen raised in 1848: "A semi-gospel, which knows how to adapt itself to anything, causes us to lose our independence."

It is noteworthy that in North America, the same developments were being noted among the Reformed people in Grand Rapids, a city with a substantial Dutch population. In the Christian Reformed Church, "conformity to the world" was also winning out. In a speech dealing with the North American church split of 1924, Rev. Herman Hoeksema declared:

A pair of brothers [Hoeksema and Rev. H. Danhof] decided to study Kuyper's doctrine of common grace in the light of Scripture and the confessions. They were driven to do so because of a growing spirit of conformity to the world which manifested itself in more than one way in our churches — through the striving of some for a broader interpretation of Reformed truth, and also through the appearance of what in those days was called the "new mentality."[33] These brothers took note of the fact that this "new mentality" wanted nothing to do with the Dr. Kuyper of the antithesis but appealed instead to his doctrine of common grace. The conclusion they reached was neither that the *name* "common grace" *(gemene gratie* or *algemene genade)* was not useful, nor that we needed a better presentation or further development of this doctrine, but that the doctrine itself, in principle, was not in agreement with the Reformed world- and life-view and therefore ought to be rejected . . . [34]

In explaining his objections to the notion of common grace, Hoeksema also wrote:

> We will not limit ourselves to the discussion of certain sporadic phenomena but will instead trace such phenomena to the principles from which they have sprung. For example, in our discussion of theater we will try to direct our thoughts to the power of imagination which man possesses as God's image-bearer . . . But we will not simply subject ourselves to the judgment of the wise men of Greece. On the contrary, we believe that in our circles an attempt must be made to throw off the yoke of the old pagan philosophers and artists . . . .
>
> Especially in the areas of intermediate and higher education, the idle philosophy and chimerical reflections of carnal reason have been deceiving us. In our circles we often hear people talking about "the divine Plato." For almost any principle of science or art, people point calmly to the ancient heathen world of Greece and Rome. I believe this is not permitted. We must make the sound of God's voice heard down the entire line of all human activities. Then it will not be possible to avoid conflict anywhere. What we want to do is put the spiritual antithesis in the foreground . . .

---

[33] This "new mentality" corresponds to what I have been calling the "younger generation."
[34] This speech, given in Dutch at a meeting in Grand Rapids, was translated into English by Rev. Herman Veldman and published by the Reformed Free Publishing Association under the title "The Reunion of the Christian Reformed and Protestant Reformed Churches: Is It Demanded, Possible, Desired?" For the passage quoted here, see pp. 12. —TRANS.

It sounds just like the situation among our people in the Netherlands in the early 1920s! The Kuyper of common grace was deified, while the Kuyper of the antithesis was rejected. Kuyper's ideas were unraveled, and the worst of them were canonized, for they were found useful for a Christianity that was externalizing itself and conforming to the world.

When the battle over these issues was being fought in North America, people in our country had not yet reached such a point in their thinking — with the possible exception of Prof. S. Greijdanus, who had understood the heart of the problem with which Hoeksema and his followers were occupied. In those days Hoeksema wrote a brochure entitled *Dr. Greijdanus Poses Important Questions,* in which he quoted from a series of articles which Greijdanus had written in *The Reformation.* From these articles it was apparent that Greijdanus also rejected Kuyper's doctrine of common grace. At that point he was about the only one in the Netherlands who came to Hoeksema's aid.

The background factor to which Hoeksema pointed, namely, the decline of church life on a practical, everyday level, was just as much present among us during the days of the first world war as among the Reformed people in the United States. We were rapidly regressing in terms of lifestyle. After 1920 materialism was rampant — also in Reformed circles. Conditions among our students were unbelievable, and the parents became lax. There developed a "parlor Christianity," complete with "parlor ministers." (I could point to depictions of such ministers in the literature of those days.) Our people had indeed raised that glass of champagne to their lips.

At the Leeuwarden League Day in 1918, Prof. Grosheide declared: "It cannot be denied that in our Reformed circles there are at present all kinds of phenomena which point to decline and regression. Among those phenomena I would make special mention of indifference to the church *(onkerkelijkheid)* and conformity to the world." Grosheide also offered some explanatory comments: "The causes of this decline and regress vary in nature. In part it has to do with the fact that there is always some weakening after a period of blossoming. Another factor is that a mistaken conception of the doctrine of common grace is operative among us. Finally, I would point to an increasing ignorance of Reformed truth."

Dr. K. Dijk also pointed to the decline and echoed part of what Grosheide had said: a law of nature was at work here. Dijk observed: "It is a law of life that after a period of awakening and blossoming, there comes an autumn of drying up and dying away. Everywhere, in every domain, you see the same rhythmic alternation of low tide and high tide, high tide and low tide — this also applies to spiritual life."[35]

Such speculative reasoning was so fully the order of the day that no one saw in it any idea that went contrary to Scripture. People simply reasoned on the basis of practice and their own rationality, without considering what should have been asked first of all and most of all: What does *the Bible* have to say about spiritual decline and the forsaking of the Word? What message would the prophets of the old covenant have been able to give to an apostate covenant people if they had reasoned in such fashion?

The men who did see something of the decline and deformation when they began to take on leadership in the churches simply had no spiritual defenses because they themselves were tangled up in the labyrinth of scholasticism and subjectivism. From the way their life and work developed in later years, it is apparent that they had no eye for church *reformation.*

Yet back in those days they did see clearly the initial symptoms of the falling away. Dr. Dijk went on to observe: "Anyone who takes an honest look at the spiritual state of affairs has to admit that the valuable struggle against the illusory principle is paired with a disquieting uncertainty and wavering with regard to the 'unchangeable truths.' Many people feel uncertain and shaken up. They can no longer say positively and surely what is true, and they do not dare to speak in specifics. They are afraid of dogmatic formulations. To be questioning and seeking is regarded as a greater indication of earnestness than to be precise about one's confession. In the area of practice, all kinds of concessions are made to the demands of life and to new forms in society. People lean toward the things we have in common with other people instead of having an eye for what specifically characterizes one's own standpoint."

Dijk then took up some concrete points and mentioned the danger of full funding for Christian elementary schools.[36] In achieving full funding, the Antirevolutionary Party[37] had struck a deal: we will let

---

[35] *The Reformation,* January 21, 1921.

[36] Christian day schools in the Netherlands have been fully funded by the government since the early 1920s. The issue was whether such schools could retain their Christian integrity while the government paid all the bills. —TRANS.

[37] The Christian political party supported by most Reformed *(Gereformeerd)* people at that time. In 1980 it joined with other groups to form the Christian Democratic Appeal. —TRANS.

the left wing have the universal franchise in exchange for full financial equality for Christian schools.

This deal has rightly been attacked as the selling of the birthright. But who in those days saw the tremendous danger in such an arrangement? Dijk saw something of it. He wrote: "The financial liberation in education is indeed a victory which cost us years of struggle, but the golden chains that will now bind us to the state are much more dangerous to our spiritual health than the iron chains with which we were confined in the house of bondage. And the way in which this 'pacification' was brought about, the 'free sacrifice' we had to make to arrange for our schools to be on the same level as the other schools — all of this indicates how much we have surrendered, and it gives the older ones among us plenty of reason to lament our step backward and to fear that a further slide is yet to come."

Men like Grosheide and Dijk, then, did see the symptoms of the deformation clearly enough. It's too bad they had their own "explanation" for what was going on. If these are all phenomena that we also see reflected in nature, if we see summer followed by winter, and low tide followed by high tide, then we may take comfort in the thought that the history of the church is also marked by an alternation of ups and downs — in which case we need do nothing more than wait for the rising tide to come in again. After winter will come spring, when everything blossoms again and we see new life everywhere. In December we can look ahead to May!

Is this prophecy — or mere speculation? The latter, I'm afraid. It's easy to talk this way, and you will not get in trouble for it. On the contrary, you can point to the decline and weakening in a very earnest way without stepping on anyone's toes or breaking any bones. But such an explanation does not fit the actual facts. After the blossoming we saw around the turn of the century in the Reformed *(Gereformeerd)* churches we did not see another blossoming as a repetition of the cycle. There was not a new springtime; we did not hear the sounds of newly awakened spiritual life — not even a faint rustle. The tide has been out now for more than forty years; the long winter does not appear to be giving way to summer. When we see synod after synod complaining about the "blurring of the boundaries," about the drying up of spiritual life, about conformity to the world, we finally conclude that the promised "rhythm" simply does not exist. It was nothing more than erroneous speculation.

We should also bear in mind that when push comes to shove and a position must be taken because of unfolding circumstances, such scholastic prophets always wind up on the wrong side. When there was finally a genuine return to the Word and the confessions during the church reformation — and thus the rustling sound of new life — people like Grosheide and Dijk opposed this "new spring" after a long winter, this rising tide which followed upon a long period of low tide. The synod that suspended Schilder for three months wanted to extend the suspension for one more month before proceeding with deposition, but Dijk opposed this step strongly and demanded that Schilder be deposed at once. In this case there were more than forty years between the root and the fruit, but we see that the fruit does not deny the root. When scholasticism fails to consult the Word but relies on human reason, it bears bad fruit.

Nowhere in the Bible do we find the suggestion that there is an alternation of ups and downs, spring and summer, low tide and high tide in the history of the Church. When there is a falling away, the Lord gets angry and sends His prophets, who declare that there will be judgment if there is no repentance and return. And if, indeed, no repentance comes about, the Lord proceeds with judgment. Nowhere in Scripture is the forsaking of the Word pictured as a normal reaction to obedience and the service of the Word. It is only scholasticism, which reasons outside of the Word, that wants to sell us this line of reasoning.

Such misconceptions made possible the misery of the 1920s and all that it led to. The Kuyper period was regarded as such an enormous Olympian high point that a decline was simply inevitable. After all, when a sick man exerts himself too much, he will inevitably have a relapse. People who talk this way point to phenomena that are not entirely in order and will even see some "dangers," but they expect a healthy reaction to come about automatically. After all, high tide always follows low tide.

Prophetic testimonies

There were others who expressed a different view. Earlier I mentioned Sikkel. There was also Rev. Klaarhamer, who thought differently than Dijk and Grosheide. In his farewell sermon on April 21, 1919, he complained about *deformation:*

> Ah, those rich, happy, beautiful days of the reformation now lie some thirty years behind us, and where is our peace and joy? Where is our overflowing saturation, and where is the comfort we enjoyed in those days? . . . . How many of us are crippled and in danger of straying from the path and the communion of the church because of the Ethical error with its mixture of Remonstrant thinking?[38] We are endangered because we do not know the Word of Truth, and because we are worldly-minded and take delight in carnal things. Can you understand that my soul is very disturbed these last days and filled with sadness? Can you understand why I look ahead to the future as frightening and threatening? Instead of continuing reformation, I see rising deformation . . .

Vonkenberg also saw the dangers looming ahead. He did not talk about high tide and low tide; instead he spoke openly of deformation and falling away. In his address at the League Day in Leeuwarden in 1918 he declared:

> There are many symptoms today which point to a decline in Reformed doctrine and morals. On the one side you hear a plea being made for concerts and the theater. Somewhere else you discover that some think it is all right to make use of public transportation on the Lord's day. Unfaithfulness in church attendance is defended on the grounds that people do not want to swallow the very old-fashioned manna that is served up in the preaching. People defend the neglect of the Heidelberg Catechism by saying that it does not properly address today's questions. Sugar-sweet conferences with people adhering to "isms" of all sorts are ideals that some manage to combine very nicely with hateful comments about their own brothers in the narrower sense of the word when those brothers propose to stick to our principles even in the realm of practice. One of the novelties is the celebration of the Lord's supper apart from the church and with the use of a "general formulary," for the sake of soldiers. This is all part of the

---

[38] "Remonstrant" is a term for the Arminian position which is repudiated in the Canons of Dort. —TRANS.

blurring of the boundaries. And why wouldn't such things be a cause of rejoicing by people who are quite offended if they are admonished for attending so many services in other churches and told that "spongers don't get fat"?

At the League Day of 1922 in Haarlem, we hear the same sound from the mouth of this man, who truly dared to be a prophet:

> You already know the tune well, even if you are hearing variations on it. Not doctrine, but life. That's the basic motif. And then come the variations: Not the confession but your walk of life. Not the form but the spirit. Not faith but the fruit. Not words but deeds. Not so much preoccupation with justification — sanctification is what's really important. Not Reformed, but Ethically Reformed . . . But we are of a different spirit! With all our hearts we cling to the confession *and* our walk, the form *and* the spirit, the word *and* the deeds of the men of 1834 and 1886. As for those repairmen who take on airs as though they were church reformers, as for those quacks who act as if they were physicians — to them we say, "Pass us by. Life is too important for us to be held up by the likes of you. The task that awaits us is too heavy for us to be able to fritter away our time by looking at the sand castle of your illusory unity . . . "

Vonkenberg dared to step on people's toes when necessary, to wake them up. He did not look to the right and then to the left to see what people were saying but dared to swim against the stream. He was not trying to deal with the rift within "Zion" by the easiest and least disruptive manner possible. Thus he knew how to choose his associates, and he realized what they were made of. On that same League Day in 1922, in the middle of the ecclesiastical confusion, which was also the time when the Reformed younger generation oriented toward the Ethical and Irenic theology began to make its presence felt, he took a firm position by choosing as his main speaker a man who would not allow the trumpet to give out an uncertain sound. That man was a minister named Klaas Schilder, at that time only 31 years of age, who gave an address entitled "Head or Tail," about which I will have more to say later on. Vonkenberg, with his eagle eye and prophetic clarity of mind, had quickly spotted the young Schilder and continued to regard him as a man who knew the times and would oppose them in a reformational spirit.

I remember very well a visit I made to Vonkenberg in the summer of 1929, accompanied by my oldest brother. At that time Vonkenberg was a minister in Huizen, and my brother, who had emigrated to the United States in 1912, was visiting the Netherlands again and wanted to see Vonkenberg once more, for he had been quite an influence on my brother in his earlier years. During our conversation in the parsonage in Huizen, Vonkenberg asked him, "Which ministers have you heard in the Netherlands?" My brother mentioned some names. Vonkenberg then asked, "Have you already heard Rev. Schilder?" My brother said no and got a typical Vonkenberg response: "Then you *must* go and hear him, for he is the best minister in the Netherlands!" I also remember that Vonkenberg had some very critical things to say that day about the policies of the Antirevolutionary Party, for it was placing the antithesis more and more in the background because of its desire for power and influence.

If it had been possible for Vonkenberg to retain his leadership role in the young men's league, things would have come out differently in the Reformed churches. In later years one could read in the magazine of this league (which Vonkenberg had founded) the occasional comment to the effect that the work of Vonkenberg was being continued. But people who talked this way were deceiving themselves and others. Their appeal to Vonkenberg did not get at the very heart of his work among the young men. The gold had indeed lost its lustre under the destructive influence of synodocracy and scholasticism.

Kindred spirits

Vonkenberg and Schilder were kindred spirits, even though the former was a spiritual child of the Doleantie (1886) and the latter of the Secession (1834). Schilder once said of Vonkenberg: "I am happy that in my life I was able to feel this very warm heart beating nearby."

It is true that Vonkenberg had been schooled by Kuyper and had many scholastic constructions in his thinking, which he simply regarded as part of the Reformed inheritance. But who could take that ill of him? He was a child of his time. Schilder came onto the scene as a thinker a little later, and he also had to get rid of some of that ballast. But the great difference between Vonkenberg and many of the

Chapter 1 — Davidic or Solomonic? 61

theologians of his time was that in addition to the Kuyper of common grace (the wrong one), there was for him also the Kuyper of the antithesis, the reformational Kuyper, and it was the second one that he clung to. So completely was this his emphasis that he got into conflict with Kuyper himself on a number of occasions. He paid Kuyper all the honor and respect that is due a great teacher, but he was not a slavish follower, as so many of his colleagues were.

If he felt he had to oppose Kuyper sometimes, it was especially in the area of practical politics, for here Kuyper often operated more as a diplomat than as one who confesses certain principles. I remember that R. A. den Ouden, who was Kuyper's secretary for a while, was once sent by Kuyper to Zwijndrecht to settle an issue between Vonkenberg and the grand old man. In giving Den Ouden this assignment, Kuyper said to him, "You have to go and visit that man for me in his 'zwijndrechtse' parsonage."[39] Such a sentence was intended to mean a great deal when it came from the mouth of Kuyper. When he wrote about his controversy with Koffyberg, Kuyper referred to him more than once as "the man in the 'muidenbergse' parsonage."[40] He did not seem to think too highly of Koffyberg.

Vonkenberg recognized the threat of deformation in his day but pointed to a different spot than Hepp did when he wrote about deformation a little later.[41] Vonkenberg also saw that things were going wrong at the Free University. When commenting on the future of this institution which Kuyper had established, he quoted what Sikkel had already written in 1916: "Unless by God's grace there is a more powerful impulse springing from the root of the unadulterated Reformed principle — and soon! — the University threatens to become a fiasco in everything that has to do with its establishment and existence, even if other institutions should think well of it in terms of ordinary criteria."

J. van Oord, who was president of the young men's league for a little while after the liberation, honors Vonkenberg as his teacher in his brochure *Secession and Appeal,* where he writes: "It is my firm conviction that Vonkenberg was shoved to the background because

---

[39] "Zwijn" is a Dutch word for swine or pig. —TRANS.

[40] "Muide" is a Dutch word for gully. —TRANS.

[41] Valentijn Hepp (1879-1950) wrote a series of brochures entitled *Threatening Deformation* (Kampen: Kok, 1936-37), which were directed against Dooyeweerd, Vollenhoven, and Schilder and in which he talked especially about common grace and anthropology (the question of body and soul). —TRANS.

of his reformational testimony, and that this is why his work in the [young men's] League came to an end the way it did — even if in *formal* respects the question of a state subsidy can be named as the reason." I agree completely with this observation.

People liked and appreciated the Vonkenberg of "common grace." What he brought about in the social domain was praised by all who were still Antirevolutionary. But as for the Vonkenberg of the *antithesis,* who wanted to draw the line clearly in the church as well as in politics and society — people wanted nothing to do with him.

Vonkenberg also entered the battle on the political and social front. People feared his influence. When he served in Barendrecht, his influence was devastating for the Liberals. In the last election held during his time there, they went down to 300 votes from 1800 votes, whereas the Antirevolutionaries got 1000 votes. When a new mayor had to be named for Barendrecht, Vonkenberg went personally to The Hague to plead with the provincial governor for the appointment of someone who was Antirevolutionary.[42] The official he talked with did not understand the situation too well and thought Vonkenberg was himself the Antirevolutionary prospect for mayor who had come to make a plea on his own behalf. He said, "I'll tell you something in confidence. Barendrecht is a very difficult community. They have a troublesome Doleantie minister there, you see, and this man is in effect the mayor . . . "

Now, Vonkenberg was the same sort of man in politics and society as he was in the church. When he came to Barendrecht, the community was under the domination of a very wealthy gentleman farmer who ruled the roost in every area of life — in the school as well as the church. Vonkenberg quickly put an end to this situation by calling the school society into action and electing a board of directors. "The school," he explained, "belongs to the parents — and not to So-and-so." When the consistory pointed out that "So-and-so" made generous financial contributions — to the church as well as to the school — he said, "We do not bow before a golden calf."

That was Vonkenberg — if he saw a wound, he would put his finger right on it. He was a prophet, and he was faithful in his office, regardless of the people and circumstances he came into contact with. The confessions he loved did not apply only to the church but to every area of life or every "sector," as we might say today.

---

[42] In the Netherlands, mayors are not elected, as in North America, but appointed by the crown. —TRANS.

Like Schilder, he has often been misunderstood and condemned out of ignorance. People called him hard and loveless — a man without feeling. Nothing could be further from the truth. People were confusing love as presented in the Scriptures with "being nice." But people who use beautiful, gentle words and streamlined language, who impress us with their velvet gloves and fine parlor manners, who act in a "loving" manner, as it appears — such people are often unmerciful, cruel, and hard as a stone. Prophets aren't like that — unless they are driven by the spirit of *false* prophecy.

Schilder was right when he wrote that Vonkenberg had a warm heart. J. Snoep, who wrote a biography of Vonkenberg, tells the following story: "Once this man (who loved to fight) stood sobbing in the consistory room after the service. When he was asked, 'What's the matter, Reverend?' he answered, 'Oh, it really has nothing to do with me, brothers. But did you see who was holding the child at the baptism? That's what has me so worked up. That girl, the granddaughter of a pious grandmother, is going into the world.' He did not say anything more — and neither did we."

Prophets of this sort lash out with the whip in an effort to beat the sin out of people, and then they cry about — and with — the sinner. Was it any different among the prophets of the old covenant, such as Isaiah, Jeremiah and Amos? Didn't Amos call the fine ladies of Israel's upper crust "cows of Bashan" (see Amos 4:1)? How Vonkenberg would rage and also weep if he could see people today ruining the work he was doing, tearing it down because of their desire for an Irenic, falsely ecumenical Christianity in which there is no place left for the Reformed confessions. Vonkenberg, too, was taken away before the great day of evil.

Schilder understood him and loved him. When Vonkenberg, shortly before his death, quietly observed the fortieth anniversary of his ordination to office, "KS" wrote in his press review: "Our paper is not exactly lavish when it comes to personal notes. But it would be a shame if we did not mention the anniversary being observed by Rev. J. E. Vonkenberg, to whose initiative, courage, determination, and perseverance our Reformed people owe an unspeakable debt."

When Vonkenberg died in July of 1934, on his oldest son's birthday, Schilder devoted an article to his death. I draw your attention to the following observations, partly because they are characteristic of the situation as "KS" viewed it at that time:

I first met Vonkenberg during my Gorcum period. It was only a few years before Assen: the pot was boiling everywhere. It was the time in which clubs were being formed, a process that was then to be distinguished from church formation, and this process was carried through. I have provided a sketch of those developments in some editorials in this paper under the title "From Church to Circle: A Falling Away." People took those articles to be a *portrait* of a *church* group" that stood on its own after Assen, but that's not what I was writing about. The articles were an attempt to sketch what was brewing and cooking long before this particular "church group" proceeded with separate formation. Naturally, the recognition of that club formation, as I had sketched it, led to separate church formation, and this indicates that it is reprehensible, in accordance with the rule that the tree is known by its fruits.

In those days, then, when the process of forming circles and clubs began, and pride led people to invent accolades of praise for "the" younger ones, it was my privilege to make the acquaintance of Rev. Vonkenberg for the first time.

How I admired this organizer back in those days! But not because he initiated me into the secrets of his organization, or showed off impressive numbers or "proved" things with statistics — not at all. I admired him because he knew his time and understood the dangers. He knew at once where a hand that had controlled the helm in earlier days had now grown weak, and where among the younger ones the club spirit had not had a chance to do its destructive work, and where there were possibilities for positive upbuilding in the *church*.

These things were all the more difficult at that time because everyone who expressed himself in a manner different from the one to which the preachers of the previous generation were accustomed was immediately regarded by the leading members of the club as one of "the" younger ones and thus was reckoned to be a member of one's own group — or at least was placed on the list of those who would be invited to join in. The *need of the hour* was the subject of an essay to be written by those interested in joining; the essay would then be the basis for admission.

But Vonkenberg sensed the coming battle and protected his young men. He knew the differences among them: he knew which ones wanted to build on the foundation of Reformed truth, and which ones wanted to carry through for themselves and for others the transition to Schleiermacher and his more recent followers. He knew whom to invite as a speaker for his league days and what he himself should say on Ascension Day in order to combine in a pure way the redemption fact of the day and the *revelational* word of the day with current questions — and then in such a way as to reject whatever was foreign to Reformed thinking and the Reformed confessions.[43] He saw the eventual outcome, and we have also seen it. If we are honest about it, we must declare that he was *right*.

What a shame that there are so many who still do not want to recognize those consequences, even though the outcome has shown us that the monster whose head Vonkenberg wanted to crush was even bigger than many had suspected. We still have to wrestle with the dangers Vonkenberg wanted to exorcize: the evil has not been overcome yet by a long shot. I know that Rev. Vonkenberg was very disappointed about this; his interest in what was going on in theology, politics, economic life, and education remained lively and pure all the way to the end.

He died concerned about the way things were going among us. Just a few months ago he and I talked about it together at his home.

To those who find it necessary to keep some distance from Vonkenberg's appeal for a return to their own Reformed past, to those who disparage his battle for their faith in a posture of Ethical arrogance, I would like to say: What would have become of our Reformed *(Gereformeerd)* churches by now if it were not for

---

[43] Ascension Day was the holiday on which the young men's societies would hold their national rally. —TRANS.

Vonkenberg's brilliant effort to take hold of our youth? What would have been lost in the Netherlands by now? How much new work would *not* have come about if Vonkenberg had *not* sent out his disciples right and left? Let us honor his memory by being Reformed and by returning to Calvinism and to God if that is necessary.

I have written rather extensively about Vonkenberg. I believe this was necessary, for he belonged to the small number of true prophets in the 1920s who saw that things were going wrong with our Calvinistic action in general and with our Reformed churches in particular. He was deeply grieved by what he saw.

When my brother and I had our remarkable conversation with Vonkenberg in the parsonage at Huizen in 1929, we had not seen or talked with him for some eight years. In my youth I had known him well, for I lived in Barendrecht while he was the minister there, and later I encountered him repeatedly through his involvement in our young men's league. He also stayed at our house when we were at Flakkee. But when I saw him again in Huizen, I was somewhat taken aback. In my mind I still pictured him as a strong, sturdy, energetic battler, tireless and unbroken, but what I saw before me was a broken old man (although he had only just turned 60!) who had to interrupt his bed rest to receive us.

He still quoted Fabius's motto based on the image of the candle: he was quite willing to be consumed as long as he was of use.[44] He was indeed a candle that had been burned out in the service of his King. But his bitter disappointment at the falling away in the churches also played a major role in his state of mind and health. Vonkenberg was very sad at what had developed — that was obvious during our visit. The one time he caught fire during our conversation, he got out of his chair like the Vonkenberg of old and underscored his words with powerful gestures. He then criticized the way things were going at the Free University and in the Antirevolutionary Party with its representatives in the national parliament, and he also complained about the policies of the Christian labor union. He regarded these forms of Christian action as straying from the path. It seemed to me that nothing escaped him. How these things filled him with pain, for in his eyes, too, the Kuyper of the antithesis had been separated from the

---

[44] "Terar dum prosim."

Kuyper of common grace in order to interpret the latter in a way contrary to anything Kuyper himself would have accepted.

Vonkenberg was indeed close spiritual kin to Schilder, and now that we have some horrible events behind us in our church life, the question naturally arises: How much did Schilder's unexpected death (he was younger at the time of death than Vonkenberg had been, and he was also a powerful figure in psychical and physical respects) have to do with disappointment at the same kinds of events? One day, when the books are opened, we will have an answer to this question, for God counts the tears of His faithful prophets.

D. P. D. Fabius

There is one more figure to be mentioned in this connection — Fabius. I can be brief about him because Rev. B. Jongeling has dealt with him in his outstanding work *Between Two Reformations* and has told us what we need to know about the life and work of this faithful prophet, who was perhaps the first to recognize the falling away and apostasy — at least in the social and political domain. I'm sure that in time we will conclude more and more that Fabius was right. He had cursed modern democracy as a poisonous plant that sprang from the soil of the French revolution. He recognized the threat posed by state socialism before anyone else did, and so people thought he was tilting at windmills. It is time we begin to study his works again, for they can open our eyes to many things around us.

I will let such matters rest here and deal with him in his battle to keep the Reformed *(Gereformeerd)* churches pure on the basis of the confessions. In his book on Fabius, Jongeling writes: "The treasures that were gathered in heaven, i.e. return to the Word of the Lord, new obedience to the Word of the Lord, were traded in for treasures on earth, i.e. honor, respect, power, influence. Fabius spoke out against this faithfully and powerfully; he fought tirelessly for the preservation of the inheritance we had received. He pointed to the decline in church life, which resulted in part from the fact that people's eyes were closed to the church in her offices and services, in her formation and reformation; instead people began to talk about a so-called invisible church, which was supposed to be present in all sorts of visible churches."

Fabius, who was one of the elders who had been suspended in Amsterdam in 1886, viewed the Church as primary all through his life, and he never wanted to hear talk about the confessions being mainly "for the church." Whoever makes confession of faith does so for his life as a whole: his commitment covers all life situations. It makes no difference whether one sits in the elders' bench or among the representatives in the national parliament or even serves in the cabinet. The confession is to be respected and followed wherever we live, work, think, and cherish our desires. Borrowing some words from Groen van Prinsterer, Fabius declared: "Like the Reformation, the Revolution touches every field of action and learning. In the days of the Reformation the principle was submission to God; in these days it is a revolt against God. That is why there rages again today one universal war in church, state, and the world of learning, one holy battle over the supreme question: to submit unconditionally to the law of God, or not."[45]

Fabius detested the practice of subordinating the Church to political ends and having her operate in a way that would allow for political gain. He remarked sarcastically: *"The Standard* recently called the National Reformed *(Hervormd)* churches the 'time-honored church,' from which the Reformed *(Gereformeerd)* churches have 'temporarily' separated themselves. This was written with an eye to the parliamentary elections coming up soon."

Commentary was not needed in this case. Fabius maintained that when church reformation took place, what happened was not that a *new* church was established but precisely that the age-old church was *continued.* "What took place in the sixteenth century was a *reformation* of the existing Christian church — not the establishment of a *new* church. The Protestant traces his family tree back to the first human couple in Paradise."

Fabius was mocked for making this comment: people drew the conclusion, in jest, that if Adam and Eve were alive today, they would be members of the Reformed *(Gereformeerd)* church. Fabius would have answered calmly: if they had persevered in their faith, they most surely would be Reformed. Anyone who is serious about the confessions could not draw any other conclusion. Such a person will likewise be sure not to gloss over church issues for the sake of forming a political power bloc.

Fabius also noted the great danger that threatened our church in the form of the Ethical and synthetic spirit. When Rev. Netelenbos, the Reformed *(Gereformeerd)* minister in Middelburg about whom I

---

[45] This quotation was drawn from Groen's *Lectures on Unbelief and Revolution.* See the translated edition prepared by Harry Van Dyke (Jordan Station, Ontario: Wedge Publishing Foundation, 1989), p. 14 of the text section.

wrote earlier, conducted a service in a National Reformed *(Hervormd)* church in 1917, Fabius disapproved strongly. In connection with this matter he wrote: "Many people seem to think that however widespread the unchurchly spirit may be, we need not be apprehensive about it in our Reformed *(Gereformeerd)* circles. Those who talk this way are deceiving themselves. Reformed life is not isolated to such an extent that the errors in circulation in our time have no grip on us. That the Reformed churches are not immune from the virus of unchurchliness is evident from what Rev. Netelenbos did and what this event made manifest. We can rest assured that this event was only possible because there was, in a fairly wide circle, a spirit of agreement with such an action."

By writing these words, Fabius was taking a strict position against *The Herald,* which maintained that the public debate about this "distasteful story" (i.e. what Rev. Netelenbos had done) should cease. *The Herald* proclaimed: "We should not keep pursuing a brother who made a mistake while acting in good faith." Fabius observed in response: "This seems a most suspicious comment to me. To characterize a battle against errors as a battle against persons promotes a pernicious clique mentality and winds up oppressing the truth. Moreover, an error is no less dangerous just because someone adheres to it in good faith."

In this exchange we begin to see the two lines that would later be taken by the *The Herald* and *The Reformation* respectively. Note that *The Herald* did not want to see the church "pursuing" an erring brother — someone who was later condemned by the Synod (and rightly so) for attacking Scriptural authority. Later there was a continual "pursuit" going on, but then it involved a brother who was *not* straying from the truth, a brother whose main desire was to uphold Scripture and the confessions. That brother was pursued by the threat of excommunication.

What came into the open in the years 1942 through 1944 was already present in germinal form twenty-five years before in the bosom of the Reformed churches. Anyone who is tolerant toward heretics and false teachers will necessarily be *in*tolerant toward those who wish to be faithful to principles. Such a person will characterize the reformational work of men who remain faithful to the confessions as deadly work in the church — "worse than in the time of Assen."

Fabius sharply criticized the blurring of the boundaries — especially ecclesiastical boundaries. Back in 1918 he offered the following characterization of the way some people think, and it is just as applicable to our time as to his: "There are some people who say that it's fine that we have the Church, provided we keep an eye open for the evil it can all too easily bring about. Ecclesiastical walls cannot be avoided altogether, but we should make sure that they do not function too much as walls. Reaching out beyond church walls is much more important than having those walls in the first place. Free gatherings of Christians in which church differences are disregarded have much more spiritual value than church services. Moreover, Christian unity is manifested in an outstanding way when people attend churches other than their own and when ministers conduct services in other churches — indeed, this sort of thing is of greater importance than church life as such. The Church only exists to inspire people. If anyone goes beyond this, he is violating the church's natural borders, and it is in the church's interest to resist him."

In those days of decline, Fabius was one of the first to understand that when things go wrong in the Church they will go wrong everywhere. Therefore he was deeply saddened at the signs of decline in the Reformed churches of his time: "There is a very serious danger threatening the church — also the Reformed *(Gereformeerd)* Church. I pray that eyes may be opened to it, and that we may become more aware of the holiness of the Church, so that the drive to unchurchliness, which keeps pushing through and threatening Christianity itself, may be checked and broken."

Fabius also objected to the kind of preaching he was hearing: "The Bible is not a textbook of morality which sometimes teaches by sketching lives, some of which we can imitate while others are warnings to us (especially in the Old Testament), and which teaches in other places through direct moral lessons and admonitions (especially in the New Testament) . . . In the strict sense there should be no preaching overtop of a text or in connection with a text; rather, the text itself has to be preached, proclaimed. The text has to be opened, and from that opened text, treasures have to be dug up and held before the people, as though they came from a mine . . ."

Those dry, dogmatic, abstract, exemplary sermons accelerated the decline in our churches and gave some substance to the critique coming from the younger generation. It was not until the 1930s, under the leadership of Schilder and others, that things began to change: over against this seemingly pious but essentially cheap exemplary method of preaching, the redemptive-historical line in the Old and

New Testaments was brought out. Exegesis, the normative power of the Word of God in its various parts and its unbreakable unity, was restored to honor and the obedience of faith. The Word was opened and restored to its unique place in the pulpit.

It was perhaps Kuyper's biggest omission that he did not realize that building constructions overtop of the Word would block the congregation's free access to that Word. He could have avoided this mistake if he had learned the proper lesson from the seventeenth and eighteenth centuries. The prophetic mind of Fabius recognized this and warned against it.

Indeed, all through his public life, Fabius took on the heavy and thankless task of prophesying against sin and apostasy. Early on he spotted the roots of the coming deformation, and what he saw placed him in an isolated position. His was the isolation of the faithful prophet.

When the Free University celebrated its fiftieth anniversary in 1930, he was present and could certainly not be ignored; in fact, he was one of the invited speakers for this celebration. But there was not much celebration to be found in the address he gave. Although he was too old to be considered an "enfant terrible," he was a stern dissenter from the mighty chorus of celebration assembled for this occasion.

His address was even included in the memorial volume published to mark the occasion. Before releasing the address for publication, Fabius added a number of notes, which was typical of him, and those notes, even more than the address itself, show us what a prophet of lamentation he was. But he did not mince words in the address itself either. His title was "Past and Future." Now, such a title leaves a great deal of room for what might need saying, and he spoke freely.

Although the Reformed *(Gereformeerd)* camp was busy chumming around with the National Reformed *(Hervormd)* people by this time, Fabius calmly quoted what Dr. Gunning had said: "the synodical organization is born of the spirit of apostasy and this is a work of the devil."[46] Fabius even called this "a manly word," which, he added, "was never sealed with a manly deed." Yet he immediately went on to say:

> This is language our Reformed *(Gereformeerd)* people understand and respond to with an amen. This is the language they want to hear in the Christian press, which

---

[46] The "synodical" organization referred to in this discussion is the National Reformed *(Hervormd)* Church. —TRANS.

they expect from our representatives in the national parliament, and which they expect will also be heard in the lecture rooms of the Free University. It is in this spirit that our young people must be educated . . .

Teach the young man the first principles demanded of his walk in life, and when he has grown old he will not depart from them.

A little further in his address Fabius said:

It gives us reason to stop and think when we realize that the battle against the synodical organization is fading away, however much this organization is in full conflict with Reformed *(Gereformeerd)* principles, as even people who are not Reformed can tell you. It also gives us reason to stop and think when we see how much the line of the Doleantie, which we always judged to be in accordance with those Reformed principles and which our people loved and understood very clearly, seems to be fading away more and more. We no longer hear any talk about setting that synodical organization aside at the insistence of consistories and of members of the congregation who appeal to the office of all believers as basis. We do not hear about Reformed ministers visiting the homes of the synodical [i.e. *Hervormd*] preachers to admonish them; what we hear about instead is friendly contact between them, and sometimes the two sides join together in church activities . . .

A little further on Fabius lashed out against the accommodation of ecclesiastical sensitivities for the sake of political power:

People feel pressure from all sides. If we do not pay attention to such sensitivities, it might cost us votes — what a catastrophe! — and perhaps even a seat in parliament. We forget what Groen said: "Do you not realize that numerical strength sometimes stands in inverse proportion to *actual power?* Do you not realize that the withdrawal of those whose faithfulness and fearlessness could not be counted on is what makes a group of fighters into a band like Gideon's?" .... Whoever wants to accommodate all ecclesiastical sensitivities for the sake of politics will feel so pressured that he is stifled. We must have the courage, where necessary, to go into ecclesiastical questions fearlessly. It is a battle not about persons but about principles, a battle in which the future of the Netherlands is at stake.

Fabius quoted Dr. Willem van den Bergh, "the conscience of the Doleantie," who regarded the National Reformed *(Hervormd)* church organization as in conflict with all ten of the Lord's commandments. In his notes he declared that the decline in the Antirevolutionary Party began back in the 1890s: "The misery dates back to 1894-96 (the franchise bills of Tak and of Van Houten). From that time on, there has been a lack of leadership; the idea that we must win the election seemed to dominate everything." He spoke of a withering process within the Party. He also directed sharp arrows of criticism against the Christian press: "And how do things stand with the Christian press? It almost never referred to my battle against democracy, which Mr. Lohman *did* note. When Dr. Nederbragt came out with an earnest writing, the press killed it with silence. The strong argument put forward by Rev. Sikkel was scarcely acknowledged."

In a note to the passage in which he talked about "friendly contact" between Reformed *(Gereformeerd)* and National Reformed *(Hervormd)* ministers, Fabius added: "The papers tell us that in the services held in the Reformed *(Gereformeerd)* church in Hooger-Smilde on November 9, 1930, the minister delivered a farewell sermon in which he addressed the National Reformed *(Hervormd)* minister, who was present for this occasion, as his 'friend,' and that the National Reformed minister also got to speak — all of this taking place in a Reformed *(Gereformeerd)* church. Especially among the younger ministers, the ecclesiastical lines seem to be blurring in a dangerous way. Could it be that when we examine candidates, we do not pay enough attention to those lines?"

Fabius said these things thirty years ago! And we know what the situation is now. But thirty years ago we were already radically mistaken. What we experience now is only the fruit of what was sown then. We live in a time in which the apostasy and falling away are coming to full development.

Davidic or Solomonic?

And now I come back to what I started with: I mentioned that in 1927, Seerp Anema published a brochure entitled *Davidic or Solomonic*. In his introduction to his well-known Biblical novel *The Shunammite,* he tells us that in the brochure he used material which he had gathered for the novel, and then he makes this comment about the brochure: "My brochure *Davidic or Solomonic,* which was published by Kok of Kampen in 1927, tried to sketch out the characteristic lines of the nature and course of the history of Solomon's reign. In that characterization we find the leading thought that must serve to bind the separate volumes of this cycle together."

Anema made a serious effort to understand and characterize the time in which he lived. This is hard to do, for a village in a valley can more easily be seen in a panoramic fashion from a point on a hillside, where spatial relationships become obvious, than from a position in the market square in the middle of the town. The writing of contemporary history — if it goes beyond noting facts and events in an effort to discuss backgrounds and spiritual directions — calls for a prophetic mind. Earlier I mentioned that Fabius was a prophet. Was Seerp Anema a prophet as well? In any event, he was a poet by the grace of God, and he wanted to study his times and understand them in the light of Scripture. Poets have keen vision. He turned away principally from the modern pagan worship of art among the members of the 1880s group and wanted to establish a genuinely Christian poetry.

I believe that Anema, as a poet, also had a visionary grasp of his time and that we can learn something from his brochure. Although it is only forty pages long, the brochure draws parallels between the time of David and Solomon, on the one hand, and the time of Kuyper and after (the 1920s), on the other.

In drawing those parallels, Anema appeals to other writers before him. Indeed, if you are acquainted with the literature of our forefathers, you will be aware how much some of our writers and poets liked to regard our land as the "Israel of the west."

There is a book called *Songs of the Fatherland* which is not widely known, even though it was assembled and published by none other than Groen van Prinsterer. Years ago a copy of the second edition (published by Kemink & Zoon in 1856) happened to come into my hands. When our country was occupied by Nazi Germany in 1940 I was trying to arrange for another edition of this book to be published. I contacted Colijn just a few weeks before the Germans arrested him

Chapter 1 — Davidic or Solomonic? 75

and asked him to write an introduction to the book.⁴⁷ I got a quick answer in the form of a letter written in Colijn's own handwriting, in which he told me that he would not be able to do it. The Germans were keeping a close eye on him and had even banned an edition of another book for which he had written the introduction.⁴⁸ His advice to us was to stay away from him altogether. That was the situation in 1940 and the years immediately after that.

In any event, I still have my copy of that book, which shows us an entirely different side of Groen van Prinsterer: he was also a literary man! He quotes verses drawn from Vondel, Huygens, Cats, Grotius, the Van Harens, Bilderdijk, Da Costa, Van Lennep, Van Alphen, Marnix van St. Aldegonde, Brandt, Vollenhove, and many others. And in these poets he finds occasions where they make comparisons between the history of our country and the history of ancient Israel.

He also quotes a number of psalms. The very first poem in the book is characteristic of the work as a whole; in it we find reference to Psalm 44:2: "They did not take the land through their own sword; their arm did not win deliverance for them. But Your right hand, Your power, gave them their prosperity. The splendor of the divine countenance allowed them to take the path of victory: for You bathed them with the light of Your gracious good pleasure."⁴⁹ When he comes to a poem on ocean navigation ("Zeevaart"), Groen quotes Psalm 107: "Those who go down to the sea in ships, who do business on great waters . . . "

Huygens, Vondel, Bilderdijk, and Da Costa, in particular, are the ones who love to draw parallels between Israel and the Netherlands. Groen quotes Bilderdijk when he rejoices over the House of Orange (Nassau): "Like a cherub with outstretched wings, covering the ark of the covenant in the temple's inner sanctuary, so you, O Nassau's house, in our Father's days, stood shining with the glow of the good pleasure of the Most High."⁵⁰

---

⁴⁷ Hendrik Colijn was an Antirevolutionary Party leader and served as Prime Minister in 1925-26 and again in 1933-39. —TRANS.

⁴⁸ The book was *Wat heeft Groen ons vandaag te zeggen?* by H. Smitskamp. —TRANS.

⁴⁹ "Hun zwaard deed hen dit land niet erven; / Hun arm deed hen geen heil verwerven; / Maar Uwe rechterhand, Uw macht, / Heeft hun die voorspoed toegebracht. / De glans van 't Godd'lijk aangezicht / Heeft hen de zege weg doen dragen: / Want Gij omscheent hen met het licht / Van Uw genadig welbehagen."

⁵⁰ "Gelijk een Cherub die, de vleug'len uitgestrekt, / In 't Tempelheiligdom de Bondkist overdekt, / Zo stondt ge, o Nassaus huis! in onzer Vaderen dagen / Omschitterd met de glans van 's Hoogsten welbehagen."

Groen also included a long poem by Vondel, which was entirely inspired by Israel's history. In this poem, entitled, "The Deliverance of Israel and the Deliverance of the Netherlands," Pharaoh is equated with King Philip of Spain: "Who shall paint Pharaoh in a life-like way, as Philip the Monarch brandishing his staff! . . . . The one honors Osiris [an Egyptian idol —RvR] on bended knee, the other wishes to honor the God of the Tiber [the Pope —RvR]. The one mows down innocent babes and sweeps them into the grave, the other kills them at their mother's breasts. The one oppresses Jacob's house with slavery; the other lords it over the Netherlands with tyranny."[51]

I am tempted to quote much more of this material, for it is certainly interesting and instructive, but such quotations would fall outside the framework of this book. I have quoted enough to make it clear that from the time we attained our national independence until the beginning of our century, poets and Christian historians found plenty of occasion to draw comparisons between the histories of the Netherlands and of Israel. (Someone should write a doctoral dissertation about this.)

Anema finds nothing unusual in this tendency on the part of our forefathers. He writes: "They wanted to live in Scriptural terms, that is to say, in Old Testament terms. The Old Testament was to them just as important a part of the divine revelation as the New Testament."

Yet this way of thinking and talking is also dangerous. Remember that Israel was liberated from slavery under the Egyptians in a miraculous way. Well then, wasn't our country liberated from the bondage imposed by Roman Catholic Spain? By God's appointment, Moses became Israel's deliverer. Wasn't the Prince of Orange *our* deliverer? Isn't the Netherlands of comparable geographical importance for the west as Israel was for the Near East? Aren't the two countries about the same size? Don't they have about the same coastline? Think also of the further history. There were battles with enemies all around. There were also battles within — formation of the Church, deformation of the Church, and then reformation of the Church again. Didn't both peoples live through all of this? Doesn't the time of the Judges make us think of the end of the eighteenth century? Isn't

---

[51] "Wie schildert Pharaoh naar 't leven af / Als Philippus de Monarch, in 't zwaaien van zijn staf! ldots / Den eenen eert Osir met zijn gebogen kniên; Den anderen zal de God des Tijbers eere biên; Den eenen maait in 't graf d' onnooz'le zuigelingen, Den anderen die nog aan 's moeders borsten hingen. Den eenen Jacobs huis verdrukt met slavernij, En d'ander 't Nederland verheert met tyrannij."

Bilderdijk in his lonely struggle against his own inclinations as well as against the enemies of the Church a second Samson? And the heroes of the nineteenth century, the men of the Réveil — weren't they judges in their often despairing and lonely battle against the power of liberalism? Wasn't Groen van Prinsterer a Samuel who prepared the people to defend themselves in principle, so that they could finally come together again as an organized community? Before that time, organization was not possible because of the oppression of the enemy. (The people of the Secession were persecuted!) And then came David. Under this mighty hero Israel became great; David defeated enemies everywhere and killed his tens of thousands. He ruled unchallenged from the Red Sea to the Euphrates.

Who can help but think of Kuyper here? David organized the work of the priests and the Levites. He brought the worship connected with the ark to Jerusalem. He led the people to inner reformation and brought about a powerful organization of the army as it faced outwards.

On the twenty-fifth anniversary of the young men's league in 1913, Kuyper himself alluded to such comparisons: "Fifty years ago, when I first came to know Calvinism with its steel heart and cutting sharpness, it was a pitiful phenomenon in our good fatherland. There was literally not a single theologian of any reputation who defended Calvinism. There was no company on the march that had Calvinism in its flag. In our organizational and civic life, there was no thread of Calvinism to be found. And no scholarly circle, however small, concerned itself with restoring the inheritance of our fathers to a position of honor. It just lay there — faded, dried out, lifeless."

Such was the situation in our poor fatherland when Kuyper stepped onto the public stage. The Philistines had seen to it that there was no smith any longer in Israel (see I Samuel 13:19). There was no university where Calvinism was taught, and no seminary where the young men could hear about it. Indeed, there was hardly a church where Calvinism was mentioned. Is it any wonder that Anema characterized the mighty time of organization under Kuyper as a "Davidic period"?

It is true that there are certain dangers in these comparisons, dangers that many people seemed unable to escape. There was the danger of exemplarism. And from Kuyper's familiar cry of "We Calvinists!" people often got the strong impression that *we* are none other than the Israel of the West. Of course this is wrong, for there is no

Israel of the West and there never will be. Fortunately, redemptive history is not cyclical: the old covenant people had the special task of bringing forth the Christ, and when that was done their task was accomplished and no other people would ever take on such a role. Here, too, exemplarism represents a hollowing out of the Word of God, which robs it of its power, and we should be deathly afraid of it. Yet Anema says — and I agree with him — that it would be hard to deny a certain point of comparison between David's time and Kuyper's.

I already pointed to some of the similarities. And it is true that God has concerned Himself with few nations on earth as fully as with the Netherlands. He has favored us in spiritual respects above all other peoples that exist now or have ever existed. Nowhere in the world did the Reformation win out so powerfully and work its will so fully in the various sectors of life as among us. And the history by which our nation became independent is also a story of church struggle and church liberation. Calvinism *is* indeed the origin of our sovereignty and our independence. No country on earth can deny us that. It was God's right hand and power that brought us our prosperity and freedom. And He chose to use the house of Orange to bring all of this about.

Thus there are indeed some points of comparison between our history and the history of the people of Israel. Our national poets had good reason to allude to events in Old Testament history when they wrote about our national struggle. Marnix van St. Aldegonde was not striking a discordant note or engaging in idle boasts when he put the following words in the mouth of the Prince of Orange, words that now form part of our national anthem:

> *Once David searched for shelter*
> *From King Saul's tyranny.*
> *E'en so I fled this welter*
> *And many a lord with me.*
> *But God the Lord did save him*
> *From exile and its hell*
> *And, in His mercy, gave him*
> *A realm in Israel.*[52]

---

[52] Als David moesten vluchten / Voor Saul den Tyran, / Zoo heb ik moeten zuchten / Met menig Edelman. / Maar God heeft hem verheven, / Verlost uit aller nood, / Een Koninkrijk gegeven / in Israel zoo groot.

Provided we distinguish very carefully between the special position, origin, and purpose of Israel's existence as a people, on the one hand, and the general position of our people as a nation among other nations in this world, on the other, we may draw attention to the points of similarity. (Groen van Prinsterer told us not to confuse comparing with identifying.) We may even draw some lessons from the comparison, for that would also be a Biblical thing to do.

The "citadel of David"

In connection with the founding of the Free University, that "act of faith," Anema speaks of the "citadel of David." As the basis for the speech he made on the great day on which the Reformed people opened this university and began to use it, Hoedemaker chose a text that again invites comparison between our history and Israel's: "Now no blacksmith could be found in all the land of Israel, for the Philistines said, 'Lest the Hebrews make swords or spears'," (I Samuel 13:19).

Kuyper concluded his powerful address "Sphere Sovereignty" with the following unforgettable peroration:

> If this business did not stem from the Mighty One of Jacob, how could it stand? What we are doing with this institution goes against all that is great, against a world of scholars; it opposes a century of unspeakable temptations. Therefore, look down on us as persons, on our power, on our scientific importance if you feel you must because of your sense of who you are. The Calvinistic confession that God is *everything* and man is *nothing* gives you the right to do so. But this one thing I ask of you, even if you are our fiercest opponent: do not withhold your respect for the *passion* that animates us. The confession that we have recently dusted off was once the cry that welled up from the soul of our oppressed nation. The Bible, before whose authority we bow, once comforted the sorrowful among *your own* forefathers. And the Christ, whose Name we honor in this institution, is He not the Inspirer and the Chosen One and the Adored One of *your own* fathers? Suppose this is not what people are writing in their study chambers and echoing in the blast furnaces; suppose that, as you confess, people are finished with the Bible, and that Christianity is no more than a defeated standpoint —

even then I ask: Isn't Christianity, in your eyes, too important historically, too majestic and holy as a historical phenomenon, to be allowed to collapse without honor and to sink away shamefully? Isn't there such a thing as "Noblesse oblige" anymore? And should we allow the banner we took with us from Golgotha to ever fall into enemy hands as long as we have not been tested to the uttermost, as long as there is still a single arrow in our quiver, as long as there is still a company of soldiers of the one crowned on Golgotha, however small it might be, that lives on this inheritance? To this question an answer of "With God's help, NEVER" arises in our souls. And from that NEVER this institution has been born. And to that NEVER, as a statement of faithfulness to a higher principle, I ask an echo in response. May it be an amen that arises from every patriotic heart!

This was David's lute and David's song. A minister who heard that address declared, "This speech, in one blow, will bring us twenty-five years further." And it was so.

Within twenty-five years Kuyper was prime minister of the Netherlands, and with his Higher Education Bill he broke the liberal monopoly in the university sector. In defense of his law concerning higher education, he spoke to the parliament. This ministerial address was so eloquent and powerful, it soared so high and was so deep in meaning, that Prof. Aalberse stood amazed that Kuyper could improvise so well, for he had nothing more in front of him than a single cue card and a blue pencil.

Kuyper won this battle by placing the right in direct opposition to the left. And after he dissolved the First Chamber of the parliament,[53] the Liberal dominance there was broken for good. A Roman Catholic paper wrote as follows about this event: "There is much in Kuyper's life that arouses our interest, but his battle for the liberation of higher education will remain the most glorious page in his history as far as later generations are concerned. The way Kuyper placed this world problem at the center of Dutch interest and discussion and made it a shibboleth in the political arena has guaranteed immortality for his name in the Dutch cultural world."

---

[53] The First Chamber corresponds to the "upper house" in some other legislative systems, e.g. the Senate in the United States and the House of Lords in Great Britain. —TRANS.

The "two lines"

The "Davidic period" in its fullest blossoming! But I spoke earlier about "two lines" in Kuyper's life. It is significant that Seerp Anema already talked this way back in 1927. And if there was anyone who knew Kuyper intimately, it was surely Anema, who was a friend of the Kuyper family. Anema says: "His opponents came forward with a foolish and short-sighted reproach to the effect that he didn't mean what he said, that he took up the cause of faith only because of clever calculations concerning his own chances for greatness through this cause. But it is a different matter to suggest the possibility that the strategy was too much bound up with his own character, that the strategy was only followed where it was demanded, than to say that Davidic simplicity and uprightness ornamented his character. Could it be that he let a cunning woman get closer to uncut locks than was desirable for someone who was a Nazirite?[54] Didn't the yearning to dominate tend too much to prevent the development of personal sympathy among the members of his staff?"

Here I think of the highly appreciative article about Kuyper's passing which Elout wrote in a leading Dutch newspaper (the *Algemeen Handelsblad*) on November 9, 1920. This liberal also saw two lines in Kuyper. When he sang Kuyper's praises as the great ringer of the chimes, he raised the question whether Kuyper always heard the chimes of the great clock of truth and concluded: "Kuyper did damage to the clock of truth in little things but was faithful to it in big things. He sinned against the truth distressingly often. In word and deed — and not least in the way he carried on polemics in *The Standard* — he often annoyed both friend and foe. And the chimes of the clock of truth do not give forth a perfect sound for Kuyper. But to suggest that a life like his could have been a lie, that he himself didn't believe the things he taught, that his inner being and his statements were always two different things — such a line of thinking is simply unacceptable. So much darkness could not possibly bring forth so much light; such an inner split could not possibly have produced so much unity in thousands of other people. When you take Kuyper's life as a whole and look at the big things, you see that it was service of what he took to be the truth. That's why, for Kuyper, the clock of truth is also striking now, however many cracks he made in it . . . Kuyper, the great ringer of the chimes, is dead."

---

[54] This reference to the story of Samson and Delilah is of course meant as a metaphor. — RvR.

In claiming that the Davidic characteristics are dominant in Kuyper, Anema does not ignore the Solomonic ones: "But they did not affect the core of his work. His work remains, in its essence and outworking, Davidic. But in its completion it suffered from Solomonic features."

On the other hand, Anema also sees human sinfulness coming out in the Davidic features: "In a regenerated heart there are two kinds of features alongside one another. On the one hand there is the childlike love for the work of God — think of David wearing an ephod, skipping before the ark of the Lord, and think of the pleasures of his heart, namely, to appear humble before the maids of his servants. On the other hand there are Solomonic features — think of the decision to count his people so that he would know the extent of his power, and also of his desire to rule the kings around him. Don't these two lines also run through Kuyper's life? The pillar that was Saul's life was completely cut by that hairline crack, and thereby it lost all of its value for God's kingdom. In David's case the split did not penetrate to the very center."

Faith triumphed within David, and so he resisted the temptation to become like the eastern despots around him. He kept the royal law, for he did not multiply wives or multiply horses (two characteristic features of eastern despotism, which strives for worldly power and greatness). Anema wrote: "In the kingship of David, the ruler (who was acquainted with eastern despotism) was subordinate to the prophet, who ate at his table. Otherwise, how would David so quickly have accepted the judgment of Nathan's 'Thou art the man!' or the choice between three punishments which Gad held before him?"

David sang the praises of the forgiveness of sins in his famous penitential psalm (the fifty-first) and later in the thirty-second, and we should continue to regard Kuyper in similar terms. He remains more the man of the antithesis than the man of common grace. His prophetic power was not broken because of a yearning for worldly fame and greatness. In these respects he was like David.

These things cannot be said of David's son, Solomon. It is significant that the Bible reports that David, before his death, had Solomon ride on his (i.e. David's) mule at the time he was anointed king (I Kings 1:38). But a little further on we read: "And Solomon had 40,000 stalls of horses for his chariots, and 12,000 horsemen" (I Kings 4:26). And how he multiplied his wives! Solomon wanted to secure his position in worldly terms, and so he sought security and alliances by marrying princesses from all sorts of pagan courts. He also organized an army in worldly style. Solomon despised the royal law, and so God could not give him the long life He had conditionally promised him because Solomon did not keep his end of the agreement. He was only fifty-eight when he died. And then came the division of the kingdom into two parts.

When Nehemiah was allowed to return from exile in Babylon many years later, he saw how the people had fallen away: people were doing business on the sabbath, and many of the men had married Philistine, Ammonite, and Moabite women. Many of the children could no longer speak the language of Judah but spoke the language of Ashdod instead. The services in the temple were neglected, and the contributions were no longer given for the Levites. The Levites and singers who were to perform the services retired to their own fields. Those conditions aroused the polemicist in this preacher of repentance. His polemic was cutting and sharp. Nehemiah cursed them, struck them, pulled out their hair, and made them take an oath that they would change: "You shall not give your daughters to their sons, nor take of their daughters for your sons or for yourselves. Did not Solomon king of Israel sin regarding these things? Yet among the many nations there was no king like him, and he was loved by his God" (Nehemiah 13:25-26).

Davidic faithfulness or Solomonic departure?

Davidic or Solomonic? Seerp Anema posed this question in 1927, seven years after Kuyper's death. Anema also understood that what is important is not strong organization or political power and influence; in the final analysis, what counts is what lives in people's hearts.

The Anema of 1927 was uneasy. He saw the Davidic line blurring and growing weaker, as the Solomonic line grew stronger. In the political sphere, the acceptance of universal suffrage concerned him: he viewed it as a first step in the direction of the idol of the people. The Davidic line, he maintained "demands the antithesis. Kuyper was the regenerator of the antithesis for our time. Bavinck weakened it, and here his personality explains a good deal. This weakening led to the conflict which came to be named after Dr. Geelkerken, a man who was entirely Solomonic and even conducted himself like Rehoboam, for he was clumsy and superficial. The foolishness of Rehoboam and his associates did not restore the church of Israel South[55] but threw it into disarray."

At the 1926 annual meeting of the Society for Higher Education, held in Rotterdam, Colijn cried out: "We will *never* let go of our university." Anema adds: "But we can only be true to that motto if the university never lets go of us — or rather, if she remains faithful to the Davidic idea of which she was born, and if she is always able to conquer the Solomonic." A little further on he says: "That the Davidic/Solomonic controversy also creates tensions within the bosom of the Free University could not remain hidden, and that the majority of the students manifest an attitude that suggests the Solomonic choice is an accusation against our university, whether positive, or negative, or perhaps both . . . May God preserve us from the triumph of Solomonic practices. If they win out, we will perish just as the kingship in Israel perished."

What would the 1930s bring — Davidic faithfulness or Solomonic decline?

---

[55] This is an allusion to Geelkerken's congregation, which was the Amsterdam South Church. —TRANS.

Chapter 2

Woe to You, My People!

"Woe to You, My People!"

If Anema's brochure *Davidic or Solomonic* was typical of the 1920s, the book that especially characterizes the 1930s was A. Ingwersen's *Woe to You, My People!*,[1] Who was this man?

I met him once in his home in Amsterdam, the very same house in which Rev. J. C. Sikkel had lived. (There was a plaque on the wall noting Sikkel's occupancy.) Ingwersen admired Sikkel because of the faithful way he fulfilled the office of prophet. The year was 1937, and I was busy gathering material for my book about Colijn.[2]

It was evident to me from Ingwersen's book that he knew the Colijn family well. He was an intimate friend of Colijn's father, who had been a farmer in the Haarlemmermeer polder. I will not soon forget the conversation I had with him.

Like Vonkenberg a few years before him, Ingwersen was very critical of conditions in the 1930s. He was aware of our decline as a people, and also of the decline of the Free University and of the Reformed *(Gereformeerd)* sector of the population. He was a well-known architect and had established a reputation as a master-builder through the modernization of Amsterdam's Reformed Gymnasium (a secondary school). He was a Calvinist of the old style, who honored Kuyper and admired Colijn. Because he was at home in the "Davidic" period, he was not happy with the "Solomonic" character that began to impress itself upon developments in the life of our Reformed people in the 1930s — in politics, in the social arena, and especially in scholarship and church life.

After the war Ingwersen became a contributor to *Elsevier's Weekly,* a periodical in which he offered his opinions freely. What he wrote was always grounded in his Calvinistic outlook on life. He found all sorts of occasions to criticize our national decline as he talked

---

[1] The second printing of this book was issued in 1935 by the Noord-Hollandsche Uitgeversmaatschappij.

[2] Eventually published under the title *De Levensroman van dr. H. Colijn* (Baarn: Bosch & Keuning, no date).

about the general corruption of style in architecture, city planning, and spelling — all of which, he believed, was grounded in the surrender of our roots in Calvinistic soil. With nostalgia in his heart he wrote about the "Davidic time" of his youth; for example, he offered a moving account of how the last evening of the old year would be spent in his parents' home. His father would open the Bible to Psalm 90, which is the prayer of Moses, the man of God, and would read it aloud as the the clock struck twelve. Ingwersen's strong conviction that the Netherlands could only be great if it lived by Calvinism, to which it owed its origin and existence, was never hidden in what he wrote for *Elsevier's Weekly*. From his pen there flowed a faithful, clear, and generous prophetic testimony.

That same prophetic testimony also came through in his book *Woe to You, My People!* Like Anema's brochure, it was widely ignored. There was a second printing, however, but not because the press devoted much attention to the book. *The Standard* carried an interview with Ingwersen, but mainly to make it clear that despite all his criticisms, Ingwersen was still Antirevolutionary and wanted nothing to do with the (Dutch) Nazi movement; the point was not to draw attention to the criticisms themselves. People knew that their toes had been stepped on, and it hurt. Ingwersen had thrown a stone into the tranquil pond of our Dutch complacency, our feeling of having arrived — and that was something he should not have done, people felt.

Solomonic glory

Things seemed to be going very well during the 1930s, and so criticizing was simply not the thing to do. The "Solomonic era," after all, was a time of great glory. We had arrived. The young people from Calvinistic homes who had gone on for higher studies were making careers for themselves as professors, doctors, mayors, government officials, and so forth.

And then there were all those celebrations. In fact, we could well call the 1930s the decade of celebrations. Let me remind you of some of the occasions we observed festively. First of all, in 1930 there was the great Free University celebration, which lasted for three days. The Free University was fifty years old, and the occasion was marked by so many speeches that they filled a book of some 220 pages. In 1933 we commemorated the birth of Prince William of Orange four centuries before. In 1934 it was the Secession *(Afscheiding)* of 1834 that we remembered, and two years later we marked the fiftieth anniversary of the Doleantie. In 1936 we also rejoiced in the engagement of Princess Juliana. In 1937 we celebrated the fact that the Statenvertaling had been with us for three centuries.[3] That same year we also celebrated the wedding of Princess Juliana and Prince Bernhard, and we did not neglect to commemorate the birth of Abraham Kuyper exactly one hundred years before. In 1938 the chimes all over our land rang out when Princess Beatrix was born. That same year was the fiftieth anniversary of the founding of our Reformed Young Men's League.

And so we went from party to party, from celebration to celebration. And there was nothing wrong with celebration in and of itself. Kuyper even wrote a book of meditations about observing festive occasions *(Viert uwe vierdagen)*. Moreover, God had commanded the covenant people in Old Testament times to celebrate festive occasions. The question I wish to raise is: *How* did we celebrate? There is a German saying to the effect that a people that celebrates many festivals forgets to create new occasions for celebration. I can't think of anything that happened in the 1930s that we would want to commemorate one hundred years later.

Ingwersen claimed that we had become spiritual "day-trippers." What did he mean by this? He wrote:

> When you visit an ocean beach, you see two kinds of people there. First of all, there are some who know the times and seasons and conduct themselves accordingly. But secondly, there are also the "day-trippers." O you day-tripper, down by the seashore, sitting where low tide and high tide alternate. A day-tripper likes to come to the beach when it is summer and the tide is out. Then there is plenty of sand, and he can sit there so peacefully. He sets up his beach chair right at the water's edge. He basks in the sunshine and becomes warm and tanned and says to himself, "Here I find 'rest.'," But then he dozes off and does not see the tide coming in. The tide approaches slowly, and in time the sand beneath his feet is soaked. The sleeper's feet begin to sink into the sand, and his

---

[3] The Statenvertaling is a translation of the Bible into Dutch which had been commissioned by the *Staten-Generaal* or parliament of the day. It is roughly comparable to the King James translation in terms of its acceptance among Protestants. —TRANS.

chair starts to tilt. But he sleeps on and notices nothing. But with the rising tide come the waves, and he is finally knocked over — chair and all.

That is how Ingwersen saw the general situation in the 1930s. Therefore he put the trumpet to his lips and sounded a loud warning that a storm was approaching. People would have to take action to save themselves if they did not want to be submerged under the rising tide. But no one listened. People simply did not believe there would be a storm, or even a rising tide. And then it suddenly swept over us in May of 1940,[4] and everything we possessed and celebrated during our easy-going rest of the 1930s was blown away.

Our national independence was gone, and so was the House of Orange. We didn't have a Christian press anymore, or Christian organizations: even the young peoples' societies were taken away. We were thrown into a raging storm and had to rely on our last bulwarks — the *family* and the *Church*. Everything else had suddenly been snatched away. We were plunged into sorrow and anguish. The prison doors swung open for many of us, and some wound up in concentration camps, torture rooms, or even gas chambers. A blind, frantic tyranny pierced the heart of the Dutch nation. "Woe to you, My people!"

A time of epigones

When we go through Ingwersen's book once more today, we can only conclude: he was right! The "Solomonic era," with all of its seeming spiritual riches, was a time of decline. The royal law was ignored, and we adapted ourselves to the world's way of doing things. Diplomacy, the desire for power, the hunger for influence, numbering the people — in short, it was all done the world's way.

And we were completely lacking in *men*. One who stood out above the common run of them was Dr. Colijn, and Ingwersen still respected him. But the rest? They were all day-trippers — epigones at best. In their hands they held the inheritance of a previous generation, but they did not have enough spiritual stature to be able to do anything with it.

---

[4] Although the Netherlands was neutral when World War II began with the German invasion of Poland in September of 1939, Germany invaded the Netherlands without provocation in May of 1940 and quickly conquered it. The German army of occupation was not completely removed by the Allies until May of 1945. —TRANS.

Listen to how Ingwersen castigated this rule of epigones and lashed out against it: "That there was a change of tidal proportions in the years right after Kuyper's death — this is not something that one of the real epigones understands. They are like the little cars that follow along behind a giant locomotive. As long as the giant was leading them, they had a direction and kept moving; but when the locomotive was no longer there, they came to a stop. If such vehicles remain motionless for long, they are shunted to the side and have their wheels removed; eventually they end up in little stations away from the main track, where flower boxes adorn their windows and a hole is cut in the wall to serve as a ticket-window. A conductor seats himself at that window and checks the tickets of the people who are traveling on a train that is still running. The space left over becomes a waiting room. And here it all comes to an end. This end is the ultimate fate of any group that had a mighty leader but does not move ahead *in his spirit*. Yet if anyone talks about this danger and wants to maintain the original spiritual direction of a group or a party, he is attacked by the epigones, who cry out that this is not the way to go about it . . ."

And then Ingwersen proceeded to point the finger at manifestations of this slack reign of epigones, whom he spotted in politics, in scholarship, and in education. He spared neither the Free University nor the Christian radio broadcasters. About the professors at the Free University he had the following to say: "And when one professor calls another an epigone, as happens today, do not ask in what era of epigones we are living now." With nostalgia in his heart he cried out: "What a spiritual garden, what a forest full of mighty oaks we grew up in! . . . It seems like a fairy tale now, as we think back to the great and eminent men we once had in politics and public affairs: Pierson, Goeman Borgesius, de Savornin Lohman, Kuyper, Troelstra, Schaepman, Nolens, De Visser, Heemskerk, Treub, Talma, Bos, Cort van der Linden, Idenburg, and so many more . . ."

And this was only in the political arena. We had our great men in every area of science, and even in art. Except for Colijn, there was no one in the 1930s who stood head and shoulders above the people. With just as much nostalgic longing, Ingwersen recalled the great men who used to work among us in the church and in scholarship: Van Ronkel, Gunning, Kuyper, Rutgers, Geesink, Hoedemaker, De Hartog, Bavinck, Woltjer, Fabius, Sikkel, and Wagenaar. There was nothing left of these men in the 1930s, and so the epigones took over this rich spiritual inheritance and fought with one another about the first place, the place of honor. We find among them "no explorers, generals, mountain climbers, or seafarers, no throwers of boulders or lighters of lamps, no fighters, no one who sets an example that makes young hearts leap into flame." All the young people ever heard was "the lowly sound of the grinding of spiritual teeth — teeth that had been ground down through the continual rechewing of what grew in the fields of the former generation."

Ingwersen also made some harsh comments about the preachers of those days: "The radio, which allows us to hear many sermons being preached around the country, makes us aware that many who seem to mean well when it comes to religion and church are afraid that the church is becoming bourgeois. All that talk about the decline in church attendance (and it is a very serious matter) and about people cutting their ties with the church (also very serious) leaves me amazed when I also hear that the blame belongs to the public, which no longer wants to hear the so-called truth. Those who talk this way never reproach *themselves* or search their own heart." Elsewhere he said of the theologians of the 1930s: "If you know what religion is and you know the people who are engaged in theology, you will realize that theology has become a fenced-off area in which the theologians do nothing but rake the paths, bind the shrubs, and water the plants which they have grown in the hothouse. In the domain of religion you do not find any who cultivate forests or fields; they are all gardeners. And for that reason they are not prophets who snatch the truth out of the hands of the lie. Now, that has never been an easy task, for such conduct is usually paid for in flesh and blood. But there are some spiritual functionaries who do their work extraordinarily well but in whom there does not seem to be any higher inspiration to spur them on."

Ingwersen talked continually about a "bourgeois religion," which he regarded as even worse for our country than Bolshevism, for it was really an offspring of it. In his own time he saw a repetition of the time in which Bilderdijk lived, when the Republic had become so bourgeois that it gave itself up to the French. Kuyper spoke out against this situation when he denounced the "Calvinists" of those days, calling them "utterly lacking in spirit, epigones of epigones, mere descendants, squandering their strength and time in hair-splitting disputes over words and in magpie-chattering, lacking any awareness of a higher calling. Dwarfs who tried to pass themselves off as giants ran the show."

In the 1930s, the tide was coming in and the storm was not far away. But no one woke up; everyone was content and at ease, and there was hardly anyone who thought of what Bilderdijk once sang in prophetic fervor: "I predicted the falling of your ramparts — Holland's Ilium. I saw the burning of your roofs, and I saw your Hectors fall."[5] There is only one difference to be noted: when the storm finally struck, there would be no more "Hectors" left to fall.

National and spiritual decline

No, we did not wish to be disturbed. We were busy with the celebration of an anniversary, or perhaps we were just beginning to look ahead to another special date. There was so much to commemorate. Things were going so well.

Wasn't it a good thing that the tension between the Church and the world was abating somewhat? We became more broad-minded about dancing and movie attendance and card playing and amusements on Sunday. And we began to see that there was also quite a bit of religiosity and piety outside our church communion. People in general were not as bad as we had once thought. And in the National Reformed *(Hervormd)* churches there were also truly pious people to be found. Mixed marriages? We didn't make as much of them as we once had done. As for drama productions and dances at special programs put on by our secondary schools, you didn't expect us to withdraw from "culture" altogether, did you? Neo-Malthusianism (in the form of the National League for Family Planning) also found some zealous followers in our Reformed circles.

At the general synods, complaints were uttered to the effect that our spiritual life was withering away. People talked about superficiality and indifference and unchurchliness among our young people. But all they did was complain, for they had no idea what to do about the situation. Meanwhile, the process of turning bourgeois continued across the board, affecting our young people as well.

In 1935 there appeared a book that was addressed to young people and was intended to get them moving: *Young Holland, Roll Up Your Sleeves!* (Dutch: *Jong Holland, pak aan!*). This anthology included an article entitled "New Times, New Demands" by Dr. Colijn, who was prime minister at the time. It is not true that he began to talk

---

[5] "In heb het vallen / Van uw wallen — / Holland's Illium voorspeld. / Ik zag het blaken / Uwer daken — / En uw Hectors neergeveld."

about living "on the dividing line between two worlds" only after the German occupation, which began in 1940. In this article of 1935 he already made such a statement. Something new was coming, and the old was disappearing. He saw it coming, and, like Ingwersen, he realized that in this time of crisis the Netherlands was not spiritually ready for the challenge in every area, for our people had grown slack.

When you read Buskes's book *Hurray for Life,* you get the impression that all the economic misery and unemployment of the 1930s was Colijn's fault. Nothing could be further from the truth. It was a consequence of the fact that we were living on the border "between two worlds." The Netherlands also had to suffer because of what Germany was bringing over the whole world. When Hitler imposed his "cannons in the place of butter" policy on his own people, promising them a glorious future with an empire *(Reich)* that would last a thousand years, he broke *our* economic neck. No one could have done anything about this. And when things got better after the war, this was not because of the wisdom of the Labor Party but because of the international situation. In the "economic miracle" *(Wirtschaftswunder)* enjoyed by (West) Germany — contrary to everyone's expectations — the Netherlands also got its share.

Now then, Colijn understood the laxness and the bourgeois spirit that had set in during the 1930s, and he was deeply concerned about it. In the article I referred to, he wrote: "There was once a mother who asked me to help her son who possessed a secondary school diploma *(eindexamen H.B.S.).* I managed to find something for the young man — a simple job with a salary of about 1800 guilders per year (thirty-six guilders per week). The money was enough — and the mother certainly needed it — but the job was not sufficiently prominent. The mother said, 'I didn't send my son to a secondary school to prepare for a job like that!' " Colijn pointed to this episode as a *symptom* of the times: the young man was spoiled and didn't know how to roll up his sleeves and get to work. He had no "grit." There were all sorts of spoiled day-trippers around, who thought that the sun would continue to shine at the seashore. They had no eye for the thunderclouds on the horizon and the flood-tide that was coming in.

Ingwersen's criticism was sharp but justified. He saw the national spiritual decline and the small-minded bustlings of the epigones who were frittering away the inheritance of a previous generation that had been made up in good measure of giants.

Unfortunately, there was one thing that Ingwersen did *not* see — the deepest cause of this decline beyond any recovery. He pointed to the "Davidic" period and declared that we lacked people of the stature of the ones who were around in those days. He believed we did not have enough classics anymore. But he did not come to the conclusion that what was going on was in essence a consequence of the forsaking of God's Word. Nowhere in his book do we find the kind of appeal for a return to the Scriptures that we find in the writings of men whom he greatly revered, such as Sikkel. And that's precisely the tragedy of Ingwersen's book. Because of it, many of the arrows he released missed their target.

How did it come about that we had poor preaching, and that after Kuyper there was nothing new to be said about theology, politics, and society, and that people really believed that in Kuyper's life and work the summit had been reached so that we could go no higher but could only keep chewing on what he had given us? Earlier I mentioned that a "Davidic" trait which Anema found in Kuyper was that there was a brokenness in his life, a split that did not reach to the very center of his existence but nevertheless was part of his make-up. Kuyper was a man who wished to live by the Scriptures and therefore developed reformational power, but he was also a man of scholasticism, for whom the Scriptures became a closed book. It was not the reformational Kuyper but the scholastic Kuyper that his successors seized on. The result was that the split was exacerbated, and so we entered a "Solomonic" period that would lead necessarily to the division of the kingdom.

The younger generation of the 1920s, i.e. the men who were dissatisfied with Kuyper's scholasticism but still remained in the Reformed churches after the Synod of Assen in 1926, became more and more influential and sought satisfaction for their heads and hearts in an Ethical-Irenic Christianity. And the older generation, which said it wanted to safeguard Kuyper's inheritance, rejected the Kuyper of the antithesis, clinging more and more to the Kuyper of common grace. These two competing directions began to place their stamp on our Reformed ecclesiastical life. People sought to consolidate our power and influence in relation to the world outside.

Soon the Federation of Calvinists was established, which welcomed the very men whom the Synod of Assen had condemned and expelled in 1926 because of their departure from the Scriptures. *Inside* the church these men were not Reformed, but *outside* the church they were. And so the confessions were reduced to documents of purely ecclesiastical value which had authority and validity only *within* the church. This represented an acceptance and canonization of the wrong Kuyper, who in his scholastic thinking had given a prominent place to the doctrine of the pluriformity of the church. Rev. W. F. A. Winckel wrote: "On one occasion Kuyper lost an argument against the late [Roman Catholic] Father T. F. Bensdorp. It had to do with the nettlesome question of the pluriformity or uniformity of the church — whether the Church Universal, in accordance with God's ordinances, was supposed to manifest itself in various forms or in one single form."[6] It is curious that in this polemic a Roman Catholic priest wound up defending the irrefutable position in opposition to Kuyper.

The doctrine of the pluriformity of the church did a great deal of damage in the 1930s. One consequence was a curious episode in evangelism which took place in Deventer and was emulated elsewhere. Four churches of four different denominations undertook evangelism together on a basis of equality. Those who were converted would then have to decide for themselves which church they would join!

The confessions as purely "ecclesiastical"

In the area of politics we were not supposed to hear anything of what our confessions said about the true church and the false church (see Article 29 of the Belgic Confession). When elections were near, efforts were made to put an end to any polemicizing between church papers representing different church groups. I remember that a school principal who edited an Antirevolutionary weekly and engaged in polemics about the covenant of grace with National Reformed *(Hervormd)* and old-line Reformed *(Oud-Gereformeerd)*,[7] people was asked to come to The Hague, where Antirevolutionary parliamentarians pleaded with him to put an end to the polemics. After all, the Church and its doctrines were supposed to stay out of politics! Politics was part of the domain of "common grace," where criteria other than the confessions were to be used.

Keep the Church out of politics — that was the theme. But when it came time to draw up a list of candidates for office, the Church did play an important role. In one instance, a man who was principial in

---

[6] Winckel makes this comment in a note in his book *Leven en Arbeid van Dr. A. Kuyper* (1919).

[7] People who are similar to the of the Netherlands Reformed congregations in North America in terms of their thinking and beliefs. —TRANS.

his politics and well educated was denied a place on the list of candidates because in Dordrecht (Dort), where there were many Antirevolutionary voters who belonged to the National Reformed *(Hervormd)* churches, Prof. Severijn would have to go on the list instead. Now, Severijn was a fine man and also well educated, but he knew nothing about politics — at least, not at that time. The Antirevolutionary Party suffered considerable grief because of Dr. Hugo Visscher, "the man with the Beggar's head," as Kuyper called him. Visscher was obsessed with the idea that *he* should be Kuyper's successor in politics, but it was not to be: Hendrik Colijn and A. W. F. Idenburg took on that role. From that moment on, things went wrong, and Hugo Visscher remained a problem for the Antirevolutionary leadership. I once heard R. A. den Ouden, the adjunct secretary of the Central Committee, say that Visscher cost Colijn many a gray hair, and that he was impossible to work with. Yet they kept him on, for he had a leading position in the National Reformed *(Hervormd)* Church. His disappearance would cost the Antirevolutionary Party votes.

Just what the Party was holding to its bosom all those years became clear during the second world war, when Visscher became a member of the Dutch Nazi party and an advisor to the Germans who ruled the country. And there were more members of the Central Committee who held on to their position within the Antirevolutionary Party because of their church affiliation, even though they were a liability and represented bad elements. Van Voort van Zijp, an Antirevolutionary representative in the legislature, also became a Dutch Nazi, as did Rev. Hofstede, a Mennonite *(Doopsgezind)* minister, who was a member of the Central Committee. That was where the doctrine of pluriformity got us in politics.

"Numbers" were everything, and God's royal law was neglected. The power of faith possessed by Gideon's band, to which Groen van Prinsterer had pointed, was despised. After all, "numbers" counted in politics. And the parliament was said to be an "arena of compromise": the Reformed confessions would not do much good there. The Kuyperian notions of common grace and pluriformity had suppressed the language of the Scriptures and of our confessions. Solomon multiplied horses in the style of the rulers around him and forgot that he had ridden to the throne on a lowly mule. The emphasis on common grace and pluriformity led to "inter-church" relationships, which in turn led to a blurring of the boundaries, which in turn led to world ecumenism. In the process the Secession and the Doleantie were denied, and also the Synod of Dort. Kuyper's work was nullified in Kuyper's own name!

Two streams

In the 1930s there were basically two streams in the Reformed *(Gereformeerd)* churches. The one stream canonized the bad part of Kuyper's inheritance, and the other one represented the "younger generation," the ones who wanted to throw everything overboard and didn't even know what it means to be Reformed.

I think of a man like Rev. A. G. Barkey Wolf, who attended a church service in London during the 1930s where he encountered Leslie Weatherhead, who was internationally known for his writings. In our church papers Barkey Wolf wrote about this man with great appreciation and observed: "I have the feeling that God is busy doing great things through Leslie Weatherhead." He ignored the fact that Weatherhead openly attacked the teachings of the apostles, emptied the Biblical miracles of their meaning, and "explained" the stories in the gospels in such a way that there was no gospel left.

Barkey Wolf was not the only one who allowed Reformed life to be infiltrated by heretical opinions stemming from a subjectivistic mentality and who tried to find a place for Humanism by disguising it as piety. The "Oxford Movement" also gained influence in our churches. Subjectivism and false mysticism were not even recognized properly by *The Herald,* for this paper proclaimed: "The Oxford Movement, with its 'quiet times' in which the ear of the soul tries to listen to what God has to say, contains an element that is not wrong in itself."

What was the "ear of the soul" listening to? The Scriptures? No, it was supposed to listen to what the Spirit says to the soul directly. Men like Toyohiko Kagawa and Stanley Jones drew a lot of attention and were read in Reformed circles and praised by our theologians. The way they were received showed that a certain Americanism had begun to infiltrate our people. Those who drifted in this direction were spiritual children of Nathan Söderblom, the man who loved to speak of a single church with a number of divisions — Protestant, Greek Orthodox, Roman Catholic, and so forth. He also proclaimed that Hindu bhakti represented a form of mysticism and love directed to God — "a divine revelation in the true and full sense of the word."[8]

---

[8] If you would like to know more about this Humanistic-mystical infiltration in the 1930s as it manifested itself especially in missions (including Reformed mission work), read Cornelis van der Waal's fine book *Antithesis or Synthesis?*

Chapter 2 — Woe to You, My People!

This shifting of position, this abandonment of the Reformed principle as we had grown up with it against the background of the Secession and the Doleantie, did not limit itself to the theologians. Such a decline may well *begin* with them, but it goes on to influence the people. We also note a shift in the kinds of books that were being issued by some theological and Christian publishers. For example, I think of a publisher who began a series of books under the rubric "A Treasure in Earthen Vessels." Writing in this series were men like J. A. Wormser and the church historian J. C. Rullmann. At first they dealt with leading figures in the Secession — Van Raalte, Scholte, De Cock, Van Velzen, and Gezelle Meerburg. These publications came out in the years 1915 through 1919. In 1921 this publisher brought out a book on the Kuyper House which was written by the adjunct secretary of the Central Committee of the Antirevolutionary Party, R. A. den Ouden, and contained an introduction by Colijn. But in the 1930s this publisher began to issue books which propagated Barthian theology, e.g. *The Revelation of Hiddenness,* to which such men as J. J. Buskes, T. L. Haitjema, K. H. Miskotte, O. Noordmans, and W. A. Visser 't Hooft contributed. In this book men like Colijn were completely repudiated.

Buskes was criticizing Colijn who had written: "In our modern times, the ordinary citizen with his ballot in his hand is also an instrument used by Christ the King. Understand me well: He uses this citizen to develop His Kingdom." J. Eykman argued that the youth work undertaken in public schools and by sports clubs can be just as much an instrument in God's hand to build up the youth as a Christian young people's society. If you reason from the standpoint of dialectical theology, this is completely logical — if, indeed, we can still speak of logic in connection with such paradoxical talk.

This reading material came from the very same presses that once issued books about De Cock and Scholte. But in the 1930s they were also putting out little books in which our people heard such false teachers as Söderblom, Leslie Weatherhead, Stanley Jones, and Kagawa glorified. These books reached thousands of people, for men like Barkey Wolf served as willing propagandists for this way of thinking.

The deep tragedy of these developments is that such teachers were just as positive in their cooperation with the hollowing out of Reformed truth as they were negative in their condemnation of faithful prophets who saw the decline and warned against it. When Prof.

Schilder was suspended in 1944 by a synod that still called itself Reformed, Barkey Wolf, from his parsonage in The Hague, sent the synod a telegram in which he urged that quick work be made of this matter: the synod should proceed at once with deposition. I know that circumstances such as this caused Schilder immeasurable pain. Not only have I heard this from his own mouth; one can also ascertain it from the special issue of *The Reformation* which commemorated its first twenty-five years of operation (October 1950). Schilder contributed an imaginary conversation with Dr. de Bondt in which he talked about "your telegraphist brother, Barkey Wolf."

When this "telegraphist brother" wrote a seemingly pious article about his longing for the "unity of the church," I wrote to him on September 8, 1948, and told him that his telegram to the infamous Synod of 1944 had wounded Schilder deeply. If he was serious about his striving for ecclesiastical unity, he could do a good deed by expressing his regrets to Schilder about that telegram. The answer I received on September 20 was that he could *not* do what I proposed: "I cannot take back the content of my telegram. I continue to regard Prof. Schilder as a source of the greatest misery. As long as this man is alive, it will be impossible for the churches to reunite, unless your churches have the courage to repudiate him and distantiate themselves from him." That was typical of the thinking of this "Reformed" minister, who apparently would rather see Weatherhead, a dissolver of Scripture, than Schilder, a defender of Scripture, teaching at Kampen.

Barkey Wolf and company represented one of the streams in our churches, a stream that had come forth from the Dutch Christian Student Union and the "younger generation" of the 1920s. Through their influence, our church life got more and more out of joint. The other stream was the older generation, which regarded Kuyper as the very pinnacle of the Reformed mountain and could think of nothing better to do than to canonize Kuyperianism. Yet they forgot that they had brought only half of Kuyper with them in their spiritual baggage — the Kuyper of scholasticism and dogmatic formulas, about which I wrote earlier.

This second stream, which was the bigger of the two, was still dominant at the ecclesiastical gatherings; it took control especially at the general synods, where the "pre-advisors" had a great deal of power. These men believed they were operating in "Davidic" style, even though they had actually gone over to the "Solomonic" approach.

Kuyper himself would have had great difficulty recognizing them as his spiritual children, despite the fact that one of his own sons in the flesh was among them.

What was most distressing about this situation was that they had brazenly denied his "Doleantie church polity." Kuyper was a strong proponent of the independence of the local church: even in his old age, he did not recognize any higher authority on the part of general synods. He set out his views on this matter in all sorts of writings, and so there is no need for me to go into it further here.[9] That was the Kuyper of the Davidic period. The centralization of governing power in a general synod was a symptom of Solomonic decline which manifested itself ever more strongly in the 1930s and eventually caused a split in our churches.

Something else which would have amazed Kuyper was the dry dogmatism that pervaded most so-called Kuyperian sermons. Ingwersen pointed to this, and anyone who remembers the 1930s clearly would be able to come up with examples of his own. Yet it is true that Kuyper himself was no exegete. He talked rather freely from the pulpit. Select a sermon of his at random, and you can see this for yourself.

His sermons were more like lectures than an opening of the Word. In the commemoration volume published in 1937 to mark Kuyper's birth in Maassluis one hundred years before (remember: the 1930s was the time of anniversaries and celebrations!), we read the following comment about Kuyper's method of preaching:

> When he preached his first sermon in Amsterdam on the basis of Ephesians 3:17, he took from this rich text only two words in the middle — "rooted" and "grounded" — and he used them to develop an interesting view of the church as *organism* and *institute*. His sermon "Freedom"

---

[9] Kuyper dealt with such matters in various polemical writings that came out in connection with the church struggle known as the Doleantie. On the church polity of the Doleantie, see especially three lectures of 1887 which were published together under the title *Het juk der tweede Hiërarchie* (Amsterdam: J. A. Wormser, 1887) and were delivered at a "Reformed Ecclesiastical Congress." F. L. Rutgers gave a lecture entitled "De Hiërarchie in haar kerkbedervend karakter," A. F. de Savornin Lohman gave one entitled "Door wat schuld de tweede Hiërarchie opkwam," and Kuyper himself lectured on the topic "Wat ons tegenover de tweede Hiërarchie te doen staat." See also Kuyper's *Tractaat van de reformatie der kerken* (Amsterdam: Höveker & Zoon, 1884), and C. Veenhof's comments on the parallels between 1886 and 1944 as reproduced in Appendix IV below. —TRANS.

(based on II Corinthians 3:17b), which deals first with freedom in *society,* then with freedom in the *church,* and finally with the freedom of the *ministers* of the congregation, is more a beautiful disquisition than an explication of the words which the apostle Paul, under the inspiration of God's Spirit, wrote to the congregation in Corinth. His sermon "The Unconscious Advent Prayer" (dealing with Malachi 3:1) has the following division into sections, which is very disputable on exegetical grounds: in the sighing of creation, in the unrest of the human heart, and in Israel's prayer. "To His temple" is the sighing of creation; "whom you seek" is the emptiness of the human heart; and "in whom you delight" is Israel's prayer.

Kuyper did not spend much time on exegesis. Take a good look at the texts he used as epigraphs for the chapters in many of his books. Their seeming relevance to the subject at hand often did not go beyond a few words within the text, or perhaps even a single word. To examine such texts in their context was a matter of secondary importance for him.

Yet Kuyper took a very different approach to some important questions than the dry dogmatists of the 1920s and 1930s. You can read about it in the same commemoration volume of 1937, which includes a chapter by Rev. T. Ferwerda entitled "Dr. Kuyper as Professor." For Kuyper, writes Ferwerda, the sermon was something living: "Wrestling with the thoughts in your own heart in order to let those thoughts be taken captive in obedience to Jesus Christ — that was Kuyper."

Ferwerda tells us how Kuyper tried to impress it upon his students not to think that he had spoken the last word, or that Reformed dogmatics had attained its final form in his (Kuyper's) work: "That when he would eventually lay down his work, it would cry out for continuation — Kuyper was much too much a man of true scholarship to doubt this for even a moment. Any suggestion that his students were to 'iurare in verba magistri' (swear by their master's words) was foreign to him. On the contrary, he continually spurred them on to study the dogmatic writings of others so that they would not fall into a one-sidedness that would paralyze them in their own study and reflection. Kuyper had no desire to train parrots who would repeat his words after him; what he wanted was thinkers who would go further, independently and relying on their own ripe judgment, in the line to which he had pointed."

But this is just the sort of emphasis that epigones can never understand. Part of the misery of the 1930s was that there was a school of thought that consisted of nothing but people repeating what Kuyper had said. And how they loved to talk! This sterile business already began in Kuyper's own time. Ferwerda tells us: "Here and there, people in the congregations began to complain about the rigid dogmatic sermons of some of the preachers trained at the Free University. There was quite a bit of exaggeration in those comments, but the complaint was not always without basis. When it reached Kuyper's own ears, he took it very seriously. That was not how he had taught his students to preach, as the hundreds of meditations we have received from him indicate. From the day he became aware that the preaching of his former students was not entirely in order, he began to warn with great earnestness against a one-sidedness that paid too little attention to the many-sided riches of spiritual life."

But his warning was in vain. The sermons of those who thought they had to pass on Kuyper's thinking degenerated into dogmatic reflections *about* the Word instead of being drawn *from* the Word. Therefore the emphasis again fell on the subjectivistic element: how am *I* saved? The inevitable consequence of Kuyper's misunderstanding of baptism and the covenant was that the "hold for" or "consider as" decision made by the Synod of 1905 as it addressed the issue of "presumptive regeneration" made everything uncertain; it removed the ground beneath the sacrament of baptism and took away the binding power in Scripture's own words about the "promise" and "demand" of the covenant.[10] The result was that everything sank away in the quicksand of subjectivism. And so we got those exemplary sermons

---

[10] The 1905 synod of the Reformed *(Gereformeerd)* churches, meeting in Utrecht, declared: "According to the confession of our churches, the seed of the covenant, by virtue of the promise of God, is to be considered regenerated and sanctified in Christ, until the contrary should become evident from their doctrine and conduct as they grow up" *(Acts,* Article 158). The Synod of 1942 took this part of the declaration of 1905 and made the decision that it was binding for everyone. The 1905 "Conclusions of Utrecht" were adopted by the Synod of the Christian Reformed Church in North America in 1908. They were challenged from time to time, given an "official interpretation" by the Synod of 1962, and finally set aside in 1968, in part as a result of discussions with representatives of the Canadian Reformed Churches. The Synod of 1968 declared that the Conclusions of Utrecht should ''no longer have the status of binding doctrinal deliverances within the Christian Reformed Church" *(Acts,* Article 86). — TRANS.

that hollowed out the Scriptures, in which the hearer would one Sunday be given a comparison with the spiritual history of Abraham, the next Sunday would hear the story of Jacob, and on a third Sunday the story of Peter or Judas or Paul or some other character in the Bible. Such preaching remained powerless because it was made up of mere human words and was no longer a proclamation of the Word.

On the one side, then, we had the "younger generation," which was importing false teachers from other countries, such as Weatherhead and Stanley Jones, who undermined in our Reformed pulpits the realization of what the church is. On the other side there were the scholastics, who did not know how to escape the deadly danger of subjectivism.

All of this was unfolding during a decade of seeming spiritual prosperity. We had a great deal of influence on political and social life; our people held key positions. There was tremendous growth in our Christian elementary, secondary and tertiary schools. Indeed, in this "Solomonic" period there was great blossoming; the Reformed world radiated its splendor outward. It seemed that we had finally "arrived," and in our beach chairs at the water's edge we enjoyed our rest, which was well deserved after so much labor and struggle — on the part of the previous generation.

But we were blind to the shift in the tide. We did not see the storm clouds on the horizon or realize that high tide would soon be upon us. "Woe to you, My people!"

Communal guilt

Now that we are a quarter century beyond those events, it is not hard to see that things back then were not going well. Yet there are only a few who can truly say, "We saw it already and warned against it." Therefore we should not try to evade solidarity in guilt or distantiate ourselves from the responsibility that rests on all of us. And so we can speak of communal guilt. There were only a few people who looked at the whole situation in the light of God's Word. The proper attitude for us to assume is that of the preacher of repentance who not only walked on the walls of the city and cried out, "Woe to you!" over the corruption of the city but also added immediately, "Woe is me!"

In the 1930s we did a great deal of celebrating and built tombs for the prophets, but who among us, in faithfulness to the Scriptures, continued the work of the prophets of the Reformation, the Secession, and the Doleantie? There were only a few who match this description. And in managing such faithfulness to the Scriptures, they had to begin with intense self-criticism and a spiritual struggle; otherwise they would not have been able to see the darkness of the continuing decline.

Genuine reformation

Among the few who saw it after their eyes were opened and who then began to see more and more of what was going wrong, one of the most important was Schilder. Who was this man, whom a colleague (Vonkenberg) called "the best minister in the Netherlands," while another colleague (Barkey Wolf) wrote that he was a "source of the greatest misery"?

In this man we see a reformer of the Church, and therefore also a reformer of the entire terrain of human life. When the Church falls ill, all of life becomes ill — in politics, scholarship, social life, culture, family life, and education. And when the Church comes to new reformation, all of human life is affected; no relationship is left as it was.

Before I say something about the life, work, and struggle of this man, there are a few other observations to be made. First of all, we must realize that Schilder did not work from some plan for reformation. In this regard he was just like the other church reformers, for they did not have a "program" or a "strategy" either. They were simply faithful to Scripture — there was really nothing more to it than that. And because of their faithfulness, reformation came in the place of deformation. When Luther nailed his 95 theses to the door of the church, he was fighting against Roman errors but did not realize that he was preparing the way for a church reformation. He was simply being faithful to Scripture. When Hendrik de Cock baptized children from other congregations and got involved in the debate about the use of hymns in worship and wrote against false teachers, he did not realize that the result would be what we now call the Secession. When Kuyper engaged in a battle against the church hierarchy and raised questions about church visitation, he did not know that the Doleantie would be the end result. Schilder fought for an interpretation of our confessions that was faithful to Scripture, and he opposed the hierarchy of the synods; yet he did not know until the last moment that the outcome would be the liberation.

In all of this, these church reformers were imitating the example of the Savior Himself, who did nothing more than preach in a manner that was faithful to Scripture, who attacked the deformation in the Church, and who was eventually cast out. And that's how it will always be here on earth. If certain people had their way and the liberated Reformed churches were reunited with the synodocratic churches without any repentance on the part of the latter, the entire sorry process would be repeated: the people in the church who were faithful to Scripture would again have to speak out against the church hierarchy and against the yearning for false ecumenism, including reunion with the National Reformed *(Hervormd)* churches and so forth, and then there would again be decrees of expulsion and the Lord would once more have to liberate His Church.

Reformation does not require a plan or program of action; indeed, if any would-be reformers started to draw up such plans, they would no longer be acting in a reformational spirit and would be judged for it. And so we can see that Schilder was acting in the spirit of the church reformers before him.

A second observation is that when we think about the work of church reformers, we must never look at *people* alone. Such a mistake would not be in the spirit of "KS" at all. Church reformation is always the work of the *Kurios,* the Lord Himself.

Prof. Benne Holwerda made some beautiful observations about this point. When *The Reformation* observed its twenty-fifth anniversary with a special issue in 1950, he wrote: "Any reformation that truly deserves the name is the work of the Lord — and not a deed of Luther, Calvin, De Cock, Kuyper, Schilder, or any other human being." He then developed this point drawing on a text from the book of Judges: "So the Spirit of the Lord came upon Gideon" (6:34). The heart of Holwerda's argument was this:

> If we read carelessly, we might conclude that Gideon stood up abruptly and took action, that he suddenly shook off his lethargy and defeatism, that a desire for battle welled up in him, causing him to seize his weapons. In that case we are reading the story of the deeds of *Gideon,* even if it was the Spirit that first set him aflame. But what we actually read in these beautiful words is something different. The Hebrew word we find here is the same one that is used when a man puts on his jacket. Now, we all know that when it's time to get to work, we put on our work clothes. The doctor has his white coat, the laborer

has his coveralls, and the maid has her smock. Yet no one is so foolish as to ascribe the work he is about to do to his *work clothes.* The act of putting on work clothes does not signify that one's uniform is about to get to work; rather, it indicates the moment at which *the workman himself,* wearing those clothes, begins work. The patient does not look to a white coat to heal him; yet when he sees the doctor putting on that white coat, he knows that he means to get to work. Well, what we actually read here is that *the Spirit of the* LORD puts Gideon on; that is to say, Gideon is to the Spirit what coveralls are to the worker. Gideon is only a set of work clothes — the one doing the work is the Spirit. And so we see that it is not Gideon who springs into action, but *the Spirit.* The Lord arises to do battle. What we get here, then, is not the story of the great deeds of a certain person but a report about the mighty deeds of the LORD.[11]

That this is indeed the correct way to read this text is also evident from how the rest of the story of Gideon unfolds. Hardly has the LORD laid a reformational mandate upon Gideon before we find him falling away into deformation. Holwerda has drawn our attention to this dimension of the story as well, and it is indeed instructive for us.

What we need to do now is listen to the Scriptural warning Holwerda has given us as we proceed to talk about the man the LORD chose to use for the work He was about to do in the 1940s, after the falling away during the 1920s and 1930s. If we keep Holwerda's words in mind, we will not confine our thankfulness to the man the LORD used but will look to God Himself, who liberated us, using a man to bring about this result.

If we do not regard the developments from this point of view, we will run stuck in our evaluation of the historical facts and of the people involved. Whenever there is church deformation and a falling away, plenty of people who are concerned raise objections to what is happening; they say they see the disease and want to approach it along "medical" lines. "You don't forsake your sick mother!" such people

---

[11] Here we see again what a rich blessing sound exegesis and a careful listening to the Word can bring us. It preserves us against all sorts of scholastic reasoning. Things would have unfolded very differently in our Reformed *(Gereformeerd)* churches if Kuyper, too, had listened in such an attentive and careful way to what the Scriptures were telling us.

then say in a seemingly tender way. They protest and are even allowed some room for their protests, for the ecclesiastical hierarchy does not want to lose any more sheep than the process of reformation has already cost it. Moreover, protesting is harmless as long as it does not lead to action.

There were also concerned priests serving as local pastors during the time of the Reformation, e.g. in Zeeland. In predominantly Protestant areas of this province you may come upon a village that is entirely Roman Catholic. How is this to be explained? Back in Reformation times the pastor (priest) of the church there also raised objections and concerns, but he did not take any action. He soothed his parishioners by being concerned, and the local church remained exactly where it was. After him came other pastors: some may have shared his objections and concerns, but others did not. The people remained Roman Catholic and still are today; even though they are surrounded by Protestants, they cannot be distinguished from Roman Catholics in heavily Catholic parts of our country, such as Brabant and Limburg.

And that's also the way things went during the time of the Secession and of the Doleantie. There were ministers who raised objections and also many elders who supported them. But they wanted to take a "medical" approach — thus no conflict. Instead they humbled themselves, and remained "faithful," and "protested," and sent in letters and appeals to the proper addresses. But their strategy was smothered, and eventually they died. Their lives remained sterile, and their congregations were devastated.

In the article I quoted from, Prof. Holwerda went on to say:

> I believe there is a profound difference between genuine reformation and all action that only *appears* to be reformational. In every age we have seen the same thing: in any situation of apostasy there are some who see the deformation but don't want to do anything about it. Many choose the "medical" approach, as people like to call it. They want to determine for themselves the point at which the attack on the problem is to begin, the moment when they will spring into action. When ecclesiastical gatherings commit sins, they think they can work reformationally by biding their time. They try to get the dangerous figures

replaced gradually until they themselves will finally form the majority.

And so they begin by subordinating themselves and joining in with the evil that is afoot. You see, they want to have the whole strategy of reformation in their own hands; *they* will determine the positions and the tactics. And so, in these last years, we have also come to know reformationally-minded people who said, "This is not the right moment; we want to choose another point as the critical one."

Yet this approach always runs stuck — it could hardly be otherwise. For such people want to hold the reformation in their own hands; they want to determine the plan for themselves. And so they take their stand at the spot which the Spirit has reserved for Himself alone. He does not make His strategy known to us; He just leads simple people to speak about a point which they had not even placed on the agenda; He leads them to give answers to questions which they have not formulated themselves. And those simple people do not know where they will wind up.

Genuine reformation has nothing to do with human strategy and planning. Those who get involved in reformational activity could get the feeling that they are caught up in a very uncertain adventure — unless they *believe,* that is, believe that the Spirit carries out His plans through soldiers who are not acting the part of chief of staff, believe that they must simply carry out the mandate they have been given at the place where they find themselves.

That's how things go in any genuine reformation of the Church. Indeed, that's the *only* way things could go.

A week after Prof. Schilder was suspended, I met him at the home of Dr. Jasperse in Leiden, where he was staying to hide from the Germans. He was completely uncertain about where he would "end up." He had no prospects; in his own words, he had been "cut off like a rotten member of the Church." Thus he was without a church home. He could not imagine how it was possible in that grim, bleak period of war and occupation that anyone was thinking of him or would declare solidarity with him. He told me that he had no idea what the future held in store for him. He had obeyed the command of the LORD, but he saw nothing of the future. His host overheard him at the organ, where Schilder sang, all alone in a room:

> *Turn to me and show Thy favor;*
> *I am lonely and distressed.*
> *From my troubles me deliver;*
> *Save me, for I am oppressed.*
> *Heal the sorrows of my heart,*
> *And regard my life as precious.*
> *Thou who my Deliverer art,*
> *Bring me out of my distress.*[12]

It is along such a path that the LORD leads His church reformers. They are blind tools — a "jacket" that the Holy Spirit puts on when He goes to work. They are soldiers who have not been filled in on the battle plan. Thus they are not diplomats or strategists who cleverly take up a position, establish a front, and place their people strategically. That sort of approach is radically mistaken when it comes to the Church of our Savior.

Misunderstanding

Church reformers are so often misunderstood and judged wrongly by their contemporaries. People who know nothing of the Holy Spirit's strategy, because they simply have not understood what blind obedience is, always have a mistaken view of the people whom God calls to the work of church reformation. You should read what Calvin's opponents said and wrote about his person and character. The same applies to Luther, De Cock, and Kuyper.

In this regard, those disciples were not greater than their Lord. Christ was despised and called a glutton and wine-bibber, someone who went around with prostitutes and tax-collectors, who despised the law and turned it inside out. He was branded a revolutionary who preached rebellion against the ecclesiastical authorities, one who stepped onto the public stage without authorization or competence. To this day people continue to bring charges against Him. No one argues any longer that He was a great sinner; the great accusation against Him is that He dared to oppose the ecclesiastical hierarchy.

---

[12] Psalm 25, stanza 8.

Not long ago I talked with someone who had been in Israel and had asked a leading Orthodox Jew what he thought about Jesus of Nazareth. This Jew praised Jesus as rabbi, as far as His person and work were concerned. But Jesus had committed one unforgivable sin, he went on to say: He became troublesome and got into a conflict with the leaders of the church. He broke the trust that the people should have in their leaders. And then it was simply necessary to get rid of Him, declared this Jew. The result, of course, is the hardening that still rests on the old covenant people today because they refused to take the road of church reformation which the great Church Reformer had opened before them.

We find no different pattern when we study church history and continue right into our own time. The tragedy repeats itself, for example, in *The Trumpet,* a paper of the synodocratic churches, with which Prof. Schilder himself used to be connected as a contributor. (It was the official publication of the seminary in Kampen.) J. D. Boerkoel, the editor-in-chief of this paper, wrote a lengthy series of lead articles devoted to the person of Schilder. The series ran for more than a year — from June of 1960 through July of 1961. Thus he had plenty of time and space in which to tell people a thing or two about this former colleague of his who had been suspended and deposed. And Boerkoel had material enough to draw on, for he had been one of Schilder's fellow students at Kampen and had had contact with him for a long time; therefore he could be regarded as a person with some insight into Schilder's character.

But Boerkoel ran stuck in a most miserable way when he began to judge — and condemn — Schilder for the struggle he undertook on behalf of church reformation. We are treated to the same arguments that were used when men like Luther, Calvin, and De Cock were condemned. He is brilliant, indeed, but a loner; he thinks he is misunderstood; he is a complicated, split character; he is suspicious, vehement, sharp, absolutistic; everywhere he sees corruption, decay, a process of undermining; he is aggressive; and so the list goes on and on — I could add a lot more to it. And can't you see that someone with such a character will necessarily get into conflict with everyone who doesn't agree with him? He was simply a troublesome person who had to be shoved aside. It was not a doctrinal question at all — just a question of maintaining proper order in the church. That was how many people judged and condemned Schilder.

When I wrote a couple of literary articles in *The Reformation* during the 1930s, I got a letter from a well-known literary lady in one of our big cities, warning me not to chum around with Schilder or to follow him, for he was an impossible person. Various psychiatrists had figured out that he was paranoid, a man who suffered from a persecution complex, and who therefore would run stuck one day. Such was the outlook of people who had no idea that the Spirit uses human beings, as a worker puts on his work clothes, when He undertakes to reform His Church.

First acquaintance with Prof. Schilder

I wanted to say these things at the outset before talking about the person and life and work of Prof. Schilder. On the one hand these comments can keep us from glorifying a person: after all, it was not Schilder but the Spirit of God that reformed His Church. On the other hand, these comments should keep us from any unfair or unjust evaluation of Schilder as a person or of his life and work. Schilder lived in a specific set of circumstances. The LORD had given him his gifts, his character and his personal qualities in order to prepare him for the work to which He was calling him.

The first contact I had with Schilder was most unusual. *The Herald* had taken over an article which I had written in an Antirevolutionary paper of which I was the editor. Schilder in turn reprinted it in his paper. Now, *The Herald* had reproduced the article incorrectly, with the result that at one point I wound up saying the very opposite of what I had actually written. I asked "KS" to correct this mistake in his paper.

I waited for some weeks and did not see any result from my request. I wrote to Schilder again and got word that because of certain circumstances my request had not been attended to: in the next issue the correction would be printed. But that didn't happen either. I got angry and wrote Schilder another letter. I got an extensive letter in return, in which he explained how it came about that the correction had not been placed. That week he had been very busy typing out a report of some eighty pages for his classis. (At that time, i.e. 1926, Schilder was a minister in Oegstgeest and was involved in a controversy with a man named Wirtz.) He had worked all through the night on this report, and had then written the correction and left instructions for the servant girl to mail it the first thing in the morning. But her alarm clock didn't go off, and so she slept in. As a result the correction could not be placed that week, but it would go in the following week.

It was a lengthy letter — so lengthy and wordy (such was my impression of it at the time) that I reacted to it in a way that was totally wrong. I believed I was not being taken very seriously, and so I wrote back, somewhat sarcastically, that I could well understand that a busy minister who had to stay up late typing an eighty-page report and who had a servant girl who did not wake up in the morning because her alarm clock didn't go off could hardly be bothered with some little editor of a paper out on one of the islands, and so it would probably be best that no correction be printed at all. I confess that I was later ashamed of that letter.

In response I got a letter that made me blush. Schilder's letter was so gentle and tender and at the same time so penetrating that I was deeply ashamed of myself. He asked why I would not simply take a brother at his word, and he went on to assure me that everything he had written in his previous letter was true. I quickly wrote back to him and retracted the comments I had made in my previous letter and asked him to forgive my outburst. Schilder, in turn, wrote back (this time it was only a short letter) and said that it gave him great joy to forgive me. He added that he wished all such incidents between brothers could be resolved in so smooth and radical a manner.

In the quarter century that followed, I got to know Schilder better and better. The more I had to do with him, the more I respected him and came to love him as a person. He was one of those rare people of whom it can be said, "The longer I knew him, the more I liked him."

I have passed on this little story because it reveals something of Schilder's character. He loved peace deeply; he was a man of great gentleness, and he had a burning desire to maintain the best possible relations with his brothers. In the 1920s I did not see this trait in very many ministers, and I got to know quite a number of them well through business dealings. My impression of ministers in general may be part of the reason why I made such a mistake in my first contact with Schilder.

Not long afterward I met him for the first time in person. On my advice, the young men's society in Middelharnis invited him to a special annual meeting being planned. But the consistory in Middelharnis refused to let Schilder have the use of the church. They were aware of the articles "KS" had written in *The Reformation* about "Church Language and Life":[13] a man who attacked "the old writers" could certainly not be allowed to use the pulpit in Middelharnis. Schilder, who had moved to Rotterdam by this point, received me, along with the president of the young people's society, at his home in the upper level of a house. As we climbed the stairs, it seemed that we were ascending Mount Olympus. Rev. Schilder greeted us from the top of the stairs, and before we were all the way up, he said, "I already know why you have come: I'm not getting the church — right?" I looked at him in amazement and said that this was indeed the case. On a later occasion he wrote to me: "I know the customers I'm dealing with."[14] He knew them already then, for he was very well acquainted with the ecclesiastical map of the Netherlands and was aware of what was going on in our churches.

He comforted us with the assurance that if we could rent a meeting hall somewhere else, he would still come, regardless of what the consistory thought. This plan went through, and the address he gave on "The Lesson of Thyatira" was a revelation for me. I wasn't accustomed to hearing this type of speech. Back in those days, speeches — even more than sermons — were reflections, expressions of the opinions of speakers, sometimes presented with flowing eloquence (think of Hepp and Wisse). Never had I heard such pure opening of Scripture and such exegesis as on that occasion.

Not long afterward I heard Schilder speak in the National Reformed *(Hervormd)* church in Dirksland in a series of winter lectures. His topic was "What is Satan?" On that occasion, too, he simply opened Scripture — without engaging in speculation or fantasizing. He simply told us what Scripture said. This he did so powerfully that I still clearly remember his last sentence: "I wanted to show you something of Christ, the King of the world, and for this reason I had to show you Satan." For Schilder, there was no reason to spend an evening talking about Satan if it were not for Christ.

His sermons

In the 1920s I also heard some Old Year's Eve sermons preached by Schilder in the big church he served in Rotterdam on the

---

[13] Schilder devotes substantial attention to this theme in *Om Woord en Kerk,* Vol. 3 (Goes: Oosterbaan & Le Cointre, 1951), pp. 96-227. —TRANS.

[14] "Ik ken mijn mannetjes."

Tidemanstraat, the one with the powerful organ. The church was full to overflowing on such occasions. The aisles and even the steps leading to the pulpit were occupied. Yet by the time the first psalm was sung, you knew that he had spotted you in your place up in the balcony; with a friendly nod he would acknowledge you as a familiar visitor from another congregation. He didn't miss a thing.

Back in those days I heard three of his sermons, and they all had the same theme, a theme that dominated his entire life's work, and also his vision of the Scriptures and of philosophy and of the whole world. That theme was: the moratorium was to become an oratorio (Dutch: *oratorium*).

The first of those sermons dealt with John the Baptist, who instructed his disciples to ask Jesus: Are You the one who was to come, or shall we await another? The answer Christ gave did not leave anything to be desired in the way of clarity. He quoted Isaiah (and John the Baptist surely knew Isaiah). Anyone who preaches the Scriptures will be listened to eagerly by those who believe the Scriptures and will be able to comfort them. But Christ added a lesson here. John had indeed said that the one coming after him would be a judge and would lay the axe to the root of the tree, and that his winnowing fork would be in his hand, but he forgot one thing, namely, that before the judgment could take place, the gospel of grace would have to be proclaimed. Therefore the most important thing was that the gospel was being preached to the poor. This meant that the judgment was being postponed — thus there was a moratorium, for people who would be saved still had to be brought into the Church.

Here we see the meaning of the old and the new covenant. God's judgment on the cosmos is not carried out directly after the fall into sin: first comes Genesis 3:15. The arch of God's judgment spans the cosmos like a dome and is buttressed and held in place by the proclamation of the gospel. That's why the world does not collapse: the proclamation of the gospel buttresses and supports that arch. *This* is the reason why the world, the evil world, continues to exist. It remains intact and possesses possibilities for development because of *the Church,* which must become full in number: the very last of God's elect must be brought in. This realization gives meaning to the old dispensation, a meaning which Christ was to bring forth. And so we also see that everything in the old dispensation had its redemptive-historical place and meaning. It all worked toward Christ and therefore is to be viewed and understood in relation to Him.

The second sermon of Schilder's I heard in those days, delivered in an Old Year's Eve service, was based on what Jesus said from the cross: Father, forgive them, for they know not what they do. Christ understood here that mankind had committed its greatest and most horrible sin by perpetrating an act of violence against the Son of the Father. If there was ever a reason for the dome of judgment over mankind to collapse, it was surely now. Christ realized this, and therefore His prayer was: No judgment yet, Father, but postponement, for there is still a New Testament Church to come — there are still those who will confess Your name. The gospel still had to be preached, and so there had to be a moratorium. The Father heard this prayer.

The third sermon I heard was based on Revelation 8:1-2: "And when he broke the seventh seal, there was silence in heaven for about half an hour. And I saw the seven angels who stand before God; and seven trumpets were given to them." Here Schilder stressed the same theme: after the six seals were opened, there was suddenly a period of silence in the heavenly work chambers. There was no divine hastening toward the end, toward the consummation of all times. But there was nothing more that John could write at this point, for there was silence. The final judgment would have to wait: there was a moratorium. First the prayers of all the saints would have to be brought before God's throne. The golden censer was brought by an angel to the golden altar before the throne, and the censer was filled with much incense and with the prayers of *all* the saints. The waiting was for the sake of the fullness of the Church. Before the end and the time of judgment could come, the prayers of the last of the elect would also have to be brought.

Thus things are not controlled by the might of the world or the powerful here on earth — not Moscow or New York or London or Berlin or East or West; rather, it is *the Church* that dominates world history. The gospel has to be preached, and world history is subordinate to this end. The Church does not exist for the sake of the world, but the world for the sake of the Church. World politics, world development, the culture of the world — it all exists for the sake of the Church.

I have given this brief summary of these three sermons because they indicate the overarching idea that dominated Schilder's work. He saw the Church as universal, embracing the entire world and dominating it. The Church could not be pushed into a certain corner or limited to a sector of life. Therefore he also wound up in conflict with the "philosophy of the law-idea."[15]

This idea can help us understand and explain what Schilder was up to in all his publications, including his treatment of the problem of culture. It is the key to his book *Christ and Culture,* in which we read: "A church magazine that, wherever necessary, does its weeding and keeps principles pure means more for culture than a gilded stage. Over against a minister who in a 'Reformed weekly' exclaims that sometimes one single drama means more than seven study outlines, the Reformed distinction of nature-grace-sin maintains that one good outline means more than seven, even good, dramas, in as much as the power of God's Word is stronger than that of the image, and doctrine is more than sign." He concludes this book, which has not been studied as much as it should be, with these words: "Blessed is my *wise* ward-elder who does his home visiting in the right way. He is a *cultural* force, although he may not be aware of it. Let them mock him; they do not know what they are doing, those cultural gadabouts of the other side!"[16]

Yes, that church on the Tidemanstraat could be full to overflowing when Schilder preached in those memorable Old Year's Eve services. Even back in those days, it was striking that the people who attended were not in the first place the "intelligentsia." Such people often found him "too difficult." Schilder preached to the "little people" *(kleyne luyden),* and they hung on his every word. Those were the people he had contact with, as he himself declared. Now, it is likely that they did not always understand him either. But what they did understand was that *the Word* was being opened and proclaimed. Thus Schilder's preaching touched them in their hearts and gripped them.

I cannot say by what means Schilder had the greatest influence on our people — through what he wrote in books and periodicals, or through his preaching. But preaching, in any case, was the work he undertook with a burning desire. And he was a very powerful preacher. As you listened to him, you got the impression that he must have

---

[15] The reference here is to the philosophy of Herman Dooyeweerd and D. H. T. Vollenhoven. The original edition of Dooyeweerd's most important work was entitled *De wijsbegeerte der wetsidee* (The Philosophy of the Law-Idea). A second edition of this three-volume work, originally published in 1935, came out in 1953-58 in the form of an English translation by David H. Freeman and William S. Young, with a different title: *A New Critique of Theoretical Thought.* —TRANS.

[16] *Christ and Culture,* tr. G. van Rongen and W. Helder (Winnipeg: Premier, 1977), pp. 53, 86.

exegeted the entire Scripture for himself. The texts he appealed to in a strict logical order were always ready at hand for him.

And he never wrote out a sermon. At most he would have a piece of paper with a few notes — often not even that. On such occasions he would rummage in one of his pockets once he was in the pulpit, looking for the piece of paper on which he had written his text and the psalms he wanted sung during the service. When he preached in November of 1951 in the Lutheran church in The Hague, the one that took on such historic meaning during the time of the liberation,[17] I asked him for permission to publish his sermon. (The service had been broadcast on the radio.) He replied with a hastily written note: "Can't — nothing on paper — had no time."

Yet his sermons were structured along strictly logical lines; they formed a firm and closed structure with a broad basis. They always moved toward a conclusion that summed everything up, and often they culminated in a peroration that sang God's praises in a most glorious manner. When you heard such a sermon you always got the impression that you were listening to someone who had plunged into the depths of the mine-shafts of God's Word and had come up with unknown riches which he now laid out before the eyes of the LORD's Bride.

His preaching was never artificial or ornamented or forced; never did one get the feeling that Schilder was reading things into the text. The material he drew from the Old and New Testaments to prove his point was so overwhelming that you could not escape the awareness that this was indeed the meaning which God's Spirit had intended to get across in this text or pericope. He could show all kinds of connections, going back to what was literally written in the original language. And he never failed to point to the Christ of the Scriptures, whom he held up as the central figure, powerful in His majesty, glory, love, mercy, and righteousness.

The church services he conducted generally ran about two hours — he really couldn't get done in any less time. And you went home with the thought that he really wasn't finished yet but had wrapped up the sermon because of the time. He never lapsed into repetition. You listened with unbroken attention; you received the material from him, worked through it in your mind, and tried to labor along with him in order to be able to understand something of the inexhaustible riches

---

[17] Not only was it the site of the original "liberation meeting" of August 11, 1944, it was also used later for many services of the liberated Reformed churches. —TRANS.

of the Scriptures. The "Amen" always came too soon, and you wished he could go on a little longer.

There was no fondness for speculation in his preaching, nor did he think he simply *had* to be original. Neither did he need to mix news items from the radio or the newspaper into his sermons to make them sound up-to-date or to hold the attention of the younger people. He did not cultivate a streamlined style or use language and terms that would make him sound fashionable. The substance of his sermons was so overwhelming that the form was automatically given with all that content.

So fully was his mind concentrated on his material that his entire physical bearing was caught up in his sermon; sometimes, overwhelmed with rich thoughts he wanted to express, he even stumbled over his words. He perspired all over his body and often needed more than one glass of water to get through a sermon. It happened more than once when he was staying at my home that he had to change his clothes after the service; my wife would then give his Sunday clothes a chance to dry out on a little laundry line so that he could wear them again for the second service.

That the sermon was never an abstraction for him nor the fruit of sheer intellectual effort but instead involved his entire personality in both its physical and psychical dimensions, and that the entire instrumentarium of his highly sensitive emotional life was drawn into it — all of this became clear to me on a certain Sunday when he was to preach in our congregation and was staying at our home. He happened upon a particularly unfair editorial by H. H. Kuyper in *The Herald,* which he later found it necessary to refute in an "Open Letter."[18] He had chosen a delicate text to deal with in the service that day but was too shocked to be able to carry through with that plan, and so he chose another.

The highly refined and sensitive feelings of Schilder were perhaps not widely known, for many have made him out to be a cold man of intellect, a fanatical extremist, a polemicist without any feeling. Those who enjoyed the great privilege of intimate acquaintance with him know better, and so do those who often heard him preach.

Yes, his proclamation of the Word was powerful. Wherever he preached, the churches were full. They came from afar to hear him — not because they loved sensationalism, and not because of his style or

---

[18] H. H. Kuyper (1864-1945) was a son of Abraham Kuyper. He taught church history at the Free University from 1900 to 1936 and was editor-in-chief of *The Herald.* —TRANS.

manner. All such interests fell away when you listened to Schilder. Sometimes he spoke so quickly in his effort to get across everything in his overflowing heart within the limited space of two hours that you could not get the sense of it all. Yet the way his sentences were put together often took your breath away; you could not fault them on grammatical grounds, even though many of them were lengthy and included subordinate clauses. He produced many of these amazing sentences, all of them neatly brought to a conclusion. But what such sentences contained in the way of meaning was sometimes more than a normal person could hold in his head. You got the main idea, and in order not to lose your hold on the overall structure and flow, you let the rest of it slip by.

A good example comes to mind. In his sermon on Revelation 8:1-2 ("There was silence in heaven for about half an hour"), Schilder explained to us what silence is. First he gave us a few sentences in which he swept away the fixed idea that so many people have about heaven, an idea that comes to mind for them when even they read this text, namely, that it is beautiful in heaven and people sing joyfully there and everyone is retired. He told us that the people in heaven work hard, for heaven stands in the most intimate relation to earth, to the struggles, labors, tribulation, and distress here. That's why John saw those vials of God's wrath being poured out over an unconverted world and saw the events in heaven moving ahead toward the final judgment. But now came stillness. John had his pen ready to write down what he saw, but suddenly there was nothing more going on, nothing to write down. Heaven was quiet, waiting.

And at this point Schilder told his hearers what silence is. When we visit one another, we are sure to keep talking without any pause, for a gap in the conversation would be impolite and cause tension. To know what silence is, you should have some contact with the people of the Orient. They are accustomed to sitting silently together without anyone feeling a need for conversation. There is nothing painful about silence when they visit one another, for they know the rest of a "blessed idleness," even when it comes to speaking. Yet this is not the tense silence of which John was a witness. The silence in heaven was a matter of sheer necessity; all were made to "wait," even though there was a divine haste to get to the very end. In that stillness there was the tension of waiting for the prayers of the last of God's elect who had to be brought in before the last trumpet of God's judgment could sound.

Small flashes, like this one on "silence," often punctuated his sermons, and they remained lodged in your mind for good — instructing, admonishing, comforting, blessing, and sometimes condemning. Yet they were only observations made in passing.

Was the content of his sermons also rich in admonition, comfort and application? It must be said that his sermons were always governed by a strict objectivity: he was completely opposed to any subjectivistic or mystical goings-on. He did not play with the feelings of his hearers and did not attach much value to tears — except in one's inner prayer chamber, before God. Nor did he believe in "applications," recognizing their uselessness. When he preached a sermon in which he laid out the riches of the demands and promises of God's Word, by way of an exegesis that drew deeply on the text, he often concluded with a mighty symphony that would make the ears of his hearers ring with the words that John had to pass on to the congregations of Asia Minor in the letters contained in the book of Revelation: "He who has an ear, let him hear what the Spirit says to the churches."

If there was anyone who taught us that only *the Word* can do it, surely it was Schilder. The man who serves as preacher can only explain and exegete that Word, making it clear what God is saying to the congregation in a certain passage of Scripture. Here, too, the Word has to do it; all human words are powerless on their own. But if that Word is to be rendered clear and understandable, it will cost the preacher quite something in the way of mental energy — indeed, it will cost him flesh and blood. And then we can well understand that a preacher will sometimes need two hours if the congregation is to find out what God wants to reveal at a certain place in His Word.

Even opponents of Schilder had to admit that he was unequaled as a preacher. Rev. Boerkoel, whose articles about Schilder in *The Trumpet* were surely not intended to justify him in the face of the synodical inquisition, wrote as follows about his preaching:

> I once heard him preach in Zwolle's East Church on Isaiah 14:12: "How have you fallen from heaven, O star of the morning, son of the dawn! You have been cut down to the earth, you who have weakened the nations!" To my shame I must confess that I hardly knew this chapter, or in any event had often read right over it. It has to do with the descent of Babylon's king into the realm of the dead. I have never forgotten that sermon. And so there are more

people who can still remember certain sermons of Schilder's very clearly.

Even when he chose well-known texts which were suggested by the church year, he brought out ideas that people had never seen in those texts before. There was always a flood of carefully chosen words within a structure and winding of sentences that dragged people along and at the same time set them to work. Part of his power was the logical ordering of his ideas: people did not always understand him, but they continued to follow him. And the verbal torrent was poured out over his hearers.

He didn't know what it was to preach a short sermon — he didn't want to try it either. One day I had preached in Amsterdam West and was going home on my bicycle when I passed the church on the Raphael Square (Amsterdam South), where Schilder was leading the service that day. I could not resist the temptation to go inside. He was preaching on another text from Isaiah: "Look to the rock from which you were hewn, and to the quarry from which you were dug" (51:1). He and I had begun at the same time, and the distance between the two church buildings was some fifteen minutes on a bicycle, but I still got to listen to him for fifteen more minutes.

I went home that day a bit discouraged. I was disturbed — not because of what I had picked up from his sermon but because of my own preaching. I bicycled the rest of the way home musing to myself: *I* had tried to put out the fire of sin with a couple of pails of water, but in the church on the Raphael Square stood a Jan van der Heyden spewing out water like a water cannon.[19] Professor Vollenhoven, who was also in the audience that day, gave me his impression in a single sentence: "It was powerful!" And it was with such an impression that thousands of people who attended services at which Schilder proclaimed the Word went home. In their response they did not place a period after what Schilder had said but a colon: they could not help talking further about it.

---

[19] Jan van der Heyden (1637-1712) was the inventor of the fire-pumps with hoses used in Amsterdam. —TRANS.

Yes, people couldn't help talking about it. And so I ask again: Did his sermons awaken people to their own sinfulness? Did they contain admonition, comfort, and instruction? These cannot be questions for us any more, for we realize that all these elements are to be found in God's Word. It is the text itself, the pericope, that must speak — not the preacher. Only then will the Word come with power, such that people will not be satisfied to put a period after the sermon but will place a colon there instead. Something will happen, whether in the way of blessing or of curse. The Word will admonish the people in a way that no preacher — not even the most gifted pulpiteer — can manage. It will comfort, and it always instructs. In every sermon the preacher must take the attitude: I must decrease and the Word must increase. That was how Schilder understood it: he did not regard himself as anything more than the one who digs the channel through which the stream of the living Word finds its way into the hearts and minds of the hearers.

I also want to draw attention to the judgment of another commentator who can by no means be counted among Schilder's spiritual kin — Dr. J. H. Gunning. In April of 1932, when Schilder was a vigorous young preacher, Gunning wrote as follows in *Peniël* about a radio sermon he had heard him deliver:

> There are some people — perhaps I am one of them — whose behavior varies with the circumstances. This very talented writer [Schilder], who is also very hard to follow, is a polemicist of the first rank: woe to the poor fellow who comes under his powerful criticism! (I challenge the ordinary person to read his three big volumes about the suffering of our Lord without asking himself whether he is dreaming or awake, and without being struck by the harmony that is naturally established between the text and its interpretation!)
>
> But he is also a preacher of the most extraordinary caliber. This Sunday morning I had a lawful reason to stay home, and if ever I have been thankful for something like this, it was today (February 24, 1932). I tuned my radio to the church in Delfshaven, and after a fairly good prelude by the organist, the powerful voice of "KS" resounded over the airwaves at ten o'clock. (Those initials

are just as familiar in the church world as the initials of S. de B. or J. Th. de V.)[20]

It's too bad that Schilder does not have a higher, "thinner" voice, for at times he is not fully understandable. In this respect — and only in this one — I am his superior, for they tell me that I am easy to listen to no matter where I am. This surely cannot be said of Schilder. You have to listen very carefully — otherwise you will miss a few words here and there.

O, what a well-thought-out and thorough piece of work he brings to the pulpit! Our Reformed worship services are lacking in many respects; we really don't have a liturgy to speak of. The only time the congregation gets to say something is in the communal singing. And some ministers seek out entirely unsuitable — I was tempted to write *impossible* — verses to sing. If such singing is only the "relaxation of attention" between the two halves of a lengthy dogmatic disquisition bawled out in an inexpressibly tiresome preaching tone — well then, surely such a sermon is *not* a refreshment of the soul. But if you once enjoy the rare privilege of listening to a man who really *has something to say,* who out of the treasure of his heart can bring forth old and *new* things, who truly makes the Holy Scriptures *live* for you, then I would not trade such Reformed preaching for even the most beautiful Lutheran service, however glorious the liturgy, however beautiful the communal singing of the choir and the congregation. For then the old psalms take on a solemnity and majesty that I would not want to exchange for anything.

And that's how it was this morning as I listened to "KS" preaching. His text was Mark 3:31-35. His introduction was already gripping and took hold of me in an understandable way, for he started out with the "Una Sancta," which he already pointed to in the beautiful prayer before the sermon, which, unfortunately, I am not able to

---

[20] S. de B. was J. R. Slotemaker de Bruïne (1869-1941), who was a National Reformed (*Hervormd)* minister. He was a professor of theology at the University of Utrecht and later served as minister of state for education. J. Th. de V. was J. Th. de Visser (1851-1923), also a National Reformed minister. This man eventually became minister of state for education as well. Thus both names were famous in the Netherlands. —TRANS.

reproduce here. For some, he said, the discussion of the "Una Sancta" leads to an emphasis on the "Sancta," on the holiness of the church, and with a one-sided love they make much of the purity and spotlessness of Christ's church. But others look so exclusively at the "Una," the unity of the church, that her holiness recedes to the background, and so they try to unify the most heterogeneous elements. (Parenthetically, I would observe that our brother "KS" does not avoid the use of "foreign" words any more than Newman did, but for a congregation that can follow such a preacher, a dozen or so theological or philosophical terms need not be a problem.)

Now, Christ resolves the struggle between these two "pious" armies. By means of a telling example — he often uses examples — Rev. Schilder explained this by making reference to Israel's sacred history. Levi had been zealous for the unity of the family, but he had forgotten the holiness of God's people, and so he had gone about in a rough and passionate way committing murder. Therefore he was sternly punished by his father Jacob on his deathbed. But later Moses could testify of Levi that after he had learned the holiness of his calling, he did not know his father and his mother — he understood his task in office. God had disputed with Levi, and now he understood that it is the holiness of God that forms the unity of the church. Even his own mother and brothers were subordinated to the interests of the kingdom of God.

In the words of the text, Christ stands before us as the Mediator between God and man. God's right comes before the voice of blood. And then Schilder proceeded to unfold these three main thoughts for us: (i) the voice of blood speaks to the soul of Jesus, (ii) the voice of blood is tested by Jesus against the standard of the spirit of Christ, and (iii) the voice of blood is subjected to the Spirit of God. After the sermon the congregation sang stanzas 2 and 13 of Psalm 22.

Dr. Gunning went on to offer a short description of the content of this sermon, and he concluded with these words:

I have written all of this down an hour after hearing the sermon. I am still freshly under the impression of this powerful address, but I know with certainty that I have not been able to reproduce the beauty of it. That's what I call *preaching!* There was no special eloquence about it; indeed, as I said, there were even times when he couldn't be heard clearly. This was not flowing, sparkling oratory. But it has been a long time since I have been gripped so fully as today by the majesty of truth, the elevation of God's thoughts, and the glory of my Savior. Yes, "Una Sancta" is a reality — God be praised! The unity *comes* because it is already there. But it only comes along the way of holiness, which is the way of perfect love . . . We concluded the service by singing stanza 2 of Psalm 133. Seldom have the Psalms seemed so refreshing and appropriate to me as this morning . . .

By way of a postscript I might add that I would love to reproduce the two prayers, but my colleague Schilder, whom I contacted about this desire, could not help me at all, and not with his sermon either, which he did not have on paper any more than his prayers. Because he will be absent from his congregation while he takes a study leave, I do not dare send him a copy of this article either for correction and supplementation. Suppose that he, sharp critic that he is, should say, "That doesn't look like anything to me!" Then I would have taken all this trouble for nothing, and that would be a shame for my readers. I'm sure that even though this is an inadequate report, they will draw a blessing from it, just as I am thankful to have heard Schilder once.

It was remarkable that although his sermons were packed full of content upon which he needed to focus his attention, nothing that went on in church while he was preaching escaped him. He saw everything. Most speakers do not see their hearers as individuals — only as a mass of people. But Schilder saw his hearers listening to him as individual persons, and a simple mother listening intently could inspire him.

I recall that in one sermon he repeated a sentence. When I asked him after the service why he had done this, he told me that someone in the church (he then pointed to the approximate place where the man had been sitting) had turned to his wife, probably with the question, "What did he say just now?" Schilder surmised that a word or a few words had escaped this man, and so he repeated the entire sentence. During the following week I had the opportunity to ask the brother in question about this incident, and he confirmed Schilder's words.

Once I was to meet Schilder in IJmuiden on a Good Friday before he preached there in the evening. The train was late (it was just after war), and so I arrived late. I had my wife with me, and we were to lodge nearby. And so it came about that I entered the church some twenty minutes after the service had begun, with my suitcase in my hand. Schilder saw us coming in, and said, "I'll just repeat briefly what I was saying." He wanted to introduce us to the material he was dealing with.

Various things in a church or a meeting hall could bother him as he spoke, such as outrageous taste in the style or color of someone's clothes. And he would much rather preach in the afternoon or the evening than in the morning. He was also very sensitive to the impression the congregation made on him. On one occasion he said to me after a preaching engagement, "I fear that it must be very hard to get that congregation moving." And it turned out that he was right!

He was well aware of *where* he was preaching, and his choice of a text was often determined by it. On one occasion, when he was to preach to a mystically oriented congregation, he chose as his text: "And last of all, as it were to one untimely born, He appeared to me also" (I Corinthians 15:8). In that congregation people loved to talk about violent conversions and sudden conversions like Paul's. In his sermon Schilder let the congregation see what Paul's conversion really was. I don't believe that after he was finished with them, there was anyone who wanted such a conversion for himself. And so his sermons constituted explication and application at one and the same time; in fact, his entire sermon was application, for when he preached he simply let the Word speak.

Nowadays there are people who have little or no appreciation for an exhaustive and thorough proclamation of the Word. They like it better when a preacher, following the modern dialectical style, describes beautiful things around the text, like a moth flying around a candle, careful not to get too close to it for fear of being burned. After all, isn't preaching a "risk"? And they regard it as both beautiful and modern when the preacher leaves a great deal to the imagination of his hearers, when he "creates a void" which we can fill with our own longings. They like vague guides who tell them, "You could go in *this* direction, but on the other hand you could also go in *that* direction." To *avoid* mentioning the thing you are talking about — isn't that the great art, as Stéphane Mallarmé has told us? Just be suggestive,[21] and leave the seeking and finding to your hearers.

And that's the poverty of so much preaching today. The Word of God remains in the mist; it is surrounded by a mysterious cloak of dialectical aestheticism. Then the "solution" is church services that hardly last an hour and contain a great deal of "liturgy." A normal person can't endure more than an hour of such a service, we are told. When the Word of God is taken away and all we have left is human foolishness, which stands in the way of the operation of the Spirit, who only works through and with His Word, then the river of life which the congregation of the Lord needs so desperately is blocked by human cleverness and cuteness and little religious "reflections" that lead people away from Religion. We get more and more "liturgy" and less and less preaching — this is seen as an urgent necessity if we are to get people into church for a little while before they return to their day-by-day agenda. Behind such preaching stands a *period* — and not the *colon* which Dr. Gunning found behind the sermons of "KS."

The third stream

Now we can begin to see that something was bound to happen through this man, especially when we consider what was going on during the 1920s and 1930s. When I discussed these decades earlier, I pointed out that there were two streams that had made their presence felt in the years after the first world war. The one stream began to canonize Kuyper — but then the scholastic Kuyper, with his mistaken ideas, constructions, and reflections; this stream soon ran dry in barren speculation about dogmatic questions. The other stream was made up of the so-called younger generation, which wanted to go in more of an Ethical-Irenic direction; this second stream had begun to feel too confined within the walls of the Church and asked for doors and windows to be thrown open toward the world. This was the group that allowed itself to be led and fed by the Dutch Christian Student Union.

---

[21] "Suggérer, voilà le rêve."

Through the work of the young Rev. Schilder, a *third* stream began to dig out a channel in our ecclesiastical life. But we should not imagine that he offered his leadership in any deliberate or methodical or organized way. He spoke and wrote in accordance with the Word and the confessions of the Church — no more, and no less. But that was enough. Then the fruits of such speaking would have to become manifest — all the more because he went about his work in such a unique and brilliant way.

His style

His massive and suggestive style would strike you immediately whenever he spoke or wrote. Then you would see that he was not just a scholar but also an artist, a poet. J. A. Rispens has compared Schilder to Prof. van Ginneken, a Roman Catholic who has been recognized in Roman Catholic circles not only as a learned researcher and philologist but also as an original stylist of interest to students of literature. Likewise, Rispens views Schilder as someone who, in addition to being a theologian, is of abiding interest from a literary point of view:

> In his works that are not specifically theological,[22] the style and handling of language form an unbreakable unity and testify to the literary powers of the author. Schilder's personality is philosophical-dogmatic, but we do him an injustice if we construct his character solely out of rational elements. Although the experiential (the element of feeling) was not uppermost and was given shape by the fiery purification of the dogmatic, there is still a dark, vital undertone of the experiential side that always comes through in him. This intertwinement of the rational and the vital, this rational sensitivity, is what determines the timbre and nature of his unique style. His style has nothing to do with a uniform eloquence (a honey-tongued eloquence) which is often (wrongly) understood to be the main distinguishing characteristic of the aesthetic. It

---

[22] In his *Richtingen en Figuren in de Nederlandsche Letterkunde na 1880*, Rispens mentions *Licht in den Rook* and *Eros of Christus* and *Bij Dichters en Schriftgeleerden*, and especially his powerful trilogy *Christus in Zijn Lijden*. This trilogy is available in English as *Christ in His Suffering* and *Christ on Trial* and *Christ Crucified*, translated by Henry Zylstra. The trilogy was published in English in 1938-40 and was reprinted most recently by Baker Book House of Grand Rapids.

is made of antithetical elements and represents a harmony of dissonant motifs that struggle toward freedom. It is also a style of imaginative ingenuity in which the life-impulse constantly strives to exorcize the tendency toward the formal and formalistic.

An artist by the grace of God

Schilder was an artist by the grace of God. In him burned the fire of a longing for beauty, the desire for harmony between content and form. But his universal spirit was not bound to a certain medium in its quest for satisfaction and for an expression of this longing. If he had wanted to, Schilder could have been a master of any one of a number of media used in the fine arts. But he subordinated everything to the service of his prophetic calling and also forced his artistic soul into this service role.

I will never forget the time I was vacationing with him in Brussels, where we visited the mighty Gothic cathedral. His eye surveyed the arches and the wood carvings around the pulpit, which depicted the expulsion from Paradise. He then sighed, "How I would love to preach in this building once!" He, who possessed so many outstanding talents when it came to preaching, could easily have had the most beautiful churches at his disposal, if he had only looked out for himself alone, which was what his enemies accused him of doing. But his faithfulness to his office and his slavish subordination to his prophetic calling led him, at the end of his life, to preach in humble meeting halls with bare walls, rickety chairs, and a modest lectern for a pulpit.

He was a master in many areas of art. He could easily have become just as great a poet writing bound verse as he was a prose stylist. In his younger years he had a great deal of interest in what went on in the world of literature. His book *Bij Dichters en Schriftgeleerden* shows how easily he could get engrossed in the modern developments in literature. But he let go of this work, which he loved, because his office required him to be busy elsewhere.

He could also have become a virtuoso in the area of music. When his friend Jan Zwart died in 1937, Schilder said of him that he had prophesied from the organ bench. The same could be said of Schilder himself, even though he had never studied music. Without lessons and without any fumbling around, he played great church organs. The well-known organist Kruithof in Kampen allowed him to play the organ of the Burgwalkerk. At the funeral of Rev. J. Bavinck, Schilder played mournful music that welled up from his imagination — not well-known tunes but music that expressed his own emotions. Wherever he preached, he tried to make his way over to the organ after the service and was as happy as a child if the organist invited him behind the keyboard.

One day he sat in the office of Mr. L. Smit in Goes, working on a lead article for *The Reformation*. The article was sorely needed — the presses were waiting for it — but it just wouldn't come. When Mr. Smit told Schilder that he would leave him behind in the office because he had to play the organ at a wedding, Schilder jumped up and asked, "May I come along?" Mr. Smit asked him how the article would then get written. "It will come to me," Schilder replied, and so he went along and asked if he could play the organ. He accompanied the singing and also played a postlude whose jubilant notes filled the church building long after the bridal couple and the family had departed. When he came out, he rubbed his hands together and declared, "Now I can get to work." And the article flowed from his pen.

Organ music moved him in the depths of his being; more than anyone realized, it became an instrumental interpretation of his deepest pain and highest joy. Only a few days before he died, he was playing the piano in the reading room of the seminary in the middle of the night. The organist Chris G. Lindeboom said of him: "A good prelude during a church service could refresh — indeed, inspire — him." Then he was the great simple man who could look at you with those gentle eyes that penetrated to the most remote corners of your soul. Abrupt as his remarks were, he then said with his humorous smile, "It was in order again up there today."[23] The Amsterdam organist Willem van Laar, a well-known musician who directed mass choirs at royal visits, said once, "In theoretical respects there are some things to criticize in his playing; but there is music in his fingers. He is a musician with originality."

Faith and scholarship

Schilder could have gone a long way in the world of art, as a poet or a musician, and he could have made quite a name for himself in scholarship as well. Even when he was a student, his tremendous talent drew attention. In the student almanacs of the years 1909 through 1913, we find various contributions of Schilder's, in which there is

---

[23] See *Gedenkt uw voorgangeren*, p. 64.

great variation. There are poems in Greek and Latin, which drove students who wanted to know what he was saying to their dictionaries. He also wrote verse in German and Dutch, his own language. Whenever he was active in some student circle, the expectations of him were very high. His lively wit, telling comments, and plays on words were unequalled.

In his student years, the course of his life already began to be marked out. Rev. Boerkoel writes:

> He rounded off this study period with an elaborate sketch about Hebrews 11:6 ("He who comes to God must believe that He is, and that He is a rewarder of those who seek Him") under the heading "Faith and Religion." . . . In this period were laid the foundations upon which Schilder was later to build. He was to develop himself ever more richly and manifest himself in an even more multifarious way. The crown of leaves and branches would become broader, and bear fruit in increasing measure. But this tree was firmly planted in the ground when he entered the parsonage. We will never know him adequately if we do not take proper account of his student days, the time when he already sent roots deep into the earth, the very roots he would later draw on regularly and repeatedly. His powerful productivity, his subtle feeling for language, his personal style, which was to take on more and more of his own stamp — all of this can be traced back to the springtime of his life.

The sentences with which Schilder concluded his last contribution to the almanac are characteristic. After asking the world of our time whether *her* faith dares to face death, and whether *her* faith has the power to both work and be still, he offered the following testimony: *"We,* who are true believers in Christ, can *work,* fight and yet be *at rest,* for our faith shows us the Eternal One, and therefore also eternity; and that eternity, because it makes us servants of God and leads us to hope for the 'crown of righteousness,' becomes our 'motif' (power) and our 'quietif' (rest) at one and the same time. 'Quiet strength' — that is *our* motto and *our* practice. Whoever believes and confesses in such a manner receives the same *assurance* as the thousands of martyrs whose death was a loud testimony to these truths. *God commands!* We *may* do nothing else! *Our own heart impels us!* We do not *want* to do anything else! In other words: *Quiet strength* — until death!"

This was already his program when he was a student. With this program he walked through the doorway of a rich and full life's work, and he remained faithful to it unto death. In that faithfulness we see God's grace in Schilder's life and toward the churches.

Apart from the grace of God, a man like Schilder with such brilliant gifts would have meant catastrophe for the church. In such a time as the 1920s, when things were on a shaky basis, when the church's confession was for many nothing more than a historical document, when many members of the younger generation stood completely open to the spiritual streams of this world, a genius like Schilder would doubtless have assumed a leading position among the members of the younger generation. With the might of his words and of his pen, he would then have helped bring about a quick and radical deformation in the Reformed world. If a genius like Schilder had allowed himself to be charmed by the seemingly beautiful religiosity of Ethical-Irenic Christianity and had been caught up in the snares of Barthian dialectical theology (as so many others did, such as Buskes), there would have been in the Netherlands no better defender and propagandist for this pernicious body of doctrines than he. And then the doors of our Dutch cathedrals would have stood open to him. The universities would also have invited him in.

For if he was an artist, he was also a man of scholarship. He was fully at home in both classical and modern philosophy. Plato and Aristotle, but also Dante, Goethe, Kierkegaard, Nietzsche, Schleiermacher, Dostoevski, Kant, Hegel — he knew them all. And for Schilder, to know a thinker meant to have grasped the very heart his philosophical system and to see its deadly danger as false prophecy. Schilder was well aware that the philosophical ideas which a student picks up are eventually worked out in daily life and can have a devastating effect on social relationships.

He was quick to see through the philosophical background of the National Socialist movement. In a pamphlet commenting on a series of leaflets put out by the Dutch Nazi movement, he wrote: "This brochure is in good measure inspired by the same philosophical paganism which seized hold of Marx and Engels at the beginning of their development, and of which the consequence is what we now see in Russia."[24]

The "world" lay open before him. If he had been in it for himself, there were all sorts of opportunities for him in the 1920s, and even more in the 1930s, when there were hardly any geniuses and talented people around anymore in the Reformed world, when the whole business threatened to run stuck in a reign of sterile epigones.

His enemies maintained that he was in it for himself all the way down to the liberation. What a mistake they made! If a universal mind like his had been looking out first and foremost for its own interests, the course of our church life would have unfolded very differently, and he would have played a very different role among us. As far as his personal life is concerned, he would have been much more successful from the standpoint of worldly criteria.

God had willed something else for Schilder, who did not seek his own interests but the will of his Father. *"God commands!* We *may* do nothing else!" That was what he had written over the doorway through which he entered his life's work. *"Our own heart impels us!* We do not *want* to do anything else!"

Indeed, there was nothing else he could do, for the Spirit of the LORD put him on as though he were a jacket. The Spirit had reformational work for him to do. And remember that Schilder did not seek such a role.

When we disregard his great talents, we also conclude that he wasn't exactly suitable for it either. J. de Waard, who was a boyhood friend of Schilder's, tells how he started out as a "Gymnasium" student at the age of twelve:[25] "On the seventh of September he came — pale, slender, timid. He was a new boy in a class of students who had already gotten somewhat used to each other. Children can be so hard, so cruel! He did not push his way in among us, and we often left him standing alone. In the five minutes during which we would get a change of teacher, we would romp and shout in the courtyard, but Schilder often stood alone staring into the sky. He came, he gave a good account of himself in his lessons, he went, he learned his lessons, he was

---

[24] Schilder's brochure was entitled *Not One Square Inch!* (Dutch: *Geen Duimbreed!*). This was a phrase Kuyper had made famous: not one square inch of creation stood outside the kingship of Christ. The quotation comes from the section entitled "Hegeliaansche evolutie-gedachten in brochure III." —TRANS.

[25] The Gymnasium was the secondary school attended by university-bound students. —TRANS.

well-behaved. Sometimes when he was present, it was just as though he was absent — living in a dream world."

When he was a university student he manifested the same characteristics. He was withdrawn, did not associate easily with people, and was often a "loner." He remained that way all of his life. Those who knew him well realize that he could not easily give himself to others, and that a sort of fear of people often brought him into isolation. He possessed a childish naiveté, was sometimes shy, and was always afraid of causing people pain. Many a telephone conversation in which he had to make an ordinary remark would begin with the following statement: "I have to say something to you, but first you must promise me that you will not become angry." At the end of his life he put a comment in his paper to the effect that we need more people with "gentle eyes." Now, Schilder himself had those gentle eyes. He was deathly afraid of having to do something that would displease someone, and if it did on occasion prove necessary, he always had his apology ready in advance. Sometimes it appeared that he was afraid of people, but what he really feared was the disturbing of relationships. It was partly this feature of his character that made him into the lonely figure he remained all of his life.

Now then, such a man did not appear at all suited to be thrown into the full stream of life, to take up positions sharply, often swimming against the stream in the process; he did not find it easy to be unpleasant to people, to have to speak the truth in a razor-sharp way, and to combat the lie. We know that when Schilder was a young man, his strong preference in terms of a career was mission work. And it would have suited his character. As a missionary he would have operated largely apart from people; he could have been free to do his own work and keep to himself, without getting entangled in relationships in which it was difficult for him to manoeuvre.

If God had not put him to work doing the things to which He called him, Schilder would never have sought such work himself. When we look at his character, we have to conclude that the Spirit of the LORD put Schilder on like a jacket. And when He did so, Schilder became a willing instrument. For *faithfulness, love,* and *obedience* were qualities that governed his character from childhood on.

Also moving is a characteristic of Schilder's about which De Waard tells us: "When we had a social evening as gymnasium students, or a club meeting, or a seminarians' fraternity meeting, he would often leave halfway through because he did not want his mother to have to overwork on his behalf. Then he would stand for a couple of hours turning the crank on the machine she used for ironing, and he was not at all ashamed to do so."[26]

"The Reformation"

When Schilder had been a minister for some years, he became a contributor to a weekly periodical which was established in 1920 and called *The Reformation*. This periodical was the chief medium he was to use in the reformational work to which he was called.

The story of the founding of this periodical is a rather strange one. Dr. H. W. van der Vaart Smit took the initiative. I still remember that when he was a minister in Zuid-Beijerland, he visited me on the island of Flakkee to discuss putting out a church weekly via the firm of Boekhoven in Sommelsdijk. He was full of criticism about the way things were going at the Free University; his criticism also extended to various church leaders and to the editors of *The Herald*. I was not able to help him in business respects, and so he went to the firm of Oosterbaan & Le Cointre in Goes, where, at his initiative, *The Reformation* began to be published as a weekly in 1920. Schilder was not involved at the initial stage.

In May of 1919, a number of men had gathered in Amsterdam, after some preliminary discussions in a smaller circle. They wanted to talk about a brochure of J. C. Aalders entitled *The Criticism of the Younger Ones*. Invitations to this meeting had been sent out by Dr. B. Wielenga, Dr. van der Vaart Smit, and Mr. P. Oosterbaan. Wielenga led the meeting, and Van der Vaart Smit functioned as secretary. Present were Dr. K. Dijk, Dr. G. Keizer, Rev. J. G. Kunst, Rev. C. Lindeboom, Rev. F. C. Meyster, Rev. J. C. Rullmann, Dr. van der Vaart Smit, Dr. Wielenga, and Mr. Oosterbaan. It was decided to start a paper, but with an expanded committee. The following were invited to join: Dr. F. W. Grosheide, Dr. T. Hoekstra, Dr. J. G. Geelkerken, Dr. G. C. Aalders, and Dr. J. C. de Moor. A small committee was established to do the preliminary work — arranging for publication with a printing company, appointing editors and contributors, and so forth. The members of this committee were Dr. Wielenga, Dr. Dijk, Dr. van der Vaart Smit, and Mr. Oosterbaan.

---

[26] Schilder's mother was a widow who earned her living as a washerwoman, taking in laundry. —TRANS.

At a second meeting of July, 1919, some of the people who had been invited to join in the project were present: Grosheide, Hoekstra, Geelkerken, and De Moor. Dr. Aalders sent word that he had no time. Lindeboom, Meyster, and Kunst were absent with notice. The ideas and plans drafted by the small committee did not win approval at this meeting. It was regarded as necessary that there be more agreement on the direction, purpose, basis, and program, that these matters be articulated more clearly, and that the paper address its voice to the "younger generation." Moreover, the paper would have to steer a positive course and be principially Reformed, binding itself to the Reformed confessions. In view of the crisis in the Reformed world having to do with such matters as the Dutch Christian Student Union, the use of hymns in worship, the prospect of a new Bible translation, and revision of the confessions and our liturgy, a certain program would have to be established which the editors could use as their guide.

Agreement on these matters was not reached immediately, but it was finally decided to go ahead and to appoint three people as the editors: Dr. B. Wielenga, Dr. K. Dijk, and Dr. H. W. van der Vaart Smit, with the latter serving as secretary. However, Dr. de Moor raised a very serious objection to appointing Van der Vaart Smit to such an important post. At a subsequent meeting held especially to discuss this appointment, with Dr. Geelkerken and Dr. F. J. J. Buytendijk also in attendance, Dr. de Moor stated his reasons for objecting to Van der Vaart Smit: he believed this man did not have the trust of our Reformed people. (Dr. de Moor could speak sharply when necessary!) As evidence he pointed to Van der Vaart Smit's brochure about Biblical criticism. De Moor had read this brochure with a sense of estrangement. He pointed out that there were many careless and ambiguous expressions in it, and that the reviews were unfavorable on the whole. Dr. van der Vaart Smit was discredited throughout the country, and his association with the paper would open the way for all sorts of misunderstandings. Van der Vaart Smit then withdrew his name from consideration for the post of secretary of the editors, and Dr. V. Hepp was named to replace him, with Dr. Keizer to serve as his alternate.

The tensions that were present in our ecclesiastical life after the first world war immediately found their echo in this paper. Dr. Geelkerken and Rev. Brussaard both withdrew from the paper before the first issue was published. A meeting was held with these two men, but no agreement could be reached. In addition to a revision of the "superstructure" of the confessions, these men wanted changes in the "substructure." Not long afterward, Geelkerken began to publish his own paper, *Word and Spirit,* which was to become the mouthpiece of the churches in "Restored Federation."

Apart from this disagreement, there was tension enough within the circle of men who began to publish *The Reformation.* At a meeting held in May of 1921 (the first issue had been published in October of 1920), there were objections to the editors: some had the impression that there was not sufficient homogeneity in their thinking. Dr. Wielenga was dissatisfied with the policies which Dr. Hepp was following in his capacity as the editor having the final say: Hepp operated too much on his own. And there were other problems as well.

I have gone to some length in telling the story of how *The Reformation* came into being because it is a most remarkable episode to look back upon in the light of some forty years of subsequent church history in the Netherlands. We now know very well who Van der Vaart Smit is and what role he has played in our Reformed ecclesiastical life, and also in our existence as a nation. In the sad and somber evening of his life we saw him disappear into the dim mysticism of the church of Rome. It is most remarkable that this man took the initiative in the establishment of a paper which, from the very outset, would serve to unmask his false position in relation to both God and man. And it is even more remarkable that he would one day approve heartily of the arrest and imprisonment of Schilder, the man who became editor-in-chief of this paper he had helped set up. While Schilder languished in jail because of his conscience, Van der Vaart Smit fraternized with his jailers and with those who persecuted him.

It is also remarkable that the goal which Van der Vaart Smit and a few others with him had in mind in setting up the paper was not realized — quite the contrary. It turned into the opposite of what they had wanted. It was supposed to have been a paper of and for the Reformed "younger generation," who found the church of the Secession and the Doleantie too narrow, who called for "open doors and windows," inter-ecclesiastical "latitude," and so forth. What actually happened is that the paper took an entirely different course: it answered the criticism of the "younger generation" in a Scriptural way; it tried to lead people through the channel of the confessions; and it worked hard to combat confessional indifference.

But all of this did not happen at once. At first no one seemed to know what direction the paper would take. When the twenty-fifth anniversary of its existence was being celebrated, Schilder wrote the following words:

> We should not forget, on this memorial occasion, that *The Reformation,* a paper that calls for reformation, itself needed to be reformed. And no editor who embarked on his work in a period like the one that began about 1920 should act as though he himself was not bound to his immediate environment with all the fibres of his being and therefore was not personally in need of reformation. Anyone who does not, at the beginning of his work, share and exhibit the weaknesses of his upbringing and milieu can at most become a revolutionary; but he will not get around to an attempt at reformation, especially not self-reformation.
>
> When this paper began to be published, the present editor was only a contributor, and he did not play any part in the setting up of the paper. And when he looks back over the course of the paper's history, he sees very clearly that in the beginning it was a weak and clumsy enterprise. It was an attempt — nothing more . . . No wonder that the initiatives undertaken often resulted in failure . . . What I mean here by "failure" is that we were not successful in coming *principially* to the proper foundation. We set out to sea without being clear on this matter. Nor were we able to be clear at that time. Although our Reformed *(Gereformeerd)* life had "run aground," it was by no means firmly grounded.

Schilder then provided various quotations, all taken from the paper's first year of publication, through which he made it clear that the Reformed people had indeed "run aground" and did not know where to go next. He commented further: "When we look back on such uncertainties in thinking and arguing and appealing to the basis, I believe we can say that in 1920 there was no one who offered a clear statement of the basic issues on which *The Reformation* wanted to give leadership — and then in conscious distinction from the kind of leadership that had been given in Reformed circles up to that point."

That's the way things were when *The Reformation* began to be published, and so it should not surprise us that there were a number of changes in the team of editors in the early years. The one wanted to be "right-wing," the other more "left-wing," a third simply wanted to be conservative, a fourth wanted to advance without conserving, and so forth. I will not take the time to trace those developments in any detail. The history of this paper is a piece of church history in and of itself, and one could easily write a substantial book about it.

But one thing is sure: the men putting out this paper wanted "reformation." The name they were using made this clear. Yet they did not ask: What is reformation? Their failure to pose this question clearly reflected the dislocated circumstances of the early 1920s. The answer to this question, Schilder once declared, "is ultimately so plain and ordinary that it almost amazes us." He then proceeded to tell us what reformation is — return to the confessions. "We want to begin with the *belief* that our thinking *IS ordered* by the reading and acceptance of Scripture — as opposed to being ordered by a theologian or by anyone else or by ourselves."

Return to the confessions

Once Schilder came to this very simple realization, he made it his starting point in his work in writing for this paper. The result was that the paper called *The Reformation* itself underwent a reformation. A different spirit came to expression in this paper than the one that had controlled it since the time of its founding. And through the reformation of *The Reformation,* the process of reformation began to spread throughout Reformed *(Gereformeerd)* life in our country. This happened gradually — not all at once. Schilder later commented: "Things happen in the field in a way we do not comprehend."

He was clear in describing the reformation of *The Reformation* as a "return to the confessions." He added: "The correctness of confronting the confessions themselves with the Scriptures, their judge, is thereby upheld from the very beginning, as soon as the confessions (whose contents form our starting point) are recognized as confessions (and as nothing more)."

Today these things may seem very simple and ordinary to us — even if we face new temptations in relation to them. We have a hard time understanding why there had to be a battle fought about such matters in the 1920s. The reason for the battle, of course, was that people no longer wanted to accept the confessions (even though they often interpreted them on the basis of their own insights and in accordance with new theological constructions). They proposed to limit the confessions to the "ecclesiastical sphere"; beyond this domain, some other, "derived" principles were to be applied.

This is also the reason for the clashes between Schilder and the other editors of *The Reformation*. I think of Hepp, who established his Federation of Calvinists, in which he calmly accepted as members people who had been condemned by the church as departing from the confessions (Synod of Assen, 1926). Men who introduced the dialectical theology of Karl Barth among us (e.g. T. L. Haitjema) and thus were in conflict with the confessions of the church were welcomed by Hepp into this Federation of Calvinists.

We could say that the great majority of the Reformed *(Gereformeerd)* people of this time had trouble understanding Schilder's standpoint and could not accept it. This shows how widespread an idea it was that there should be a separation between the Church, where the confessions were held to be valid, and the domain of common grace, where they played no role.

Return to the Scriptures

Early in his career, Schilder himself went through an inner struggle concerning this matter. How did this come about? At first the change in his thinking happened unconsciously and very simply: it came about because he *believed the Scriptures.* He read what was written there, exegeted without prejudices, and yielded willingly and obediently to the Scriptures. When he did all of this, a breakthrough was inevitable.

To manage to read Scripture apart from the spectacles of *a priori* dogmatic constructions was quite something in that time. Reformation was needed if this was to be possible — a reformation that began in one's own head and heart. It is worth noting, then, that at the very beginning of his ministry, Schilder bowed his head and heart before the majesty of the Scriptures. His life became strictly determined by *one* line, *one* motif, *one* style.

When he had come to the end of his life, Schilder faced a very sad task: he had to find a new name for the student union he loved so much because some of the students who were unfaithful (remaining with the synodocratic church and its Theological School on the Oudestraat) had, through a court order, managed to take wrongful possession of the property and name of this organization.[27] Schilder's

---

[27] See *The Reformation,* September 30, 1950.

brilliant response to the situation was to come up with a play on words that was at the same time a change in name for the student corps: "Fides *Quaerit* Intellectum" became "Fides *Quadrat* Intellectum." The change involved only two letters. "Faith seeks understanding" was the slogan of Anselm, the "father of the old scholasticism," who lived in the eleventh century, but in the small change introduced by Schilder, Anselm's phrase was replaced by one with a radically different meaning.

The change meant that faith no longer *sought* intellectual comprehension or understanding but rather *rounded off* scholarship, set it in the proper context or framework, and gave it its structure and proper place. Schilder wrote: "It is the faith that the God of the Scriptures is the one who orders our intellect, who establishes order among things, who cleans the stable of reason, which is corrupt by nature, and sweeps out our natural foolishness, removing the gaping lacunae by way of filling-from-above, who fills the valleys and levels the mountains, who regenerates and rounds off our intellect and makes it harmonious. He does all of this in the way of faith, whereby the 'man of God' accepts the content of the God who speaks and says 'yes' to it."[28]

That was what Schilder had to say, then, about the new name for the student union. Here he showed again that God is able to make good come forth from something that in itself is evil. The new name was even more reformational and Scriptural than the old one!

When we use this Kampen incident, which is significant in itself, as our starting point, we are able to see something of how Schilder rounded things off at the end of his life — or better, we see the content of faith that governed his life's work. He never regarded his faith as a process of "seeking" knowledge, for he realized that faith may seek a "sharpening, advancement and purification" of intellect but must never seek intellect itself or understanding itself. Understanding is given by God in the Scriptures. This starting point is all-determinative for Schilder. If we do not bear it in mind, we will not understand his life's work and the struggle he underwent.

---

[28] The name of the student union was another instance of "occupied possession" *(bezet bezit)*. The majority of the students at the Theological School in Kampen had joined Schilder and Greijdanus in 1945 as they continued their instruction in a building on the Broederweg. The court case about the name and property took some years to process: an extensive report on it was given by Dr. Jelle Faber (then a student) in the annual almanac of the student union (see *Almanak van het Corpus Studiosorum in Academia Campensi "Fides Quadrat Intellectum"* [Kampen: Drukkerij en Boekhandel P. Zalsman], pp. 85-103). The same book contains Schilder's own illuminating discussion of the change in name and of the meaning of Anselm's phrase (see pp. 72-84). —TRANS.

Yet this starting point, this basis for his life, also set him apart from most of his contemporaries. When we read what was written in *The Reformation* in the early years about the "problem" of the younger generation, we see that the problem was approached from all sorts of different angles. Faith was seeking knowledge, but it seemed to forget that this knowledge is already to be found in the Scriptures.

Schilder never forgot this. When he wrote about the younger generation in one of the very first issues published,[29] he simply opened the Bible and read what we find in Zechariah 7:1-6. This pericope has to do with the first years after the end of the exile of the covenant people in Babylon. A mission comes to ask about the prospect of doing away with some days of penitence that had been observed faithfully in the years before that. The answer is not given by the official advisors but by the prophet Zechariah, who teaches the members of the younger generation that they are not to be critical of essentials but should restrict their criticism to peripheral matters. Iconoclasm is always part of the backwash of reformation. And to the older ones he said: Whoever calls reformation revolution is himself a revolutionary.

In that first year he also published a series of articles on the aesthetic view of Christ in which he showed the members of the younger generation that what they wanted could be accepted in part, provided that the old Reformed confessions were not ignored. On the contrary, he pointed out that those confessions also set a direction for life in the modern age. And in the second year of publication, he wrote a series of five lead articles on the language of the Church. In those articles, which drew a lot of attention, he again made it clear that when it comes to burning questions about the confessions and the liturgy, there can be no reformation unless we listen to the Scriptures.

Head or tail?

In 1922, when he was only thirty-one years old, Schilder addressed the Reformed Young Men's League at its annual League Day in Haarlem. His speech was entitled "Head or Tail?" On this occasion, too, he drew on the Scriptures in giving an answer to the questions of the day. He took his theme from Isaiah 9:14: "So the LORD cuts off head and tail from Israel."

The head, Schilder explained, "stands for those who are aged and are held in high regard, while the tail stands for the prophet who

---

[29] *The Reformation,* October 29, 1920.

teaches falsehood." False prophecy may stir itself and act important and be held in honor and look modern, says Isaiah, but the false prophet is a "tail person." For all his energy and prominence, he *follows* the beast as the least important part of the body. Here Isaiah compares the people to the body of a ponderous animal. That big body is not without movement. See how it shakes its head and moves. That head is the governor, the one raised aloft. The head is the person who leads and directs and goes first. Wherever the head turns, the entire body has to follow — each of the parts of the body must come along, including, of course, the tail. The false prophets are the tail, says Isaiah. They sometimes act as though they are very deliberate about what they do; yet, despite their show of being busy and their reckless haste, they are people who are doomed to play a passive role. They are the tail; they come dragging along behind. Sometimes a man may think he is a head person whereas in fact he is nothing more than a tail person.

In this League Day address, Schilder proceeded to offer the following lesson by way of application: "My friends, try to hold this calling high: don't be the tail, but be the head. Take hold of the Word tirelessly. Draw from it not simply what the *older ones* want you to find there nor what the *younger generation* is yearning for. For in both cases that would amount to trailing along behind — tail prophecy. Try to find and bring out what lies *within* it."

Forty years ago this was for many people a brand-new sound — that's how thoroughly accustomed they were to living by "derived principles" instead of by Scripture itself. But this message is also of great contemporary relevance for us, for today there is a lot of "tail prophecy" around. We have National Reformed *(Hervormd)* synods sending out resolutions about nuclear weapons, world peace, the question of racism, ecumenism, and so forth. They are tail prophets, for they are simply following the leading of the great and mighty of this earth, who represent the "head" of the ponderous beast that is our nation. These church bodies do not speak the Word of God when it comes to *internal* matters, so why would they follow the Word as it applies to *external* matters?

And when we turn to the synodocratic churches, we also find a lot of "tail prophecy." There is much movement and excitement and hubbub about all sorts of "cultural questions." Their prophets draw on films, liturgical services, youth meetings, mass evangelism meetings, and study committees about burning issues; they defend themselves against spiritual erosion and unchurchliness; they call for world ecumenism and contacts between churches, and for pastors to be placed over pastors, and for reorientation in the evaluation of their own history (Secession and Doleantie) — all of this because the church's young people complain about "narrowness" and cry out to have the boundaries expanded, to have more ventilation, more open windows and doors, more appreciation for culture (which often turns out to be a desire to engage in worldly amusements). And it may look as though those prophets are standing at the head of the parade — aren't they up-to-date, contemporary, modern, sensitive to what our new age demands? But Isaiah calls them tail prophets! They follow the ponderous beast that in turn follows the head, that is, the great and mighty of this earth in whom the spirit of the beast resides.

Schilder was not yet fully cognizant of his own position and commitment at the time he began to take a stand. Remember that faith does not *seek* knowledge, for it already possesses it in the Scriptures. What it seeks is to order knowledge and to put it to work by applying it in every part of daily life.

Whoever does not care to take his place among the tail prophets with their exaggerated sense of their own importance but wishes to offer "head prophecy" will have a hard time of it. In the address he gave on that League Day, Schilder manifested an awareness of this and made the following statement, which we can read as a prophetic comment on what awaited him in life: "Naturally you will have to face the scorn of people — perhaps even of people who are very close to you, perhaps even of people (who can say?) who have been marching alongside you in the ranks." The changes in *The Reformation*'s editorial team represented a direct fulfillment of this prophecy, as did many things that happened later in Schilder's life.[30]

Outwardly directed polemics

At first, things went well as Schilder engaged in polemics against those who were outside the federation of the Reformed *(Gereformeerd)* churches. For example, after Dr. G. Wisse left the federation, Schilder took him on and satirized him in a masterful way: he took over Wisse's phrase "the regeneration of the presupposition" *(de wedergeboorte van de veronderstelling)* and used plays on words to demonstrate to

---

[30] This speech was published in Schilder's *Om Woord en Kerk,* Vol. 1 (Goes: Oosterbaan & Le Cointre, 1948), pp. 147-162. —TRANS.

Wisse the emptiness of his "shining lights" *(schijnende lichten),* which were no more than "sham lights" *(lichten van schijn).* The article in question had been published in the church paper of Classis Gorcum, and Prof. Hepp took it over in the press survey he included in *The Reformation,* expressing his full agreement with it. And when Schilder published a brochure defending the Synod of Assen against an attack by a Reformed minister who chose to remain anonymous at first, the brochure was welcomed with great thankfulness and expressions of agreement.[31]

When he published a series of articles in the periodical of the Reformed young men's societies, in which he warned against dangerous tendencies in Johannes de Heer as manifested in *The Searchlight,* he could count on warm approval throughout the Reformed churches. (Schilder's conclusion was: "We want to be one with Mr. de Heer in many things, but what we want even more is to be one with the Word that says: hold on to what you have.") He wrote critical, Scripturally-based articles about various currents and sects.[32] He was applauded gratefully in his own circles, and many of the articles he wrote for regional papers were taken over by the bigger Reformed papers, where they were quoted and reprinted with appreciation.

As time went on, he was allowed more space in *The Reformation.* Not only were his articles pervaded by a pure Reformed outlook, he was also a feared debater and polemicist. His argumentation was based on tight logic, grounded in an extensive knowledge of facts and states of affairs, and formulated in a brilliant style backed up by an unparalleled intuition for using exactly the right word in a given setting.

What made his publications so hard to oppose was the way he argued from Scripture and the confessions. He was above all an exegete and a student of the confessions. Whether he was defending something or on the attack, he did not take refuge in "principles," in Kuyperian constructions, Reformed ideas, or *a priori* theories; in-

---

[31] Schilder's brochure was entitled *Assen Overturned?* (Dutch: *Een hoornstoot tegen Assen? Antwoord op een "Conscientiekreet"*) and was published by Kok of Kampen in 1928. —TRANS.

[32] He wrote about Tagore in the Netherlands, about Rubinism and spiritism, about Roman Catholicism (in connection with the commemoration of the St. Bartholomew's Day massacre), about a Reformed political party known as the *Staatkundig Gereformeerde Partij* (under the heading "Merkwaardige tegen-strijdigheden"), about Freemasonry, about an attack from without based on alleged contradictions in the Bible, about the National Reformed *(Hervormd)* Church as she called for the other Reformed churches to return to her (his article was entitled "Ons aller Moeder"), and about various other things.

stead he drew exclusively on the Word and the confessions of the Church. He did not give the last word to that which now counts as "science" or "scholarship" but to what Scripture and the confessions say.

Because he took this approach, it was inevitable that he would get embroiled in conflicts within his own circles. At this point I cannot go into such conflicts that emerged. (In Chapter 1 I already discussed the decline and deformation in our ecclesiastical life.) For the most part, our people no longer lived by Scripture and the confessions but by what had come forth from Kuyperianism. We had our theories about "common grace" and the "pluriformity of the church" and "presumptive regeneration." We knew the scholastic distinctions that were made in connection with the covenant, the divine in man, and the Church. Moreover, what Kuyper had once offered to us as ideas that might — or might not — be helpful were now accepted among his epigones as "Reformed doctrine"; they became universally accepted in the practice of our church life and were passed on as "our" view.

In the process we bowed before science and scholarship as before an idol. When Prof. Waterink published his study *Christology and Anthropology,* in which he proceeded from a dogmatic construction about the Ego conceived of as the Nucleus *(Kern)* of Jesus and speculated about an "Ego as the Nucleus in every man," Mr. A. Janse, a Christian school principal in a small village who knew Scripture and the confessions well, opposed him. But Janse was dismissed as not competent to enter such a debate, for he had not enjoyed a "classical education": he was not a "scholar."[33]

Inwardly directed polemics

As we saw, Schilder was held in high regard as long as he carried on the battle against forces outside the Reformed *(Gereformeerd)* churches. But when he began to lay his finger on the wounds within the Reformed camp, he lost the support of many.

Prof. J. Waterink, who was one of the editors of *The Reformation* during the 1930s, commented on the rejection of inwardly directed polemics. After he made some observations about "church awareness" within our own circles in connection with an incident in Lisse, where Reformed *(Gereformeerd)* office-bearers were present when a

---

[33] It is well worth reading how Dr. R. J. Dam took up Janse's cause over against Mrs. H. Kuyper-Van Oordt in *The Herald.*

Christian Reformed *(Christelijk Gereformeerd)* minister was being installed in office (Waterink was still quite sensitive to such issues in those days!), a number of angry letters were sent in. In response to those reactions, Waterink observed that as long as polemics were directed against people *outside* our circles, they were appreciated:

> But here we encounter a most remarkable phenomenon, namely, that on this occasion, when I feel I must lay a finger on an open wound in our own circles, the result is a stream of letters, many of which outdo one another in being ill-mannered. Even the most polite of the expressions people are throwing at me are still too rude to be printed in this paper. I received some postcards lacking postage (and so I had to pay the postage myself) which contained nothing more than a few abusive words and a reference to the article about the Lisse incident. What kind of a strange mentality is manifesting itself here? We let people polemicize right and left, but as soon as someone dares to warn against the blurring of the boundaries within our own church life, people begin to carry on in a heartless manner — and all of this in the name of love, so they say, or in the name of the communion of saints which they desire.

Such was the situation at the beginning of the 1930s, when *The Reformation* began undertaking reformational work in our own circles. It's too bad that Waterink soon grew much more lax and left it to Schilder to do what needed to be done. In this same period Schilder continued with polemical articles in which he criticized people inside the Reformed *(Gereformeerd)* churches; for example, in one of his articles, he pointed out that the Lutheran idea of the church was slowly beginning to win out in Reformed *(Gereformeerd)* circles: to each his own life sphere, with the church left standing somewhat to the side:

> When it comes to politics, art, science, and social interaction, everyone says that we have our own leaders and that we hold high the name of Calvin, but there is also a church sphere where we maintain a strict neutrality. Let the churches tell us, with each one attending his own Sunday services, how the distinguishing marks of spiritual

life are to be found deep within us, so that when our time comes, we will have good reason to hope we will rest in Abraham's bosom. But the Church must stay out of our own sector. And so the Church winds up in a dead-end street, removed from the busy traffic of everyday life.

Schilder ended his article with these words:

> Have mercy on us, Lord; preserve us, for we perish. We are bold enough to talk about Moscow and to send telegrams to Geneva, but beyond that we don't dare do much *here*. We don't demand much either. We are happy that the judgments we utter are not taken any more seriously than the quarrelsome chatter of a senile person — in his home, set back from the busy street. We do not expect that the traffic in the street will pay attention to what we say for even a moment. Our home away from the street does not make many demands. And we find it quite normal that there should come to be more and more of these homes set back from the street; if someone grows troublesome in one of them, we can find him a place in another one — we don't mind giving him that place at all. His salvation is taken care of wherever he is, and on the same basis. The porridge that is used everywhere to nourish the mystical life of the soul is easy to make: it doesn't give rise to any controversial issues. And as for our confessions, they are meant for internal use; that is to say, they only apply within our little home away from the street. We old folks will close the windows. Then we won't hear the cars honking their horns out in the street. And the neighbors will not hear us playing "Take Time To Be Holy" on our own record player, while another person in his home away from the street plays another such song on his. Meanwhile, life seethes out there in the street. Lord, have mercy upon us![34]

---

[34] This article was entitled "De kerk in het slop" and was published in *The Reformation*, Vol. 11, No. 18 (Jan. 29, 1932), pp. 138-139. It has been reprinted in Schilder's "Verzamelde werken," first volume of *De Kerk* (Goes: Oosterbaan & Le Cointre, 1960), pp. 142-148. —TRANS.

Lord, have mercy on us!

That's how things began in the 1930s. The Word and the confessions were again made central for the full richness of everyday life, including every sector and every situation. Prof. Greijdanus had once said, "Apart from the Word I am nothing and can do nothing and know nothing." This claim had also taken on flesh and blood in the person of Schilder. This meant that there would have to be *reformation*.

But reformation involved picking up the knife and doing some cutting. Favorite ideas and sacred cows and constructions that may have seemed beautiful and pious to us had to be eliminated. And that was a painful process, for it led to division among those who appeared to be one. When we think back today to the situation at the beginning of the 1930s, which was the middle of the time I have been calling the "Solomonic era," the era of self-sufficiency, of the feeling of having arrived spiritually, when our people thought they knew everything and had laid it all out in schemas and programs and dogmatic assertions, when they had gained in power and influence over political and social matters, when it had gotten so easy for them in spiritual respects precisely because the Church had been brought back to the dead-end street of religiosity and meditation and "taking time to be holy" — if we bear all of this in mind, it will not surprise us that a battle eventually broke out.

And yet, there was no other way for Schilder. In his polemicizing directed outward, he had allowed Scripture and the confessions to speak; he would have to do the same when the polemic was directed at people within the camp. And then he soon came up against certain peculiar Kuyperian constructions which had virtually become common coin (the accepted view), such as common grace, the pluriformity of the church, and Kuyper's ideas about the covenant and baptism.

The epigones, who believed they had to take up Kuyper's cause, accused Schilder of trying to ruin Kuyper's life's work. But in advancing this claim they made a great and fatal error. *They* were the ones who were ruining Kuyper's work by simply repeating uncritically what he had said — and then choosing to elevate to the level of "the accepted view" exactly those parts of Kuyper's spiritual inheritance which had the least basis in Scripture and the confessions.

Schilder's intention was to work for a purification and strengthening of what Kuyper had left to our people in the way of a Scriptural inheritance. His great appreciation for the genuinely reformational work in Kuyper's legacy demonstrates that he was trying to maintain the good, to purify it, and to work it out further wherever necessary. Of Kuyper's "Stone Lectures"[35] he wrote: "There is so much that is charming in the broad flourishes with which it draws those bold lines. Yes, and it all continues to speak to us today in its clear Scriptural lines . . . There is so much here that is good and is faithful to the revealed Word in a wonderful way that it almost seems audacious to ask whether there are not also some dangers in it." But what Schilder opposed in Kuyper's work was only that which he regarded as in conflict with Scripture and the confessions. Schilder took aim at the scholasticism in Kuyper in order to be able to preserve Kuyper as reformer of the Church.

Back to the Word! That, and nothing else, neither more nor less, was the motto for his life when, in the 1930s, he took up the battle through his writings in *The Reformation,* opposing everything he regarded as in conflict with Scripture and the confessions. What was at the very heart of this battle was stated clearly in the issue of *The Reformation* that celebrated its twenty-fifth anniversary (October 7, 1950),[36] when he wrote: "We *know* (from the Scriptures), and we can and may 'systematize' that which we know. But when we do so, we may not build it up from an 'idea' or 'principle' or 'ground-motive' or 'Leitmotiv.' Neither may we go about our work of systematization on the basis of a slogan — not even if that slogan should be a Bible text (e.g. Proverbs 4:23) that seems to us a nice expression of a thought that had occurred to us already, for then *Scripture has far too little to do.* It misses out on the glory of daily 'operation' and 'purification' and 'instruction' as a permanently opened and functioning divine tribunal over our mind. *Scripture* comes into play *too late* and much too briefly with such hearers of the Word."

Schilder wanted to listen to the entire content of the Scriptures in context and to read them in the original languages. For Kuyper, Scripture still functioned too much by way of approving what he himself had first set out in the way of a system and laid down as "principle." Schilder writes: "It is better to wait with the 'rounding off' of a closed system, and then 'only' to publish in separate chapters what we have found in the Scriptures, than to build a tower on a text which really

---

[35] Published in English under the title *Lectures on Calvinism.* These lectures were delivered at Princeton in 1898. —TRANS.

[36] There is a disparity of five years here because the Nazi rulers of the Netherlands forbade the publication of *The Reformation* during the occupation period. —TRANS.

serves to introduce or illustrate an idea. When we use 'a Bible text' as our starting point, we will not build up a coherent system of universal breadth."

When Schilder spoke in such a manner, the trumpet gave out a radical and different sound in the 1930s, and so he found himself coming into conflict with much ecclesiastical and "Calvinistic" practice, for now *the Church* began to speak again. She emerged from the dead end and took up a position on the main street along which the traffic flowed.

In the traffic of the 1930s were the great international actions undertaken to promote a general "Calvinism." This was the time of the establishment of a Federation of Calvinists and the organization of congresses for those who are Reformed *(Gereformeerd),* which included participation by people from National Reformed *(Hervormd)* circles, Barthian theologians, and members of the Churches in "Restored Federation" (the very people whom the Synod of Assen had rejected as unreformed). Schilder wrote: "The generals have applied the 'ecclesiastical' ban to Dr. J. G. Geelkerken, but when it came to university matters, politics, culture, and finance, they quickly wanted to bring him back, for the Federation of Calvinists was being set up. The general staff (this way today, different tomorrow) again ordered the prophets around." By the prophets, he meant the Church.

The Church is only there for our salvation, of course. This is how Schilder explained this mentality in 1932: "Furthermore, the sermon must deal with the question: How can I be saved? My salvation means that I am not left out in the end. Demands for *this* life? Do you mean the life of the street, the school, the world of art, the novel, and the church that argues against your church before God? Be a little more practical — I mean, be more edifying. A good minister should preach a sermon about the distinguishing characteristics of the spiritual life, and he must do so in such a way that all orthodox churches can find 'satisfaction' in it. Beyond that, he should serve up meditations as requested. But there is one condition: they must not be concrete in terms of what they say to workers in another sector. In other words, there must be no concrete application made on the basis of the confessions. As for the confessions, what they present us with is just the business of theology, and theology is only one of the five faculties of the university. Indeed, our fathers claimed that the *confessions* apply to *all* the faculties and *all* groups — but that was precisely the confessionalist streak in their thinking . . ."

Because Schilder chose this reformational standpoint, a battle with people in his own circles could not be avoided. Even the narrower circle of the editors of *The Reformation* was affected. In 1932 Hepp resigned as one of the editors, and in 1935 Dr. C. Tazelaar and Dr. J. Waterink followed suit. The editors were not able to agree with one another about the policy that should be followed in *The Reformation*. Because the paper was ultimately the property of the publisher, he had to make a decision: he chose to stick with Schilder and to let go of the others. In 1937 Hepp founded his own paper, *Credo,* which was to serve the cause of "progressive" Reformed *(Gereformeerd)* life, and Waterink established the *Calvinist Weekly.*

Schilder was now alone at the helm of *The Reformation. Credo* and the *Calvinist Weekly* limped along in a sorry state with too few subscribers, but *The Reformation* had more and more of them — between 3500 and 4000 in those days. That was an incredible total for a church paper in a time of depression. There were more and more people who wanted to listen to the reformational sound Schilder was sending out. He found a following among the younger ministers who, whether they had studied at the Free University or at Kampen before Schilder taught there, had not picked up what Schilder was now teaching them via his writings. Among the simple church people there were also many who noted the clear appeal to Scripture and the confessions in what Schilder wrote.

And so a third stream began to dig out a channel in our ecclesiastical life. Alongside the diminishing stream of a fossilized Kuyperianism and the growing stream of the younger generation, which first sought refuge in an Ethical-Irenic Christendom and then began to go over more and more to Barthianism, there came the stream of those who loved the Reformed confessions and wanted to live by the norms of Scripture and the confessions, applying them universally and fundamentally in every area of life.

Schilder's influence

It is remarkable that by the middle of the 1930s, most of the local church papers had come to share the standpoint of *The Reformation.* Schilder's influence grew greater than ever. Reformed life had run stuck, but he opened up some space and gave people perspective, for he knew how to get a generation excited about Reformed thinking. The confessions again became a source of living, streaming water for many people in our churches.

At a ministers' conference, Dr. C. Bouma and Rev. C. B. Bavinck complained that some of the younger generation were preaching about the covenant in a very one-sided manner. Rev. E. T. van den Born responded as follows: "We were students of Prof. A. G. Honig and Prof. T. Hoekstra, from whom we learned dogmatics and homiletics, and they were mainly the ones who taught us the theme of the covenant — I could almost say: hammered it into our heads and hearts — so that it became dominant for all of our work, including our *preaching*. Moreover, since our student years we have become readers of *The Reformation* and have thus learned to think of the covenant in a still broader and richer way through the articles of one of the current professors, Dr. K. Schilder. Thus, when it comes to dogmatic instruction and the homiletic method used in preaching, I and many others should be regarded as having undergone a development from Prof. Honig to Prof. Hoekstra to Prof. Schilder."

Rev. van den Born was speaking in the name of many of the younger preachers in the 1930s, who had been gripped by the reformational work of Schilder. This work was not the formation of a faction or a church within a church or a group apart; it was pure reformation. Rev. van den Born hit the nail on the head when he concluded his article about this matter with these words: "In Scripture we read, 'And He will restore the hearts of the fathers to their children, and the hearts of the children to their fathers' (Malachi 4:6). I would paraphrase this text as follows: Christ the Lord brings the hearts of the older ministers again to the hearts of the younger ones so that they listen to us in these matters; and He brings the hearts of the younger ministers again to the older ones, so that they will carefully consider and test the answers that are given. He brings us together through obedience to the Scriptures, so that we may also be converted daily in our work of preaching." What was underway was not some action undertaken by the younger ones, then, but a reformation of the whole Church — the younger ones along with the older ones.

Not a controversy between the Free University and Kampen

It has been suggested that the work of Schilder was really an offensive on the part of old Kampen (i.e. the Theological School) against the Free University of Amsterdam. Schilder always contradicted this idea. He showed how witty he could be in his polemics when he once observed: "Someone was afraid that the Free University would suffer because of my publications; I share that fear, and that's exactly why I publish. I am not 'hanging out dirty laundry,' but I want to make sure that the wash water is not polluted."

When Prof. H. H. Kuyper wrote his notorious and very personal article in *The Herald* against Schilder and insinuated that Schilder's polemicizing was intended "to shake the trust of our Reformed people, especially when it comes to firmness of principle on the part of the professors at the Free University," Schilder answered: "Such things make me sad. And this while I have repeatedly said, at the risk of being tiresome, that at the Free University there were also people who have turned away from what the Federation of Calvinists has actually become. I said that because I did not want anyone to think this was a quarrel between Kampen and Amsterdam. I thank God that the front lines are drawn differently today than they were earlier."

Those "front lines" were indeed different. The reformational work of Schilder called for reformation all down the line. There was decline in Kampen just as there was in Amsterdam. The insinuation that Schilder was out to build a power base and to gather a group around himself caused him immeasurable pain. There was nothing in the Church he hated more than such accusations.

No Schilder party

In one of his interesting articles surveying what had appeared in other papers, Schilder quoted with approval what Hendrik Algra said in a Leeuwarden church paper. Algra was defending Schilder against some loose talk emanating from a ministers' conference where it had been suggested that a new group was forming in the church. Schilder observed: "There is nothing that needs to be added to this article. The 'Schilder party' does not exist. But those who get things mixed up do run the risk of forming a party themselves."

Rev. D. Zemel was not edified by what had taken place at that ministers' conference either. In a Gorcum church paper, he wrote: "The report on the ministers' conference at Utrecht presented us with an alarming sample of this pasting of labels, in which the labels seemed to be completely justified. And it was without animosity. If there had also been animosity in the picture, imagine how many labels would then have to be hauled out! It's incalculable. But they were still careful in what they said about the Dutch Nazi movement, for it is something new. No general discipline against it. We are not to label it censurable. Fine — but then shouldn't we also be terribly cautious in the way we deal with our own brothers? Shouldn't we be very careful in how we try to refute them? Shouldn't we convince them by way of Scripture and the confessions, instead of throwing large-scale general accusations at them? Or could it be that people were thinking that since Dr. A. Kuyper Sr. had spoken, the matter was now fixed and finished until judgment day — Kuyper has spoken, and that's the end of the matter? But Kuyper himself would have been the first to oppose such an approach."

Zemel was getting at the heart of the matter here. A rigid Kuyperianism defended by epigones who themselves could take the ideas no further was being attacked, but they thought the criticism they were getting represented an attack on Kuyper himself!

And so people did not understand each other any more, for Scripture and the confessions were no longer the norm for their ecclesiastical actions and discussions. Instead the well-being of the "Solomonic glory," with the Free University as its Zion, its fortress (Seerp Anema), came first.

People seemed more inclined to play political and diplomatic games with one another than to deal with each other openly and honestly as members of the church of the LORD. Private meetings were typical of the diplomatic games that went on. On one occasion Hepp spoke in a closed circle about the "current dogmatic problems" among us. That the meeting was closed meant that Hepp himself was not even allowed to pass on his notes to Schilder afterwards, even though Schilder was the man he was combatting and had been invited to this meeting as the second speaker. On various grounds, Schilder had refused to come. One of his grounds was this: "I have publicly promised to teach nothing that runs contrary to God's Word and the confessions, neither in public nor in secret meetings. The first speaker for this meeting made the same promise. The Reformed people must therefore be allowed to see what I have to say and what I teach." Yet because he did not want anyone to interpret his refusal to attend this meeting as a manifestation of a strictly negative attitude, he proposed some conditions through which his objections could be overcome, so that he could attend and speak. Schilder hated any secrecy when it came to public ecclesiastical matters.

Contra semi-public discussion

Rev. H. A. Wiersinga issued a warning in a Leiden church paper against "semi-public polemics." He agreed with "KS" that a semi-public treatment instead of a public one would weaken the church.

He wrote: "I believe Prof. Schilder is right in speaking out against this sort of thing. Come on, Prof. Hepp and the rest of you, admit in the paper that you did something wrong, that you made a very serious mistake."

Rev. J. M. Spier wrote: "I am in complete agreement with Prof. Schilder. In opposition to the spirit of the times, he has recently defended, in broad outline, the necessity of honest, open-hearted polemicizing. Many took this ill of him and said unfriendly things about him in the press. Yet, as time goes on, it appears more and more as though the opponents of polemics cannot do without it after all. But when it nevertheless takes place, it may happen in the way sketched above, which is much more dangerous. For now, in semi-darkness, distrust is sown, and the person against whom it is directed cannot defend himself." There were more papers that printed articles in this vein.[37]

In this context Schilder quoted with approval a comment which C. Veenhof had made in a discussion of Rullmann's *Voices from the Doleantie*. Veenhof used just the right phrase when he said: "Semi-public discussion supplants public discussion." This is an indication of church decline, to say nothing as yet of apostasy, for it shows that people are no longer recognizing that the Church has a style of her own. Instead they think they can properly discuss church affairs and do the cleaning up that is needed by operating with a club mentality and having closed meetings and exchanging impressions among themselves (whether they choose to call such activities conferences or press association meetings). And we should remember that all of this happened more than a quarter of a century ago.

Since that time the liberation has taken place, but we are still dragging the same sinful heart around with us, and so we must make sure this history does not repeat itself. Whenever "semi-public discussion" takes the place of public discussion (C. Veenhof already saw it back in the 1930s), corruption creeps into the Church and distrust is sown among our church people, who are then regarded as incompetent, unable to have a say in church matters. When this happens, we are resisting the Savior's statement that we are all brothers.

We have ecclesiastical gatherings, and they are public, open to all. We have church papers, and they are also public: anyone can read them and follow what is going on. But in the Church there is no place

---

[37] Among them were *The Watchman* and the *Enschede Church Messenger*.

for "clubs" of like-minded people who deal with ecclesiastical matters in a "semi-public" way, for such activity corrupts the Church. Schilder saw this very clearly in the 1930s and dissociated himself from it. We should be thankful to God for this, for now reformation can progress. The people — by which I mean the *entire* people — can be involved.

The necessity of polemics

Schilder has been much criticized for all the polemicizing he engaged in, but he really had no choice about the matter. If prophecy is not to be "tail prophecy," it will often cause pain; yet it has a healing effect.

Well worth reading — also in the light of the situation today — is what C. Veenhof wrote in *The Reformation* about the necessity of polemicizing. The context is the battle that broke out in 1936, and he made his remarks while discussing Rullmann's *Voices from the Doleantie*. The title of the series by Veenhof is "Reformational Polemics." Typical of what he wishes to say is this quotation from Fabius: "We say that someone is getting personal not when he opposes persons because of what they teach but rather when he leaves their teachings undisturbed for the sake of the persons who are propounding them." Another quotation: "Groen van Prinsterer declared repeatedly that polemicizing is a necessary condition for healthy church life." Also: "To polemicize against internal corruption, says Groen, is a condition of life for the Christian and also for the Church." But Groen also saw right through the false loving posture adopted by those who act as though they love peace and who sigh about polemics and division: "I recall that I have often found an appeal for Christian love offered at the end of an argument by an author who was clearly guilty of lovelessness. It has been my own experience more than once that love was recommended at the same time that hatefulness was being manifested."

Veenhof wrote in his younger years: "Groen was convinced that Christ wants us to do battle, to engage in polemics. Behind the disinclination to engage in polemicizing there lurks a misunderstanding of the task Christ gives to His children in this world." Veenhof quotes Groen as follows: "People don't want polemics; but here on earth, as long as the truth has not triumphed, Christians will always have to polemicize against the sin in the world, within themselves, and in others." Groen detested the *tactic of silence,* says Veenhof, and in the section of *Voices from the Doleantie* in which he discusses Rev. J. C. Sikkel he observes: "Read the fragment of Sikkel's sermon entitled 'Ye Are Christ's.' With the passion that was typical of him, Sikkel spoke against everything that threatens to come between Christ and His Church and dismissed it, everything that might separate the body from its Head. This sermon is polemical, relentlessly polemical in its attack on certain forces both within and without. But that's precisely why it is such an earnest sermon, so gripping, appealing to thousands to combat the lie and fight for the truth."

From this series of articles I could draw quite a few quotations about the necessity of polemicizing, but I will limit myself to one more observation from Veenhof. He writes that the most painful kind of polemicizing for Groen was the kind that was directed against his own brothers and closest friends. "Groen's cross in life was having to work continually against his own 'brothers.' But this did not lead him to be silent. The truth came first for him."

At the end of his discussion of Rullmann's book, Veenhof draws the following conclusion: "This is an unconscious but therefore all the more powerful proof that every reformation is ultimately a battle against 'brothers.' When things get tense, those 'brothers' become the fiercest opponents. It is also a proof that every reformation is opposed by the 'peace-lovers,' and that every reformation is effectual and is blessed only if the opposition of the peace-lovers is resisted in firm obedience, and that such brothers become raging lions toward all those who do not wish to sing along in their choir of peace . . ."

We have seen that when things became tense in the 1930s and people began to complain about the polemicizing and the leadership offered by *The Reformation,* a group of young theologians took their stand next to Schilder, not just to defend what he was doing but also to declare that he could only do reformational work in the Church in such a manner. And that was indeed the truth. Without polemicizing, without the leadership of *The Reformation,* no reformation would have come about in the churches and there would have been no liberation.

How could it have been otherwise? We are the "militant church." To be militant means to be engaged in battle — a battle against foes outside but also, and even more so, against foes within. The only question that still must be be raised is this: Did we conduct the battle in a lawful way?

Schilder contra H. H. Kuyper

Schilder conducted himself in a lawful way in the battle, for he was not fighting persons but causes; he was not seeking power for a group of his own but was trying to preserve and purify the Church through faithfulness to the confessions. Unfortunately, the same could not be said of all the church papers. In particular, *The Herald* carried on the battle in much too personal a way in the 1930s.

A very sad example of the strongly personal tone in battle was the article which Prof. H. H. Kuyper wrote in the May 24, 1936, issue of *The Herald*. Schilder answered this attack, which was directed mainly against his person, with an "Open Letter" published in *The Reformation* on May 29. From his answer it is apparent that the accusations of H. H. Kuyper were unjust, for his claims were preposterous. He made mistake after mistake when it came to the "facts," and as for the personal attack on Schilder, it was without any basis and served mainly to create an atmosphere of hatred. Yet despite the fierceness and personal character of the attack, Schilder remained sober and objective in his response. In defending himself he said at one point, "I believe I am maintaining control of myself."

His eyes were "gentle" and remained focused on purely objective matters. When we go back today and read this material, we cannot understand how people could have accused him of being unfriendly or unbrotherly or of engaging in excessively sharp polemicizing. Such charges could be made against his opponents, but not against him. He continued to cling to his brothers because he continued to cling to the Church, which he loved above all as the Bride of Christ. But he did suffer a great deal personally because of this unworthy opposition.

At the time H. H. Kuyper came out with his very sharp personal attack, Schilder happened to be staying at my house because he was to preach in our congregation on Sunday. That Saturday evening I passed him *The Herald*. He looked at the paper for a while and then asked if he could take it along to bed with him. When he came downstairs the next morning, I could see immediately that he was very dejected and taken aback. I asked him at breakfast what he would be preaching about that morning. His answer was: "I had planned to preach a sermon in connection with Pentecost about the prayer of the Church in Revelation 22: 'Yes, come, Lord Jesus.' But that article by H.H. in *The Herald* has upset me so much that I cannot deal with that tender material now. I'll have to preach about something else this morning." And so he chose a pericope from Micah 6 to preach from that Sunday morning; his sermon was entitled "The Vocative to Reformation." The passage tells us how God appeals to the mountains and the hills as witnesses in His lawsuit against His people, who are unfaithful to the covenant of grace. That covenant is not a pillow for us to rest our heads on peacefully; on the contrary, in all the world there is no sharper goad to our conscience than the covenant of grace. In the vocative we find in this text ("O man!") we hear man being addressed in the most essential way, for he is addressed as he stands over against God. Here Schilder was pointing back to what he had said in his address "The Principle, Justification, and Meaning of the Secession," which he had delivered to commemorate the hundredth anniversary of that act of reformation in 1834.

The sermon he preached that Sunday morning was like his other ones in that it was lengthy: the service went on for two hours. It was a mighty proclamation of the Word, and it appeared that the burden of the article in *The Herald,* which had lain on his shoulders throughout the night, now slid off him.

That evening, after the second service, Schilder said to me, "I have resolved that each time I go out somewhere to preach, I will try to come home with one hundred guilders for the hospitium in Kampen.[38] Do you think it would be possible to raise this sum in Baarn?" (Baarn was where I was living at the time.) I replied, "We can try." And so we went out together. From a well-to-do man living on an independent income he got ten guilders. I then said, "We could also call on Mr. X, for he is quite generous." Mr. X was surprised to see Prof. Schilder at his door. Upon hearing what Schilder wanted, this brother said, "When you as a professor go out for this cause personally after preaching two sermons like the ones you delivered today, you're surely looking for more than a couple of guilders — right?" Schilder looked a bit embarrassed, took a deep puff on the fine cigar he had been given, and mumbled, "I would like it best if you would not regard it as a gift but as a sacrifice." Mr. X smiled and handed him a bank note of one hundred guilders. When we stood in the street again, Schilder said to me, "This makes a new man of me. I could dance." Then he was like a child again. Yes, that's the way Schilder was.

---

[38] The hospitium was a residence for the seminary students in Kampen. When people contributed funds for it, they were helping make education for the ministry possible. —TRANS.

A worker for his "School"

As both a battler and a builder, he bore the entire burden of the Church in the Netherlands. Not only was he a polemicist who battled for the truth and defended it, he was also a toiler who labored in unseasonable times for the School (seminary) in Kampen and for "his boys," whom he loved dearly. Rev. Boerkoel, who offered many criticisms of "KS" in *The Trumpet,* had to admit: "Through the labors of KS, the School in Kampen went from strength to strength. In 1939 a chair in missiology was added, and a 'sixth' chair was also planned; that it would come along in due course was beyond doubt. The period of blossoming enjoyed by the School was due in good measure to Schilder."

Elsewhere Boerkoel wrote: "The School also took on more academic airs. Its decorum had to correspond to its state. Gowns for the professors, a silver chain of office for the rector magnificus, and a mace for the mace-bearer [one of the administrators] all enhanced the School in terms of appearance. To what extent Schilder had a hand in all of this I cannot say. He was probably not the only one who pressed for these decorative touches. It is clear that he attached great value to such insignia. It is also clear that he did what he could to preserve what was there already and to make available what he thought was needed. By gathering gifts diligently, he buttressed the hospitium in its shaky existence. There was a suppletion fund to help cover the cost of living in the hospitium; by raising fifteen thousand guilders, he was able to keep this fund solvent. He yearned for an organ for the great Aula (auditorium), and in response to his appeal for a freewill offering, it became possible to install a complete pipe organ that is still in service." And so we see that Schilder not only wielded the sword but also worked with the trowel. He was both a battler and a builder as he toiled for the School and the Church, and thereby for our Reformed people.

How little his opponents understood him! How deeply they often wounded him! I can well imagine that the personal attacks made upon him publicly did not teach his attackers much, for they were practicing an ecclesiastical diplomacy that belonged to the "Solomonic" era we lived through in the 1930s — a time of great blossoming combined with inner decline. Because Schilder abhorred diplomacy and ecclesiastical politicking and only did battle in prophetic faithfulness to the truth, fighting for the effective upholding of our confessions, such attacks wounded him very deeply as a person. Those of us who knew him intimately are convinced of this.

Ready for battle

It should not surprise us that his opponents sometimes did battle in unworthy ways; within the framework of the overall ecclesiastical decline, their conduct is somewhat understandable from a psychological point of view. They simply did not know how to get at him. In no polemical exchange could they defeat him. There he stood before them, fully equipped and ready for battle. Immediately his vision penetrated to the heart of the matter. He knew what the key to the issue was, and with irrefutable arguments he would soon checkmate his opponents. His arguments always went back to the confessions of the Church, to which his opponents had bound themselves with their signatures.

When polemics broke out over the Calvin commemoration (Paris, 1935), which included participation on the part of a number of people who did not base their stand on the confessions, Schilder commented on H. H. Kuyper's radical change in standpoint: he pointed to what Kuyper had written in *The Herald* back in 1909 and contrasted it with what he was now writing. It was not Schilder who was bringing in something new but those who maintained that they were actually securing Abraham Kuyper's inheritance.

He had a very neat way of checkmating his opponents. During a time of polemical exchange concerning the issue of self-examination, Schilder quoted Dr. A. Kuyper Jr. (another son of Kuyper Sr.) and caught him in his own net. Kuyper had opposed Schilder on a number of occasions in connection with Schilder's view of self-examination, namely, that it can only take place *after* there is faith — and never *before*. Now, Kuyper had once written an article in a church paper about key sayings. He had read that the key saying for the ancient Greeks is: Know yourself. A key saying can be found for a number of nations, and in each case it indicates the nation's religion and morality. The Greek says: Know yourself. The Roman says: Control yourself. The Chinese says: Improve yourself. The Buddhist says: Extinguish yourself. The Hindu says: Sink into yourself. The Muslim says: Subordinate yourself. Kuyper Jr. then added: "It is interesting that all these nations have a key saying about what you must do yourself. But we should note that for the Christian, the key saying of the Savior is:

Without Me you can do nothing. It is certainly worth taking the trouble to think carefully about this key saying."

Schilder drew attention to Kuyper's comments in his ever current and always interesting review of what had appeared in the other church papers, and he offered the following commentary: "I am in full agreement with this gripping article. The Christian does not say that you must do it yourself, and then leave it at that. Neither does he say that you must bring your own existence to an end, or that you must qualify yourself, e.g. through self-examination, and then you are done. He always confesses: Without Me you can do nothing — you can't even engage in self-examination. Faith, conversion, self-examination — I am in full agreement with the Synod."

There is an interesting incident in the background to Schilder's comments. Kuyper Jr. had proposed that the question of "self-examination, faith, and conversion" be dealt with by the Synod. Later Greijdanus, who had been assigned to study this matter, asked Kuyper whether he would have any objection to reversing the order and making it faith, conversion, self-examination, for this was logically more correct. Kuyper said he had no objection, and so the Synod declared its unanimous agreement with this proposal.

Hence Schilder could write that he was in full agreement with the Synod. This in turn made Kuyper suspicious, and so he wrote in *The Herald* about a "lawyer's trick." Yet Schilder had given this piece of advice to Greijdanus not as a "lawyer's trick" but because this order was the logical one and conformed fully to Scripture and the confessions.

There was polemicizing week after week. Some theologians wanted to see an end to it and sighed over this matter in a very pious way. Dr. H. Kaajan of Utrecht wrote: "A polemicist must write in a *prayerful* way." Schilder offered his decisive and irrefutable commentary on this observation in a couple of short, telling sentences: "This last statement is completely correct. One could add: one must also keep silent in a prayerful way. We could even say this about concealing things. Let us never suppose that it is only when we speak that we come near the high-tension wires of God's law. His law always applies — even *when we are silent*; it even applies to pensioners and 'gardeners' (Sikkel, J. C.)." And so keeping silent was also a "high-voltage" activity.

When the *Calvinist Weekly* came into existence, it was on the basis of misconceptions about polemicizing. This paper was founded by people who had withdrawn from an editorial role in *The Reformation*. In the very first issue they wrote that they would not engage in polemics — at least, not in any polemicizing directed against those within their own circles.

The Watchman (actual Dutch title: *De Wachter*), which was a Dutch-language paper published in North America under the auspices of the Christian Reformed Church, drew the sword against this paper, with Rev. D. Zwier asking what such an attitude had to do with the paper's name. He wrote as follows: "I regard polemicizing as a vital necessity — not least in our time and our country. I have let the brothers know this. When polemical bread no longer tastes good to us, there is something wrong with our health . . . But we are told again that this paper intends to seek and defend the truth without engaging in polemics against persons or against statements issuing from its own circle; that is to say, it wants to build up in a thetical way, defending and protecting, while avoiding any polemical tone. And now I am completely in the dark. If errors are propounded by Reformed people, somehow the paper will not name names but only defend the truth — without polemicizing. I don't understand it. But I do know that the phenomenon we are dealing with is the same disease that plagues so many people in the United States — the abhorrence of polemicizing."

People wanted no polemics directed within. Polemicizing directed against people outside our circles was still to be tolerated, but within our own circles there was to be only peace. The Solomonic empire was supposed to shine in all its glory and power for the world out there to see; there was no place whatsoever for a "palace revolution." Such goings on would diminish our influence in the world.

The initiative from The Hague West

The consistory of The Hague West also got into this public discussion. Now, this church had long represented a weak point in our ecclesiastical life, for it saw no place for polemicizing in relation to those who were within. In any event, this consistory sent a request to both the Curators of the Theological School in Kampen and the body in charge of the relationship between the Reformed *(Gereformeerd)* churches and the Theological Faculty of the Free University. This communication from The Hague West expressed sadness over the polemicizing in which the professors were engaged in the press and asked that a stop be put to it, to bring them all back to reason and gentleness and unity.

Prof. Greijdanus pointed out in *The Reformation* that the action taken by this consistory was contrary to Scripture and the church order. Prof. Schilder predicted that the initiative from the Hague West would have the effect of increasing polemicizing substantially, and this turned out rather quickly to be the case.

All the church papers began to deal with this matter. Schilder wrote that refusing to polemicize was tantamount to standing outside of history. The initiative taken by The Hague West, he argued,

> has not been thought through in a Reformed way. It is Reformed to recognize that all creatures of God (including exchanges of words, such as polemicizing intended to correct people) are good. Only sin, which misuses polemicizing, is bad. What is unreformed is the thesis that we should render some of God's creatures inoperative (e.g. by banning polemical exchanges of words aimed at correction) and that we should rejoice in the blossoming of the rest of God's creatures (e.g. the exchange of words in which the dominant tone is praise and peace). Such a position is *unreformed:* it has the audacity to embrace one work of God while rejecting the other, which amounts to being self-willed. Something that God has commanded and given it now rejects.
>
> It does not thereby prolong the course of the kind of prophecy that breaks our allegiance to our own self-willed opinions; what it prolongs instead is the back-and-forth movement of self-willed diplomacy. It pulls the sinner back from the storm-wind of the law, and, with its false interpretations of the law, hands him an umbrella so that he can shield himself from the storm that is the law. Because the initiative from The Hague did not set out prophetic lines on this point, the first result has been that polemicizing is now in a position ten times worse than the one it was in last week, before The Hague got mixed up in this business.

Schilder certainly gave The Hague West something to think about, but it did not understand his prophetic language. Some years later, when Schilder was suspended, this church spoke up again. It then became apparent that the sweet irenicism of The Hague West did not stand in the way of joining in when a brother was assassinated in terms of his office. Again I quote Veenhof's observation: the peace-loving brothers "become raging lions toward all those who do not wish to sing along in their choir of peace . . ."

The political leaders also began to concern themselves with the polemicizing — not because church life interested them so much but because their efforts to gain political influence might be undermined. It is well known that Dr. H. Colijn sighed that the theologians should really conduct their controversies in Latin, as their colleagues in the seventeenth century had done. He forgot that although the disputes were indeed conducted in Latin in those days, the common people were as deeply concerned and involved as the theologians themselves. And it's a good thing they were.

It also appears that Dr. Colijn himself did not understand the ecclesiastical questions that were at issue. He told me once, "People should not compare me to Kuyper. He was a theologian; I am an economist." Colijn went to church to receive "edification for his soul," believing that the church's reason for existence was simply to provide such edification: the church's task was to preach the message of salvation to lost sinners — nothing more. Therefore when he was in Gelderland he could calmly spend a Sunday listening to the rather heavy preaching of a *Gereformeerde Bond* minister.[39] He could also be "edified" by such preaching.

For Colijn the church had its place in the dead end street — not on the main thoroughfare. Particular grace and common grace were for him two entirely distinct and separate sectors of life. In every way he was a Kuyperian. At the same time, he was an upright man and told me sincerely, "My faith is just as great as Kuyper's."

The tragedy of his life was that because he believed there were those two sectors in life, he regarded the Reformed confessions as strictly "ecclesiastical" in character. He simply did not realize what was at the heart of the matter in the ecclesiastical battle, just as it was beyond most of the Reformed politicians in the 1930s. Thus they regarded the duel between theologians simply as a threat to the unity that was needed if they were to be strong politically.

Now, Dr. Colijn had his say about polemics in an address given at the Free University Day (an annual rally) in 1936. He hoped, of course,

---

[39] The *Gereformeerde Bond* or Reformed Federation was — and remains — a conservative wing of the National Reformed *(Hervormd)* Church. —TRANS.

that there would be an end to the battles. But that this hope had gone up in smoke he must have realized as soon as he read the article H. H. Kuyper wrote against Schilder (the one I discussed earlier).

Colijn also found a good part of the church press opposing him. Rev. J. M. Spier wrote: "We do not have the right, on the basis of our own desires, to draw a distinction between what happens *within* our own circles and what happens *beyond* them, so that we resolve to use our weapons only against attacks from *without,* while *within* our own ranks we allow free play to the father of lies, who also rummages around actively within the Church." And many people agreed with him.

This should not surprise us, for the eyes of many people were being opened to what was going on within the Reformed *(Gereformeerd)* churches. They saw that people were turning away from the principles of the Secession and the church order of the Doleantie. People were rejecting the Kuyper of the antithesis in order to embrace the Kuyper of common grace, whom they then proceeded to interpret more and more along the lines of an inter-ecclesiastical Christianity that had a great deal in common with this world. Irenic subjectivism gained a great deal of ground among many of the ministers, for whom the confessions of the church were relegated to the background and disregarded.

And it was not the case in the 1930s that only Schilder polemicized and pointed to the dangers. The church papers included polemicizing about various questions. When the literary bells chimed to herald the arrival of the so-called "Third Réveil,"[40] it was not just a literary movement that was declaring its independence from the first Réveil (1834) and the second one (1886). K. Heeroma found quite a few followers and disciples on Reformed turf for his Third Réveil (Karl Barth). Mr. A. Kuiper of Utrecht correctly pointed out in *The Reformation* that the children of the Third Réveil had denied their fathers in the first and second ones.

Rev. I. de Wolff made the following observation about the Reformed *(Gereformeerd)* churches: "A Humanistic Christianity orienting itself toward practice is in the process of raising its head. We find a

---

[40] "Réveil" is a French word used to refer to the revival of Dutch Calvinism in the early nineteenth century, in which the poets Willem Bilderdijk and Isaac da Costa played a role, as did Groen van Prinsterer and Abraham Kuyper a little later. The term is also used by historians to refer to spiritual revivals or reawakenings in other parts of Europe, such as Switzerland. — TRANS.

spirit of synthesis, which seeks cooperation and association with elements that do not live in obedience to the Scriptures. There is a melting away, a blurring of the boundaries, a resting on past accomplishments without continuing the battle, a bowing before the iron necessity of practice. What we do not find is the courage of faith, as spiritual descendants of stalwart earlier generations, to oppose someone when our eternal spiritual goods are at stake." De Wolff went on to say that under the influence of *The Reformation,* a movement of reformation seemed to be afoot, and that this movement "intends to lead our people away from the road that runs downhill toward the abyss for which they are headed, and to get them to walk again on the path of covenant obedience."

Rev. O. Bouwman commented as follows on the work Schilder was doing by writing in church papers: "In reality there are hundreds and thousands of people who follow his reformational program with agreement and subscribe to his stand in virtually all cases; moreover, more and more people are becoming aware that there is a task here for *all* Reformed people, all Christians." That Rev. Bouwman was not exaggerating is apparent from what Schilder himself was able to write in an issue of *The Reformation* that inaugurated a new publishing year: "I am grateful to be able to announce, as this new year begins, that since April 1, 1935, *The Reformation* has more readers than it ever had before."

It should not surprise us that when The Hague West asked the Curators of the two theological schools (Kampen and the Free University) to put a stop to the polemicizing between the professors, a fresh round of polemics was unleashed in the papers. There were many who took up a position in defense of Schilder: when we look back at the list today, we are surprised at some of the names we find there. For example, Rev. C. J. W. Teeuwen argued that Reformed *(Gereformeerd)* polemicizing is necessary: "Surely it is not possible to take a clear position without formulating that position carefully! Haven't our great predecessors in earlier years always spoken out against inauthentic liberal irenicism, when people appeared to be acting so tolerant whereas they were actually using that guise of tolerance to have their own world- and life-view established as the regnant one? Is the danger of a false Reformed irenicism just an imaginary one?" This article was a sustained defense of the work Schilder was doing in the press!

In *The Watchman,* Revs. Rietberg and Feenstra also set out to answer The Hague West. This paper played off the Dr. Dijk who served as a minister of The Hague West against the Dr. Dijk who wrote in the church papers and who himself opposed his colleague Rev. H. L. Both when the latter wrote his infamous brochure promoting the Oxford Movement.

Mr. H. Algra pointed out ironically that Dr. Dijk must have been absent when The Hague West decided to make its request, for Dijk had himself written an elaborate study about the battle between infralapsarianism and supralapsarianism in the Netherlands. Thus he knew how people had once polemicized. Algra concluded: "I'm afraid that those who love the polemics of our fathers will find *The Reformation* rather insipid fare." In connection with this remark Schilder observed: "Moreover, it is clear that no one can pretend that Dr. Dijk was not a party to the request by the consistory. Mr. Algra must have meant it in an ironic sense."

Rev. A. M. Boeijinga wrote: "In *The Reformation* Schilder raises his objections and argues for them in a compelling way. His blows are *objectively* on target, even though he gives his piece the rather tame title 'Puzzled.',"And there is a great deal more along these lines that I could quote.

Manifestations of deformation

In his book *Around the Reformation,* A. Janse mentions various symptoms of deformation in the 1930s:

> I think, for example of book reviews in the leading papers, such as the favorable review of Prof. A. H. de Hartog's book *Modern Paganism.* I think of the Calvinist Congress to which Prof. T. L. Haitjema was invited as one of the Reformed *(Gereformeerd).* I think of the advice a certain minister (Rev. Barkey Wolf) has given us about Weatherhead. I think of the influence Karl Barth was able to exercise when he first emerged. I think of the often weak defense embodied in our practices vis-à-vis the Reformed *(Gereformeerd)* people who were inclined toward National Socialism and also what we did vis-à-vis the Christian Democratic Union. I think of the undisguised sympathy of many of us for the Oxford Movement (Rev. H. L. Both and others). I think of the

modern consequences of subjectivism, for example, the doctrine of the reborn Ego in us (an Ego "smaller than we can imagine"!), which Ego is not capable of sinning, we are told. I think of the toleration of "parties" among us, so that those who "think differently" are honored for thinking differently, with the eventual result that we brand as intolerant only those who, in the midst of all this tolerance, claim to know the truth of God. And in connection with this weakening of the principal divisions between spirits we also have to understand the weakening of our Calvinistic mores in relation to movies and newsreels and so forth. Worldliness always starts at the core of our religion. For Israel, idolatrous unfaithfulness to the God of the covenant was the beginning of all sorts of other deviations. The religion of Jeroboam was the sin that caused Israel to sin in all areas of life.

That was what Janse had to say. And there were indeed some deplorable things going on in the 1930s — the "Solomonic era." In his book *Antithesis or Synthesis?*, Dr. van der Waal has written at length about the great changes in our approach to missions after we became members of the Dutch Mission Council. At the Synod of Middelburg (1933), Rev. K. van Dijk was warned for making a powerful protest heard all the way from Indonesia about the degeneration in our Reformed *(Gereformeerd)* mission work. The Synod protected his "ecumenically" minded colleagues. "The great danger that threatens us lies not in an acute heresy but in a permanent one," declared Schilder. Yes, things were indeed going wrong in those days.

Prof. J. Waterink and Dr. C. Tazelaar, who had resigned from editorial involvement in *The Reformation* because they could not agree with the policies of "KS," started a new paper called the *Calvinist Weekly,* in which they said there would be no polemicizing — at least, not against persons and statements *within* Reformed circles. Rev. A. M. Boeijinga commented as follows:

> No polemicizing against those of like mind! That statement was surely intended as a small bow toward The Hague West, which may respond at once with an approving nod. And many very irenic heads will nod along with them.

I must now look down the road and try to imagine a situation in which there is no polemicizing. It would surely be a situation in which *the truth* is no longer at issue. As long as the truth is still a matter of concern among us, also within Reformed *(Gereformeerd)* circles, I would rather appeal to Hebrews 10:24 to set the tone than to this irenic attitude, which I believe is incorrect. We read in this verse: "Let us consider how to stimulate *one another* [that is, within our own circles] to love and good deeds." This statement is made in the context of the previous verse ("Let us hold fast the confession of our hope without wavering"); thus it has to do with *the truth.* And so it also applies to the exchange of ideas in the press, where we are supposed to be serving the cause of truth.

If there was to be no polemicizing in the *Calvinist Weekly,* what would there be instead? In the very first issue, the one containing the promise of no polemics, Mary Pos reported on an interview with Mussolini, in which we read: "And great as the Duce always was in my eyes, despite the differences between his political convictions and my own, I first came to recognize his true greatness in the conversations I was able to have with this simple, thoroughly human, and, fortunately, also deeply religious man whom we now know as the Duce . . . May God grant this great man, who realizes his personal dependence upon Him, as we all must do, and who always has a Bible lying within reach, the wisdom to carry out his awesome task, namely, to seek the material and spiritual welfare of his millions of people, and also to cooperate with other heads of state to seek the welfare of our poor, confused world."

Schilder commented as follows: "Some people ask: 'The world is on fire — how can you polemicize?' I ask, 'The world is on fire — especially because of such views of 'religion' — how can you irenicize?' " We now know how much significance to attach to the cute story about Mussolini always keeping a Bible on his desk.

In the 1930s there was also an author of so-called Christian novels who came out with a book entitled *The German Church Struggle — Truth or Lie?* He reported on a number of "interviews" with leading German figures in the Nazi regime, and he told us that Hitler, too, kept a Bible on his desk. Later it came out that all the "interviews" were imaginary, and the publisher had to withdraw the book from the market. But in the "Christian press" people had already greeted it with rejoicing!

In this context I also think of Dr. van der Vaart Smit. He had become the director of the Dutch Christian Press Bureau, and until his treason was unmasked, he was protected by Dr. H. H. Kuyper. Under the pseudonym Willem van Dalen, he regularly defended Hitler and tried to win our Christian people over to National Socialism. J. J. Buskes writes about him as follows: "No one knew that the director of the press bureau was the same person as Willem van Dalen. Dr. van der Vaart Smit continued to deny it, even though I produced the documents to prove it. Right from his student days Van der Vaart Smit was a rascal and a terrible liar. He hoped to become Minister of Religion in the new order for the Netherlands under Mussert.[41] We already had him figured out when we were students. When the Second Christian Social Congress was held in Amsterdam in 1919, Van der Vaart Smit, who was still a Reformed minister at that point, stayed at the hospitium of the Free University, for he was one of the participants. He told a group of students that he was thinking of going into politics. I can still hear Gerrit Kruiswijk, who, unfortunately, died young, shooting back: 'That would be tough luck for politics, but a blessing for the church!' "

In the Solomonic era it was possible for such a man to be accepted and to be quoted repeatedly in the paper *Kuyper* had established. This was an indication of how blind people had become to the real dangers that threatened us.

These things were possible because people were living by power concepts, so-called derived principles, and not by the Word and the confessions of the Church. How often and earnestly Schilder warned against Van der Vaart Smit and his so-called Dutch Christian Press Bureau! It was not that Schilder somehow had keener vision than the rest of us or possessed so much more knowledge about people; rather, he saw through Van der Vaart Smit because he was faithful to the Word and brought the Word into play in every concrete situation in which he found himself.

But there were many in the 1930s who were blinded by the seeming greatness, power, and influence of our Reformed life. They saw

---

[41] Anton Mussert was the leader of the Dutch Nazi movement, who hoped to become the *Führer* of the Netherlands after the anticipated Nazi victory in World War II. After the war he was tried and executed by Dutch authorities. —TRANS.

no inward degeneration and falling away; all they had eyes for was the greatness of our position, as manifested in the cabinets under Dr. Colijn as prime minister, the great commemoration days (as mentioned earlier), and our strength at the ballot box. People like Dr. H. Kaajan and Rev. C. van der Woude were also impressed by the initiative from The Hague West and wrote that it was our task to "attack the Philistines communally." Schilder responded by asking: "But one of the points of the polemic was this: How can we do so if that which is called Philistine is now proclaimed to be of Israel (in the broader sense)?"

Rev. H. A. Wiersinga then remarked: "If we read objectively, we see that after the reading comes the prayer 'God preserve our churches.'" To which "KS" responded:

> Indeed, but let us not forget that this prayer lived in the hearts of many before The Hague West stepped forward and forced them to deal with these questions. We have to pray, and therefore work. In the stillness of the grave no one sings the Lord's praises, nor do people praise Him when they are being smothered or when they are lost in a labyrinth.
>
> The peace of the churches is promoted when that which divided them is *kept from advancing* because it is discussed in public. If no one had polemicized against Barth, many a minister in the younger generation would have been lost to the Reformed confessions. Exaggeration? I have letters from more than one such minister that demonstrates this in a spirit of heartfelt gratitude. If there had been no polemicizing against the Calvinist Congress, some people would be even worse off than they already are when it comes to testing the spirits. Why would we advise the *students* not to become members of the Dutch Christian Student Union, and why would the synod ask the professors to press this warning home to the students, and meanwhile ask the professors themselves, through public deeds, to rob the objections against the influence of the Dutch Christian Student Union of their power and their appeal to conscience? For the Ethicals walk arm in arm with Barth nowadays.

How faithful to Scripture Schilder was, and how concretely he taught our people from the Scriptures! It was because he was faithful that he repeatedly had to polemicize, as we see from a small article published in the Pentecost issue of *The Reformation* in 1935. In this article, entitled "A Pentecost Sigh," he wrote:

> Some ministers, drawing on an inheritance from the past, fill out the formula somewhat when they pronounce the benediction. Thus they don't speak simply of the "communion of the Holy Spirit" but of the *comforting* communion of the Holy Spirit." But of all the *many, many* operations of the Holy Spirit, what gives us the right to pick out *one* as the most glorious and the one that needs to be stressed the most? For example, the Holy Spirit also instructs us. Why not speak of the *instructive* communion of the Holy Spirit"? The Holy Spirit also makes us able to discover things, to be discerning, to grow in conviction and determination, and so forth. Let us no longer apply the Holy Spirit to the "quatenus" (the insofar) of our short-sighted feelings of need. That's not a manly Christianity. And it isn't pious either, for it flatters us "after the flesh" (it is self-willed). If such predicates as "instructive" and "leading to discretion" could have been used in the benediction as often as "comforting" was used, the voice of The Hague West might perhaps not have been heard in the way it was heard recently. Moreover, the Biblical concept of comforting on the part of the Spirit is always a question of an objective legal action (Paraclete = Advocate). Come, *creator* Spirit *(Veni creator Spiritus)*, and *renew* the face of the earth, and renew us.

And so this battler both prayed and toiled on all sides in an effort to make God's word and the confessions of the Church authoritative again. On *all* sides.

Also a battle against outside enemies

In his struggle to bring about reformation and restoration in the church, Schilder did not forget about the foe outside his own circles. The Philistine needed to be attacked. And so he continued to warn against the principles of National Socialism, whose corrupt, pagan philosophical background he was easily able to recognize. His constant attacks on the Dutch Nazi movement, especially in terms of the principles that drove it, even forced this movement to withdraw one of its brochures as untenable.

One result of his battle against the Nazis was that *The Reformation* quickly came to be placed on the blacklist in Germany. Schilder once wrote the following postcard to his publisher in Goes: "Mr. A. Schram of Maassluis informed me that when he crossed the German border, the November 6, 13, 20, and 27 issues of *The Reformation* were taken from him by the police at Emmerich. He is asking whether he can get those issues replaced." And this was not the only such case. At one point Schilder told me that in his travels he no longer went to Germany, for it was not safe there anymore. Later we saw how right he was about this.

His battle against the Dutch Nazi movement and the Christian Democratic Union was principial in character, as was all of his reformational work; that is to say, he did not proceed from ideas or derived principles but from the Word of God and the confessions of the Church. Therefore, even though the Dutch Nazi movement and the Christian Democratic Union stood diametrically opposed to one another, he could accept neither one but branded both as unacceptable to anyone who believed the Scriptures. In his brochure *Not One Square Inch*, Schilder concluded: "In its conception of the state, the Dutch Nazi movement began with Hegel and thereby managed to draw many people away from the banner of, 'Christian politics.' The Christian Democratic Union began with the radical opponents of Hegel (i.e. Barth, Brunner, Kierkegaard) in its conception of the state, and thereby also drew many people away from the banner of 'Christian politics.' Between Hegel and the anti-Hegelians lies our poor Bible, which manages to do no more than *indicate the direction* for locating the place where the revolutionary will is 'bounded' by the anti-revolutionary will."

The battle was about "ideas" concerning the Bible — and the Bible itself did not have the final say. Schilder wrote a revealing article about this matter in *The Reformation* on March 25, 1932. Although this article is now thirty years old, it is as relevant today as it was then.

That there was good reason to make an issue of these two rising movements is apparent from the fact that at the time Schilder was writing (1936), there were already 8000 confessing members of the

Reformed *(Gereformeerd)* churches who were also members of the Dutch Nazi movement. Many of them held prominent positions within the movement.

When the Synod of Amsterdam (1936) made some positive decisions regarding membership in these two movements, we may calmly say that this was in part the result of Schilder's polemicizing in *The Reformation*. A number of separate requests and proposals regarding the Dutch Nazi movement and the Christian Democratic Union, some of which touched on the church order, were brought to this synod. The synod decided to reject both movements as incompatible with the Scriptures and the confessions of the Church. The church members who belonged to either of these movements were to be admonished, and if they did not respond properly to the admonition, they were to be barred from the Lord's table. Of course certain general rules were to be borne in mind in the process, and every case would have to be looked at separately.

In his brochure Schilder made it abundantly clear that this was not just a matter of political direction or a case of the Church involving itself in the political sphere. He demonstrated this by discussing the leading principles which these movements had accepted. Anyone who confessed the Christ of the Scriptures could not possibly confess those principles as well, as the later history of those movements has shown us. Thankfully, he could write: "The situation is becoming clearer. Various consistories and classes are beginning to speak out and say that the principles of the Dutch National Socialist Movement cannot be combined with the Reformed confessions or with the Scriptures, and they have decided to act in accordance with this recognition. Good! From this time on, the muzzle now being prepared for placement over the mouth of the church, to keep her from speaking, will be made and held ready only outside the church."

Growing influence

And so Schilder's influence grew all throughout the Reformed churches. Those who still thought in truly Reformed terms began to associate themselves more and more with what he said and wrote.

The establishment of such papers as *Credo* and the *Calvinist Weekly* also turned out to be a hopeless business. The editors who had withdrawn from *The Reformation* and sought to maintain their influence through these new papers, hoping to silence Schilder in the process, did not achieve their objective. Their papers could continue their pitiful existence only through special contributions and gifts. It did not help the *Calvinist Weekly* that it had announced that it was not called to give any leadership through the press and that it would engage in no polemicizing against those within the Reformed camp, for this amounted to striking an "irenic," and therefore unreformed, note.

But didn't those who made this promise have a "past"? At the time the *Calvinist Weekly* was established, Schilder reminded Prof. Waterink that he was hardly in a position to say that polemicizing is inappropriate and useless: "When we remember how Prof. Waterink polemicized against his colleague Prof. Vollenhoven, and against Rev. H. Steen, and against Mr. A. Janse, and against Mrs. H. Kuyper-Van Oordt[42] . . . we sigh and say that Prof. Waterink should not have allowed the editors of this new paper to set aside his previous work. In my student days I once read a note in an almanac to the effect that there are animals that eat their own children. I would look like such an animal if I were to write a piece in opposition to polemicizing. But Prof. Waterink is in the same situation."

I will resist the temptation to ask to whom that note in the almanac really applied. Unfortunately, the Reformed population of our time also includes some people who have "eaten their own children."

In the meantime, the establishment of the new paper did *The Reformation* no harm. In March of 1936, the publisher was able to announce: "We have been successful in our efforts for this paper. In the past year we received more than 500 new subscribers!"

Fully armed and at full strength

In those days Schilder developed his amazing energies and used them to the fullest. He certainly was not a scholar who restricted himself to the study. A note in an almanac once provided us with striking pictures of the homes of Schilder and Greijdanus late in the evening. In Greijdanus's house there was a brightly lit room at the front, but at the home of "KS" it was completely dark — not because he lay in bed but simply because he wasn't home. It remains a mystery how someone who was on the go as much as Schilder was still able to do so much academic work and put so much on paper, all of it equally thorough and scholarly in character.

---

[42] When Dr. Tazelaar gave a favorable evaluation of a novel by "Hendeck Sönne" (a pseudonym used by Waterink), Mrs. Hendrika Kuyper-Van Oordt took issue with it from a literary standpoint, and she was right to do so, in my judgment.

He literally worked night and day — as a slave in the King's service. Even his vacations involved work — for the Church and for the people. His publisher at Goes has overwhelming evidence of this: bits of paper with copy for *The Reformation,* with requests, with corrections, with changes on proofs — and they came from everywhere. They were written in trains, in waiting rooms, in homes where Schilder lodged, in hotels in Paris, Rome, Berlin, Erlangen, and Venice.

There is a postcard that begins with the words: "Being in Holland for one day . . ." Another one, sent from a point far outside our country, concludes: *"Word and Spirit* is busy promoting itself. Hundreds of free copies are sent out, going to, I hear, local agents of the Free University, among others. Of late it is also making use of advertisements." From Berlin this postcard: "Please send Dr. H. Colijn in The Hague a copy of the various issues in which I have said something about *The Standard* in my press review. —KS." Another postcard from outside the country: "I don't get the *Franeker Church Messenger* any more, yet it is worth reading." Another postcard: "Could you see to it that from now on I get the periodical *The Watchtower* for *The Reformation?"* He even included the exact address of this paper in Potchefstroom, South Africa.

He did all of this while he was busy in Erlangen (Germany), completing his work for his doctorate in philosophy. While he was there he sent this telegram: "Absolutely opposed to any advertisement re Chiliasm [millennialism] —Schilder." Another telegram from Erlangen: "Disregard the copy first sent, another version on the way —Schilder."

Just how seriously he took his relationship to his publisher and to his readers, despite the incredible busyness in the midst of which he lived, is evident from the following postcard, which he also set from Erlangen, apparently after a few days of "vacation" in the Netherlands: "I am sending you some copy for *The Reformation.* This time it is largely taken over from what I have written elsewhere. I find this a nuisance and therefore do not want to send in such copy without at the same time giving you my excuse. I went to Rotterdam for a few days of vacation, but they made it even busier for me there than it already was in Erlangen. I just didn't have any time to write something new. Hence this way out, although it does have this in its favor, that I already had this topic on my list, and there is not a lot to be said against it because the paper in which I published this material does not have a wide circulation. It just wouldn't come for me this week, and you know that I am not often guilty of this sort of thing. —KS."

Isn't it moving to see someone who works so hard making excuses because, for once, he had to send in some copy that had already been published in another paper? And why was this necessary? Because he had no time to write!

How deeply his work in the press on behalf of the people occupied him also comes through in a letter in which we read: "I wanted to let you know that my promotion is scheduled for this coming Friday morning."[43] But in the same letter we almost get the impression that this piece of information is merely a detail of secondary importance, for he also writes: "In recent weeks I have not received my copy of the Reformed young men's magazine. That paper interests me at the moment because it contains something against my brother, and someone told me I was also mentioned."

When he was home again from Erlangen, he continued on the old footing. He usually wrote his copy for *The Reformation* late in the evening or at night, and then sent it in with the very last postal pick-up. On a postcard he explained: "I'm sorry you didn't have the copy in hand on Thursday at 1 P.M. I'm sorry, but I could not foresee what happened. You know that when I came back from my leave of absence, I was under the impression that the train leaving on Thursday morning at 8 A.M. is still a postal train, as it used to be, but it turned out that it's not. Acting on this assumption, I mailed the copy on Wednesday evening, just after 8 P.M. The mailboxes in Rotterdam still had to be emptied — I took note of this . . ."

Another postcard: "Please send me, as soon as possible, the official reports of the general synod's session beginning with Tuesday, August 29 — if this is possible for you. Please send the reports to my address for this week: the Hotel Magdeburg Hof, at the Bahnhof Friedrichstrasse, Berlin. I want to write an article about this synod for the next issue of *The Reformation,* and so I need those reports. I leave on (Wednesday) evening, and so I don't have time any more to read the papers. I'll be back on Saturday, September 16." He adds the following note: "If you receive papers which you're familiar with and which I can use for my press review, may I have them?" The synod he is referring to here is probably the one that met in Middelburg in 1933.

And there was always the concern to maintain good relationships. Note the following excuse to the publisher: "This meditation is

---

[43] A "promotion" is the defense of a doctoral dissertation. Success in this enterprise means that candidate has completed his doctoral studies and can be given his degree. —TRANS.

also too long — I know that, but there's nothing I can do about it. I will not remind you that last week I didn't take all the space for that one column. I will only say: Don't let me upset the regulations you have established for the paper. Therefore please leave it out until next week (then we can abbreviate the department dealing with church life) — that's fine with me. Or if you want to use half of it, that's all right. In that case, make sure you indicate in small letters at the bottom that the article is to be continued. Whatever you do, it's fine with me — just so long as you aren't angry at me."

So long as you aren't angry at me! How often he said this in telephone conversations when asking for something, or when he thought someone might have reason to be upset with him. But how could we ever have been angry at such a man — someone who worked so hard, virtually consuming himself in the process? He concluded that letter with this sentence: "Please forgive me for using such a grubby piece of paper. It's all happening tonight in great haste, and I want to get it into the mail."

He was a hard worker, but he was also businesslike. Consider this comment from a letter probably written in 1934 (he never dated his letters): "Yesterday I spoke in Utrecht about the Dutch National Socialist Movement. In the meeting I was asked if I would allow the speech to be printed. I said I would publish it in *The Reformation,* and that anyone who wanted a copy would have to subscribe temporarily, or regularly. Applause from our friends . . ." In another letter dating from about the same period we read: "Could you let me know how many new readers we have picked up in the last three months? I'm thinking of publishing this figure in an article this week, to oppose the foolish claim made by some to the effect that our people are no longer interested in theological questions. From various sides we are receiving sympathetic responses from readers."

That this comment was justified is apparent from various letters I have read. Let me quote one here which was sent by a minister who remained with the synodocratic churches (as did so many who knew the right way). In this letter of April 5, 1937, he said: "I am not sending you this material to put pressure on you but to give expression to my great thankfulness to God our LORD for the work you have done in your writings on behalf of our churches. Your writings have given 'guidance' to me (and to many colleagues). I know that many would join with me in thanking God for this and would add their prayer that you may be strengthened. I send you hearty greetings in Christ." There were so many whom Schilder influenced and moved during the 1930s, pressing them to make a choice, whether for good or for bad. Doesn't the Word always affect people in one of these two directions? Doesn't it force us to make decisions, whereas irenic half-heartedness and a posture of broad-mindedness all too often gives us a way of evading the choice?

How Schilder struggled and labored to restore the Word of the Lord to the place to which it is entitled. He fought on all fronts and used all lawful means at his command — not just the pen but also the spoken word. Every Sunday he was out somewhere preaching, for preaching was his favorite kind of work. He gave lectures and speeches in many places on behalf of many kinds of organizations and on numerous commemoration days. And always he spoke with great authority — there was just no getting around it. His speeches were relevant to the situation and got to the heart of the matter; they always proclaimed the Word and honored and applied the confessions.

How skilled he was at giving his hearers an overall grasp and perspective on a topic! He knew the situation well and knew the people involved. Nothing in the ecclesiastical or political domain escaped his eagle eye. He read all the church and political papers every week. When he traveled, he would take many church papers and newspapers with him in the train (and he always went third class!). He would pull a little scissors from his pocket and cut out the articles he wanted to use or save. All the rest went out the window, and if you walked along the railway track connecting Amsterdam and Zwolle (near Kampen, where he lived), you might come upon the papers Schilder had discarded.

He was a man who made good use of time, even to the point of conducting oral examinations of his students in the train station near their home when he happened to be out that way. He often traveled to the place where he was to preach early on the Saturday so that he could collect some money in that area for his hospitium or for other causes that might help needy students.

One Friday he telephoned me and asked if I could pick him up at the station the next afternoon so that he could go to Bunschoten and there try to collect his weekly hundred guilders for the hospitium. In the homes of the fishermen of Bunschoten and Spakenburg we ate our fried fish. How "KS" could enjoy himself as he ate in a humble home! How completely he fit in! One of the fishermen invited us to have some of the fish his wife was preparing just then. When this man, wearing a blue sweater, put a ten-guilder note on the table as we were enjoying the delicious fried fish, Schilder gave him a broad smile of satisfaction and said, "Thank you! Thank you! That's money with the fish."[44] And so he was constantly in contact with the simple people of the church, who understood him better and loved him more than the intellectual element, who often understood nothing of what he was about.

In his articles on Schilder in *The Trumpet,* Rev. Boerkoel maintained that Schilder was only happy behind his typewriter and did not care for conversation and personal contact with people. That was not the Schilder I came to know. Moreover, it is also incorrect that he carried on his polemicizing only by way of his paper. When necessary, he did have personal contact with the people who did not agree with him — or at least, he *sought* such contact.

This was true, for example, in his relationship with his great opponent Prof. V. Hepp. When the differences of opinion around the time of the Synod of 1936 were pending and Hepp came out with his notorious series of brochures entitled *Threatening Deformation* and insinuated to a synodical committee that secret meetings were being held involving members of the committee, Schilder tried repeatedly to have personal contact with him, but he didn't succeed. Not even with the help of an intermediary was he able to arrange an appointment with Hepp, who could not substantiate his accusations but did not withdraw them either.

Schilder conferred a great deal with people and carried on a lot of personal correspondence. He wrote innumerable letters which went out to all parts of our country. If a biography of Schilder is ever written, those letters should be placed at the biographer's disposal, for then people will have a chance to get to know Schilder thoroughly and see what kind of person he really was. We have the correspondence of Groen, Bilderdijk, Da Costa, and others; why should we not pass on to our posterity the correspondence of the man who dominated and led the reformational movement in our churches for thirty years?

From a letter dated April 6, 1930, which is in my possession, we see how consumed and preoccupied Schilder was in everything he did in carrying out his task in office, serving in the churches, prophesying faithfully, and fulfilling the mandate of testifying to the Truth in

---

[44] There is a play on words here that is lost in English. —TRANS.

every area of life. It is clear from this letter that he already saw the rising danger in our church life, even though at that point almost no one else among us was aware of it. Consider the following sentence: "I believe a new distinction is emerging, also among us — unless we have a change of course . . ." Also this sentence: "The Federation of Calvinists will probably not flourish to any great extent. But that should give us no comfort. The Federation is a fact that cannot be undone, and it has already caused much damage . . ."

From a letter of September 1932, written while he was in Erlangen, we see his great interest in the question of the organ bought by the National Christian Radio Association. He wrote to me: "I am completely in agreement with the criticism, and I deplore the purchase." A vibrating, theater-style Vox Humana sound in an organ was an abomination to him!

He was interested in anything that served to promote purity, principles, style, and beauty, and he opposed whatever stood in the way. When various things went wrong in politics, he did not just write about it in the papers. In one of his letters I came upon this sentence: "Over the years I have written extensive personal letters to Dr. Colijn about various things on my heart." Elsewhere we read: "Things have gone amiss to quite some extent among our older generation. Our beloved Dutch Christian Press Bureau also defended the 'causes' of its director by taking over articles advocating what amounts to an impotent and quintessential irenicism and by flirting with the people who tear things apart, and then talking, every day, in an endearing way, about unity."

Everywhere he went, he found ways and means to write copy for *The Reformation.* The publisher received copy from Schilder on all sorts of paper — on the back side of wedding and funeral announcements, on the proofs of books written by him, on lesson rosters of the Theological School in Kampen. And the copy often came from his pen under situations of great pressure. A roughly composed note in pen, almost illegible: "Not in Kampen tomorrow Thursday 2 o'clock. Perhaps in Middelburg, phone number 238 (Olthoff). If possible send proofs by *express* to Middelburg. I can then correct them and send them back toward morning. Badly written in the train, therefore correction by me needed. —KS." Such notes were not an exception. Yet everything he wrote was responsible, well thought out, and completely to the point. Often he would set something straight that had been slanted in the press under the cover of pious words.

That he never left his paper in the lurch is apparent from the following note, also written on the back side of a lesson roster: "Please send *The Reformation* to the Hotel Royal Danieli, Venice, Italy. Please let me know Friday at the latest when I'm there how much of the press review column is left over, if any at all. —KS." A telegram from Amsterdam: "Advise meditations for June ask Van der Vegt, Goes — KS."

Nothing escaped him, and he thought about virtually everything. No matter where he was, he always came up with copy — it was abundant, and it was topical, up-to-date. His commitment on this matter is apparent from the following scrawled note: "Suddenly, unexpectedly, I find that I have to make a trip out of the country this week. Thus I cannot telephone you next Thursday. By my calculations you still have one meditation of mine. There are also lead articles. The rest runs by itself . . ." At the end of the note he adds: "Let me thank you again heartily for your kindness, which I have put to the test. I'll see to it that you get copy. —KS." Was it really necessary to add that assurance?

Schilder as a person

This child of God was a slave of his Savior, working day and night. If there was anyone who could apply Paul's word to himself, it was Schilder: "In everything commending ourselves as servants of God, in much endurance, in afflictions, in hardships, in distresses, in beatings, in imprisonments, in tumults, in labors, in sleeplessness, in hunger, in purity, in knowledge, in patience, in kindness, in the Holy Spirit, in genuine love, in the word of truth, in the power of God; by the weapons of righteousness for the right hand and the left, by glory and dishonor, by evil report and good report, regarded as deceivers and yet true; as unknown yet well-known, as dying yet behold, we live; as punished yet not put to death, as sorrowful yet always rejoicing, as poor yet making many rich . . . " (II Corinthians 6:4-10).

Did he have any opportunity to relax and enjoy himself? I can report that when he stayed at my house (which happened often, to my great delight), his only enjoyment was a good cigar. He smoked quite a few of them. There was no other personal pleasure he permitted himself. If he had an hour free, he liked to read the papers he carried with him, or he studied books. He never went anywhere without books, and so the suitcase he dragged along with him when he went out to preach was impossibly heavy. And if you went to meet him at the train (we didn't always have a car available), you almost had to wrestle with him to get hold of that heavy suitcase.

On a number of occasions my wife found that the bulb in the lamp by the bed had been unscrewed slightly. The reason was this: Schilder had continued to work for hours in his bedroom, and when he finally went to sleep he did not want to disturb anyone by going over to the light switch — and so he quietly unscrewed the bulb instead.

Did he ever take a vacation? On the two trips he made to the United States, he also kept working, making the most of every hour and conferring with people wherever he went. In 1939 he labored to bring the churches of Hoeksema into contact with the Christian Reformed Church again — and succeeded. In 1947 he went all over the United States, attending conferences and giving speeches and lectures about such topics as common grace, the covenant, and the concept of the church.

On one occasion just after the war, my wife and I, along with an American friend, invited Schilder to come with us to Belgium for a few days. He spent a whole day in a large Roman Catholic book-room where, on his knees, he looked through the books piled up around him to find works he could draw on for his commentary on the Heidelberg Catechism. We finally went into Antwerp without him. Because he bought some 500 guilders worth of books, the fathers who ran the book-room also let him have a beautiful original Luther Bible; he was happy as a child to own it. Father Henri de Greve later smuggled that exquisite work over the border for him and brought it to his home.[45]

There was no rest, no relaxation for him. He made no demands on his own behalf except that he wanted opportunity to *work*. Even with exhausting work piled up all around him, it was moving to see how he did not still the impulses of his loving, priestly heart. His interest always went out to the individual who was in need or in pain. Once when he was preaching in Apeldoorn, he visited a member of the congregation whose wife was dying. He comforted this man by drawing on the Scriptures. When he received word not long afterward that the man's wife had died, Schilder sent him a handwritten letter (very legible), which made it abundantly clear how fully he could enter into someone else's pain and feel his loss. The letter offered true comfort.

---

[45] The book wound up being smuggled because considerable duty would have to be paid on it at the border. —TRANS.

It appears that Boerkoel did not know Schilder very well, even though he had enjoyed ample opportunity to make his acquaintance when they were both students, for he wrote that Schilder sought his friends among rich and prominent people who coddled him and took him along in their "Cadillacs." Now, if that was really what he had wanted, if that had indeed been his inclination, he would not have had much trouble assuring himself of much more luxurious living conditions. Earlier I commented that if Schilder had been been out for his own honor and fame, the world would have opened its doors to him. But on the contrary, he sought *nothing* for himself and never made personal demands.

I still remember very clearly that I needed to have a discussion with him about business matters on Good Friday of 1946. Train connections were still poor at the time, and so a trip to Kampen was almost an impossibility for me. Schilder therefore suggested that I meet him in IJmuiden, where he was to preach that evening. Unfortunately, he had had a small accident just before that and wound up with a fractured shoulder-blade. That his arm was causing him pain was obvious from his gestures up on the pulpit.

I had to stay in IJmuiden myself that night because I couldn't get transportation back home. The next morning I talked with Schilder again at the place where I was staying. During this conversation, two brothers from IJmuiden came to offer him a taxi to take him to Bussum, where he was to preach on Easter Sunday. They had collected the money for the taxi fare among friends, and it amounted to quite a sum for that time. They had seen how Schilder, with his shoulder causing him pain, still dragged a heavy suitcase full of books along with him and, as was his custom, traveled third class in drafty old trains, which were the only ones available just after the war. But Schilder wouldn't hear of it. He asked them to turn the money over to him so that he could pass it on to needy students or use it to build up the library of the seminary, which was in dire straits.[46] He would take the train to Bussum.

It took the brothers quite a bit of talking before they finally persuaded him to accept their offer. One of them finally managed to cut the knot by saying, "Now listen here, Professor. This money has been collected for a special purpose, and we're not free to turn it over to

---

[46] The seminary established by the liberated Reformed churches after the events on 1944 (in Kampen, on the Broederweg) is the one being referred to here — not the one on the Oudestraat (also in Kampen) at which Schilder taught before the war. —TRANS.

you for any other purpose. You're going to Bussum in the taxi, and that's the end of the matter!" Schilder yielded, but he continued to regard it as a shameful way to use the money. His students needed that money so much! That's the way Schilder was — and not the way Boerkoel pictured him.

Whether a person was prominent or not made no difference to him — people were creatures of God. He was well aware of what the LORD had said to Samuel: "Do not look at his appearance or at the height of his stature, because I have rejected him; for God sees not as man sees, for man looks at the outward appearance, but the LORD looks at the heart" (I Samuel 16:7).

For Schilder there was no distinction between rich and poor, between the mighty and the lowly. The people of Kampen could surely give us some striking anecdotes to illustrate this. Schilder's lifestyle was not dominated by a yearning to fulfill his own desires but by his determination to live in conformity to the demands of the Scriptures.

During the 1930s there were many people who could no longer understand such an attitude. People in the Reformed *(Gereformeerd)* churches had become so worldly that his way of life, in which he set his personal desires aside, made no sense to them. It did not fit in with the "Solomonic glory" of those days when everyone was out for himself, when it was the accepted thing to seek honor and prominence. Schilder, too, was measured by such yardsticks, and so people did not understand what he was up to; they wound up offering completely mistaken interpretations of the intentions that motivated him.

Boerkoel wrote that Schilder sought recognition, that he wanted to assert himself and have a group of his own which would follow him through thick and thin. His seminary would have to grow, for any decline in the number of students could snuff out his passion and excitement. He had to be carried along by full churches and packed lecture halls. Now, these things he said about Schilder could indeed be said about many of his contemporaries, but in no way do they apply to *him*. If those were indeed the sort of things he wanted, nothing would have prevented him from attaining them, for he was *primus inter pares* (the first among equals), as Boerkoel himself recognized.

People no longer understood him because they had no eye for the work of the Spirit in the churches. Thus they came up with a completely mistaken and distorted picture of Schilder as a person. The influence he achieved, especially among the younger generation, was dismissed as a "temporary phenomenon."

Boerkoel explained it in this way: "Earlier I pointed to Schilder's inclination toward the absolute . . . The desire for absoluteness was also a characteristic of the movement of the young people around 1930, and it still characterizes the liberated churches. And let us not forget that in 1930 absoluteness was in the air as far as the political sphere is concerned. There is no movement that lives in isolation from the time in which it has arisen; to that extent, there is something relative in every movement."

H. H. Kuyper struck the same note: Schilder had certain features in common with the Dutch Nazi movement, for he, too, thought in absolute, black-and-white terms. A minister of the synodocratic churches serving the congregation in Berkel would later write in a church paper about the "New Schilder Movement."[47]

Throughout the 1930s, this misconception was operative in certain circles, and it was also a factor at the time of the liberation. In 1944 I was placed under discipline in Goes because, after Schilder's suspension, I had passed on information in various places in our country about what was going on. I was visited by an elder who came to inform me what the consistory had decided in my case. This elder told me that Schilder's great sin was that he had opposed "the highest authority in our churches — the Synod." When I went into the facts of the case, this man, who was an architect and thus well educated, shrugged his shoulders and assured me that he himself did not know much about these things. He had no time to go into them. But there was one thing he did know: the Schilder movement had the same sort of appeal for the younger people as the Dutch Nazi movement. His own sons had also been sympathetic toward the Dutch Nazi movement in the 1930s. The movement was young and had fresh ideals and dared to take action. It was the same way with the Schilder movement, and so it was attractive to the young people. But the church had to preserve a conserving element. And so this elder stuck to his guns.

That was how many people judged and condemned the reformational work of Schilder. They simply did not have the capacity to understand the meaning of Scripture and the confessions in their application to a time of decline and conformity to the world. People were not thinking in categories derived from the demands of the cov-

---

[47] The Dutch Nazi movement was usually referred to as the "N.S.B." (National Socialist *Beweging,* i.e. Movement). This minister used the same acronym to refer to the "New Schilder *Beweging* or Movement." —TRANS.

enant; instead they were concerned with power relationships and influence and personal authority in relation to the masses. They saw their own influence on the people declining, while Schilder's influence was growing.

Boerkoel himself describes this growing influence in one of his articles on Schilder in *The Trumpet:* "At the outset, long before the synod began to take up the questions that had been raised, the members of our churches were drawn into the movement — and sometimes very intensely. But not everywhere to the same extent: the people in the cities were especially involved. Through their gifts in preaching, and perhaps through some other means or connections as well, the most fiery of Schilder's followers managed to get calls to the big congregations, which were the key positions. Yet there were many villages in which a younger follower of Schilder would wind up as minister and then gather a group around himself."

I will not respond to the insinuations in this quotation. The fact of Schilder's growing influence was simply not to be denied. Young preachers who looked up to him were indeed being called from small places to big congregations. C. Veenhof went from Harkstede to Haarlem and then to Utrecht; B. Holwerda from Kantens to Amersfoort; E. T. van den Born from Loosdrecht to Helpman, Heemstede, and Amersfoort; J. Kapteyn from Kralingsche Veer to IJmuiden and Groningen; M. B. van 't Veer from Zevenbergen to Groningen and Amsterdam; P. Deddens from Brielle via Rijswijk to Groningen; J. Groen Jr. from Kralingsche Veer via Bilthoven to Groningen; C. Vonk from Baarland to Schiedam; I. de Wolff from Mussel to Enschede. And there are more I could mention.

They did not make these moves through "means" or "connections" other than their gifts in preaching. The people could hear that they brought the Word and opened the Scriptures. This was not the sound of a "new movement"; rather, it was an old sound — reformational, delving into the Scriptures. And it was spoken in faithfulness to the confessions of the Church. There was nothing more to it than that — and nothing less. The people were listening carefully.

Thus these young men were also asked to speak at society meetings and rallies. Van 't Veer became the president of the Men's League. At League Days for the women and the young people, speakers from this circle were invited because people knew they had something to say. All down the line the ordinary church people were involved in what was happening, and there was great joy and thankfulness on their part that the message of the Scriptures was being proclaimed again; the people were delighted that they no longer had to listen to dry speculation and subjectivistic experiential religiosity that was measured by standards not derived from the Word.

Boerkoel writes: "The growing stream did not yet encounter dykes to block it. The movement could advance calmly; it saw no hindrances placed in its path. In many sectors of our ecclesiastical life, its influence penetrated, and it moved ahead." And indeed it was so.

This also applied to the church press. Despite the fact that first Hepp and then Waterink and Tazelaar had withdrawn from *The Reformation,* to establish *Credo* and the *Calvinist Weekly,* Schilder's paper not only maintained itself but grew steadily, so that the numbers of subscribers hovered between 3500 and 4000 in the years when the battle was fiercest. Now, this was an unbelievably high number for a national church paper: no other paper could match it. *Credo* eventually failed because of lack of interest, and the *Calvinist Weekly* managed to keep publishing only through great effort. *The Herald* was also having its share of difficulties.

During this time I used to visit Mrs. Hendrika Kuyper-Van Oordt, an exceptional and very charming elderly lady, at her home on the Provenierssingel in Rotterdam. She was a very capable literary figure who wrote excellent prose. The daughter of an old Rotterdam aristocratic trading family, her own inclinations were more Arminian than Reformed. During one of these visits she appeared, as was her custom, in a thick old cape and a fur stole, with a cigarette the length of a cigar in her mouth. We were in her private chambers, and she pulled up her chair right in front of a blazing fireplace, next to which I saw a huge stack of back issues of *The Herald.* I had come to discuss the novels she was writing for us, and when we were done with this topic, she said she wanted my advice as a businessman about *The Herald.*

This paper was the property of the Kuyper family, she told me, and it cost the family about 2000 guilders a year — money that would otherwise be at the disposal of the two Kuyper daughters. But the paper was in serious financial difficulties, for it had just 800 subscribers and was able to keep going only because of the goodwill of its publisher, who wanted to maintain the tradition. What could be done to raise the number of subscribers? I tried to give her some advice, and she nodded, agreeing. "That's just what I wanted," she said, and then added, "but the difficulty is that when we have a family meeting about the paper once a year in a hotel and I come forward with such proposals, Herman [H. H. Kuyper] wants to eat first. He loves a copious dinner, and when that's over it's too late, for he has fallen asleep . . . And then we go home with nothing to show for our trouble."

The Synod of 1936

It was at the Synod of Amsterdam in 1936 that certain "differences of opinion," which soon came to be called "disputes over doctrine," were placed on the agenda. This happened in a most unfortunate way that went completely against the church order.

At the beginning of 1936, Rev. J. D. Wielenga made the following observation in the *Franeker Church Messenger:* "At the moment there is a campaign underway against Prof. Schilder. And it's not the first one — oh no! Do you still remember the decision made by the consistory of The Hague West? And there are other things that could be mentioned. But now, before the year 1935 draws to a close, our press, that is, our church press, feels it has to issue one more strong blast against this Kampen professor. He wrangles, he cuts people up, he . . . Of course he does — when people cry, 'Peace, peace, there is no danger.' But others call it providing principial information, or sounding a warning, or maintaining the Reformed confessions, or pointing to small deviations that can lead to much bigger ones, and so forth."

Various papers defended Schilder against the personal attacks and provocation he endured. The *Free Frisian* wrote: "Weren't De Cock and Dr. Kuyper also driven by such a 'zeal'? How often mud was thrown at the men of the Secession and the Doleantie because they 'wrote so sharply' and did not let any human being stand in the way of the Lord's honor! Wasn't Prof. Schilder right in warning us as Reformed believers against a congress of *Reformed* people in which someone like Prof. Haitjema, a Barthian, was a speaker? Has Prof. Schilder been too sharp in his writings against Barth and the Dutch Nazi movement? We believe that today the danger of a *blurring* of the boundaries is great — very great. People call for *synthesis* at the expense of our Reformed confessions."

But the defense did not produce much in the way of results. The synodical robot simply *had* to be put into operation while it was still possible. After all, what would happen if action against Schilder was delayed for some years?

How did the matter of the differences in opinion come before the synod? We know that what happened was contrary to the church order of Dort. Two greenhorns named H. W. van der Vegt and A. D. R.

Polman respectively were the ones who brought it about. Rev. A. M. Boeijinga described it as follows in a Haarlem church paper: "During the discussion about the polemicizing, two synodical Benjamins (no disrespect to them as persons is intended here) came up with the idea of putting a proposal before the synod to intervene in the matter of the 'disputes over doctrine.' And that's what happened. Will this whole course of events really leave anyone thinking that the synod was deeply convinced there was a dangerous deviation from the confessions underway? Will anyone suppose that the synod was aflame with holy zeal to carry out the 'task and calling' mentioned above?"

I still have the impression that one of those greenhorns (i.e. Van der Vegt) was not fully aware of the consequences when he let himself be used to get the robot into motion.[48] Van der Vegt was sympathetic to Schilder and was a faithful reader of *The Reformation* even after the *Calvinist Weekly* had been established. In the matter of the covenant, he thought along the very same lines as "KS." But he was naive, not possessing much insight into people, and not having a good feel for ecclesiastical diplomacy, which formed the background to this entire synod. He was used.

Mr. H. Algra put it rather sharply in the *Leeuwarden Church Messenger:* "At the latest synod there were hours and days devoted to questions that did not come up from the churches but were directly or indirectly placed on the agenda by various professors by means of their stalking horses." He came back to this matter on a later occasion and took back the comment about "stalking horses" because one of the men in question felt insulted by it. But in substance he stood by his judgment that the proposal had gotten onto the synodical agenda through certain professors, albeit indirectly.

Was there "agitation"?

A very remarkable phenomenon is that although H. H. Kuyper and others declared at the synod and in the church papers that there was great agitation among the people, which in turn made synodical action necessary, the great majority of the people involved with the

---

[48] Schilder foresaw the consequences very quickly. Years later Polman reported that Schilder accosted him angrily at the very first opportunity outside the actual session of synod: "He was in radical disagreement with my proposal. His chief objection was that a synod was now doing what should actually be taking place in the academy and in the discussions theologians have with one another" (see N. Scheps, *Interviews over 25 jaar vrijmaking* [Kampen: Kok, 1970], p. 25). —TRANS.

church papers were of the view that "agitation," or whatever one might care to call it, did *not* exist among the people. It looked a bit like the tactic Hitler was using. He would stir up some agitation by having his satellites create a hubbub in a neighboring country — and then maintain that he had to intervene, for revolution was on the horizon and the borders were threatened. In this way he brought almost all the countries east of Germany under his control.

J. G. Feenstra wrote that the questions had been "blown up" and asked: "Wouldn't it have been better if the men who were so concerned to go into all those disputes over doctrine had paid more attention to the *dangers* threatening us from the side of dialectical theology? I cannot understand how some people who wanted to defend the last Calvinist Congress now see all these disputes over doctrine, but do not have an eye for the great dangers that really do threaten us from the side of Barth and Brunner."

It was simply a fairy tale that there was agitation among the people. At the synod even Dr. Dijk declared: "No lesser assembly has placed this matter before the synod, and if the proposal of Polman and Van der Vegt had not been brought to the synod, it would not have formed a topic of discussion."

A very sharp judgment came from no one less than Rev. IJ. K. Vellenga in a church paper serving Drenthe and Overijssel. Vellenga commented on the manner in which this matter was handled. If there are complaints about deviations from the confessions, the proper thing to do is to take up the matter with those who are proponents of the deviations. He ended with a sharp question: "Or is this perhaps a view that will also lead to my being counted among the fair game which the [synodical] committee has been licensed to hunt, even if it is not stated in so many words in its mandate?" Thus it appeared that the "hunt" was on.

Rev. D. Sikkel, who was certainly not a "Schilderian," did not detect any "agitation" either. He wrote: "Moreover, it strikes me as strange that the professors tell the representatives of the churches that the churches are agitated, while those same representatives, upon returning to their homes, are asked on all sides what this ecclesiastical agitation is all about." Dr. Kaajan took the same position and expressed himself in virtually identical words in the *Utrecht Church Messenger.*

It was Sikkel's view that the things said at the synod had *caused* whatever agitation there was in the churches. Indeed, the agitation came not from below, that is, from the people of the church, but from the synod. That was basically Hitler's tactic, and it was also successful in this case.

What Boerkoel later wrote about this matter was absolutely incorrect: "In many a heart there arose a concern over the future of our Churches; and many people were filled with fear. The anxious question 'Where are we headed?' could no longer be suppressed. Those were days of pain and sorrow, and they became ever more painful and sorrowful." It is striking that back in 1936, the same Boerkoel held an entirely different view on the matter of polemicizing in the church papers. He found it only natural that all the questions should be dealt with in a polemical setting in our papers — after all, we have a "living theology."

Dr. Dijk, in his church paper, made the same comments he had made at the synod itself: "Not a single church or classis or particular synod had raised the alarm about 'uneasiness in our churches' or had brought forward a gravamen against an impure doctrine which was being propounded among us. And so I ask: Was there reason to sound the alarm bell so loudly? If the evil was so frightening that the situation was much worse than in 1926, surely a number of churches would have voiced their concern to the synod. But not a single voice was raised. For this reason I believe that the outcry about uneasiness did not correspond to the actual condition of our churches, in which a great number of people are asking what is *really* going on."

Consider also what Rev. S. J. Popma had to say in the *Amersfoort Church Messenger:* "At the synod some people created the impression that there was anxiety in our churches about existing differences of opinion. I don't believe a word of it myself. The anxiety we currently see results from the way people were talking at synod. The thought arose in many minds: 'What's really going on there?'"

I could cite still more voices in the press, all of them of one mind on this matter, but I will refrain. I quoted these particular writers because they all walked into the trap which the unholy synod of 1936 had set: We want Schilder in the dock! And so they must share the responsibility for what followed — including both *what* was done and *the way* in which it was done, even though they had originally protested against this Hitler-like strategy.

The reason such deplorable actions and attitudes were possible was that we no longer lived in the reformational "Davidic" period but had fallen back into a "Solomonic" period of deformation. Ecclesiastical questions had turned into power struggles, and the reformation that was underway in the 1930s could no longer find an open channel in the churches of the Secession and the Doleantie. Solomon bought many horses, took many wives, offered sacrifices on the high places, and died at the age of 58. The distressing Solomonic era was followed by the division of the kingdom.

Loyal cooperation

Schilder, in his pure innocence and simple uprightness, did not realize what was actually going on. When today we go back and read the articles he wrote at that time in *The Reformation,* we see that he struck an optimistic note because there were, in his judgment, so many things that went well at the synod.

When his battle for a sixth professor at Kampen was finally getting some results, he wrote: "I am personally delighted at this course of events. I asked for water, and they gave me milk and butter." In a positive spirit he plunged into the work entailed by the agenda of synod, e.g. in relation to the question of hymns. In evaluating the report on this matter he wrote:[49] "The report itself is a model of calm and brotherly explanation — may it restrain many in their impetuousness." That the catechism instruction books were not to be introduced was another decision with which he agreed: "Given the circumstances, I am personally happy with this decision."[50] He was even happy about the rather meagre progress on the ticklish question of introducing doctoral-level programs at the seminary in Kampen. "The decision that was made represents a step in the right direction," he wrote.

He was in good spirits and was unaware of the dark clouds gathering over his head. He even saw something positive in the debate about "polemicizing" and quoted a comment made by the president of the synod: "Tomorrow afternoon we get to the business of polemicizing — then we can polemicize about that." Schilder explained: "When the public session of Thursday morning came to a close, that was what the president said with a twinkle in his eye as he glanced at the gallery."

---

[49] Synod had decided not to increase the number of hymns approved for use in worship services. —TRANS.

[50] Synod had decided not to approve some proposed new catechism instruction materials because the underlying concepts were not sufficiently oriented toward the Heidelberg Catechism. —TRANS.

The synod's decision to issue a general admonition was also accepted calmly by Schilder: "As things stand now, it may not accomplish as much good as was intended, but it certainly cannot do any harm. Only lack of clarity will harm us." Even the fact that the matter of the differences in opinion had come up at the synod did not meet with much objection in what Schilder wrote. All he said was: "A conclusion in which the synod speaks of *disputes about doctrine* can be expected to lead to more uneasiness." But he could be comfortable with a conclusion that spoke of "differences of opinion."

The "dark day"

Schilder did not realize that there was rough weather ahead until H. H. Kuyper began to speak. Rolling out the heavy artillery, Kuyper declared that "we have to face the fact that the situation in the Reformed *(Gereformeerd)* churches is even worse now than it was in the days of Assen." He talked about a "new generation" operating as a faction on its own and declared that it would turn out to be a curse in our churches. He explained that he had received letters "in which young preachers and others wrote that they were through with Kuyper and Bavinck." Even Calvin did not appear to have any authority anymore. What these men wanted, after serving in the ministry for only a couple of years, was practically to tear down the temple and build a new one. And such talk was coming from "beardless youths." It was the spirit of revolution, which wants to turn everything upside down. And it was a movement that would poison the church. He maintained that it was wrong to speak of the "true church," for then we could no longer work to become closer to other churches, since, strictly speaking, there would then be no other churches. Such thinking represented a shattering of the "catholicity of the church."

In the report on the proceedings we read: "In deep silence the synod listened to this speech." Schilder responded in a speech in which he declared that it was "one of the darkest days in the life of the Reformed churches in recent times — as much because of what was concealed as because of what was said." Later he also addressed this issue in *The Reformation:* in the column on church life he talked about "that anxious Thursday."

But he did not spend much time on the expression "beardless youths." He observed: "I don't know to whom this is supposed to refer, but I do know that Timothy, and John Calvin at the time he wrote his *Institutes,* could well have been addressed as such, given their age at the time they stood in the front ranks of the holy universal Christian church."

He took the comment about the formation of a "faction" somewhat more seriously. In his speech Kuyper had mentioned the newly established paper *Pro Ecclesia* (For the Church), which was popularizing the ideas of Schilder and Vollenhoven. Schilder observed: "But the fact that this paper wants to look at some ideas in the light of *two* authors, one in Amsterdam and one in Kampen, seems to me to be sufficient to refute the charge about a faction being formed."

As for the charge that things were worse in the church now than they had been before Assen, Schilder maintained that such sentiments did not manifest sufficient gratitude for God's work in our churches. Moreover, this comment was rather unfair toward some of the people who had joined in that work.

When we reread Schilder's article today, we are struck by the exceedingly sober, objective and even gentle tone he adopted in the face of H. H. Kuyper's very personal attack and insinuations. People have often complained about the "tone" of Schilder's writings. I have never been able to find a strident tone in them: that they possessed such a tone was simply a story that was passed on from one person to another.

Schilder was irrefutable in his argumentation and was hard to resist because he got right to the heart of the question. But he was never personal or bitter or vulgar or a diplomatic smoothy or a speculator out to win cheap applause or a few laughs from his public; no, he regarded all such devices and aims as in conflict with Christian ethics, even though there were plenty of others who did use them in an effort to save face or to prove themselves right after all.

And when he gave H. H. Kuyper an answer about his complaint that things were even worse than in the days before Assen, he remained very businesslike; yet at the same time he got to the heart of the matter in such a thorough way that there was nothing left of Kuyper's complaint. The result was that the sword turned back upon Kuyper himself, without any suggestion to that effect on Schilder's part.

What did Kuyper mean, and *whom* did he have in mind? In reflecting on this question Schilder wrote:

> The speaker was not talking about the public disregard
> of an earlier synodical decision, namely, that the leaders

in our church life were to point earnestly to the dangers connected with membership in the Dutch Christian Student Union. (It is clear that this decision is being disregarded here and there.) Neither was he pointing to the deplorable neglect — at least, I fear there is such neglect — of earnest "self-examination" in connection with the question whether one's life, including its political and social aspects, is being lived along the *Scriptural* line of obedience to Christ our King, the line which Dr. A. Kuyper drew so vigorously.

When I see our people joining the Dutch Nazi movement or the Christian Democratic Union, I fear that there are many who have fallen away completely from the solemn earnestness that was expressed by Dr. A. Kuyper in the speech he gave at the opening of the Free University, when he spoke those familiar words that are featured so prominently on the calendars handed out by the Free University: "There is not one square inch anywhere in human life about which Christ, who is Sovereign over all, does not exclaim, 'Mine!' " It was the same speech in which Dr. A. Kuyper so vividly sketched the dangers of a state that seeks its own power, and one can still use that speech today in direct opposition to those who have joined the Dutch Nazi movement and those who have not entirely turned away from Fascism. Neither was the speaker [H. H. Kuyper] talking about the Buchman movement, or about Barthian theses — the kind of talk which some younger members of the flock Christ has entrusted to us are offering us in their writings or in their first efforts at preaching, giving us reason to fear that they are threatening to drift away from the green pastures of God's Word.

No, he was talking about still others, whose ideas he did not mention specifically, people who, if you do not ask them what they mean by their terminology, may *appear* to be opposing what we all accept as our confession but of whom we can attest publicly that they have made important contributions, also of dogmatic significance, and that they harness all their energies to work out the idea of a Reformed university (one that fights the battle against a synthesis with unbelief all down the line), and that they expose the roots of the dangers of the Dutch Nazi movement, the Buchman movement, pietism, Methodism, and the drive to synthesis — and indeed, that they do more of this than many other brothers. Furthermore, it can be said of them that neither in the circle of our churches nor in the circle of those who exercise supervision over higher education has any complaint ever been brought against them. And I believe I can say of them that they, with great satisfaction, could make the very same declaration, *mutatis mutandis,* that Prof. Waterink gave us in his debate with Rev. H. Steen, if such a route should appear desirable to them.[51]

Finally, in regard to H. H. Kuyper's complaint that the ideas of Abraham Kuyper and Herman Bavinck were being surrendered, Schilder wrote:

> I ask again: By whom? I don't deny that some people are giving up those ideas. There are the people who follow the Dutch Nazi movement or the Christian Democratic Union. And then there are the few, some of whom have attained lofty positions, while others of their ilk are striving for them, who have been enchanted to some degree by Barth and Brunner. But as for the people clearly indicated by the speaker [H. H. Kuyper], I can't think of a single one to whom his comments apply.
>
> What I do know about them — and I am going by what they have written — is that they realize that the basic ideas of Kuyper and Bavinck are not finding much of an echo among certain of our people, and in the light of this situation they have decided to go back to those ideas, although they want to bring in certain corrections in the case of Dr. A. Kuyper, corrections that are needed in order to get back to the real Kuyper. Is that so strange? Does it count as "letting go of Kuyper"? And has he [H. H. Kuyper] not acknowledged at the outset that we have to go in such a direction?

---

[51] The debate in question had to do with the pluriformity of the church. —TRANS.

To the low point

I have quoted Schilder at some length here because it is apparent from this article published in *The Reformation* how the problem was being posed at that time. What we encounter here on the part of H. H. Kuyper is an incomprehensible blindness to what was going on in our church life. And the tragedy of his short-sightedness was this: on the one hand he wanted to fight to preserve the spiritual legacy of his father, while on the other hand he placed himself on the side of those who had long been busy shoving that legacy aside as worthless. And those who were discarding it did so largely because they wanted to follow Karl Barth instead of Kuyper. Yet H. H. Kuyper directed his accusations against the very people who, in faithfulness to the Word and the confessions, wanted to continue the genuinely reformational work of Abraham Kuyper and thereby safeguard his legacy!

H. H. Kuyper saw nothing of this. On the contrary, he himself did the very things he feared in others. Here I am thinking especially of the position he took in relation to the so-called Doleantie church order which his father had posited in such a pronounced way during the struggle for church reform, emphasizing the "autonomy of the local church" over against the hierarchy of major assemblies (see Appendix IV below). Via this emphasis, Kuyper Sr. had combatted the old sin that had often devastated the church, the sin that led to the Romanization of the early Christian churches and the denaturing of the churches of the Reformation era, thereby making the Secession and the Doleantie so bitterly necessary.

H. H. Kuyper saw nothing of this anymore, and there were others who were equally blind. What they did "see" was that only through the power of a governing hierarchical synod could a halt be called to the influence of those whom they, in their blindness, regarded as the agents of a "threatening deformation." And so the "claw of the beast"[52] began to come out of its sheath. Eventually, the unbelievable actually happened: the churches of the Secession and the Doleantie became deformed to the point that they followed in the footsteps of the church from which they had separated and turned into a hierarchical body, a body in which not false prophecy but true prophecy is always persecuted and cast out.

It would fall outside the framework of this book to narrate the utterly depressing church history of the years 1936 to 1944. A good

---

[52] This phrase is the title of a brochure in which Rev. J. S. Post of Axel, following in the footsteps of our fathers, criticized the ecclesiastical hierarchy.

deal has already been written about those events. What I want to say here in brief only serves to show what a low point the church of the LORD had reached in this time of national and ecclesiastical decline. When such decline takes place, the battle sinks to the level of a gray loss of propriety, accompanied by petty-mindedness, plots, and intrigues (which some people regard as diplomacy). In such a time, there is no longer any shadow of the conduct which the Sermon on the Mount requires of us. One can well imagine that a faithful child of the Lord like Schilder, who wanted to live and act in the spirit of the Sermon on the Mount, must often have felt discouraged by what was happening.

In the first place, there is the way in which the so-called differences of opinion got onto the synodical agenda, directly contrary to the written church order. A tactic borrowed from the world was used when it was suggested that there was "agitation among the people," which made it "urgent" that this matter be dealt with. There was already an unlawful power grab in the opening address at the synod, when Dr. B. Wielenga said: "But as soon as your gathering has been lawfully constituted, you are not just a combination of representatives but a corporation equipped by your King with *independent power* which, more than *any other authority,* determines the course of church history."

And then there was Hepp's series of brochures, which began coming out at the same time that the synod was meeting. Hepp published accusations without being specific as to what was said and who said it, and he opposed fellow members of the committee on which he served; he even opposed his colleagues on the faculty of the Free University, people among whom he moved day by day, without once discussing his objections with them. When Prof. Greijdanus declared that, because of what Hepp was doing, he could not continue to work with him on the committee (the one that was to deal with the "disputes over doctrine," which had started out being called "differences of opinion"), his stated motives were *kept a secret.* And then there was the strong possibility that "current opinion" would become the touchstone for testing teachings, whereas only the *confessions* of the Church could properly function in such a capacity.

Further, there was the fact that complaints about the teachings of Schilder were brought in by a committee that had two members who also served as curators of the seminary in Kampen, while a third served as an alternate curator. Those men were among the people who were responsible for supervising the instruction at the seminary, where Schilder was teaching dogmatics and philosophy, but they had never made a single comment about his teaching, to say nothing of telling him personally that they disapproved of what he taught. But now they suddenly put accusations against him on paper in the Acts of Synod, which meant that the people of the church were supposed to find out about it.

Schilder had enough of a sense of propriety to see the impossibility of serving as a judge in his own case and so he asked to be relieved of his role on the committee that was supposed to make a report about the matter of the "differences." But people did not understand his compunctions and pressed him not to withdraw. When I took up this topic with a lawyer who works with formal legal questions in the world outside the church and asked his opinion of this ecclesiastical due process, his answer was, "It's incomprehensible! Under due process in non-ecclesiastical court procedures, a judge who had earlier given written advice in a matter on which he must rule would be relentlessly challenged — it would be best if he would disqualify himself."

Moving ahead now to 1938 and 1939, which was not long before the world war plunged our country into the abyss, we see that nothing came of the complaints to the effect that Schilder had gone astray in his teachings. The whole business was eventually shelved. And Prof. Jan Ridderbos wrote to a delegate of Classis Appingedam that one reason why the Synod of Sneek decided not to publish the reports about this matter is that they contradicted one another. He wrote, literally, "Personally, I was all the more convinced that the publication of those documents would not do honor to our church, and that was for me a reason to propose not to publish them. Only the result should be served up: the rest of it could remain in the kitchen. Perhaps there was some dirty laundry in the picture as well."

The testimonies brought forward were not in agreement, then. That was the situation at the end of the 1930s. The petty-mindedness and finicky quibbling of 1938 and 1939 represents a low point in the life of our churches. It was reminiscent of what Abraham Kuyper had said in a devastating judgment about the end of the eighteenth century: "Squandering their strength and time in hair-splitting disputes over words and in magpie-chattering, lacking any awareness of a higher calling. Dwarfs who tried to pass themselves off as giants . . ."

In October of 1938, which was the beginning of a new publication year for *The Reformation,* "KS" wrote that the number of subscribers was again higher than it had been the year before. And he added that Hepp had noted in *Credo* that an announcement to this effect was made periodically in *The Reformation.* Schilder's answer: "He did not realize that it was only a response to 'periodic' assurances to the contrary — also from 'leaders' in personal conversations. If those myths would cease being repeated, our refutations would also cease." Many people indeed wished *The Reformation* would decline in readership, and so they whispered to one another that it was actually happening. But the contrary was the case, as the management of *The Reformation* can still prove today. The influence of Schilder continued to grow.

Also indicative of that influence was the fact that H. H. Kuyper warned against "glorifying persons" and worried about the possibility of "dictatorship." People understood well who it was that he had in mind. But from which side was "dictatorship" being exercised? Kuyper admonished the youth organizations not to allow speakers who thought along the lines of Schilder or Vollenhoven to address them, and even the consistories were advised to take measures of this sort. Schilder lamented: "There is only a deep feeling of shame about the things that are possible in the Reformed churches — and these things are being done by the very people who for years have drawn attention away from the *real issues* by complaining endlessly about the manner in which the polemicizing is being conducted."

Journey to the United States

At the end of 1938, just when narrow-mindedness was at its peak in Dutch ecclesiastical life, Schilder received an invitation to give some lectures in the United States. The Reformed people there had for decades followed the custom of inviting prominent figures from their fatherland to come over: Kuyper, Bavinck, Bouwman, Greijdanus, Hepp, Aalders, and many others had been there. Hence there was nothing unusual about "KS" also receiving such an invitation.

But then came the reactions in the Netherlands. H. H. Kuyper placed in *The Herald* an article which had originally appeared in the United States in *The Banner.* This article, written by H. J. Kuiper, the editor of *The Banner,* warned against Schilder. Kuiper feared that Schilder would bring the "differences of opinion" across the Atlantic with him and would cause new difficulties, especially in connection with the doctrine of "common grace," which had been the point at issue in 1924 when Rev. H. Hoeksema and some others were thrown out of the Christian Reformed Church. In taking this article over, H. H. Kuyper translated it in a tendentious way, sometimes introducing outright errors, and adding emphasis in places where it was not present in the original text. Prof. S. Greijdanus criticized H. H. Kuyper for doing this, after he had first called *The Banner* itself to order.

The controversy in the church papers in turn became the occasion for more clamor. Rev. S. O. Los sent a piece to *The Herald* in which he opposed the article that H. H. Kuyper had taken over from *The Banner*. Los wrote that he was familiar with the United States through a visit he had made there and therefore could state that *The Banner*'s "Not welcome" policy in relation to Schilder would sound most unamerican in the ears of the people there. American sensitivities have to be taken into account. Los summed up the American point of view in the following words: "The personal element in your battle about dogmatic questions leaves us cold. We do not say that we choose for Hepp or for Schilder; rather, we choose *both* Hepp and Schilder, in accordance with the rule 'Everything is yours.' We want to see argument placed over against argument, so that we can judge these differences in accordance with the rule that two or three prophets are to speak while the others judge. Prof. Hepp has been here, and we have heard him. Now we are glad to have Prof. Schilder come here as well so that we can meet him and listen to him."

Rev. Los also sent this piece to Schilder and invited him to place it. He did so, and added a note of his own: "I thank him for this. And I can assure our readers that my American travel program is very full and that there has been a reaction against the article in *The Banner,* a reaction which *I* have not unleashed and which is, for that very reason, all the more gratifying. It is also evident from *The Banner* that there is a circle of ministers who have decided to publicly oppose the wishes of the editor of *The Banner*."

Schilder was not exaggerating. Shortly after his journey to the United States I also made a trip there and visited virtually all of the places he had visited. In a word, I found that people there were enthusiastic about what he had to say, and also about Schilder as a person. He was an American among Americans. In that great, expansive country, he fit right in.

I heard amazing stories about him, stories that had *one* purpose — to show how much of an "American" he was. People remembered what it was like when certain other professors from the Netherlands had come over with their unamerican, unapproachable sense of dignity and self-importance, how they would wait calmly until the driver of the car in which they were being transported would open the door for them to get in or out. But Schilder made a game of it to try to get out of the car before the driver so that he would be able to open the door for his host, who was behind the wheel.

On one occasion, when Schilder was staying at the home of a minister, his host excused himself after the meal: he was going to assist his wife with the dishes since she had no help in the house. (This is not at all unusual in the United States.) When Schilder heard that, there was no keeping him out of the kitchen: his hostess provided him with an apron, and Schilder helped both of them with the dishes, and did a good job of it! That was Schilder as a person — he came, he saw, he conquered. He won the hearts of Americans.

Rev. Herman Hoeksema told me that at first he had been angry at Schilder because he had promised to speak in Hoeksema's churches (Protestant Reformed) but proceeded to spend his time speaking and preaching in Christian Reformed churches. Now, Schilder undertook to arrange a meeting between leaders of the two groups, which had parted company back in 1924 over the three points on common grace adopted that year by the Christian Reformed synod. When March 29, the day for this meeting in Grand Rapids, finally came, Hoeksema went there with some angry feelings because he felt Schilder had been neglecting him. Hoeksema tells what happened next: "When I entered the meeting room and encountered Schilder for the first time, he jumped up from his chair, extended both his hands to me, and came toward me with a broad smile on his face to bid me a most hearty welcome. At once all my anger fell away, and this man managed to disarm me through his friendliness alone."

When we consider what Schilder's warm greeting meant for Hoeksema, we must bear in mind that this was the first time since 1924 that he was meeting with his former colleagues from the church that had expelled him: they had never taken the trouble to seek him out since then. Thus there was a very tense relationship between those two groups of churches. That Schilder should go over to Hoeksema and greet him in such a way in the presence of all those Christian

Reformed dignitaries was a gesture that indeed "disarmed" Hoeksema.[53]

After Schilder had spent some weeks preaching in the United States and speaking virtually every evening, Rev. J. Weidenaar of Grand Rapids wrote in *The Watchman:*[54] "He has been zealous for the unity as well as the holiness of the Church . . ." Weidenaar had understood Schilder well. He also wrote: "By this point in time it no longer occurs to any of us to place a question mark behind the name of Dr. Schilder."

How busy Schilder was during the time he spent in western Michigan is apparent from the following notice in a local newspaper: "Prof. Dr. K. Schilder, one of the leading Dutch theologians, will speak in the Dutch language on January 22, 1939, in the Fourth Reformed Church on Ionia NW at Coldbrook, at 8:45. On Sunday afternoon, January 22, he will conduct a worship service in the Dutch language at the Eastern Avenue Christian Reformed Church. On Tuesday evening, January 24, 1939, at 7:45 P.M., he will speak in the Twelfth Street Christian Reformed Church on the topic 'Faith and Mysticism.' On Wednesday, January 25, 1939, at 7:45 P.M., he will speak in the First Protestant Reformed Church at the corner of Franklin and Fuller on the topic 'The Pluriformity of the Church.' On Thursday evening, January 26, 1939, he will speak at 7:45 P.M. in the Twelfth Street Christian Reformed Church on 'Christ in Biblical History.' On Friday evening, January 27, 1939, at 7:45 P.M., he will speak in the Berea Christian Reformed Church of Muskegon, Michigan, on 'Faith and Mysticism.' " We also read that Schilder was to conduct three worship services on Sunday, January 29.

---

[53] In his opening remarks at this meeting, Hoeksema paid tribute to Schilder's desire to promote the unity of the church: "The immediate occasion of this meeting of certain leaders of the Christian and Protestant Reformed Churches was, no doubt, the visit of Dr. K. Schilder among us. Now and then, also before the coming of the professor at Kampen, the sentiment was expressed that the difference between both churches was not sufficiently important or fundamental to justify their separate existence. Never, however, did this lead to any definite action. It was Dr. Schilder who in his lectures among us not only expressed the idea, but also urged, that both groups should seek one another anew, should try to arrange a conference at which the points which had caused their division would be discussed, and, if possible, once more live together under one ecclesiastical roof" ("The Reunion Idots," p. 5; see also p. 16). —TRANS.

[54] The real title of this periodical is *De Wachter*. It was published in Dutch by and for members of the Christian Reformed Church in North America and ceased publication in 1985. —TRANS.

Rev. Zwier wrote in a church paper: "The cloud created by misconceptions and incorrect suggestions and ungrounded accusations about the *real* situation is beginning to disappear." And that was how virtually everyone regarded Schilder's visit.

Just as in the Netherlands, people came strongly under the impression of his *preaching*. Here they saw him at his best. In *The Watchman,* Rev. Weidenaar wrote as follows about his preaching: "Sunday afternoon, for the first time, I heard Prof. Dr. K. Schilder. Or better: on Sunday I listened with rapt attention to Rev. K. Schilder. But what I would really like to say is that on Sunday afternoon, in the Eastern Avenue congregation, the Word was proclaimed by K. Schilder, V.D.M., that is Minister of the Divine Word." In these three sentences written by Rev. Weidenaar are represented the three stages through which the hearers of Schilder found themselves moving.

Weidenaar reports that the first thing to be noticed in the great crowd assembled that day was curiosity. Long before two o'clock, people began to stream into the church building. Shortly after two, there was no room left. Those who managed to get a seat congratulated themselves on having come on time. People looked around curiously to see whether this or that person was present. When Prof. Schilder, accompanied by the pastor of the church, Rev. W. P. van Wijk, went up to the front, it was quiet in that large, full building. After a short and pertinent introduction by Rev. van Wijk, Schilder took his place in the pulpit. By that point the curiosity had been replaced by expectation.

But first, during the prayer, the proper mood set in. The people understood at once that what counted here was not Prof. Dr. K. Schilder and people's curiosity about him. In his prayer Schilder struggled, and the people with him, through the power of the Spirit, to banish all ulterior motives and carnal thoughts from his own heart and the minds of the people assembled for worship.

And God heard that prayer. Through the simplicity and uprightness of His servant the people quickly came to the awareness that a congregation had gathered to hear what the Spirit was saying to the church. What mattered was not Dr. K. Schilder, but the word he spoke. That day the Word of God laid hold of the hearts of the people.

The text was Exodus 4:24, which deals with Moses, Zipporah, and the circumcision of their second son. Rev. Weidenaar seems to have understood very well what the Word is saying here, for he gives us the following report on this sermon: "Two mediators in the inn.

Chapter 2 — Woe to You, My People!

That covenant is rich, but it is also costly in terms of its obligations. Two parts in the covenant, as the baptism form teaches us . . ."

Other ministers were also enthusiastic about Schilder as a preacher and speaker. In *The Standard Bearer,* a minister wrote: "He fits in completely among our people!" and "Schilder conquers the hearts of our people" and "From everything it is apparent that he loves God's Word and the Reformed confessions and tries with all his gifts and powers to defend them against the attacks of the Evil One and his henchmen." About a sermon for which Schilder had chosen "Love: The Way of the Church" (I Cor. 12:31b) as his main thought, Dr. Henry Beets wrote: "This beautiful sermon has set our minds at rest about those rumors to the effect that Dr. Schilder would prove to be a divisive force through his presence among us and would drive our people even further apart; on the contrary, he functions like cement to bring and hold our people together."

Rev. Emo Van Halsema tells us that when Schilder conquered the hearts of those who were truly Reformed in the United States, it was not only through his speaking and preaching but also through his "smoking." In commenting on this matter, Van Halsema gives us an indirect indication of the excellent spirit surrounding Schilder at this time: "Here was a man with smoking power. While he was talking and enjoying a cup of coffee and the good-sized piece of cake that is traditional in this country, the Dutch Theological Master would smoke one 'Dutch Master' after the other.[55] And that really means something, for our American cigars are rather heavy-going in comparison to the light fare they smoke in the Netherlands. More than one Dutch smoker has given up halfway through after setting out to smoke an American cigar right down to its bitter end. Whoever may have fallen when enveloped by the smoke of this battlefield, it was not the man from the studio [i.e. Schilder]. He seems to be accustomed to this sort of thing."

Wherever Schilder went in the United States, the judgment was the same. One minister wrote in his paper: "If you ask our impression of the man and of what he had to say, we would note in the first place that this professor's appearance is ordinary and simple, and that he has nothing of the citified 'elegance' *(deftigs)* that we sometimes see in scholars from the Old Country (the Netherlands), or expect from

---

[55] Despite what its name suggests, the "Dutch Master" is an American brand of cigar, and not a Dutch import. —TRANS.

them." Another minister wrote: "I believe I am expressing the sentiment of all the ministers in this area, and also of hundreds of our people, when I say that Prof. Schilder's stay among us was a very pleasant visit. What he left behind is the impression of an eminent, brilliant Reformed theologian, and at the same time a humble — and therefore great — man of God . . . His stay among us has been a blessing for our church."

Rev. Hoeksema wrote in *The Standard Bearer:* "The reception received by Dr. Schilder in this center of Americanized Reformed people was much warmer than it appeared it would be at first, for it seemed that the notorious *Banner* article would do its work. Dates that had already been set for Dr. Schilder to speak were cancelled, and it appeared that the professor would not be very busy among us. But then the situation changed quickly. Especially after he preached to an overflowing crowd in the Eastern Avenue church, where hundreds of Protestant Reformed people heard him, and shortly thereafter gave a lecture in another overflowing church where the undersigned normally preaches, the professor's program quickly became full — somewhat too full, in my judgment. Four or five lectures in a week, and then conducting three services on Sunday, plus all kinds of meetings and conferences — who could keep that up in the long run?"

Hoeksema described his impressions of Schilder as a person in the following words: "If you give him your hand and say in the Dutch manner, 'Aangename kennismaking' (instead of our 'Pleased to meet you'), you are not disappointed later. Whether you agree with him or not, making his acquaintance *(kennismaking)* is and remains something pleasant *(aangenaam)*. You feel drawn to his personality. He could well be an American — and I do not mean an American in the sense of an 'uncircumcised Philistine.' He circulates in our midst with ease and seems to feel at home. And we quickly feel at home with him. He has nothing about him that we here in America would call 'put on' or 'hot air.' He does not have any affectations. He is hearty, generous, open, friendly, and lively in his dealings with people."

Hoeksema also honored him as a "peace-maker." Schilder took the initiative to arrange something that had not been possible since 1924: a meeting between representatives of the Christian Reformed and Protestant Reformed churches respectively. Hoeksema's gratitude for this initiative on Schilder's part comes through in his general estimate of his visit: "I am happy, and many are happy with me, that Dr. Schilder's trip to the United States went through. I wish he had been able to stay here a little longer." Instead of a *breaker* of the peace, which is what some people called him in the Netherlands, he came across to Americans as a *maker*.

Schilder spent some very pleasant months in the United States. His spirits revived. From the letters he sent to *The Reformation* while he was away, we became aware of a softening mood graced by subtle humor. He relaxed among all that free and easy, brotherly cordiality and affection — the great hospitality he encountered among the Reformed people in the United States. Finally he traveled back home on the steamer *Zaandam* and stepped back onto Dutch soil on April 24, 1939.

In his seventh (and last) travel report, which demonstrates strikingly his wonderful qualities as a language virtuoso and a fluent journalist, we read (among other things) this passage characterizing the United States: "Everywhere you encounter vivacity and a sportive character in contacts between people. If you have breathed American air for a while, you can finally begin to understand that an eight-year-old son of Van Halsema could write a letter to the President of the United States with a request to support the Netherlands in case it is attacked by Germany and could even get an official answer (I read it myself)."

In case the Netherlands is attacked . . .

The sky above Europe was growing darker. The promise of peace through the negotiations at Munich turned out to be a deceptive illusion. Chamberlain, the English prime minister, came back to London with his umbrella and a scrap of worthless paper from Hitler and was received with flaming enthusiasm. But it was not long before poor Poland was betrayed, overrun and divided between Moscow and Berlin.

In case the Netherlands is attacked by Germany . . . An eight-year-old boy in the United States was worried about this possibility and kept talking about it — but not the professors and ministers in the Netherlands, who kept up their campaign against Schilder and even intensified it while he was across the ocean on his American journey.

I think again of Ingwersen's book. Those day-trippers at the beach did not see the thunderclouds; they were not aware that the tide was coming in again. All they saw was their own little life, and they wanted nothing more than to safeguard their own existence, which seemed to be threatened only by that one trouble-maker, that polemicist, who was gaining more and more influence, even in the United States.

In case the Netherlands is attacked by Germany . . . The eight-year-old son of an American minister wrestled with this concern. But what certain people in the Netherlands were concerned about was the question: How will we maintain our place among the people? Such was the anxiety of those day-trippers in their beach chairs as they enjoyed the Solomonic rest and glory of the 1930s.

Not Reformed?

In the United States a minister allowed Schilder to read a letter which he had received from Prof. Hepp. Part of what Hepp had written was this: "Now, about Prof. Schilder. You asked whether I believe he is orthodox. Yes I believe he is, but I do not believe he is 'Reformed' *(Gereformeerd)*. But I believe you mean 'orthodox' in the sense of 'Reformed,' and then I do not believe he is wanted here."

This abominable, petty-minded scheming caused Schilder inexpressible pain. It also touched off an explosion of anger within him. There were two reasons for his anger. In the first place, he believed he was being attacked in his office. As a professor of dogmatics, he held a position of trust among our Reformed people and was charged with the task of instructing ministers who were to preach the Word. He was being dishonored in his office.

But he was also grieved *personally* to the very depths of his being. To suspect him of *not* being Reformed was one of the worst things that anyone could do to him, for the Reformed confessions were inexpressibly dear to him. In his commentary on the Heidelberg Catechism, he would later conclude a chapter with the hearty exclamation: "What a great joy it is to be Reformed!" And in his book on heaven we find a similar statement: "It is a great blessing to be *Reformed.*" [56]

When he celebrated his twenty-fifth anniversary of ordination to office in the Rotterdam-Delfshaven church in the summer of 1938, he made the following comment in a speech: "I must thank God that He led me out of the fellowship of the National Reformed *(Hervormd)* church in Kampen, in which I was baptized, and led me into the fellowship of the Reformed *(Gereformeerd)* churches, which are the churches I still love with all my soul and which, through God's grace,

---

[56] Entitled *Wat is de hemel?* second edition (Kok: Kampen, 1954), see p. 229.

still stand as a pillar and support of the truth in our country."[57] These were not cheap words coming out of Schilder's mouth. Something that one should not casually say of people could certainly be said of him: he would be willing to lay down his life for the Reformed *(Gereformeerd)* confessions. Therefore he was deeply wounded and felt as though he had been stabbed in the back when a "colleague" wrote about him: "I do not believe he is 'Reformed.'"

Hepp had already pronounced the sentence on Schilder back in 1939. His letter represented an ominous prognosis with regard to the events that would follow inexorably.

The Reformed churches and people in the United States received Schilder, despite the scheming in the Netherlands, and they were genuinely pleased to have him in their midst. They were reminded of what we read in Isaiah 52:7: "How lovely on the mountains are the feet of him who brings good news, who announces peace and brings good news of happiness." There had indeed been happiness, and the unanimous judgment was: there is no question mark behind Schilder's name anymore. This man is Reformed; he is one of us.

In 1947, when Schilder made his second journey to North America, all the churches there (with the exception of the small Hoeksema group) closed their doors hermetically to him. This was done on the order of the Christian Reformed "synodical committee," and the order was published in *The Banner,* which is the official paper of the Christian Reformed Church. Those actions were taken without paying any attention to Lord's Day 43 of the Heidelberg Catechism, which deals with the ninth commandment. Such slanderous conduct has had a poisonous effect, also in the Christian Reformed Church in North America.

This battler for Reformed truth, for the truth and purity of the churches of the Secession and the Doleantie, was forced into a position of isolation by people and churches also rooted in the Secession and the Doleantie. Schilder's isolation applied not just to the Netherlands but also to the Reformed people in North America.

Rev. Maarten Vreugdenhil wrote as follows about the controversy that surrounded Schilder's American journey: "How small-minded we are! The world is in the greatest upheaval, and we

---

[57] Here Schilder is alluding to I Timothy 3:15, where Paul speaks of "the church of the living God" as "the pillar and support of the truth." —TRANS.

Reformed people make life and the study of God's Word impossible for each other. How gracious the LORD is when He still blesses us despite all of this! Let's make sure we do not misuse His grace, for won't His great wrath be kindled against us if we do?" The Lord's response came on May 10, 1940, when Germany invaded the Netherlands.

In case the Netherlands is attacked by Germany... Well, the Netherlands *was* attacked. The tide came in, and all the beach chairs were knocked over. But dwarfs cannot be made into giants.

Could it be that the Lord used the beautiful American journey of 1939 to allow His faithful servant a short time of refreshment, a time of strengthening in soul and body, before he went into that dark tunnel as black as night, the tunnel of suffering, with the bitterest suffering for the sake of the Church he loved so deeply? Could it be that both Schilder's suffering and his American journey are to be understood in terms of God's unsearchable providence?

Chapter 3

Occupied Possession

May 1940

About seventy years after the birth of the Lord Jesus Christ, the Roman general Vespasian, who was soon to become the emperor, marched on Jerusalem with a large army, after he had first subjected all of northern Palestine to his control. His son Titus took charge of the attack on the mighty bulwarks of the "holy" city after Vespasian returned to Rome to be crowned emperor.

The situation within the walls of Jerusalem was perilous. In the city were thousands of people from all over the country because, in accordance with Jewish custom, it was the time for the celebration of the Passover. The Jewish people remained "pious" and "religious" after all that had happened, even though their fathers, some decades earlier, had attacked the Son of God, crying out before the pagan governor Pilate: "His blood be upon us and upon our children!"

That cry was now coming to fulfilment in the siege of Jerusalem. But in their blindness and foolishness, none of the Jews in the city realized that this was indeed so. Those who had seen it and believed had already fled far from the city, in accordance with the Savior's word of warning. They left Jerusalem and took refuge in the stronghold of Pella: from there the Church of the Lord would eventually spread far and wide.

The conditions in the city were frightful. Because so many thousands had come into the fortress, the supplies of food were quickly exhausted. The defenders on the wall had to remain strong, and so they received most of what was edible.

It was exactly in this period of time that the religious disputes and battles between the aristocrats and the Zealots in the city and in and around the temple flared up most fiercely. A historian describes the situation as follows: "The racially pure Israelites, with drawn swords stained with Jewish blood, stood on opposite sides of those doors, confronting each other over the world-shaking question whether only a Jerusalem native who had been appointed by a half-Jewish governor should be allowed to be the high priest, as opposed to a pious and simple priest who hailed from the country and who had been elected by the people." This historian also tells us that when Titus conquered the city and entered it, he encountered a "threeheaded monster that bit itself and rooted around in its own flesh." Another "party" had emerged on the scene. It was then that the "continual burnt offering" (see Daniel 11:31) was taken away, and the temple was totally destroyed after a Roman soldier tossed a burning torch through one of the windows.

Even while the enemy held the bloody sword to the throat of the people, internal debates and disputes between the theologizing aristocracy and the Zealots continued to rage. The historian concludes with this observation: "Such was the caricature that had been made of one of the highest religious feasts, just when world history was at the point of putting a complete end to the services in the Temple . . ."

On May 10, 1940, the Friday before Pentecost, Hitler's hordes, heavily armored and equipped with bombers, tanks, and cannons, crossed our borders. Behind this fearful German army came the even more feared Nazis whose assignment was to "Nazify" our country. In a mere matter of days, everything we had rejoiced over during the 1930s was taken away from us.

There was no House of Orange anymore: the Queen had gone into exile in England. We were no longer independent but were ruled from Berlin. We had lost our spiritual freedom: everything came under strict control, including the press, radio broadcasts, books and other writings, and even sermons, which were monitored carefully by Nazi hirelings. There were no political organizations or young people's societies. Before long there was persecution, and the Jews (there were more than 100,000 of them living peacefully in our hospitable country) began to be hauled away to the gas chambers. There were also a great many people deported to Germany to work for the war effort there. Hostages were taken. The prison doors swung open to receive our people, many of whom were tortured. Concentration camps were filled up, with sadistic bullies in charge. And then there was the hunger that made the entire country cry out in anguish, with its victims collapsing in the streets and on the roads. There was even a shortage of coffins for the countless dead.

In the first bloody week, the old, faithful, hard-working heart of Rotterdam was burned out by some sixty bombers flown by German vandals hardly twenty years old, who later declared that they had had a lot of fun watching Rotterdam burn below them. The heart was also cut out of the beautiful historical city of Middelburg. At the Grebbeberg Line, hundreds of our young men bled and died. And then the Netherlands could breathe again for a while: there came an end to the fighting and destruction.

On June 7, 1940, Prof. Schilder finally had an opportunity to address our people by way of his paper *The Reformation*. The first thing he did was to extend his hand to his accusers, who had been "disturbed" in the middle of their "synodical" work by the German bombers. He wrote: "Given the current circumstances, should the Reformed churches want to carry through their synodical program of 1939 from A to Z? Apart from a few quick matters, should they still try to deal with well-known differences of opinion by way of synodical channels? . . . As for me, if my advice should be asked, I would say: Bury all that material as quickly as possible. And I will immediately add that part of my reason for offering such advice is that I have said from the very beginning that the raising of this question back in 1936 was a serious mistake." That was a wise, peace-loving statement by this great man!

If only the synod had accepted this brotherly hand, extended so willingly and in the cause of peace! Schilder concluded this article, which he entitled "A Shield and My Reliance,"[1] with these words: "We lay the future of our church and our people, of our schools and our Christian societies, in God's hand. That the synod of Sneek of 1939 lost not only Dr. H. Kaajan, who died early in 1940, but also its president, places the current situation in an especially sorrowful setting. I, too, would want to remember the good that was given to our churches in the person of Rev. J. L. Schouten. He did not experience much of the conflagration of warfare — who knows what we may yet go through? When I was still in my first congregation back in 1914, very soon after my ordination, I led my first war prayer service and chose as my text Matthew 18:7. Who would have thought that in May of 1940 I would choose that text again? May that text remain in the minds of all of us, for it will keep us from hiding behind the mass of people and evading our individual responsibility."

The text to which Schilder referred reads as follows: "Woe to the world because of its stumbling blocks! For it is inevitable that stumbling blocks come; but woe to that man through whom the stumbling block comes!" This text applied to Hitler and his henchmen — but

---

[1] "Myn schild ende betrouwen," which is a phrase from the "Wilhelmus," the national anthem of the Netherlands. —TRANS.

also to those in the Church of the Lord through whom the stumbling block comes.

How many stumbling blocks the people of the Lord, the lowly along with the great, the sheep along with the lambs, would have been spared if the Reformed people and churches of the Netherlands had heeded this wise, God-fearing advice of Schilder and put an end to the petty quarreling, burying everything that had to do with the disputes before the war. But the greatness of soul needed for such a decision was not there.

On August 6, 1940, the synod was already in session again. The particular synods of North Holland and Gelderland both asked the general synod not to deal with the differences of opinion, but the synod decided not to accede to their request. It also decreed that the treatment of this matter was to take place "in strict secrecy."

While the pagan legions were breaking through the first, and then the second, and then the third wall around Jerusalem, while the battles were taking place in the temple square, fanatical Jews continued to fight against each other and stick swords and daggers into each other's bodies. There is in principle no difference between what happened in 70 A.D. in "Zion," where the LORD used to dwell, and what took place in the Reformed Netherlands in the years 1940 and 1941.

Our conduct during the occupation

During the 1930s we had used many big words. Two synods had taken up the question of the sort of discipline that was to be exercised toward those who were members of both the Reformed (*Gereformeerd*) churches and the Dutch Nazi movement. They could not be left undisturbed.

When the polemicizing was underway at full tilt, there were some who said it would be best to call an end to it so that we could "communally" attack "the Philistine." Well, after the dark days of May 1940, "the Philistine" stood on Dutch soil, and so we had more reason than ever to put an end to that wild hubbub in order to join together in resisting the Nazi poison being injected into our people in such a clever way.

What came of those great and bold words about Nazism spoken during the 1930s? I will quote what Rev. Hermanus Knoop wrote on July 31, 1945, a day to commemorate the liberation of the Netherlands from Nazi rule, about our poor record during the German occupation:

Chapter 3 — Occupied Possession

> The great and sorrowful tragedy of the leadership in Reformed (*Gereformeerd*) circles during the time of the occupation was that there soon took place a desertion on the part of the leaders — and on a major scale, at that. How our Reformed people yearned for leadership and looked to her leaders and awaited their words and deeds! But in vain, in the case of many of them, for they forsook their leadership positions, which they owed in part to the Reformed people, and went into hiding in deadly fear for their lives, or they collaborated and entered into a prudent arrangement with the enemies of God and His Word. They wanted to *save their lives*!
>
> And so our Reformed people had to struggle on their own with questions which the National Socialist occupying forces placed before them. They had been left in the lurch by so many of their leaders. That was the bitter experience of the time of occupation, an experience our people will never be able to forget. Is it any wonder that many of the sheep also began to stray? What good did *The Standard* do us? Or *The Herald*, which had become a German paper? Or *Credo*, whose editor-in-chief was so insolent that he tried to secure his own safety by declaring in public, without anyone asking him to do so, that he had freed himself from the decisions which the synod of 1936 had made against the Dutch Nazi movement? How our people grieved when A. A. van Schelven, another professor from the Free University, went over to our enemies with bag and baggage![2] Our people saw one leader after the other seeking refuge; now that their own lives were endangered, those leaders forgot that whoever seeks to save his life will lose it . . .[3]

Was Rev. Knoop using too many dark colors here as he sketched the situation? Was he exaggerating? We shall see.

Consider the remarkable change in attitude on the part of *The Herald*, which had been Abraham Kuyper's paper, once Germany and

---

[2] In the interests of what he understood as Dutch nationalism, Van Schelven joined a fascist organization and then made secret overtures to the Germans in hopes of having them appoint him rector of the Free University. He did not get his wish. —TRANS.

[3] See Knoop's introduction to *Occupied Possession,* a collection of articles which Schilder wrote and published during the occupation period. —TRANS.

the Dutch Nazi movement took control in our country. On February 4, 1940, some three months *before* the invasion, this paper still played up the heroic role of the small nation opposing Germany, when it quoted and praised an address given by Prof. Anema in the First Chamber of Parliament. In this address Anema pleaded for the Netherlands to give up her neutrality when tiny nations were overrun by a mighty nation eager for power. Prof. H. H. Kuyper wrote: "It would not be hard to demonstrate from our own history that Prof. Anema is completely correct in what he says. Calvin pleaded for something of this order, and our princes of the House of Orange put it into practice, for they never hesitated to apply this right of intervention when some nation was being oppressed by a tyrant."

On March 15, 1940, less than two months before the invasion, *The Herald* declared: "The demands Hitler is supposed to have made, i.e. to keep Bohemia and Poland permanently and to get back Germany's former colonies, while England, on the other hand, is supposed to give up Gibraltar, Malta, and Singapore, which guarantee its secure journey to, and possession of, India, are of the sort that could be made by a conqueror, but not by a nation that must yet win the decisive battle." A little later the editor of this paper wrote about "the secret plans of Hitler, which go far beyond what he has already managed to pull off, and which call for all the small states of Europe to be incorporated into Germany."

On May 6, 1940, H. H. Kuyper wrote: "May our people unite themselves all the more firmly in allegiance to our Queen and government. May they see to it that no traitors or spies are tolerated in our midst . . . ." But only a few weeks later, on May 26, after the German invasion had taken place, he wrote: "Our Queen, along with the Crown Princess and her small daughters, fled to England. It was not given to her, the Queen whom we loved as the Mother of our country, to play the heroic role earlier played by our princes of Orange in times when the greatest perils threatened our people, perils of the sort which caused the Father of our country [William of Orange] to say,

> *I bide the sight so pleasing*
> *Unto my princely heart:*
> *That when I death encounter*
> *I honour find therein*
> *And as a faithful warrior*
> *The eternal realm may win."*

Note his use of the past tense: "the Queen whom we *loved*." But note also the mistake made here in reference to Prince William of Orange. It is hard to accept that so keen a historian as H. H. Kuyper would have forgotten that William of Orange also fled on one occasion — to his castle Dillenburg, in order to be able to *continue* to offer resistance from there.[4] Moreover, Kuyper would also know that the "Wilhelmus" (the Dutch national anthem), of which he quoted a few lines here, was indeed a song which the poet Marnix put in William's mouth — but he had him recite these words at a very dark time in our national existence, a time when this prince was still far from being the prince who speaks to us in this song. He had yet to become the William of the "Wilhelmus."[5]

How graceful in the face of this gracelessness, how grand when contrasted with this pettiness, were Schilder's comments when he also addressed himself to the departure of Queen Wilhelmina and her house. In *The Reformation* he wrote:

> Those who listen to the Word in these days will be preserved from many a disastrous mistake. And the mistake of an overly hasty judgment is not the least of them. In this short period that has so perplexed us, how much evil has resulted from rash judgments! I think here especially of the ease with which some have condemned the departure from Dutch soil of Her Majesty the Queen and her ministers. Who knows the facts? Who knows what conclusions had to be drawn in the interests of maintaining Dutch sovereignty? Who knows to what extent the will of the one was bound by the will of another or of the Queen herself? *Let us not judge this matter prematurely*, and let us bear in mind that we know virtually nothing about the background of, or connections between, the various catastrophes that have come over us at such a distressing rate. If the citizen, even in normal times, regardless of the system of government, finds it impossible to make correct judgments regarding recent facts as they have been reported, how much more is caution called for when, on the same day that Rotterdam is on fire, we get pictures in the press of temple ruins in Asia, tender

---

[4] William of Orange (1533-1584), the hero of the Dutch revolt against Spanish tyranny, was a German nobleman who had his ancestral seat in Nassau-Dillenburg —TRANS.

[5] *Wilhelmus* is a German form of the name William. Kuyper quoted part of Stanza 9 which is here given in a translation by A. J. Barnouw. —TRANS.

blossoms in a garden, pretty birds in a zoo, and a bumper market of garden crops? The bond between the Netherlands and the House of Orange is too precious for improvisation even in days of peace, but especially in a time of war . . .

Here Schilder's judgment towered over the remarks that were typical of the press in general in the first days after the occupation began.

Note especially the first line I quoted: "Those who listen to the Word in these days . . ." That was the secret to Schilder's approach; it did not lie in any personal brilliance on the part of this faithful prophet. And here we also see how these events are related to the situation in the 1930s, for in the previous decade the very same starting point governed the battle he fought, the vision he presented, the convictions he expressed.

"Listen to the Word," which sheds light on all concrete situations. It was because Schilder remained faithful to that Word that he was able to write as he did after May of 1940, and that was also why he was completely vindicated in the later events which at that point still lay in our country's future.

His opponents during the 1930s did not let themselves be led by the Word and the confessions but relied instead on scholastic constructions, human speculation, and calculating diplomacy. After May of 1940, there was no conversion on their part, and so in their thinking and reflecting they continued to allow the overwhelming power of the facts to dominate them. In the affairs of both church and nation, they went on making mistakes and causing misfortune. They thought exclusively in terms of the facts and persisted in a worldly *Realpolitik*[6] in accordance with the wisdom of this age.

When Schilder asked himself what he must do as the editor of a church paper now that the German hordes had occupied our country, he did not have a hard time reaching a conclusion. But for those who preferred to hide out in bomb shelters and now wanted to forget about "wearing the uniform,"[7] there were problems enough.

---

[6] A "realistic" approach to political questions (often associated with figures like Bismarck and Machiavelli) without any trace of idealism or emphasis on transcendent principles. —TRANS.

[7] The author is here alluding to an article entitled "Out of the Bomb Shelter and Into Uniform," which Schilder wrote during this tense time and published in *The Reformation* on June 21, 1940. —TRANS.

Speak — or keep silent?

One of the most important questions which people began to discuss directly after the occupation was whether to speak out or keep silent. But this question was also stated in another form, one that is almost unbelievable, and yet real. There were some who asked: Is it *permissible* for us to speak now?

Prof. Hepp wrote in his paper *Credo*, which collapsed not long after this for lack of subscribers, about the "strong man." According to this professor, who in the 1930s had spotted so many manifestations of a "threatening deformation" and had dedicated his paper to "progressive Reformed life," the "strong man" was not the one who spoke and wrote (which was what was really needed now) but the one who "kept silent." Hepp explained: "Scripture says that the man who is in control of his own spirit is stronger than the one who captures a city.[8] Thanks to common grace, self-control is also to be found among non-Christians, even if it is scarcer among them. But the control over one's own spirit of which I speak here is a fruit of particular grace. People who have learned this holy act through the exercise of their faith are the ones we need especially in this time. Today we are looking for strong men. Here they are . . . ."

The writer of this most remarkable article certainly earned the unconditional right to be called a "strong man" during the frightening days when Germany overwhelmed our country. He became an example of the man who is the most eloquent of all because of his profound silence.

In sharp contrast to him stood his old opponent Schilder, who could once again be castigated under the heading of "threatening deformation." Now that the crisis involving the Germans was upon us, it was clear that Schilder did not manifest any of that "particular grace" of which Hepp spoke — indeed, he even trailed behind people on the terrain of "common grace," in whom this "fruit" of keeping silent was also to be found, even if it was rare among them. And so Hepp again found reason to point a finger of reproach at "KS."

The Herald took over Hepp's article spontaneously, and Rev. J. H. Telkamp reprinted it in the *Utrecht Church Messenger*. Rev. A. J. Bouma also found something that appealed to him in this line of talk about the amazing "strong man," this clever fiction concocted by

---

[8] He was referring to Proverbs 16:32: "He who is slow to anger is better than the mighty, and he who rules his spirit, than he who captures a city." —TRANS.

Hepp, the Amsterdam dogmatics professor. In the *Frisian Church Messenger*, Bouma offered this opinion: "We do not transgress any divine command when we conclude that it is a time to keep silent. After all, there is a time to speak and a time to remain silent. Solomon says that the man who rules his own spirit is stronger than the man who captures a city."

There is hardly an assertion anywhere that is so absurd that it does not find some enthusiastic disciples to take it over and propagate it. In addition to enjoying a "Scriptural seal," this posture of heroic silence also had the advantage of being useful. It appeared that utility and the Bible came together very nicely this time.

On September 15, 1940 (by which time Schilder was already prison), *The Herald* allowed the utility angle some open exposure: "There is good reason to issue this warning [about keeping silent] for otherwise our churches may get themselves into trouble needlessly. This applies especially to the servant of the Word. If, through careless words or actions, he should give occasion for the imposition of punitive measures, not only he but also the congregation he serves would be affected. The flock would be deprived of its shepherd."

How do you suppose those words struck the wives of ministers who, for the sake of conscience, did not observe this caution and therefore wound up in prisons or concentration camps? How did the wives of such ministers feel when they read those words? Were they encouraged by them?

On July 26 the *Calvinist Weekly* had already warned against the impulse to "seek martyrdom." But in the very same issue of this paper, which bore such a proud title, the press review department let a different sound be heard, for it quoted Dr. Brillenburg Wurth, who had written: "We have so long repeated: 'There is not a square inch of human life of which Christ the Sovereign does not say, Mine!'[9] It will now become apparent whether those words were meant in holy, deadly earnest."

On November 10, 1940, *The Herald* again warned all editors ofchurch papers to exercise caution. A number of church papers had already been forbidden to continue publishing, and so *The Herald* commented: "We may well point out that here lies an indication for the editors of our papers to exercise greater caution. When one of our

---

[9] Brillenburg Wurth, in turn, was quoting from Abraham Kuyper's famous address on sphere sovereignty, entitled *Souvereiniteit in eigen kring*: see p. 32 of the third printing (1930). —TRANS.

church papers just recently gave the advice not to keep silent but to speak, we saw what the consequences can be . . ." What were those consequences?

The actual developments have shown that the "strong men" who knew how to keep silent did not manage to save the papers they were publishing either. Only *The Herald* saw its silence and — what is even worse — its compliance with the orders of the occupying forces (I gave some examples above) rewarded to the point that it was allowed to keep publishing in its prewar format, using the same materials. It was the only paper that did not suffer under the heel of the occupying forces. Did it pay too high a price for its safety?

In addition to the question of being careful, there was also the exegetical question. Those who were on the side of the "strong men" sometimes quoted the text about being "shrewd as serpents and innocent as doves" (Matthew 10:16). But Rev. J. A. Vink, of the church of Berkel, brought out the proper meaning of this text when he wrote in his church paper:

> The word "shrewd" in Matthew 10:16 means that those who confess Jesus Christ and believe in His name and acknowledge Him as their Lord must be keenly aware of the situation in which they find themselves. They must be in their right mind and have the presence of mind to be able to see just what is going on around them. When a serpent is in danger, it does not easily let itself be fooled, for it is on the lookout in every direction. This is the shrewdness Jesus is talking about. The situation is that the Church community, made up of those who confess Christ, finds that it is surrounded on all sides by enemies.
>
> The Church finds herself facing temptations, and also opposition. She must now manifest the proper presence of mind and be on her guard. She must be on the lookout in all directions to see what is tempting her and what is opposing her. She must not allow herself to "get off track." Such is the "shrewdness" of the Church. She works out her shrewdness not by being passive but, on the contrary, by being active, in order to be able to persevere in faith when facing the dangers of temptation.

Rev. Vink also quoted Calvin on this point: "Christ makes it clear to His disciples that their caution and wisdom must be kept within certain bounds so that they do not forsake their duties because of great fear. All too often we see that people who wish to be cautious and circumspect wind up being fearful and slow to act."

Mr. H. Algra, the editor-in-chief of the *Frisian Daily*, came right out and declared that the silence of those who were supposed to be leaders of our people was sinful. He expressed himself very sharply about such "zwijgstras"[10] in a meditation on Philippians 1:12-14, where Paul writes as follows: "Now I want you to know, brethren, that my circumstances have turned out for the greater progress of the gospel, so that my imprisonment in the cause of Christ has become well-known throughout the whole praetorian guard and to everyone else, and that most of the brethren, trusting in the Lord because of my imprisonment, have far more courage to speak the word of God without fear."

This meditation, written when Prof. Schilder was arrested and imprisoned, was certainly intended to be read with a specific background situation in mind. Judge for yourself:

> Paul was in prison. That was grace, for he was put there because he had been a faithful servant of Jesus Christ. He knew that the proclamation of the gospel, as long as it was done faithfully, had to lead to a clash with the Roman and pagan state. For this pagan state demanded religious veneration for earthly powers. The crash simply had to come, and Paul knew it. Yet he persisted. And so he found himself in chains.
>
> He wrote to the congregation at Philippi about his imprisonment. They had already heard that Paul had been locked up. But Paul comforted them. Brothers, it does not matter. You are thinking that now I must keep silent. You are thinking that I, the man who loves to be active, am now doomed to do nothing — the battler who was busy day and night redeeming the time is now idle.
>
> No, congregation of Philippi, I am still proclaiming the gospel, for my presence in the praetorium is itself a

---

[10] Many people in Friesland, which was Algra's part of the Netherlands, have last names that end in "stra," while "zwijg" is the Dutch word for keeping silent. A rough equivalent in English would be McSilence. —TRANS.

proclamation. The officers and guards are not in a state of uncertainty regarding me. I have become publicly known as a captive for Christ's sake. Yes, but . . .

Such an arrest also has a preventive effect. Others are frightened because of it and resolve to keep silent. Fear will come over the congregation. They will say to their leaders: Woe is us! Be very careful and keep silent. Where are things headed? Before long we will have lost all our leaders.

No, brothers, do not worry. The effect of this arrest will be quite the opposite. Most of the brothers have become *bolder* through it. They are speaking up much more powerfully than they did before. It is as though they now realize that Paul used to be braver than they were. If they had been compared with him, they would have fallen far short. But in God's strength this will now change. Because persecution has come over the congregation, they find themselves able to be bold in a way that could lead, via martyrdom, to victory. And this can be said of the majority.

Yet there were still some cowards — Paul had to admit it. There are always a few of them. But something frightening is written about them in the Bible. In Revelation 21:8 we are given a list of those whose lot is the burning pool of fire and sulphur. Heading the list are the cowards!

Unfaithful to the Fatherland

The *Frisian Daily*'s editor-in-chief, like his counterpart at *The Reformation*, remained faithful right to the end. Instead of allowing his activities to be coordinated[11] with those of the Nazis, which was what *The Standard* ended up doing, the Frisian Daily ceased to publish. Better to put out no paper at all than to publish a paper using the antirevolutionary banner while serving up the lies of the Dutch Nazi movement and the German occupying forces! On January 23, 1941, the faithful editor of this paper put down his pen rather than get in-

---

[11] The author here uses the term "gelijkschakelen," which is the Dutch equivalent of the infamous Nazi word "gleichschalten." When this process was applied to organizations, they were swallowed up and made part of the Nazi state organization, maintaining no substantial independence in their objectives or operations. —TRANS.

volved in spiritual prostitution. He was not in favor of finding a pious meditation to place on the front page (preferably by a famous minister), which was what *The Standard* did, and then filling up the paper with lies and propaganda for principles which, if triumphant, would stamp out even world-flight pietism.

Why did the other papers not follow the example of the *Frisian Daily*? After May 14, 1940, there was nothing at all to be found in *The Herald* by way of warning against the spiritual dangers of National Socialism — in fact, one found the opposite. In the issue of September 15, 1940, *The Herald* rejoiced at the fact that "through the intervention of Italy and Germany, the injustice done to Hungary has largely been set right." The editor-in-chief offered "the Hungarian brothers heartfelt congratulations on this outcome of the negotiations and the arbitration award made by the Axis powers."[12]

In the issue of September 22, 1940, *The Herald* again expressed its gratitude to "the occupation authorities for the freedom they have promised for our religion and our churches — the freedom to come together in houses of prayer, to proclaim God's Word and administer the sacraments, to pray together, to take care of our poor, to do house visitation. We are left unhindered in all these activities."

This servile attitude is all the more repugnant when we bear in mind that by this point Prof. Schilder had already been stripped of his freedom and imprisoned in Arnhem for some weeks. In the issue of September 7, 1941, the editor-in-chief even went so far as to express his sympathy to Germany in its battle against communism, and he characterized England, our ally, as an "adulterous mistress" seeking Russia's favors. He wrote: "It is a reason for thankfulness that now, before it is too late, the battle is being undertaken not just in Germany but on the domestic front in virtually all the nations of Europe."

In an article of March 6, 1942, we read the following words in the context of a discussion of the war between the Dutch East Indies and Japan: "Not because Japan attacked our East Indies empire and we therefore felt called to defend ourselves but because our government[13] believed it had to make common cause with England and

---

[12] Hungary tried to maintain its independence from the Axis powers (Germany and Italy) but was enticed into a half-hearted cooperation in the early stages of World War II: the reward was to be a territory Hungary had lost in the aftermath of World War I. This country was of special interest to Christians in the Netherlands because of its substantial Reformed population, with which Dutch Reformed people had traditionally maintained many contacts. —TRANS.

[13] The reference here is to the Dutch government in exile, operating in London. —TRANS.

Chapter 3 — Occupied Possession 227

America . . . And then comes the following judgment: "The outcome of this world war will show whether the condemnation of our government for declining to stay out of this struggle was correct or not."

Here H. H. Kuyper was reasoning on the basis of pure opportunism. Principles of justice that led us to take the side of England and the United States played no role for him at all. This was nothing other than conformity to the world, and it came from the pen of the same man who, in the issue of February 4, 1940, had written: "To think only of your own safety and therefore not to take sides would surely not be a moral high point and would be in conflict with Christian thinking."

In the issue of December 1, 1940, he took up the question of the "Winter Help" program, which was the Dutch version of an initiative already underway in Germany under the same name. The purpose of this program was to pry money out of private pockets through intimidation, and to make propaganda about a seeming pose of "charity" and mercy on the part of godless people. In the Netherlands, fortunately, this program never caught on in the way the Dutch Nazi movement had hoped it would. Yet H. H. Kuyper wrote as follows about it: "The 'Winter Help' program which the Reich Commissioner has put in place to take up an extra collection for the coming winter, so that families that are impoverished or in need can be helped, is surely an action which, in itself, is to be applauded."

In an article of January 5, 1941, he appealed to the Synod of Emden (1571) and advised the churches to be careful in the matter of censuring members, for they might complain to the government, and then the church would be endangered. His conclusion: "We must think about the preservation of the Church."

It was quite clear what he had in mind. In 1936, the Synod of Amsterdam had declared: "There is no place for members of our Reformed churches in organizations which proceed from unscriptural errors, such as 'the leader-principle, the nationalistic and totalitarian power state, or the anti-militaristic rejection of warfare in any form,' while the members of the Church, 'for the sake of the Lord and His Word,' are admonished to keep themselves far removed from any such organizations. The consistories and other ecclesiastical assemblies are instructed to see to it that they keep away from anything of this sort; they are to bring people back from it with the power which they, as supervisors of the Church of Christ, have received from her King."

H. H. Kuyper's stand was all the more remarkable when we read what he wrote only a few years later about the "authority of synods" and the upholding of their decrees. But on that later occasion it was no longer a matter of deeply antichristian and thus unscriptural teachings; rather, it was a matter of pushing a brother who remained faithful to the very end into the deepest anguish of soul. If anyone makes comparisons here, he cannot help but be struck by the shrill dissonance of the lies that ran like cracks through the "Bell of Truth" — dissonants that finally drowned out the Truth. And so things went from bad to worse.

In an article published in *The Herald* on September 3, 1940, the government-in-exile in London (along with the various pre-war cabinets that had been led by Colijn) was criticized for not being active enough during the 1930s in combatting unemployment, which had become a cancerous wound under democratic governments. Now that the Germans were in control, the article went on to explain, this cancerous wound was eliminated at one stroke, and so "a foreign power had to come and solve this problem."

But in the issue of September 29, the editor had to back away from this position. Apparently his comments had proven too much for many of the readers of *The Herald* to swallow. He wrote an additional piece to explain what he was getting at and to "take away any offense that was given."

Now, just how the Germans put an end to our unemployment was something that hundreds of thousands of our men and boys found out the hard way, for they were sent to Germany to engage in forced labor. Some might say that Prof. H. H. Kuyper didn't know about this conscription of forced labor back in September of 1940. But he *could* have known if he had not been blinded by his desire to please the German occupying forces by what he wrote.

If Germany had no unemployment under the Hitler regime, it was only because people were busy making weapons. And that we *did* have unemployment was not the result of any passivity on the part of our government (no country worked as hard to combat unemployment as the Netherlands did) but was due to the fact that the enormous market on which the Netherlands was so dependent economically was closed to its goods. Germany did not allow anything across its borders. "Not butter but guns!" was the slogan.

I could go on like this for page after page, listing more and more frightening manifestations of servility. The shining glory that had once radiated from *The Herald* in its spirited service to the threefold office of prophet, priest, and king under Dr. Abraham Kuyper had been badly tarnished. It was not just silent about its principle — it even *denied* it.

How can this sad phenomenon be explained? It was not that the editor-in-chief did not have an adequate understanding of the spiritual danger to the Christian Church which National Socialism represented. When we read issues of *The Herald* published before May of 1940, we hear an entirely different sound. In the issue of September 3, 1939, this same editor declared sharply: "National Socialism may make it a slogan that we must stand for a positive Christianity, but its actual practice in Germany has made it abundantly clear how little one can build on this slogan." On September 17 he quoted with approval an article that had appeared in a North Holland church paper and went on to talk about "the work of carrying the Biblical message in the Third Reich, which people risk their lives to carry on. When we pray for righteousness and peace among the nations, we may not neglect to be mindful especially of the need in which the *Christian Church in Germany* now finds itself." (The emphasis in this quotation is H. H. Kuyper's own.)

But in the issues of *The Herald* published after May 14, 1940, there were quotations almost every week taken from the infamous (Dutch Nazi) Christian Press Bureau, under the directorship of Dr. van der Vaart Smit, quotations which tried to show that the German Nazis left the churches alone, and that the people in the Ukraine were very happy when the Germans came along and allowed them to open their churches again. Perhaps the saddest manifestation of all, was the striking about-face which *The Herald* executed in the matter of Rev. Niemöller.[14] On September 3, 1939, *The Herald* had printed a poem of Rev. Barkey Wolf, which is striking enough to be reproduced here (in English translation). The poem makes it apparent how *The Herald* thought at that time about the "friendly attitude" which the Nazis took toward churches that remained faithful.

Go forth, go forth, O man of God,
Serve out your dreary term.
And if your prison cell be dark,
The world is free and open.

---

[14] Rev. Martin Niemöller was a pastor in Germany and a prominent leader in the Confessing Church, which was a group of Protestants who resisted the Nazi treatment of the Jews and opposed other Nazi measures as well. He was harassed and arrested in 1937; he spent the war years in concentration camps. —TRANS.

Your credo, your confession,
Your prayer, uttered softly,
Is not blocked by any door
But breaks out of the prison.

And out at sea, where we still
Sail along in the mist,
Everyone now plays
The role of marconist.[15]

We listen . . . listen . . . listen for a long time.
We hear your words from afar.
And as we listen to your voice,
We go forth encouraged.

You say, Maintain your courage in the storm!
Face the wind! Fly the flag
At full mast! And in your heart
Is the certainty that God will win!

And so you are still a captain.
The Command is, Never turn back!
The church of Christ is your ship,
The chair in your cell is your bridge

So you have still reached your goal.
You have fulfilled the destiny of your youth:
You are and remain an officer,
One of God's commanders.

What did *The Herald* say about this poem when it printed it back in December of 1939? The following words: "Rev. A. G. Barkey Wolf, who feels great respect and warm sympathy for the German Confessing minister Martin Niemöller, long imprisoned for his faithfulness to the gospel, wrote the following poem, reproduced here with his permission." That was in 1939. But on June 8, 1941, when the same Nazis who held Rev. Niemöller in a concentration camp were in con-

---

[15] Niemöller had been a submarine captain during World Wax I. Marconi was the inventor of the radio. Niemöller, then, was sending out messages that were still being received by the "marconists" beyond the prison walls, whom he could not see. —TRANS.

trol in our country as well, with the result that ministers were already being murdered, while others were held in prisons inside and outside our country, the same man wrote: "There was even a report that Rev. Niemöller, the well-known minister who is glorified as a martyr of sorts because of his imprisonment, was planning to go over to the Roman Catholic Church."

"Glorified as a martyr of sorts . . ." Could it be that when Prof. H. H. Kuyper wrote those words, he was under the influence of a certain article that Van der Vaart Smit had written in a "religious" paper which he published on behalf of the Dutch Nazi movement? In that article entitled "The Niemöller Case Clarified Once Again," which appeared on April 30, 1941, he declared that Rev. Niemöller was being glorified as some sort of martyr. Did *The Herald* serve as a channel along which the poison dripping from the pen of Van der Vaart Smit made its way into the living rooms of our simple Reformed people during the war years?

In his writings in *The Herald*, Prof. Kuyper complained about "whisper campaigns." In the issue of March 29, 1942, he told his readers that there were reports that he had joined the Dutch Nazi movement, and he bemoaned the fact that such a report could find some credence. But was this really so strange when we consider the flagrant contrast between what the readers of *The Herald* found in their paper *before* May of 1940, and what they were asked to swallow *after* the Germans took control?

After the Netherlands was freed from German rule, the general synod of the Reformed churches judged it to be necessary to confer upon H. H. Kuyper, who had died during the last days of the war, a "posthumous restoration to honor."[16] It is my conviction that this son of the great Abraham Kuyper reflects much of the spirit of what I described earlier as the "Solomonic era." When people become "Solomonic," their concern is not for the Truth alone, or for belief in the Scriptures and faithfulness to the confessions; no, other factors play a major role for them, such as power positions and utilitarian considerations. A diplomatic game is begun as people seek to hang on

---

[16] H. H. Kuyper's son Willem was also much more open to the Nazi cause than one would expect: he joined a SS (*Schutz-Staffeln*) unit and died on the eastern front around Christmas of 1942 or January of 1943. Many of his countrymen made a similar choice for German military service by volunteering for the SS: see N. K. C. A. in 't Veld, *De SS en Nederland* (Amsterdam: Sijthoff, 1987). There is considerable debate about the actual numbers who joined: see pp. 404ff. —TRANS.

to positions they have attained. Then some people are very good at calculating instead of trusting in God. And some people are very good at calculation. H. H. Kuyper was certainly a diplomat. In his book *Hurray for Life*, Dr. J. J. Buskes writes:

> Moreover he [H. H. Kuyper] was very familiar with Dr. van der Vaart Smit. Kuyper was a slippery one, for he saw to it that the first announcement from the pulpit on October 27, 1940 (protesting measures which the Germans had taken against the Jews) was omitted in the Reformed (*Gereformeerd*) churches.[17]
>
> I had a lot of fun debating with Prof. Kuyper about the question of offering public prayers for the Queen. Before May of 1940 I had almost never — and this was wrong on my part — prayed for the Queen, for such prayer was almost always misinterpreted in Reformed circles. It was usually taken as a political testimony directed against the Reds (communists). But such a man as Prof. Kuyper had, before May of 1940, prayed every Sunday for "our beloved and revered Queen." In may of 1940, Prof. Kuyper stopped doing it, and I started. When the question of praying for the Queen came up at a meeting of the I.K.O.,[18] Prof. Kuyper said that it was by far the best to pray for the government without being any more specific, and that the Lord would know whom we had in mind. I replied somewhat sarcastically to my former teacher that the Lord would then also know at once what sorts of people were addressing Him. It was nothing short of disgusting . . .

Faithful to the Fatherland

It was indeed most distressing. But it was even more deplorable that the same sort of "diplomacy" had to play a role in the fierce battle against Prof. Schilder — and that these things were happening in a time when the nation was in an upheaval.

A few weeks after *The Reformation* began to appear again (once the horrible events of May, 1940, were behind us), Prof. Schilder

---

[17] This announcement was a protest on the part of the churches against measures the Nazis had instituted against the Jews. —TRANS.

[18] An organization for churches to consult together on matters relating to the government. —TRANS.

came to Goes for some discussions of business matters. I traveled with him on his journey back to the north. We were on an antiquated, ramshackle, little train (the good train stock had already been carted off to Germany), with rattling, drafty windows, and so an ordinary conversation was all but impossible. Yet I asked him whether he realized what the consequences would be if he continued to write in *The Reformation* in the same way as he had been doing during the past few weeks, and I reminded him that his paper had been on the blacklist in Germany for some years already. The response he gave me — without thinking the matter over first — was completely typical of him. He said: "I *have* to go on writing in this vein. We used some loaded words before the war, and the young people expect nothing other than that we will honor those words. Where else could they turn?"

For him that was the end of the matter. It was simply not a problem. In his faithfulness, he was blind to what might happen; he allowed himself to be led along in obedience. He did not hesitate for a moment. While we were on the train that day, I also said to him, "Professor, you realize what the consequences are, for the Germans will not let you continue to write in the long run." He replied, "Yes, I understand that. They will have to put an end to what I am doing, but I believe I *have* to do it."[19]

He knew that he had used "loaded words" back in the 1930s — heavily laden words that he directed toward the Church of the Lord. He had used them when speaking to the young people, and also when polemicizing. He had used such words whenever he was engaged in a conflict with people in any area of life. He had used such words because he saw how far the Church had sunk from the high ideals that had once been proclaimed during the "Davidic" era. How deeply disappointed he had been to hear the children of the covenant speaking half the time in the "language of Ashdod" when they were no longer able to speak the "language of Judah" (see Nehemiah 13:24).

Church . . . Office . . . Covenant . . . Grace . . . Calling . . . These words — and many others like them — had become worn-out clichés through the insipid writing and talking of the generation of epigones, who were impotent when it came to further elaboration and reformational development, and who, in their subjectivistic sterility,

---

[19] See N. Scheps, *Interviews over 25 jaar vrijmaking*, p. 28; see also *Gedenkt uw voorgangeren*, p. 67. —TRANS.

allowed Reformed life to sink away into formalism and flat bourgeois dullness. But this faithful prophet gave fresh outline and definition to these words; he made the deep meaning of such loaded words speak again to the heads and hearts and instincts of our Reformed people. That was why he and his followers had the ear of the people: the "little people" *(kleyne luyden)*, who still possessed the "Reformed instinct" of which Abraham Kuyper had spoken were listening to him.

This "Nehemiah" also accomplished a great deal in his prophetic office when he turned to forces and movements outside our circles. At once he saw through the antichristian philosophical foundations of National Socialism and warned our people against it. He even forced the Dutch Nazis to withdraw their notorious "third brochure."[20] In his brochure *Not One Square Inch,* he laid out the principles by which the Nazis and their followers in the Netherlands lived, and he proclaimed the calling of the Church in the face of this movement — a calling that did not just include the service of the Word but also disciplinary measures.

In the face of the Barthian theology that was busy infecting our students and theologians, he issued a timely warning and pointed to the disastrous consequences of dialectical theology for both the Church and the state. How necessary such warnings were! There were many students who needed to be warned, for they were caught up in the thinking of Barth and seemed to believe that Kuyper was obsolete.

With kingly, prophetic, and priestly faithfulness he struggled for the *unity of the Church.* I think of his brochure *Dr. A. Kuyper and "Neo-Calvinism" Condemned at Apeldoorn?* in which he defended Kuyper against an attack made by a professor at Apeldoorn named J. J. van der Schuit — while *The Herald* remained silent! In this brochure he polemicized in a gentle and principled way against the brothers in the seminary at Apeldoorn[21] and made a deep impression on the young people studying there, who finally began to understand something of what a *split in the church* really means.

---

[20] The brochure in question was published in January of 1933 by the (Dutch) National Socialist Movement. Its theme and title was *The National Socialist (Fascist) Doctrine of the State.* —TRANS.

[21] This seminary served the churches known in the Netherlands as "Christian Reformed." These churches stem from the Secession of 1834 but did *not* go along with the merger of 1892 between the Doleantie churches of Kuyper (dating back to the events of 1886) and the Secession churches. The corresponding federation of churches in North America is known as the Free Reformed Churches. —TRANS.

I think of his brochure *Our Mother*,[22] in the *Year of Our Lord 1935*, in which he struggled, together with all those who are close to us, to show something of the true unity of the Church and to lay bare the real sin in splitting the church. While there was much pious talking and praying about the "unity" of the church going on in many a congregation, Schilder showed by his deeds that he yearned for this unity, and he took upon his shoulders the giant burden of working toward it.

How clearly he recognized the dangers of a so-called Christian Press Bureau, with which some leaders who called themselves Reformed *(Gereformeerd)* cooperated right to the end, until Van der Vaart Smit was finally forced to drop his mask. And how beautifully he defended the Synod of Assen over against the direction represented by Dr. Geelkerken, as he warded off the attack on Assen in his brochure *Assen Overturned?* In the process he defended Kuyper with some powerful arguments.

Like a hero in full battle dress, he fought against all sorts of dangerous influences emanating from the spirit of the times as they bore on the Church, the state, social life, the press, scholarship, art, the school, and the family. If a historian one day does some research into the causes of the frightful decline in the spirit of our Reformed *(Gereformeerd)* life during the 1920s and 1930s, he will find a lot of valuable material for his story in the pages of *The Reformation,* for they constitute a written record of a tremendous struggle on the part of one giant who knew the times.

Honoring the past

Prof. Schilder had indeed spoken and written quite a number of "loaded words" before the war. But what was his attitude and position *after* May of 1940? Even the giant in Ibsen's drama hesitated for a moment when he had to choose between his child and his office, and so someone had to say to him, "I understand your words, but not your deeds." How did Schilder react?

I have already pointed to the spineless attitude in such papers as *The Herald.* How deeply ashamed we as Reformed people would have to be when recalling our lofty pretensions of earlier days if we indeed had no other testimony to place over against it.

---

[22] The title used here comes from Galatians 4:26, where we read: "But the Jerusalem above is free; she is our mother." —TRANS.

In the very first weeks of the occupation, right after we had been defeated on the field of battle by our enemy, it was most urgent that a manly call be issued, a call that would have the effect of neutralizing the poison that was already being injected into our national bloodstream. Our people lay there, bewildered and partly paralyzed, looking to see whether their leaders would speak a word of deliverance which the people could seize hold of as they tried to get to their feet.

It was a moment of great danger, for the very first public address by Seyss-Inquart[23] seemed much more hopeful than people had expected. The papers responded to it with gentle words and pledged "loyal cooperation in reconstruction." And so, in this moment of great danger, it appeared that our spiritual resistance to Nazi rule might be broken before any sort of concrete action was undertaken. Firm leadership was sorely needed at this moment. And it appeared.

Prof. Schilder wrote in the same way *after* the black days of May as he had done *before*. He gave the leadership that was so badly needed. Earlier I pointed to the manly statement he made about the Queen's departure to England, a statement that was diametrically opposed to what *The Herald* said about this matter.

How thankful our Reformed people were for what Schilder wrote! And how his writings contributed toward the purification of an atmosphere in which, even at the highest levels, things appeared murky! Against the background of comments about being "shrewd as serpents" and about the "power of the strong man who knows how to keep silent," Schilder soberly pointed out the way in an article published not long after the invasion:

> The Reformed pulpit has never "gotten involved in politics," but has only wanted to proclaim *principles* which are derived from God's Word. In this regard, let the pulpit calmly go its own way, sensing its responsibility to both God and man.
>
> "Know how to avoid giving offense." This word from Scripture, which rejects unreflective action when it comes to taking a principial attitude in church matters, must be placed alongside another word from Scripture which Peter

---

[23] Arthur Seyss-Inquart (1892-1946) was an Austrian Nazi whom the German occupying forces installed as the military governor of the Netherlands. His title was Reich Commissioner. He was eventually executed as a war criminal after being tried at Nuremberg. —TRANS.

introduces as a beatitude concerning suffering for *Christ's sake,* namely, that if someone must suffer, he should not undergo his suffering as a murderer or a thief or an evildoer or as one who busies himself with the affairs of others, and so forth. If someone suffers as a *Christian,* he must not be ashamed to glorify God in his suffering. For it is the time in which judgment begins with the household of God. Let each one remain *in his office,* and remain faithful *in* that office. And indeed remain *faithful.* Shrewdness and caution are not the same as servility.

Schilder then took a prophetic look at the future, at what awaited us in the ecclesiastical arena. With great tenderness he turned his mind to the Reformed churches of Rotterdam, and to the damage which the fire in Rotterdam had caused indirectly even to the theological school in Kampen.[24] He showed his concern for missionary work, and for the richly developed works of mercy, and for the many Christian organizations that could only live by way of freewill offerings. He thought of Christian periodicals and the church papers.

As he surveyed all these developments, he could easily have become afraid and discouraged. Yet he wrote:

> Nevertheless, A shield and my reliance, O God, Thou ever wert *(Mijn schild ende betrouwen / Zijt Gij, o God, mijn Heer.).*
> The current upheaval will not leave the church either empty or fruitless. It will have a purifying effect and will sift us. If the present interim circumstances, with our relatively great powerlessness in the way of principially thought-out reconstruction, persist for long, we will lose some fellow-travelers. But we will gain in depth what we lose in breadth. Don't we have promises to that effect?

Prof. Schilder was an example to all of us in prophetic, kingly, and priestly respects. He was aware of his "personal responsibility," and he faithfully carried out his office among us, even when the cir-

---

[24] The material devastation was so extensive that even the seminary in Kampen, which had many supporters in Rotterdam, would be financially affected. Moreover, the treasurer of the seminary, who kept many of its important records, lived in Rotterdam and saw his records go up in flames (see Schilder's *Occupied Possession,* p. 4). —TRANS.

cumstances were very difficult for him and when the "offenses" were great.

I think of a certain article which our people passed from hand to hand, an article which saved the situation for many of our churches and our young theologians, an article which was both moving and authoritative in its title, an article which can be regarded as a follow-up to the one I have just quoted, and which also appeals to our national anthem: "That I may stay a pious servant of Thine for aye."[25] In the first place, this article is a *prophetic* testimony written with an eye to Seyss-Inquart's decree of May 29, 1940. In the article Schilder said that it would be easiest to "look the other way"; that is to say, act as though we knew nothing about it. He went on:

> Writing is responsible work in a time like this. Keeping silent . . . is also responsible work. For others can be affected not just by the consequences of our writing or speaking, but also by the consequences of our remaining silent. If the shepherds speak in the *wrong way,* the sheep will bear the consequences, says Ezekiel. And if they do *not* speak, the sheep will also bear the consequences. This Ezekiel says as well. If the prophecy is false, the people are laid bare, but they face the same danger if there is *no prophecy* at all. And our poor people are already "exposed" enough.

Schilder then pointed to part of Seyss-Inquart's decree which stated that judges, public officials, and teachers at both public and private educational institutions would have to swear an oath to the effect that they would strictly obey the decrees and other regulations issued by the Reich Commissioner and by the various bodies subordinate to him, and also swear that they would refrain from any deed directed against German rule and the German army. He commented as follows:

> Swear an oath. The time may come, then, when many of "our" people will have an oath demanded of them. Then

---

[25] The previous article quoted "myn schild ende betrouwen" from the "Wilhelmus." This one quoted "Dat ik doch vroom mach blijven." Both are statements made by William ("Wilhelmus") of Orange, who "speaks" in this anthem. —TRANS.

they will *have* to open their mouths, knowing that not just the representatives of the *Führer* of the German Reich but also the angels of God and the congregation bought with Christ's blood, and Christ Himself, will be listening to hear *what* comes out of their mouths. And they will all listen to *what* is sworn. The situation will then become extraordinarily serious. It will all depend on the concrete content of the decrees, on whether the oath demanded of them, at whatever point, represents a denial of the one who has said, "But whoever shall deny Me before men, I will also deny him before My Father who is in heaven" (Matthew 10:33).

Schilder also addressed the question of the *kingly* office among our people, by writing:

And we hope first of all that *if* there *should* come conflicts of conscience, God the Lord will find us faithful. Our soldiers — we remember sadly the ones who were wounded and killed — have performed their stern duty. Their wives and children, brothers and sisters, friends and betrothed, have made a sacrifice for the cause of our Queen. They have had a hard time of it. *If* there should come conflicts of conscience, then it will be important to be reminded at the right time that we are *all* soldiers — soldiers of Christ our King.

A little further along Schilder wrote:

I believe I can say that our Dutch people, especially those who are Christians, are sufficiently disciplined to object to any rioting, to condemn all outrages, and to wish fervently that all armed resistance would end. There is no need to search for hidden weapons among our people who attend church. Our people will still have their desires for the future and will hope the day is not far away when the "Wilhelmus" is again sung before the balcony of the Royal Palace in The Hague. Yet they will not strive for this worthy objective through means that are dishonorable or unfaithful to the decision of General Winkelman.[26] Our people in the occupied territory will not take this hour into their own hands but will place it in God's hands. Insofar as they pray, they will want to see this hour "calmed with weapons," but the weapon they will think of is the one mentioned in Revelation 11, namely, the weapon of prayer. We know that others find prayer to be a dull weapon and will laugh at the idea. In any case, such people will regard this weapon as posing no threat whatsoever.

Our people will not provoke anyone either. They will not aggravate the oppositions that exist or make accusations where they have no factual knowledge, and they will not defy anyone, *not even those* of whom our prime minister, currently in residence elsewhere, has said in a radio broadcast that they have personally committed un-Dutch deeds.

But they will not allow themselves to deny their God. They will not preach every Sunday about the differences between National Socialist doctrine and Reformed doctrine, which are certainly deep enough. Yet when the occasion arises in the course of their ordinary work in office (e.g. when preaching on the first commandment as dealt with in the Heidelberg Catechism), they will not deliberately remain silent about those differences either. They will try to hold on to their young people — their *free* young people under the authority of their parents.

Insofar as they are antirevolutionary, they will not want to give up their view of authority and of the government as ruling by the grace of God, nor will they want to suspend the principial application of this doctrine in order to get along with people, for obedience to God comes before obedience to people. They will not try to provoke people or stir up feelings of hostility by dwelling on the relation between the mysticism of Jacob Böhme and the philosophies of Fichte and Hegel, on the one hand, and

---

[26] General Winkelman was the Dutch commander-in-chief who capitulated to the German invasion forces, after the German army overran the Netherlands, and ordered Dutch citizens to lay down their arms. The government that fled to London (along with the Queen) did not surrender political sovereignty and thus did not recognize the occupying German forces as the legitimate rulers. —TRANS.

the book of Alfred Rosenberg, on the other, a book that has already found a great many readers in Germany.[27] Yet if the question should come up or if circumstances should call for it, (e.g. if our booksellers should be forced to carry this book, or if we should lose our freedom in working with our young people), they will *not be silent* about those principial connections either, nor will they cease to reject a *doctrine* which we cannot accept. In other words, they will do no harm to members of the Dutch Nazi movement as *persons,* nor will they overlook the difference between what they did personally and what they did as part of the Dutch Nazi movement. But they will continue to condemn the doctrines of the Dutch Nazi movement. The *visible* weapons they will leave untouched, but not the *spiritual* weapons.

And they will suffer persecution rather than be unfaithful to their living God. They will also continue to pray for the Jews, and when Jews present themselves for baptism after being converted, they will not turn them away. They will declare that blood and race and soil are all subordinate to the Word and the Spirit.

After honoring the kingly office, Schilder went on to a powerful conclusion, in the form of a prayer, in which he pointed to the exercise of the *priestly office:*

> O Lord, Your Word is in eternity, and Your works praise You. You have gathered a people here that on many occasions and in many ways has said much good about You. O Lord, do not let those words now come down upon their heads. The sons of a Reich which in recent years has sometimes favored a *doctrine* that goes against Your Word pass by our house. They may also desire to come in. Among those sons are some who confess Your Name. Do not let our oaths or theirs, when we gather together, turn against You. Vindicate us, O Lord, vindicate

---

[27] Alfred Rosenberg (1893-1946) was the chief ideologist of Nazism. The book referred to is *The Myth of the Twentieth Century* (1934), which is an exposition of the Nazi position on race. Rosenberg was eventually tried as a war criminal at Nuremberg and executed. — TRANS.

us.[28] In whatever is to come, glorify *Your* Name, for that is the purpose for which we have come to this hour, Father. And let us seek the good also for Germany, the only good, which is truly confessing Your Name and the name of Jesus Christ, our supreme Leader[29] and Archeeg and King. And let us seek the good for our own defeated people so that they will not feel even more defeated and scattered through our silence.

Preserve us, Father, from treason committed against You. Preserve those who crossed our borders — for how long? Preserve them against that which would hinder our prayers and against that which would subject our conscience, which is made free in Christ, to a service that is *not* of Christ and is not compatible with the service of Christ. Preserve our children so that those among them who have fallen in battle will not come to be envied as the ones who were taken away before the evil day arrived.

Lord, let us live, *live.* Let us live with a free conscience. And take away our sins, for they are great — our sins of speaking and *no less of remaining silent.* And bless our Sovereign, our Queen Wilhelmina and her House, and give us peace in Europe, and make us believe firmly that the peace which You proclaimed in the fields of Bethlehem Ephrathah is already here. And bind us to Your Word. Amen.

A Reformed church paper published for North Brabant and Limburg reprinted this prayer and added the comment: "Blessed is the church that still has such intercessors. And let all the people say, Amen, yes, Amen."

Rev. H. A. Wiersinga reprinted Schilder's article in the *Leiden Church Messenger* and added the following comment: "I do not understand why the following article is not reprinted in all our Christian dailies in boldface type; in any case, not one of our church papers should neglect to reprint it." He also wrote: "If there is one person who gives leadership, it is Prof. Schilder in *The Reformation* . . . The

---

[28] Here Schilder echoes the language of Psalm 26: "Vindicate me, O LORD, for I have walked in my integrity; and I have trusted in the LORD without wavering." —TRANS.

[29] Schilder uses *two* terms for leader here: *Leidsman* and *Leider.* Thereby he is emphasizing that for a Christian, Hitler cannot be recognized as the supreme Leader (*Führer*). —TRANS.

things he writes about the current conditions and our principal attitude in this time give our people something to hold on to. And so we can continue to speak about the meaning of the Christian press in our national life — in no other way. Such words are of much greater benefit to our people than what many other newspapers and church papers have written. This man is loyal because he reckons only with the Word of God." Such loud, spontaneous "Hosannas" also came from the lips of the very people who, four years later, were to cry out: "Crucify him!"

A clarion call

To many of our people, this faithful statement from Prof. Schilder was a clarion call. Various ministers saw the way clearly again; both from the pulpit and in their church papers they spoke faithfully in the manner that was expected of them as leaders. Some of them remained faithful right to the end — winding up in a prison cell or even dying a martyr's death.

And *The Reformation* did not restrict itself to a single trumpet call: This article was followed by others like it. For example, there was one entitled "Out of the Bomb Shelter and Into the Uniform," in which Schilder declared that "the one hour of catastrophe is not the very worst thing of all. After that hour comes the real danger — the danger of the gradual disarming of the spirit, the gradual psychical and spiritual infection of our people, as we get used to the idea that although we can leave the bomb shelters that protected us from shrapnel, still, because of the uncertainty in the political atmosphere, we would do well to buy tickets to a spiritual bomb shelter, tickets good for an indefinite time until — who knows? — the storm has passed."

Then there followed an article on our *legal position,* in which the question of "lawful government" was posed keenly. It was followed by an article in which Schilder warned against making our national life "corporate." One example of what he was talking about was the establishment of a "corporate press agency." This was to be a "newly built organization through which the Dutch press would be able to fulfill its task of enlightening the people to the fullest extent." This organization would "embrace the entire press corporately and, in its public legal competence, would give leadership in a 'folkish' sense."

The word "folkish" was enough to get Schilder going. He wrote: "The National Press Bureau (which passed on the news) is violating our beautiful Dutch language here: Germanisms ('folkish') do not belong in our language any more than Gallicisms." He also observed: "We talk about these things now, for we may not do otherwise. It is necessary to be ready: any 'press person' who today merely waits to see what will happen will be too late when, on some subsequent occasion, he joins our Christian people in a chorus of complaints about the battle that has been going on here, a battle with Dutchmen on both sides, with a small group helping to exclude a large majority."

Schilder went on to show that the issue here was not an incidental case but a spiritual manifestation of National Socialism. He appealed to a study by Prof. A. Anema, entitled "The Foundation and Character of the Italian-Fascist Theory of the State." In his criticism of the corporate state, he also drew on a study which Dr. J. W. Noteboom had written in a journal of the Antirevolutionary Party. Here was an appeal to the principles which our people had learned, the principles which had sustained and maintained the foundations of our Calvinistic national life.

At the end of this article, in which Schilder called people to exercise the authority of their kingly office, he wrote: "Let our Christian papers speak, for God's sake. Let us hold meetings — the National Socialists do it. Let us carry our cross in public (so that people will at least be able to see us) rather than remain silent. And let us not forget what Prof. Diepenhorst once wrote: 'The error made by large groups of (German) Christians is that they accepted the idea [of the totalitarian state] on the assumption that it would not be applied to the church and spiritual life. They wanted to both swim and remain dry. Not even the best Dutch swimmer could manage that.'"

In a subsequent article he warned against a circular that had been issued by the National Dutch Federation (an organization that sprang up during the occupation) about centralization in cultural life. This centralization represented a new attempt to take over private societies. Schilder pointed to the dangers involved in allowing our youth organizations to be "coordinated" *(gleichschalten)* and made part of the new order: "According to their principle, they *cannot* allow themselves to be centralized or coordinated or incorporated into an organization, even if that organization should (provisionally) call itself a 'federation' — federative as long as is necessary! Moreover, 'federative' comes from the Latin word 'foedus,' which means covenant. A federative organization, then, always remains a covenant organization. And what foundation can there be for a covenant between Jerusalem and Athens, between Christ and Antichrist, between God and Belial?"

Next, Schilder published a broadly conceived article in which he settled accounts definitively with the former Reformed *(Gereformeerd)* minister Dr. H. W. van der Vaart Smit, the man of the "Christian Press Bureau." The article was entitled "The Sorrows of a Reformed Minister." Van der Vaart Smit, who openly sided with the Dutch Nazi movement, had sent an "information kit" to the press (dated June 21, 1940) in which he maintained that it was abundantly clear by now that German military might had won the war. By this point, he maintained, the power of Germany and Italy was so overwhelming that the war's final outcome could easily be foreseen. The renegade then made the following application:

> I am not asking whether everyone finds this prospect pleasant or stands ready to embrace the new view of the world. I can well imagine that people of firm character, who all their lives have felt bound to a certain political outlook, do not now consider crawling out of their old skin in order to reappear within a couple of weeks in a new skin. That would not get them much respect; rather, people would despise them for it. An honest person cannot do such a thing, even if he might want to!
>
> But this does not take away from the great fact that the future — once we acknowledge that Central Europe is not able to lose the war at this point — will be determined by National Socialism and Fascism, and that every Dutchman living in the Netherlands must take account of this, whether willingly or under the press of circumstances.

The conclusion offered by Van der Vaart Smit was this:

> I believe there is much to be said for taking a positive attitude and cooperating in a positive spirit. Given what was said above, such an attitude must be seen as the way — indeed, the only way — to the freedom which the German Reich Commissioner has promised our country and people. Many will have a hard time with this. But we must reckon with the fact that things have changed. And then we have to look at what is before us, relying on the sober realism that has always characterized our people.

Prof. Schilder posed a question for this man:

> What would Dr. H. W. van der Vaart Smit say if English propaganda sent the following message to the subjects of the German Reich? "There are so many Russian tanks on your eastern border that once the skies there turn 'sorrowfully red,' you must give up your attempts to block *Bolshevism,* the Russian *doctrine.*" And what if a German citizen or some German Peacock should declare: "We must swallow this line like candy — because of the realism that has always characterized our people"?
>
> I think someone who talked that way would simply be called a traitor. I think that if a pastor in Germany said, "In case a Russian victory appears *probable,* do not resist Bolshevism any longer but cooperate positively," he would soon find that he had to leave his house!
>
> Let us not look to the hidden things and base our conduct upon them, but let us be guided by *the Word,* by what has been revealed! Thus also the confessions, which are even the confessions of this minister, whom one can telephone at Koninginnegracht 70.[30]
>
> But here — O shame! — the "conduct" prescribed for us is based on *calculations of what is probable!* Germany is going to win. Anyone who does not change his tune will be annihilated.
>
> Well, better to be annihilated for the sake of faithfulness to our confession, Dr. van der Vaart Smit, than to be spared by the grace of Koninginnegracht 70.

In a subsequent article Schilder quoted from a German newspaper (the July 4, 1940, issue of the *Frankfurter Zeitung)* which published an article about the legal foundation for German rule in the occupied territories. He declared that the German military forces in the Netherlands would have to observe strictly the provisions of international law which were agreed on at the Convention of The Hague (1907) and were signed by Germany. (Nothing came of "strictly observing" those provisions, but at that point the German press still wanted to make the German people think that German rule in the occupied territories was humane and cultivated.) Schilder observed:

---

[30] This was the address of Van der Vaart Smit's Christian Press Bureau.

Chapter 3 — Occupied Possession 247

> I have written repeatedly about the legal position of our people so that, in addition to maintaining a correct stance with regard to the occupying power, we can know exactly what our attitude must be over against that small group of Dutchmen who are now misusing this difficult situation in order to do harm to the church, to the family, and to religious convictions in the interests of their own theories — theories we must reject on the basis of our faith. We believe that we are called to this attitude for the Lord's sake, and that we would not be doing right by the Lord and by our people and churches if we neglected to assume this attitude.

And to the Dutch press Schilder said:

> Do not take a single step to meet these gentlemen halfway, and be especially careful not to let yourselves be intimidated. We want to respect the German army and to conduct ourselves correctly. But those Dutchmen who conduct themselves incorrectly [the members of the Dutch Nazi movement — RvR] must be kept at arm's length. And we have the right to keep them at arm's length, as the domestic edition of the *Frankfurter Zeitung* implies. What we want is for Dutchmen who think otherwise than we do to leave our religion alone and not to hinder the cause of Christ in our lands by their semi-official acts and their influence on the press.

On a later occasion he issued a warning to our university students, whom the Nazis were trying to take over and incorporate into the new order *(gleichschalten)*. On yet another occasion he raised a finger of warning against those who were inclined to join the newly established "Netherlandic Union," which was led by three men who themselves were fairly well regarded and who believed that the new organization could serve as a counterweight to the ever growing disastrous influence of the Dutch Nazi movement. This organization wanted to get rid of political differences and debate. Schilder judged this element of its program to be out of the question, and argued: "From a religious standpoint this desire is unacceptable; we have been too long in the school of Groen and Kuyper to embrace such a thing."

Schilder also regarded it as an insuperable obstacle to cooperation that his countrymen were not supposed to express the wish that the House of Orange would return one day and that the country would get its independence back.

Meanwhile, he was bold in attacking the follies of the Dutch Nazi movement. Among the many brochures with which the newsstands at the train stations were flooded, all of them serving the cause of German and Dutch Nazi propaganda, there was one which had been translated from French and was attributed to a certain "Michel Nostradamus." Its title was *How Will the War End? An Important and Contemporary Reflection Based on the Prophecies of Michel Nostradamus.* The unusual thing about this brochure was that it had been sent out to all the press, accompanied with some words of commentary stemming from the "Council for Enlightenment of the Dutch Press." The editors of the paper were encouraged to reprint the commentary which this Council included. This was the mode of operation that had been adopted by this "Council for Enlightenment," which was of course made up of members of the Dutch Nazi movement. And so it was official and in good order.

In this brochure, the author (who had lived in the seventeenth century) prophesied back in 1688 how the war of 1940 would end. In physical appearance the brochure was a very attractive publication. Hundreds of copies had been printed on hand-made old Dutch paper, with a bleached vellum cover, and the title was printed in red letters. It could hardly be any more antique or authentic in appearance! Thus this little publication became a popular item that was much sought after.

What was the truth of the matter? This "Nostradamus" read the history of peoples and great personalities in the stars! He had also read the destiny of Germany and of England in the stars, and had prophesied that in 1939 a war would begin in which England would be defeated, with Germany emerging as the victor.

Meanwhile, all sorts of his prophecies about times that had already passed had not been fulfilled — but then, one should not take every prophecy literally! But the most amusing thing about this whole case was that Prof. Schilder discovered that this famous astrologer was a Jew! And he proceeded to make fun of his enemies, just as Elijah had once made fun of the priests of Baal: "Erect a statue for this Parisian Jew, and let Mr. Goedewagen lay a wreath before it, and let Mr. Rost van Tonningen deliver a stirring address. 'Let the best man of the people be placed in the front rank,' he said not long ago." Schilder then continued: "My friends, laugh and cry. Laugh at all the nonsense. And cry for the Dutch press, which is as silent as a mouse when a pair of gentlemen enlighten the press and, like sharpshooters, try to clean up the press street, threatening that any and all who refuse to dance to their tune will receive punishment and still more punishment. When will our papers again get around to speaking the truth to such countrymen of ours who disparage the Jews and do not even realize that they are importing a Jew in these days when Mr. Mussert acts as though he is very important?"[31]

The result was that the Nostradamus brochure disappeared without a trace from the Nazi propaganda stable. It appeared that our people would not so easily surrender to the foolishness of superstition as the German people had done.

Edgar Ansel Mowrer, an American who lived for many years in Germany, has said the following about the German people: "To the outside world Germany is the land of organized scholarship. But it is also the land of arch-superstition. The German people are rich in intellect but impoverished when it comes to healthy judgment. They radiate intelligence, but there are many minds among them which are open to cosmic darkness." Hitler's belief that his destiny was "written in the stars" was the belief of the German people. A book by Dr. F. Schwab entitled *Stars and the Fatherland,* in which he tells us with full earnestness what the destiny of Europe will be in the coming years, had a great deal of influence in Germany.

Imprisoned

It the meantime it had become clear that the Dutch Nazis, with Dr. van der Vaart Smit leading the parade, would not sit still. They passed up no opportunity to try to muzzle Prof. Schilder. But they could not get at him with weapons of the kind he was using: they lacked the wit and intelligence, the sense of truth and feeling for just procedure to do so. They would have to seek a solution by the raw use of power. And with the German sword now on their side, they had an easy time of it. What hollow victories they won!

For two and a half months Prof. Schilder had enlightened our Reformed people week after week, without fear or favor. Never did

---

[31] What Schilder is alluding to here is the disappointment of Anton Mussert, the leader of the Dutch Nazi party, at not receiving a more prominent role in his country's affairs once the Germans had moved in. —TRANS.

he take back what he had written about National Socialism in 1936 in *Not One Square Inch*. In the issue of *The Reformation* dated August 16, 1940, Schilder wrote a principial article about Dr. Colijn's recent brochure entitled *On the Border Between Two Worlds*. That article ended with the following words, written in a style that was so typical for Schilder: "Only God knows whether *they* [the Dutch Nazis] will be able to seize *'power'* here, using their means. But we know that *we* will retain the 'authority.' Fortunately, *power* and *authority* are not the same thing. Ultimately, the Antichrist will have the *power,* and the Church will still have *authority.* And then will come the day of the great harvest. Come, Lord Harvester, yes, come quickly, come over the Channel and the Brenner Pass, come via Malta and Japan, yes, come from the ends of the earth, and bring Your pruning knife along, and be gracious to Your people. Your people do possess authority, but only from You, from You alone, for Your eternal good pleasure."

When we read these loving words, it is as though we hear the threefold office woven into one, as Schilder wrestled for the right of the Church. In these words the prophetic, kingly, and priestly offices spoke a single language, in which priestly intercession is ultimately dominant, in which the loving heart, overflowing with cares, ultimately pours itself out before God's throne and pleads for grace for the people. Anyone who prays in such a way must be overflowing with love.

But this prayer also remains bound to the Word. It is not a prayer in which human arbitrariness and human desire reveal themselves apart from the Word. It is not a prayer in which God is told how He must solve the appalling world crisis. It is a prayer according to the Word, a prayer prescribed by the Word, a prayer for the great Parousia, the return of the Lord, and so it is ultimately a repetition of the prayer which the Word of God lays upon the lips of the Church at the end of the book of Revelation: "Lord Jesus, come quickly!"

Every Christian who read this prayer understood at once that it came straight from the Bible. Van der Vaart Smit, who had once been a student at the Free University, could not have overlooked its Biblical inspiration either. All the same, that very week Prof. Schilder was arrested. German police hauled him away from his home, giving him the impression that he was to come to Arnhem for just a little while and then would be allowed to go home. But that was not how it turned out. He remained locked in a cell until the middle of December, with no more than a half-hour hearing, for the sake of appearance. Nor was he ever convicted of any offense. Such was "German justice." And that same week, *The Reformation* was seized: further publication was forbidden.

There were only a few papers that had the courage to do as much as mention the silencing of Schilder and *The Reformation*. Prof. K. Dijk was one of those who dared to say something. In *The Trumpet* he wrote:

> For those who follow events intensely *(meeleven)*, it will not be a secret by this point what has happened to our highly esteemed and beloved Prof. Schilder. The authorities regarded it as necessary to take him away from his family and his work; he went as a "brave Christian" who has fought with a free and good conscience for his heavenly King. I am not allowed to put down my judgment regarding this arrest, but I cannot refrain from expressing my inward sympathy and concern for this brave battler and his family, who may be assured of the heartfelt sympathy of all our people and of the continuing prayers of all who know the open way to God's throne of grace . . .
>
> "That I may stay a pious servant." In these last days I reread that powerful article by my colleague. A deeply moved soul speaks in it, and a strong childlike faith glories in the Lord. In communion with that faith we think of him whose mouth may no longer speak and whose pen is doomed to idleness. It will be a severe test for him, but one in which he may yet taste the great grace of Him who confirms His Word to our brother: "If you are reviled for the name of Christ, you are blessed, because the spirit of glory and of God rests upon you" (I Peter 4:14). To them He is being slandered, but to you He is being glorified.

Prof. Dijk used some loaded words here. It was the time for shouting "Hosanna!" Yet when cries of "Crucify him!" went up only a few years later, the voice of this professor was also heard in the cacophanous choir. If only Prof. Dijk, before the synodical session of March, 1944, had taken the trouble to reread that article entitled "That I may stay a pious servant"! Wouldn't he then have wondered whether the stirring words he wrote at the conclusion of his article in *The Trumpet* ("To them He is being slandered, but to you He is being glorified") might not be applicable to a Reformed synod as well as to Dutch Nazis and renegades?

The pettiness and small-mindedness that pervaded the synod of 1944 apparently also hindered this colleague from asking the question whether the "faithfulness" of Prof. Schilder, which he praised so highly in the year 1940, when Schilder was defending our holy principles and proclaiming them to the world out there, might not have sprung from the same source and had exactly the same character as the faithfulness he manifested in 1944 when he was defending the principles of Reformed church order against attacks from within.

As long as Nehemiah prayed and fought for his people against foes on the outside, he was popular with the people. But when he pointed to deviations within the ranks of his people, such as marriages with women of Ashdod, Ammon, and Moab, and heard the children in the streets speaking half the time in the language of Ashdod and saw that they could no longer speak the language of Judah, and he became angry and contended with his own people, hitting some of them and pulling out their hair (see Nehemiah 13), then the people forgot that he had prayed to God *for* his people. They forgot all about his struggle to persuade King Artaxerxes to allow him to participate in the rebuilding of Jerusalem and the temple.

Reactions to Schilder's imprisonment

After Prof. Schilder had been in prison for some weeks, Van der Vaart Smit wrote as follows in *Gospel and Folk,* his "religious" periodical:

> Prof. Dr. K. Schilder was arrested a while ago on the orders of the German authorities, and the publication of *The Reformation,* his paper, was forbidden. Some people are calling this incident a case of "religious persecution." Anyone who does this is lying. And any church that does this is lying.
>
> It is no secret how fiercely Schilder conducts the political battle and how fiercely he has attacked National Socialism on the political front. I have found out that when Prof. Schilder printed in *The Reformation* a prayer asking the Lord of harvest to come with the sword of judgment over the Channel and from Malta and by way of the Brenner

Pass, that was the last straw. He was praying openly for an English victory and the defeat of Germany. At once the German authorities intervened.

I can suggest a way whereby Prof. Schilder can be set free again. Let his friends begin by admitting that, in column after column, he went directly against what the occupying authorities had decreed, and that he did not show the government the respect he is obliged to manifest toward it. Let them also admit that he wrote in a way that is not permitted for a Christian, and finally that his prayer for England's victory makes it completely understandable that he should be taken prisoner. If his friends would write these things openly and clearly — in all sincerity — they would pave the way for his return. But if they write, as they having been doing up to this point, about religious persecution (which has nothing to do with this matter), they are putting an extra lock on his cell and will have to accept responsibility for any further suffering on Prof. Schilder's part.

From this vulgar, pedestrian piece of prose it became abundantly clear that the director of the "Christian Press Bureau" had indeed been in contact with the German "government," as he liked to call the occupying power.

Rev. Hermanus Knoop, a Reformed minister in Delfshaven, responded to Van der Vaart Smit by way of an article which he placed in his church paper on October 26, 1940. Knoop spoke up in a very positive, faithful and courageous way. He began by expressing his thankfulness that Van der Vaart Smit had let it be known *who* had undertaken to arrest Prof. Schilder. Since it was done by the Germans, the order came from Seyss-Inquart, the Reich Commissioner. Thus our people now had an address they could turn to in pleading for the release of Prof. Schilder.

Knoop went on to say that although it was true that Schilder had opposed the ideology of National Socialism, this was no more than his duty since this ideology is in conflict with Scripture and the confessions. Thus Schilder's opposition stemmed from "religious constraints" and not from any love of political battle for its own sake.

Knoop also took issue with the way Van der Vaart Smit quoted Schilder's prayer: he had twisted the reference to Malta by quoting incorrectly. Moreover, the "pruning knife" in Schilder's prayer was not the same as the "sword of judgment." And then there was the question of Japan, which, at the time Schilder wrote his article, was still neutral in relation to the war in Europe. (The pact between Japan and the Axis powers of Germany and Italy had not yet been made.) And Schilder's reference to "the ends of the earth" had been left out entirely by Van der Vaart Smit. Finally, Knoop wrote:

> If we take the trouble to read, sentence by sentence, what Prof. Schilder actually wrote, we rub our eyes in amazement at what has been made of it. "How it is possible?" we ask. Does Dr. van der Vaart Smit, a theologian and a former minister in the Reformed *(Gereformeerd)* churches, a man who was educated at our Reformed university, *really* believe that Schilder, in the part of one sentence which has been quoted, was "praying openly for an English victory and the defeat of Germany"? Come on now! The simplest catechumen would shake his head over this conclusion and say to him: "It is abundantly clear that this is nothing other than a prayer for the return of our Lord Jesus Christ, a prayer offered in the *manner* of the Scriptures, and that the prayer is being made concrete by way of place names which are concentration points of world traffic in the modern era."
>
> The path recommended by Van der Vaart Smit for securing the release of Prof. Schilder will not be followed by our people, for they know of another way — the way of prayer. And they will use that other way, so that, in God's time, the prison doors will swing open. They will avail themselves of that way of prayer both in devotions conducted in their homes and in congregational worship services on the Lord's day.
>
> And they know that the decision about the fate of God's servant does not lie in the hands of any human being but only in the hands of the One who is Lord of lords and King of kings.

The week this article came out, Rev. Knoop's church paper was also forbidden to publish, and it was not long before this faithful servant of the Lord was arrested. After being held in a cell for a short time, he was shipped off to the notorious concentration camp at Dachau (near Munich, in Germany), where he remained for two full years, until he was finally released in October of 1943. In this death camp, which held about 20,000 victims at the time, including Rev. Niemöller, Rev. Knoop shared the grim lot of many ministers of the Word from virtually all countries of occupied Europe and also from Germany itself. And he was there long enough to witness the deaths of young Rev. Kapteyn and Rev. Tunderman.[32]

Rev. Knoop himself became deathly ill while he was in this concentration camp, and eventually his weight dwindled to a mere forty kilograms (about ninety pounds). The camp doctors had already given up on him as a hopeless case. Therefore the Germans transferred him to the section of the infirmary they reserved for "travelers to heaven," as they liked to put it mockingly. But God heard the prayers that were offered, and Rev. Knoop was given back to his congregation.

Only a few church papers had the courage to continue the work of Prof. Schilder during the time he was in prison. Rev. J. A. Vink published a church paper for Berkel, in which he continued faithfully to combat the principles of National Socialism. About the work of Prof. Schilder he wrote: "As we read all those pages in *The Reformation,* our hearts were thankful that Prof. Schilder, as a faithful member of the church, acting in the obedience of faith, warned our church people against the seductive, unscriptural outlook on life which National Socialism represents."

In the *Frisian Church Messenger,* Rev. Herman Veldkamp used his pen to combat National Socialist ideas, eventually getting embroiled in a polemic with Van der Vaart Smit, especially on the question whether the synodical decisions of 1936 were to be understood as touching on "politics," as opposed to being purely "ecclesiastical." Rev. Veldkamp wrote: "It is on the basis of his principles that a Christian confesses and lives, and he is supposed to do so not just in his inner chamber but in every area of life. No one can adhere to Christian principles in the church and to pagan principles in the state. If anyone tries to do this, he gives evidence that he is off the rails; it is the church's loving obligation to admonish such a derailed person and to try to heal him with the medicine of church discipline if he persists in hardening himself. This is all so simple and clear that it is utterly

---

[32] Another minister who died in Dachau was Dr. K. Sietsma, the author of *The Idea of Office,* trans. Henry Vander Goot (published by Paideia Press in 1985). —TRANS.

amazing to see that someone calls it a 'political decision.' The church does *not* concern itself with politics." The only answer which Van der Vaart Smit could think of was that the Calvinists in earlier eras had accepted and praised a "leader (*Führer*) principle" in connection with the House of Orange.

Unfortunately, Rev. Veldkamp was opposed by a professor in his own circles, who told him to quit polemicizing. That was how far the people from whom leadership could have been expected had fallen. They had crawled into "bomb shelters" to hide from the danger.

It was reported that one of the professors at the Free University made the following observation when he heard about Prof. Schilder's imprisonment: "He could have avoided it. Daniel didn't pull the tails of the lions either when he sat in the lions' den." This is one of the sad and sorry specimens of the hopelessly petty outlook that emerged from the fading and leveling of our national life. What Daniel had done *before* he wound up in the lions' den had apparently escaped this theology professor.

This little episode also reveals something about the mentality in the circles in which Van der Vaart Smit gave leadership, for he was able to take over this insipid comment in his own paper, *Gospel and Folk,* just as though it was his own, writing: "We know how many have compared the imprisonment of Prof. Schilder with Daniel's stay in the lions' den. Those who make this comparison are ignoring an important difference, namely, that Daniel did not continually pull the lions by the tail to provoke them."

Meanwhile, our people heard very little about the condition of Prof. Schilder while he was imprisoned. His nearest blood relatives were allowed to visit him only a few times, and then always with guards present. In time it became known that the man who had gone to Schilder's house to take him to Arnhem, for a "brief interrogation," as he was told on August 23, actually took him to the Security Police building to be questioned. Nothing more was revealed about the "legal" end of his imprisonment.

But Rev. Knoop, responding to Van der Vaart Smit, had written that our people know about prayer as a path to follow in such a situation and would indeed take this path that was open to them. In thousands of families continual prayers went up for the release of this faithful witness.

In the *Frisian Church Messenger,* Rev. Veldkamp wrote as follows concerning Prof. Schilder's imprisonment: "The book in the Bible called 'The Acts of the Apostles' could just as well be called 'The Mistreatment of the Apostles.'[33] Yet they indeed acted, for suffering is often the highest act of faith. Think of the imprisonment of Peter in Acts 12. What was the activity of faith in this case? Do you read anything in the way of a bitter judgment against the imprisonment? No! Do you read anything about a mediator intervening, or about someone speaking up for him? No. What happened was this: 'Prayer for him was being made fervently by the church to God' (vs. 5). No more than that. If someone asks who it was that saved Peter, we should not reply that it was the angel; no, Peter was saved by those powerless folded hands of the believers who were praying." How our people did pray!

While Prof. Schilder languished in prison, a poem which had been widely distributed among our people somehow reached him. This poem entitled "Do Not Forsake Him, O Lord" was one of the first illegal poems in the body of "resistance literature." In English translation it reads as follows:

> *Do not forsake him, O Lord; be at his side.*
> *Be in his cell with Your favor and love.*
> *Be his support and strength, make all things well,*
> *Now that he must suffer for Your name and honor.*
>
> *He was always an armored battler for You.*
> *He feared nothing and no one, and proudly held up,*
> *As God's standard-bearer, Your banner of war.*
> *And showed himself to be your brave confessor.*
>
> *Now his voice is smothered by drab prison walls.*
> *We do not hear him speak; yet we know that You*
> *Hear every word, every sigh, which he*
> *Sends up to his King in silent, frightening hours.*
>
> *Do not forsake him, O Lord; do not forsake him, O King.*
> *Direct his way, his path, his mouth, his lot.*
> *Fill his cell with Your presence, O God,*
> *That it may be a bethel, a divine dwelling-place.*

---

[33] Veldkamp's play on words cannot be reproduced in English. The difference between the "Acts" *(Handelingen)* and the "Mistreatment" *(Mishandelingen)* of the Apostles is only the prefix "mis," which indicates in Dutch, as in English, that something is amiss. —TRANS.

Give him, if need be, the strength to testify.
And let each one who has learned to pray,
And who obeys Your direction and leading,
Bow before You, praying for help for Your servant.

We do not seek Your help and support in vain.
We know — and Your servant knows it too —
That though the world rage, He gives the heart Your peace,
And that all things are ordered by Your good pleasure.[34]

It was prayer that made the prison doors swing open for Prof. Schilder. Four and a half months after he was arrested, he was suddenly released, as by some miracle, and we got the good news: Prof. Schilder has been set free! Yet for him this freedom was not much more than the freedom of an eagle that has been crippled and cannot fly, for when he was released he was also forbidden to do any more writing. If he should publish as much as one item, he would be hauled away to one of the dreaded German concentration camps. The eagle's wings had been clipped! The fighter had been disarmed!

Yet there was still one thing he was allowed to do: he could speak in public. When it was still possible to hold a meeting of a men's society or a young people's society here or there, Prof. Schilder would be invited to speak. On Sundays he preached in churches all over the country — until the time arrived when the authorities were looking for him again. Then there was only one thing left to do — go into hiding and become a "diver."[35] Like so many thousands of others, Schilder became a fugitive in his own country.

If the enemy had had his way, this faithful witness would have been rendered harmless. Not only had his wings been clipped, his mouth was also stopped. The battler was not just disarmed, he was also bound hand and foot.

Prometheus is pictured for us on a crag in the Caucasus Mountains daily undergoing an unknown torment: an eagle feeds on his liver, which keeps renewing itself. What could be worse than thinking ahead (the offense of Prometheus)? What could be worse than want-

---

[34] This poem was later published in a collection of such literature entitled *Gedenckclanck 1940-1945*.

[35] The standard Dutch verb for living in hiding during the occupation is "onderduiken," which means to dive down or sink until one is out of sight. The people who did this are referred to in English as "divers." —TRANS.

ing to give people the light from heaven?[36] Not only would such a deed awaken the fullest wrath of known enemies and open opponents, but it would not be tolerated either by petty, small-minded people in a time of "descendants of epigones" (Abraham Kuyper).

The position of a Prometheus is one of the very worst imaginable. What we see pictured in this story is a fire god who is no longer dangerous: even dwarfs can torment him and belittle him. And where was the Hercules to kill the eagle and give this benevolent giant his freedom and place again? It was not a time of Herculean figures but of dwarfs.

There is a very sad piece of "church" history that needs to be inserted here if we are to sketch the situation that obtained during the occupation years. When Prof. Schilder was arrested, it was on the initiative of a German named Hushahn who was already living in our country before the war as the son of a German merchant in The Hague. Hushahn had received his education in this city and was one of the Germans who had been busy before the invasion of May, 1940, looking the country over carefully, which he was in a good position to do because he was attached to the German embassy in The Hague.

Hushahn knew Dutch as well as he knew German. His task, even before the war, was to read through the main Dutch church papers on behalf of the German government. Naturally, his eye was drawn to Schilder's articles in *The Reformation,* and the article of August 16 (especially the concluding lines) seemed to him to be a reason to put Schilder out of action. What he read there was that Schilder was praying for an English victory and a German defeat.

At that point it was still conceivable that there should be no arrest of Schilder, for this German spy could have been informed what Schilder really meant by such a prayer. Early in the occupation period, the Germans were not eager to take stern measures against the population in the Netherlands: they still hoped to win our people over by a gentle approach.

Now, Van der Vaart Smit, as a former theology student at the Free University and a regular reader of Schilder's writings, knew enough to see that the offending words were set in an eschatological

---

[36] The author's comparison to Prometheus, a Greek mythological figure known to us through the poetry of Hesiod, turns on the desire of Prometheus to make fire (and thus the many benefits that go with it) available to men on earth. Schilder was being tormented for upholding the fire of truth. —TRANS.

framework. H. H. Kuyper, who had contact with the German authorities in the name of the churches, could also have pointed this out. But what actually happened at this juncture?

Schilder was originally under the impression that his relatively quick release from imprisonment was in part due to the efforts of H. H. Kuyper, to whom he sent a friendly letter of thanks when he was home again. Dr. J. Ridderbos told Schilder that H. H. Kuyper had done his very best for him while he was in prison. But in 1941, when Schilder was present at the Synod of Sneek as an advisor, Rev. Veldkamp acquainted him with the contents of a significant letter he had received from H. H. Kuyper. The letter dealt with the brave stand Veldkamp took in his writings in the *Frisian Church Messenger.* Kuyper warned him to be very careful about what he wrote and declared that Veldkamp's impression that Schilder was in prison because of his confession was incorrect. This is literally what he wrote: "As for KS, the idea that he is a martyr just as the apostles were is in conflict with the truth. You are probably not aware of the grounds on which the German authorities arrested him, and you probably don't know how KS responded to those grounds, for if you knew these things you would realize that it has nothing to do with confessing Christ. It is therefore a thoroughly mistaken conception that he is suffering as a martyr for the cause of Christ."

There was an extensive exchange of letters between Schilder and Kuyper having to do with this sorry affair; those letters have been printed in a supplement to the yearbook of the liberated Reformed churches published in 1946. The letters did not accomplish much in the way of clarification and bringing out the truth. Schilder defended himself against false ideas and stated the truth sharply. But he still continued to use a brotherly tone, as we see from the conclusion of his last letter to Kuyper: "I do not write this letter gladly; I wanted so much to live in peace with you, and I thanked you in a spontaneous, trusting way after my return. I don't make judgments about your person now either. But I do have to condemn certain actions of yours, as well as certain omissions. In the final analysis, there is a difference between you and me in relation to the question what God's people needed in these times of oppression. And since there are many who talk about you behind your back, please count it in my favor that I have never wanted to do that, not even after you wrote to Rev. Veldkamp and said things you never said to me."

Here Schilder remained the man with the "gentle eyes," even though he had to declare in one of his letters to H. H. Kuyper: "I simply cannot understand it — and therefore it is all the more painful to me — but I must now conclude that you lengthened my time of imprisonment."

Right after the war, when our own government was in control in our country again, a number of ministers sent a letter to the Department of Internal Affairs in which they drew attention to the faithfulness and brave resistance work of Prof. Schilder during the first months of the occupation and suggested that some sort of recognition or honor by the Queen was in order. It would not be an exaggeration to call Schilder a "resistance hero."

There was a great deal done during the occupation in the way of resistance work — and we should be thankful for it. But to undertake such work in the very first months after the German invasion, when there was nothing to indicate that we would ever get out from under German control, was not the same thing as opposing the Germans later on, when we could be sure that Germany would lose the war.

The government never responded to this letter. The climate of thought had changed in Europe, and our government-in-exile operating in London had also been affected. There was a flood of "unity dreams," and much talk of "renewed brotherhood" throughout Europe. The "breakthrough" was to be a fact, a reality.[37] There was to be no more quibbling between "factions." I suspect that this short-sighted outlook is the reason Schilder was never officially recognized. Hadn't his "quibbling" led to yet another "faction" (the liberated Reformed churches) when there was now supposed to be unity?

Eventually Schilder was honored for his resistance work, but it happened after he had already died. Dr. Louis de Jong, who was well known as a radio speaker for Dutch broadcasts originating in England (called Radio Orange) during the occupation years, and who was himself a Jew and a member of the Labor Party, worked hard to ensure

---

[37] The "breakthrough" (*doorbraak*) was a feeling and conviction that divisions along lines of religious conviction, e.g. in education, were obsolete after the grand war effort in which Christians and Humanists and Communists and members of other groups as well had worked shoulder to shoulder to overthrow Fascist oppression. This "breakthrough" mentality did not have much sympathy for Schilder's emphasis on faithfulness to Scripture and the confessions. —TRANS.

proper recognition for Schilder. He saw to it that the whole Dutch population heard about his contribution to the resistance effort.

Dr. de Jong, as director of the Office of War Documentation, was commissioned by the government to write a book about resistance work during the occupation. In this capacity he came to see me in Goes. He had already read "KS's" resistance articles, which had been reprinted in the book *Occupied Possession,* and he told me that he had not found such highly valuable material anywhere else in the Dutch press of that time. He spoke about Schilder with the deepest respect.

He also made it apparent that he was well acquainted with the suspension and deposition of Schilder, and he knew about the subsequent church split. To inform himself about this matter he had labored through the acts of the Synod of 1939-42, meeting first in Sneek and then in Utrecht. He expressed disappointment that such events could have taken place during the occupation period, and that such treatment was meted out to a man like Schilder. I was scarcely able to tell him anything new about Schilder's resistance work; he already knew practically everything there was to know. The only thing he had not yet read was the exchange of letters with H. H. Kuyper, which was reprinted in the supplement to the 1946 yearbook. I gave him a copy to take along.

In October of 1960, Dr. de Jong presented a television program in which Schilder's portrait was shown to millions of viewers. They were also shown the paper he loved — *The Reformation.* In the course of this program, Dr. de Jong declared:

> Nowhere in Reformed *(Gereformeerd)* circles was sharper and more principial polemicizing published during the first months than in the weekly periodical *The Reformation.* Ten [weekly] issues appeared before it was banned. The content of the paper was the work of one of the professors at the Theological School in Kampen — Prof. Dr. K. Schilder.
>
> When the Dutch press, at the beginning of July, received a warning not to write about the Queen anymore, Prof. Schilder wrote the following words in his paper: "I hope that the God of the ages will be gracious to Her. Tomorrow I will pray for Her publicly in the church, where you do not come. [He was referring to the people who had issued

the warning.] Speaking straight from the shoulder, I want to express my best wishes for the Royal House." A little further on, he wrote: "If this issue gets through to the people, a ban will have been broken among those whom I reach." And it was so.

A ban is broken

Was Schilder honored posthumously by the authorities? No, nor was such honor something he needed. Yet he did receive due recognition posthumously in the forum of the entire Dutch nation as the people watched on television. I hope Dr. de Jong's program was also watched in the royal palace at Soestdijk.[38]

Dr. de Jong quoted Schilder with approval when he spoke of a ban being broken. This was surely no exaggeration on his part. The publication of Schilder's articles made it clear that in this first year of the occupation, the Dutch Nazi movement did not have nearly the power it boastfully claimed and pretended to possess while using its methods of intimidation. Our people were given fresh courage. Other papers became a little bolder and dared to say something here and there.

People in many places and representing many directions were suddenly taking an interest in this weekly called *The Reformation*. The number of subscribers increased dramatically. Even people in liberal and socialist circles began to pay attention to what Schilder was saying. A socialist alderman in the city of Groningen said to Mr. A. Zijlstra: "I now read *The Reformation*. I see only one man who gives us courage and power again, and that man is Prof. Schilder."

On July 22, 1940, Mr. Scheps of *Church News* (a weekly publication offering church news and information), wrote as follows to the publisher of Schilder's paper: *"The Reformation,* which is surely worth its weight in gold these last weeks, just flies out the door here. Even my colleagues who write about labor and business come to borrow my copy, and although they always return it neatly, my own copy does suffer from heavy use. Could you perhaps send me a couple of copies of the most recent issues? There should be a way to get copies of these most timely recent issues of *The Reformation* circulating

---

[38] Later there was a posthumous honoring of Schilder in Kampen. On September 30, 1981, a stone was placed before the old city hall, with an inscription informing people about Schilder's significant role in the resistance effort against German occupation during the war. —TRANS.

among the people [who don't already subscribe]. Perhaps you can think of something. For example, could they be sold at train stations?"

On August 2 the publisher received a postcard from the bookshop at the train station in Utrecht: "Someone just telephoned us and asked why we don't sell *The Reformation* in stores at the train stations. We would very much like to know whether you would be interested in having the paper sold at kiosks at the stations, and then we would also like to receive a copy of the paper first so that we can look at it ourselves."

The answer that had to be given to Mr. Scheps was this: "We are overwhelmed with requests for copies of the most recent issues of *The Reformation,* which have almost all been sold by now. We cannot even supply copies of the June and July issues for our new subscribers. Of course reprinting them would not be possible. We are sending you a few copies of what we still have on hand."

"The Reformation" is forbidden

The same day that Prof. Schilder was hauled out of his home in the manner then current — "just for a hearing down at the station" — and was locked up in a cell, the publisher of *The Reformation* received a visit from two individuals — a German in uniform and a Dutchman in civilian clothes. The Dutchman did the talking; the German seemed to have come along for intimidation purposes. I happened to be in conversation with the manager in his office when these "gentlemen" walked in and, without any words of introduction or explanation, demanded the archives and administrative materials that went with *The Reformation*. They also declared that the paper was no longer to be printed and published under any conditions.

Now, it happened that we had a special room devoted to *The Reformation,* where we kept the back issues and the addresses of the subscribers. When the two men saw the tremendous collection of old issues and all the other material in that room, they looked at each other and shrugged their shoulders. Apparently their original plan was to take everything along in their automobile, but that would clearly be impossible. They took some administrative papers, including the addresses of the subscribers, and then locked and sealed off the room devoted to *The Reformation,* warning the publisher expressly that he was not to open that door.

And that was the end of the matter. They had also intended to seal the press on which the paper was printed, but when they were informed that the printing of *The Reformation* occupied only a few hours of the press's time and that it was used mainly for ordinary commercial work, they let the matter rest.

That was how *The Reformation* ceased to publish — it had just finished its twentieth year. Dr. van der Vaart Smit, the man who had taken the initiative in the founding of the paper, was now fraternizing with our nation's deadly enemy. And the enemy, surely at the prompting of the Dutch Nazis, had shut the paper down.

Within a few weeks reports began to appear in the church press that *The Reformation* had been banned. *The Herald* "deplored" this but pointed out to readers of *The Reformation* that there were other church papers to which they could subscribe. It also devoted an article to pointing out that after *The Reformation* was banned, a new paper called *Confession and Experience*[39] was founded under the editorship of Prof. F. W. Grosheide. *The Herald* went on to say that this would be an excellent paper to subscribe to.

The Herald was not showing much consideration for a colleague who languished in prison, with his paper closed down. It was plain as day that people saw a chance to lure subscribers away from the *The Reformation,* in the hope that instead they would read papers that took the side of H. H. Kuyper.

Right after *The Reformation* was banned, Rev. W. W. Meynen of Dordrecht raised the question: What are we to read now? First he drew attention to H. H. Kuyper's paper, *The Herald,* which, he explained, "provides illumination and leadership for our time." He then went on to recommend *Credo* and the *Calvinist Weekly,* and finally *Confession and Experience.* This pastor who took a position sharply opposed to Schilder's did not mention that there was still a paper called *Pro Ecclesia,* which took the same direction Schilder had chosen.

Here we see the same diplomatic game being played that was underway throughout the 1930s. The notion of dividing the inheritance of a dying man before he has even passed on is regarded by us as contrary to proper style, form, and manners. Yet here an inheritance was indeed being divided by people without any scruples, while the

---

[39] Most of those Dutch church papers had names that can easily be translated into English. This one *(Belijden en Beleven)* drew on a word ("beleven," parallel to the German word "erleben") with no strict parallel in English. This word as used in the title of this paper does not just mean experience but also suggests an emphasis on one's confession coming to expression in everyday life. —TRANS.

man to whom it properly belonged — still very much alive — sat in prison. They made haste to divide the spoils! From such incidents we can draw our conclusions as to what was really going on. What inconsiderate, merciless treatment to inflict upon a man who had to endure it while imprisoned in a cell just a couple of meters in length and breadth!

Fortunately, the subscribers to *The Reformation* did not need much advice. Within a few months, the publisher of this paper had taken over the paper *Pro Ecclesia* from the Boersma Company in Enschede. The purpose of this paper was to "popularize" the scholarly work of men like Schilder, Dooyeweerd, and Vollenhoven; thus it had the same orientation as Schilder's own paper. It was possible to arrange for a suitable expansion of the editorial team by drawing on younger members of Schilder's following, which was something the readers of *The Reformation* understood very quickly without anyone having to draw it expressly to their attention.

Almost all of the subscribers to this paper went over to *Pro Ecclesia,* which was able to continue publishing until June of 1942, when it, too, was banned by the Germans.[40] The editor-in-chief of this paper was Dr. R. Schippers, who unequivocally rejected the decisions regarding "disputes over doctrine" and the "new church order." He continued to hold this stand right down to the year of the liberation and was even present at the gathering of August 11, 1944, in The Hague.[41]

Harassed from two sides

In June of 1942, our papers were discontinued, and we were left only with the satellites of the German Nazis. (Van der Vaart Smit had by this time set up a "religious" paper of his own: *Gospel and Folk.*) In this barren time, our poor, exposed people were harassed from two sides at once when it came to the press. On the one hand there was the weekly paper *Storm,* and on the other hand the paper put out by Van der Vaart Smit. The former was a raging lion, and the latter a wolf in sheep's clothing.

Hitler once wrote the following with regard to the churches in Germany: "I will not give them the pleasure of persecution. The

---

[40] The author comments further on this paper in *De braambos,* Vol. I, p. 132. —TRANS.

[41] Yet Schippers did not join the liberated Reformed churches. In 1950 he became a professor at the Free University of Amsterdam. —TRANS.

churches must be rooted out by making them laughable in the eyes of the masses. Our movie theaters will help us in this effort. We will need films which make it clear just how laughable the priests and parsons are, as parasites preying on the people. In the meantime we must hollow out the ecclesiastical system as much as possible from within."

This tactic, which was a new invention of the antichristian world power, was also applied zealously by the Dutch Nazis and their masters during the occupation years. That the effort failed even more completely in our country than in Germany was probably due to the fact that our people had a stronger (Calvinistic) foundation to stand on than did the Christians in Germany, who were mainly Lutheran, although we should certainly respect the many German Christians who did manage to maintain a firm stand.

In the two-pronged effort to render the Dutch churches laughable and to hollow them out from within, the Nazis had two papers at their disposal, as we saw. The one was *Storm,* a weekly which served as the publication of the Dutch SS. (I have copies of all of its issues in my own archive.) The other was the weekly *Gospel and Folk,* which was under the direction of Van der Vaart Smit, a man who had studied at the Free University, had been one of the founders of *The Reformation,* and had written a book entitled *The Future of the Elementary School* (for which Dr. H. Colijn wrote an introduction) and some other works as well.

Until 1940 Van der Vaart Smit enjoyed all the privileges and prerogatives of a minister in the Reformed *(Gereformeerd)* churches, which he then resigned voluntarily. I add this latter fact deliberately, for the contrast between the treatment of Greijdanus and Schilder, on the one hand, and the position of Van der Vaart Smit among our people, on the other, needs our attention. Greijdanus and Schilder, both professors at our theological seminary in Kampen, were persecuted and suspended because, in their faithfulness to Scripture and the confessions and Reformed church order, they opposed that which they regarded as unscriptural and unreformed. Van der Vaart Smit, a betrayer of his church and people, continued to hold all the privileges of membership in the same church, despite the fact that the well-known decisions of the Synods of 1936 and 1939 condemned the kind of work he was doing. He even helped to persecute the children of God and to scatter the sheep that made up Christ's flock.

This double standard, which is an abomination to the Lord, caused Schilder a great deal of pain when he saw it applied in the church he loved so dearly. How he felt about it is evident from *Occupied Possession,* a book in which the articles he wrote during the occupation years are collected. When we turn to his article about Van der Vaart Smit, which was published in *The Reformation* on July 12, 1940, as reprinted in this book (pp. 44-54), we see an important comment: "Note carefully the date, and note also who were and were *not* suspended during the war years."

Just how far people like Van der Vaart Smit dared to go during the occupation years is evident from his paper. As logo for the paper he used the shining Morning Star, accompanied by the phrase "Christ Before All." As his motto he used Acts 1:8: "But you shall receive power when the Holy Spirit has come upon you; and you shall be My witnesses both in Jerusalem, and in all Judea and Samaria, and even to the remotest part of the earth." His paper advertised itself as "the most widely distributed religious paper in the Netherlands" and as a publication of an association known as the "Order of Witnesses of Christ."

These two papers — *Storm* and *Gospel and Folk* — were let loose upon our people, including the youth of the Church. In *Storm* the Roman Catholic priests were consistently referred to as "cross moles" and pictured as moles in cartoons, while the Protestant ministers were called "preaching tigers" and were ridiculed in cartoons as tigers with sharp claws and mean, bloodthirsty faces, and so forth.[42]

That this paper had great influence behind the scenes was abundantly clear to anyone who read it carefully and kept an eye on what was happening. If the paper started a hate campaign against some priest or minister, you could be all but certain that the poor man would lose his freedom within a matter of weeks.

A striking example was the hate campaign against Dr. H. Colijn, which was unleashed after he spoke at a meeting of the League of Reformed Young Women's Societies. That this grey-haired statesman was so loved and honored by the young people and that his words were received with so much respect was more than the Dutch Nazi scum could tolerate. And so there appeared an article in *Storm* in which we read: "He [Dr. Colijn] is shameless enough to feel no uneasiness when the Reformed youth sing to him: 'The Lord will always watch over you . . .'" (Psalm 121). Boiling with anger because this

---

[42] Moles burrow underground, uproot things, and are hard to catch. As for the tigers in the pulpit, raging against Nazism, they did their "evil" work more openly, according to the propaganda in this paper. —TRANS.

statesman was able to influence the young people while *they* could not, the editors of *Storm* warned: "Up to now you have been treated in such a way as to suggest that your former conduct did not call for any special measures. Therefore the thing for you to do now is to make sure that you are forgotten as quickly as possible." A few weeks later, Dr. Colijn was arrested and exiled to Limburg, where he had to live in a Dutch Nazi hotel under constant surveillance — until he was taken away to Germany. He did not return alive.

The same sort of thing happened to a number of ministers. And we could be sure that whenever *Storm* unleashed a new hate campaign against the Jews, new measures imitating the notorious "Nuremberg Decrees" would be applied to those poor victims of Nazi hatred. And so there came the law that they were to wear the yellow six-pointed Star of David — just a few weeks after *Storm* had pronounced it a "scandal" that the Jews in the Netherlands still walked around without any mark to distinguish them from other people.

One by one the ministers who, in speech or in print, still testified to their confession, were "finished off" in this paper. Dr. J. Koopmans was branded "a dangerous saboteur" in a headline, and Rev. D. J. Couvée was accused of committing a misdeed "while hiding behind a Biblical mask." He was attacked as a blasphemer because of what he said about a drive to increase production.

In such a manner, this lugubrious paper carried out its task against the Church. But right next to it, unashamed, stood Van der Vaart Smit's church paper, *Gospel and Folk,* which spoke of "trusting in God" as it was busy with its impotent effort to "hollow out the church from within." In this paper one could find threats, pleas, intimidation, appeasement, slander, and harassment.

As an example of the way in which Van der Vaart Smit misused the "exegetical" knowledge of the Scriptures he had acquired, consider the following excerpt from his "meditation" published in the issue of January 1, 1941. His "basis" was Revelation 21:5, where we read: "And He who sits on the throne said, 'Behold, I am making all things new.'" This is what was made of it: "There is a tide in world history. Sometimes its movement looks sluggish to us. In recent decades the years seemed to creep by listlessly. But those who wait for the Lord do not lose hope. *Today* we see what a remarkable time we live in and how God's footsteps ride the storm that shakes the world. The date of this new year is a date full of promise for us. A renewal is underway, and it will embrace the entire world. Event follows event, and it is our privilege to be able to join in the forward march into this new time."

Here Van der Vaart Smit was equating what God has revealed to His faithful Church about the new eternal Kingdom of Peace with what Hitler was trying to establish. God was "joining in the forward march" into this "new time" in which all things were being made new. The devil also approached Christ in such a manner, with the words "It is written" on his lips.

What did this "new time" of which Van der Vaart Smit spoke actually bring us? 1941 was a year of horrible suffering for many of the finest servants of the Lord. They were thrown into concentration camps, incarcerated in tiny prison cells, beaten and tormented, and hauled away to Germany, where most of them would meet their death. Their daily martyrdom and the carefully calculated tortures to which they were subjected grew beyond measure. While these things were being done to his colleagues, Van der Vaart Smit rejoiced in the "new time" in which all things were being made new.

In the same period of time in which Prof. Schilder wrote his article addressed to Van der Vaart Smit, as a last attempt to restrain this man in his deep fall (the article was entitled "The Sorrows of a Reformed Minister"), he also wrote a meditation entitled "The Power of Delusion," which was based on what we read in II Thessalonians 2:11: "God will send upon them a deluding influence." We do not know whether Prof. Schilder was thinking specifically of Van der Vaart Smit as he explicated this word from Scripture. Yet we do know that there was generally some reason or special circumstance or occasion behind what he wrote; sometimes a note or observation in one of his articles in an issue of *The Reformation* would be the key to understanding another article in the same issue.

In any event, what he wrote in this meditation can certainly be taken as fully applicable to the editor of *Gospel and Folk:* "We confess concerning that church that when she is viewed from the aspect of grace, she is not only a *coetus* (i.e. a free gathering) but also a *congregation* (i.e. a group brought together by a higher and stronger hand). The same applies to the aspect of wrath, also in the present, when we look at the enthusiasts who follow the Antichrist. They are a *coetus,* for they 'admire the signs and wonders of the lie,' the signs in which the power of Satan has its 'parousia.' But they are also a *congregation,* for a higher, stronger hand herds them into a single mass.

Such is the dynamic of the power of delusion *sent* by God. They cannot help looking first in this direction, and then in that direction. They wander around, and 'to this they are also set.' "

When we bear in mind that Van der Vaart Smit, late in his life, sought refuge for his burdened soul in the intoxicating incense of Roman Catholic mysticism, this exposition of Scripture takes on a special significance for us. To the very end, this man continued to look first in this direction, and then in that direction.

On July 15, 1941, his paper *Gospel and Folk* made itself heard again very extensively, for it was distributed among all our ministers. This was three weeks after Hitler broke his "eternal pact" with Russia and crossed the Russian border with his armored vehicles and shock troops. *Gospel and Folk* then published an article entitled "To the Ministers," which was intended as a manifesto. The article declared that the time had come to make a choice. Hitler had himself formulated the alternative: Whoever is not with me is a Bolshevist. The streets in our country were stained with the slogan "Orange is Bolshevism,"[43] painted in red letters.

Naturally, Van der Vaart Smit could not resist adding his share to the new wave of Nazi propaganda. Therefore he wrote in this article: "Pastors and teachers, shake the dust off yourselves! It is soiling you! Clean yourselves up. Think in a Christian way! Act in a Christian way! This is a time of great decisions. You cannot continue to hesitate between[44] Stalin's weapons, on the one hand, and his worldview, on the other, balancing them off against each other in self-deception. If Baal is God, follow him and choose *both* his weapons and his worldview. And if the Lord is God, follow Him and choose *both* weapons and worldview accordingly. Be consistent, and fully honest, and Christian. If you hesitate between two opinions, you will fall behind and lose the prize of the calling of God which is in Christ Jesus."

What horrible language! Satan had indeed been given power over our people to sift them as wheat. It was the time of stumbling blocks and of a great upheaval, such as our people had not known since the Eighty Years' War through which they shook off the tyranny of Spain in the seventeenth century.

---

[43] The royal family was the House of Orange. The term "Orange" is used in Dutch to stand for the royal family, and also for support for the monarchy as part of the Dutch political system. According to the propaganda, then, to be a monarchist was to be a Bolshevist (Communist)! —TRANS.

[44] Van der Vaart Smit was here alluding to the language Elijah used in his encounter with the priests of Baal at Mount Carmel: see I Kings 18:21. —TRANS.

It was an epoch reminiscent of the time of Vondel,[45] whose poem "Now Threatens . . ." ("*Nu dreight . . .*") depicted the history of his day in the following words:

> *Now threatens a hellish and blind night*
> *Of errors and idolatries.*
> *To extinguish the light of the main altar,*
> *With force, by the overthrow of ruling powers,*
> *For the amusement of pagans.*
> *O bitter lot!*
> *Now the emissaries of the cross stand exposed*
> *As targets for the blasphemers.*
> *The domes of the churches are in distress,*
> *And so are Christ's bloodless altars.*
>
> *Let us go to the altar in the courtyard,*
> *In such a sudden change of state,*
> *To offer up to heaven our supplications,*
> *And submit to the will of the Most High.*
> *It is God who sets limits to empires;*
> *This is the supreme law.*

"The domes of the churches are in distress . . ."
"Let us go to the altar in the courtyard . . ."

Even so, Synod meets

During this grim time of anguished cries for help, wailing sirens, police vehicles, prisons, concentration camps, gas ovens, mass executions, and the spiritual poisoning of our national life, a general synod of the Reformed *(Gereformeerd)* churches came together on May 26, 1942. What was the purpose in meeting? Were the delegates gathering in the "outer court," where they could lift their hands in prayer as they begged for deliverance? Were they driven together by the cutting lash of a wrathful antichrist? Were they brothers who were taking refuge together, herded together like sheep?

No, the Synod had come together to "deal with the disputes over doctrine." There had been requests — many of them — *not* to do this.

---

[45] Joost van den Vondel (1587-1679) was one of the greatest Dutch poets and is known for his strong opposition to tyranny. —TRANS.

Two particular synods, comprising twenty-one classes, and sixteen consistories had brought forward pressing requests *not* to deal with the "disputes over doctrine." The following arguments were offered in support of these requests. First, the particular synod of Oost-Friesland could not be properly represented because of the wartime circumstances.[46] Secondly, there was no great uneasiness in the churches about "disputes over doctrine." It was simply not an urgent matter. In a time of occupation there were other matters demanding attention. Thirdly, the churches would not be able to follow the discussion or join in. The war and occupation made it impossible. Fourthly, the church papers had been silenced by the Germans. Fifthly, the churches feared that great disunity would result from an untimely treatment of this matter.

Nonetheless, by a vote of twenty-seven in favor and twenty-three opposed, the synod decided to proceed. The arguments that had been adduced were swept aside. The decision to proceed was accompanied by the following cynical argument: "The synod, bearing in mind that there were no new points of view in the materials that had been submitted, decided first of all to proceed immediately to deal with the matters which it had assembled to discuss, and secondly to place in the hands of a committee the materials which had been submitted as pertaining to this matter, so that the committee could advise the synod what to do in relation to those materials."

The extent to which proper procedure was being twisted here is apparent when we take a good look at what was going on. A synod decides to take up a case and will only *later* investigate whether it has the competence and capacity to deal with such a matter. Indeed, what this synod decided in relation to arguments that it should not proceed with this matter could almost be called cynical. When it was pointed out that in such a time the churches would not be able to follow the discussion and feel involved, the simple answer was: "That is why the synod has decided to deal with this matter *in secret*"![47]

---

[46] There were some Reformed churches in areas of Germany near the Dutch border which were affiliated with the Reformed *(Gereformeerd)* churches in the Netherlands and had their own classes. For more on this "German Reformed" population, see Herbert Brinks, "Ostfrisians in Two Worlds," in *Perspectives on the Christian Reformed Church*, ed. Peter De Klerk and Richard R. De Ridder (Grand Rapids: Baker Book House, 1983), pp. 21-34. — TRANS.

[47] See also what Rev. Geert Janssen has written about this matter in his book *The Facts of the Case* (Dutch: *De feitelijke toedracht)*, third edition published in 1955 by De Erven A. de Jager of Groningen, pp. 22-23.

As for the fear that synodical action on the "doctrinal disputes" might create disunity in the churches, a similarly cynical response was offered, namely, that fear is a poor advisor. An attitude of great condescension with regard to the people of the church was expressed. The synod, as the "highest body" in the church, would decide what was advisable and would act accordingly.

Necessary rebuttal

The disastrous synodical decisions which were intended to destroy the life work of Prof. Schilder were made in the absence of the man who was being condemned. He was not heard at the time he was condemned, and he had no opportunity to defend himself. People knew that he had to stay out of sight because he was being sought by the Germans; he lived the life of a wandering "diver," as many thousands of others had to do as well.

It was a sad and sorry thing that Schilder, after the war, found it necessary to defend himself against malicious talk to the effect that he had gone into hiding unnecessarily during the occupation period, and that he had used the wartime conditions as an excuse to stay away from the synod. I recall an occasion when an elder who had been a member of the general synod that condemned Schilder spoke at an "information evening" and declared that Schilder could nicely continue to harass the synod from his "bomb-free" shelter. (He was referring to Schilder's status as a "diver.").

The truth was just the opposite: it was not that Schilder was harassing the synod, but that synod could harass him and remain unscathed. Schilder had no opportunity to reply — neither in the press (he had been forbidden to write) nor by taking part in church meetings, for he would run the risk of being arrested by the Germans and winding up in a concentration camp. In 1946 he wrote his brochure *Necessary Rebuttal,* in which he revealed just what happened.[48]

That such revelations had not been superfluous but most necessary became apparent to him in 1947, when he was in the United States, where he was making a tour to tell people about the events in the churches. While addressing an audience in Rev. Hoeksema's church in Grand Rapids, he encountered another Dutchman who was also on tour, who engaged him in debate. The other man did not restrict him-

---

[48] The Dutch title is *Afgeperst.* Abraham Kuyper had also written a brochure with this title. Schilder's brochure was intended to serve as an appendix to the 1946 yearbook of the liberated Reformed churches but published as a separate item. —TRANS.

self to ecclesiastical matters, as Prof. Schilder was trying to do, nor did he make it his business to defend the synod that condemned Schilder. He simply reproached Schilder for not being present at the synod: Schilder, he suggested, had chosen to stay in hiding, only to emerge once the liberation was a reality in 1944. The same kind of talk had also circulated in the Netherlands. And so Schilder addressed these matters in *Necessary Rebuttal.*

The facts of the matter are as follows. Until July 13, 1942, Schilder continued his labors at the theological seminary in Kampen undisturbed. His church paper had been banned, and he made no effort to defy the ban on publication because he viewed his work as a teacher at the seminary as his highest and most important task. But what happened next? On Monday, July 13, 1942, early in the morning, which was the usual time for the Germans to be out and about, a German police truck pulled up in front of his house. The Germans rang the bell, with the intention of arresting Schilder. When their summons was not answered, they withdrew; a Dutch policeman persuaded them that Schilder must have preached somewhere the day before and had not yet returned. That day the Germans arrested some other people in Kampen. Prof. Schilder was warned and took advantage of an opportunity that presented itself that same morning to disappear from town unnoticed: he went to Amsterdam by boat.[49] His intention was to return to Kampen some weeks later when the lectures at the seminary resumed (it was the vacation period).

But a month later the order to arrest Schilder was repeated, and the Kampen police came by for his ration card.[50] A loyal, trusted policeman let the members of the Schilder household know that there was a standing order to arrest Prof. Schilder just as soon as he returned to Kampen. And this created a new situation for him. He had to give up his intention to return to his duties at the seminary once the vacation period was over. Prof. Schilder was not willing to stay away from his place of work because of a *possible* arrest, but when it came to *certain* arrest he really had no choice. Because there was a standing order for his arrest, he drew the only possible conclusion.

---

[49] See De Vries, *K. Schilder als gevangene en onderduiker,* pp. 43-44. —TRANS.

[50] People could not buy food and other consumer goods freely during the occupation years, but only in set amounts. For every purchase, one would have to pay with money plus a ration coupon. The coupons were issued monthly, and one would have to present a ration card to get them. Underground resistance workers periodically raided ration offices so that they would be able to supply divers with the ration cards and coupons needed to survive. —TRANS.

At that point he wrote a letter to the Curators of the seminary explaining the state of affairs and asking for their judgment in the matter. They answered *officially* that in such circumstances they regarded it as unavoidable that he should stay away from his work. The secretary of the Curators was Rev. F. C. Meyster, who, along with Rev. N. Duursema, another member of the Curators, was also a member of the synod that met in 1942. Because he had received such a letter from the Curators, it must have struck Prof. Schilder as rather strange that synodical pre-advisors, along with Curator Duursema and other members of the synod, began to say publicly that they questioned Schilder's reason for going into hiding.

It was indeed a very sad history that was played out here. And if all of this was not already enough, this brother who was pursued by the external enemy was declared an outlaw within his own camp. In Reformed *(Gereformeerd)* circles, people sowed distrust about the uprightness of Schilder's intentions, even though he had never been anything less than upright in all he said and did.

The fact that Schilder's ration card was taken away by the Germans when they did not find him at home was proof that he was being sought for arrest. During those occupation years, a person without a ration card was a pariah, unless others took compassion on him. For it was only with a ration card that one could have one's identity pass in proper order and also get the requisite stamp affixed to one's pass. Without such papers, travel was virtually impossible, for papers could be checked at any moment or any place. Moreover, without a ration card it was impossible to obtain the coupons needed to buy food.

Fortunately, there was an underground resistance movement that could produce falsified papers when necessary. What was happening during the occupation years was a fulfillment of what was prophesied in Revelation 13:16-17 about no one being able to buy or sell without the mark of the beast: thus the servant of the Lord was not excluded. Instead of being able to count on comfort, love, and an understanding of his perilous situation, Schilder encountered distrust, malice, and the continuation of the fatal ecclesiastical action that was being taken against him by the synodical robot.

It is virtually incomprehensible when we look back at it, but it happened. In those days Rev. J. van Nieuwkoop still took the opportunity to warn the general synod that Schilder really was being sought by the Germans. This minister had been summoned to Apeldoorn by the authorities for a hearing. Mingled with the usual stream of ugly expletives to which he was subjected there was a clear indication that there were a number of young Reformed *(Gereformeerd)* ministers who still refused to reconcile themselves to the National Socialist ideology. Their refusal was ascribed to the influence of Schilder, and so, if he could once be arrested, his destiny would be sealed.

Rev. van Nieuwkoop told this to the people in Schilder's household and also made sure that Dr. K. Dijk found out about it. But it didn't help one bit. The ecclesiastical proceedings were pushed ahead, even if the "accused" was not only under an order not to write but couldn't even appear anywhere to defend himself orally.

In *The Reformation* issue of February 2, 1946, Schilder wrote a meditation entitled "Flee Bravely," which was based on Matthew 10:23 ("But whenever they persecute you in this city, flee to the next; for truly I say to you, you shall not finish going through the cities of Israel, until the Son of Man comes"). He wrote: "Thus the question whether a Christian may *flee* came up for discussion continually; I myself also had to face this question during the occupation years." In this meditation he went on to demonstrate what "fleeing bravely" involves: "If staying in one dangerous place makes action impossible for you, then do not seek another dangerous place. You must not seek out the next city in order to challenge the demon of persecution in a playful spirit. No, you have to seek the place where there is a task for you, where there is work awaiting you." The conclusion he drew was this: "To flee before the carnal powers before they are able to silence you permanently and then at once to make a new beginning — that's fleeing bravely. For outside are the cowards."

That was how Schilder understood his task during this period of hiding, and he carried it out in the faithful spirit for which he was known, with the very few means that were still at his disposal. He no longer had a paper to write in, and travel was impossible for him.

Rev. Hermanus Knoop gave the synod a written warning about these things and pointed out the errors being made. In a letter dated July 22, 1944, he declared: "It disappointed me bitterly to discern from the choice of words in the official proceedings of the synod as concerns Prof. Schilder's being in hiding that people in synodical circles have put a question mark (to put it mildly) behind his status . . . The synod does itself no honor when it calls his honesty into question . . . You must respect his secret. You must in no way cooperate with anything that might lead Prof. Schilder to come out of hiding and expose himself to danger — not even in the name of so-called needs of the church. For the church does not have to be in need when it comes to this matter. The matter in question does not necessarily have to be dealt with now but could properly be put off until a calmer time. Believe me, if the church were truly in need, Prof. Schilder would not hesitate for a moment to risk his life for her — in fact, he would be the first to do so. There are some people who talk about such a thing rather glibly: I wonder whether they have ever gone so far as to risk their own lives . . ."

Alone

It must have been very bitter for Prof. Schilder to have to defend himself against the slander emanating from his opponents. The people at the synod knew perfectly well what the circumstances were. They had been informed about the events in Kampen, and they knew Schilder well enough to realize that he was not a man who would lie or who was too cowardly to appear in public when it was necessary. Moreover, he did his part to cooperate with what people were asking of him. He never refused to respond to anything the synod asked of him. And whenever he could, he made himself available for discussions in secret locations.

Only a few days after he was suspended by the synod on March 23, 1944, I was invited to see Schilder at his address in hiding. To me and to everyone else, it was a complete secret where he had been hiding all this time. From July 13, 1942, through March of 1944, the only people who knew where he was hiding were the people immediately involved in his day-to-day existence.

Because I had business dealings with him, a meeting was necessary after the suspension, for it would inevitably lead to deposition, in Schilder's opinion. And so it appeared that he would soon be without any way to support his family. He had to think not only of himself but also of his family's welfare. On top of all his other worries, this concern was a very heavy weight on his shoulders. Therefore he regarded it as necessary that he and I have a business meeting to talk about the publication of books and writings just as soon as the war was over.

That he wanted such a meeting also indicates that after his suspension in March of 1944, he saw no prospect whatsoever of a liberation of our churches. That he did not then regard this as a possibility was clear to me from the conversation we had on that occasion.

He had gone into hiding in the home of a friend, Dr. P. Jasperse of Leiden. I was told to ask for "Mr. de Priester," for this was the name he had taken as a diver and thus the name by which the servants knew him. I still see him before me in Dr. Jasperse's study — plunged into misery. He sat in a sunken posture in an armchair. In his mouth was a big, wooden pipe containing homegrown tobacco. When I asked him how he viewed the situation now, he shrugged and said: "They will naturally proceed to depose me. I am regarded as a rotten member of the Church." Dr. Jasperse reports that in those painful days Schilder also used to say: "I am a rotten apple and I'm not good for anything anymore in the eyes of the people of the church."[51]

To hear such words from a man who had devoted his whole life to the service of the Church and had never viewed her as anything other than our Mother and had said and written such glorious things about her cut right through my soul like a knife. I said to him: "But Professor, surely our people will not put up with this! You have friends, people who are of the same mind as you, people who stand behind you."

He responded by saying: "I know that, but what can they do? The time has been very well chosen. People don't know what's going on. There is a cloud covering our country. People can't come together because the trains are being shot at from the air. They can't read about this business either because I'm not allowed to write and

---

[51] See N. Scheps, *Interviews over 25 jaar vrijmaking,* p. 41; see also a letter Schilder wrote in April of 1944 (in W. G. de Vries, *K. Schilder als gevangene en onderduiker,* pp. 156-157). The depth of Schilder's anguish during this period is likewise apparent from an episode dating from a year and a half later that has been related by Prof. J. Kamphuis: "As praetor of the student corps I had asked to see him, and he received me in his study. But the lordly joviality that usually characterized the contacts between this professor and his students was not there this time. Prof. Schilder was upset, and he told me why. Just before I arrived he had been visited by another student. I should add that this episode took place in October or November of 1945, when seminary studies in Kampen were just starting to get underway again after the war and the seminary on the Oudestraat [the one belonging to the synodocratic churches] was reassembling its people. Prof. Schilder, then, had been visited by a certain student who proceeded to say that he had come to say goodbye and wanted to thank Prof. Schilder cordially for the instruction he had enjoyed under him. Schilder — and here we see his spontaneous cordiality — immediately responded by saying something like: 'Are there then some difficulties which make it impossible for you to continue your studies?' The answer he got was: '*No — I am studying at the Oudestraat.*' This meant, of course, that this man had chosen for the synodocracy. Prof. Schilder showed him the door, without saying another word. 'Believe me,' he then told me, 'I cannot recall a single occasion before this when I have cut off a conversation with a guest in my home, but in this case I didn't have words to reply. To regard me as guilty of the sin of public schism, as dry rot infesting the Body of Christ — and then to come and thank me in such a friendly way for all the instruction I have given! Then to pay a polite visit with a cigar and a nice little talk!' " (in *Verkenningen,* Vol. 2, pp. 186-187). —TRANS.

publish. I am alone." He even said: "I am on the outside; I am without church."[52]

It turned out later that Schilder's assessment of the situation at that moment was too dark. He did *not* stand alone; many thousands stood ready to support him. This would become apparent within a mere matter of months, to the unpleasant surprise of the synod, which must have proceeded from the conviction that *this* was the time to silence Schilder, for now he was all alone.

If they had realized what the consequences of their miserable decisions would be, I wonder if they would have allowed things to go as far as they finally did. But in March of 1944, the developments were not yet at their ultimate end. And so Schilder believed that because of the wartime circumstances, he stood all alone.

Some years later I thought back to this conversation when I read what Dr. Jasperse wrote about Prof. Schilder after his death: "On a late afternoon, some weeks after his suspension, I came into the room where he was, but he did not see me. He was sitting at the harmonium and singing from Psalm 25:

> *Turn to me and show Thy favour;*
> *I am lonely and distressed.*
> *From my troubles me deliver;*
> *Save me, for I am oppressed.*[53]

"It was so touching," Dr. Jasperse continued, "to see the great 'KS' singing to his God about his deep disappointment, crying out in his pain like a child."

Why have I emphasized that Schilder was alone at that moment? Because it appears that no one — not Prof. Schilder, and not the protesters either — suspected or realized that there would be a "liberation." There was no one who regarded this as a possibility.

The real developments, then, were not as they were later portrayed by Dr. Louis Praamsma in his book *The Foolishness of God*.[54] When he deals with the liberation, he creates the impression that when certain synodical decisions were made about the "disputes over doc-

---

[52] See *Gedenkt uw voorgangeren*, p. 67. —TRANS.
[53] English words taken from stanza 8 of Psalm 25 in the *Book of Praise*. —TRANS.
[54] Dutch title: *Het Dwaze Gods*. This book is a history of the Reformed *(Gereformeerd)* churches in the Netherlands from the beginning of the nineteenth century to about 1950, when the original edition of this work was published. The passage referred to occurs on page 376 of the revised edition. —TRANS.

trine" in 1942, those who objected to those decisions had already made up their minds that there would be a "liberation." Praamsma writes: "The protesters did not hesitate to break the ecclesiastical federation when they realized that in the short run they would not get full satisfaction for their feelings." This statement makes it appear as though the decision that there would be a liberation was made back in 1942. Praamsma also writes: "The *moment* for the break was not chosen in connection with the rejection of the objections to certain teachings; the moment was chosen in connection with the outcome of a disciplinary matter that will now concern us in the second place."

The actual course of events is thoroughly misrepresented here. In the first place, the protesters never "broke" the ecclesiastical federation: they were simply put outside the federation. Suspensions, depositions, and disciplinary measures were applied by the dozen. In the second place, the protesters did not choose the "moment" (in the passage quoted above, Dr. Praamsma placed this word in italics) for the break — neither in the case of the decisions regarding the disputes over doctrine, nor in the case of the disciplinary action against Profs. Schilder and Greijdanus. They simply had no other choice: it was "like it or lump it," to put it bluntly.

This little piece of church "history" is nothing other than historical falsification, and it is in conflict with the facts. Not a single one of the protesters who appeared at the meeting of August 11, 1944, had planned on "breaking" the ecclesiastical federation or "liberating" the churches. The facts of the matter are clear: from the way this whole matter unfolded, it is apparent that not human beings but *the* LORD chose the moment. Insofar as it had to do with the deliverance of the Church, it was not human work.

When it comes to the actions of the synod that cast out so many office-bearers, the words which Joseph spoke to his brothers in Egypt bear repeating: "As for you, you meant evil against me, but God meant it for good in order to bring about this present result, to preserve many people alive" (Genesis 50:20). Those who were faithful to the confessions were *placed* by God on the path they trod. When the moment of the liberation was suddenly there, they had not foreseen it or considered it in advance as a possibility — not even Prof. Schilder.

In hiding

Right up to the day of the liberation, Prof. Schilder was a solitary wanderer in our land. When he fled his home in Kampen on July

13, 1942, he did not know that it would be a long, long time before he would be able to come "home." His plan was to return to Kampen after a few weeks to continue his work at the seminary. But when the attempt to arrest him was repeated by the Germans after a month, he understood that if the enemy ever managed to seize him, he would wind up in a concentration camp. So where was he to go?

If he stayed with relatives, he would easily be found, and so he had to turn elsewhere. He went to one of his former congregations, Oegstgeest, in the hope that he could find a place to stay among the people there, even if only temporarily. But the people realized that he might well be sought in the areas where his former congregations were located, and so Mr. Kranenburg, a member of the congregation, brought him to the home of his sister and brother-in-law (a man named Groeneveld), who lived on an out-of-the-way farm near Giessendam, on the Merwede River.

After the war I visited the Groenevelds at their home. It was an ideal place for divers to hide out — as long as there were no traitors around to report their presence! To get to their home, I had to ride along a dyke until just before Giessendam. I left my car in a concrete parking place along the river and hoisted a white flag on the dyke as a signal to the solitary inhabitants on the other side of the broad river that there was someone who wished to be ferried across. Then I had to wait until a little boat came along from the other side.

It was the middle of winter when I made this visit. At the foot of the dyke were some ice-floes, and there was a sharp northeast wind. Groeneveld manoeuvred his boat neatly between the ice-floes and helped me step over some slippery paving stones and into the boat. And so you see that it was no simple matter to get to this farm: there was no road leading to it.

On the far side of Groeneveld's land was a wetlands area called the Biesbos. His house was somewhat elevated and commanded a good view of the river. If one also has a good telescope available, like the one Mr. Groeneveld showed us, nothing need escape the watchful eye.

Yet our host told me that on the day he suddenly saw his brother-in-law standing before him with someone he did not know, he was not too keen on giving shelter to divers. The Biesbos may be fairly isolated, but it was also a strategic area, and the underground resistance movement made good use of it. Groeneveld was willing to hide the diver for a week or ten days, but then he would have to be brought to some other place — that was the agreement.

"Uncle Gerrit" was left with the Groenevelds, who gave him a small room of his own upstairs. But within a week, his winning ways, his friendliness, his willingness to help, and especially his great simplicity had stolen the hearts of his host and hostess so completely that they decided to take a chance and *not* send him on to some other hiding place. Schilder, in turn, dedicated the second edition of his trilogy on the sufferings of Christ to the Groenevelds.

The Groenevelds hid Schilder until the end of 1943, for about a year and a half in all. While I was there visiting, I must have heard the hostess say ten times: "He was such a dear man!" or "He took such a personal interest in our little family!" or "He helped out with everything — even though he was such a learned man!"

In all the time that "Uncle Gerrit" lived there, nothing unusual or distressing happened. A couple of times, relatives of the Groenevelds who knew nothing about the arrangement happened upon him, but quick thinking and ingenuity on the part of Mrs. Groeneveld, who was not afraid to tell a white lie if need be, saved the day. On one such occasion, a friend of hers came by unexpectedly and found the professor sitting in a chair in the Groeneveld home. She then said: "That man looks just like Prof. Schilder." Mrs. Groeneveld replied quickly: "If only he *was* Prof. Schilder!" And it took some talking to convince this visitor that the man she saw before her was a distant relative, somewhat retarded, who needed a place to stay temporarily.

"Uncle Gerrit" caught on at once and must have thought of David so long ago when he was brought before Achish, the king of Gath. (On that occasion, David acted like a madman to save his own skin.) In any event, when he preached once in Giessendam after the war and wound up drinking coffee after the service with this woman who had unconsciously played the role of a troublesome third party while he was in hiding at the Groeneveld home, he recognized her immediately and said: "Here you have that madman again." Fortunately, he had not lost his sense of humor!

Now, Schilder certainly needed a sense of humor in the situation in which he found himself. It was a sad and sorry business. The friendly concern and devotion of the Groenevelds did a great deal to make his lonely diver's existence easier to bear; yet we should consider carefully what he was enduring. Here was someone who was accustomed to working eighteen hours a day — indeed, there were weeks in which he also worked right through two of the nights — who was now forced to do virtually nothing, and that in a time of great tension, when there was so much going on that concerned his person and work. He did manage to arrange for reprints of a couple of his books, in which he was assisted by the cleverness of his hostess, who also managed, via her doctor, to have some study books Schilder needed brought from a library to her home.

For someone like Prof. Schilder, it must have been a daily torment that his own beautiful library was not accessible to him (it had meanwhile been plundered by the Germans) and to have no contact with his brothers or with the churches. He was dependent on radio reports and an occasional secret visit from an intimate friend, who could bring him nothing but the most unfavorable reports about a synod which, despite all these circumstances and restrictions, continued to hound him. And he had to live this way for a year and a half!

Is it any wonder that he always strongly desired news, both national and international, and that when a local minister visited him periodically in secret, Schilder always asked him about the latest developments in the news? This minister, who understood Schilder's hunger for contact with the outside world, said to him once: "Professor, it is written that those who believe are not in a hurry" (see Isaiah 28:16). Schilder did not reply to this statement but went over to a different topic of conversation. But here we get a glimpse into his pure, childlike faith and his humble, upright heart, for in saying goodbye to this minister, Schilder tugged at his sleeve and said, "Thanks for the admonition you gave me a few moments ago."

What a weight it must have been on his sensitive soul to be so alone during this period in hiding! His friendly host and hostess gave him what they had and watched over his welfare with the kind of love found in a parental heart. But what he really desired and hated to be without was something they could *not* give him, namely, an eagle's flight over the land, and the opportunity to join in the intense struggle with the spirits of the age, whose threatening danger he understood so well.

He knew that his people, in both ecclesiastical and national respects, had been cast into the furnace of the most abominable temptation. He saw the dangers to which the youth of the church were more subject now than ever before. He also saw the foolishness being perpetrated by the general synod, which was leading the churches he loved so dearly along the path to a binding dogmatics and in the process making a separation between the Word and the Spirit, with the result that the operation of the Word was hindered.

He had to remain quiet, hidden, unemployed, alone. No one will ever really know what a struggle Schilder endured there in that upper room in the farm house behind the river dyke near Giessendam, as those long, long, grim months dragged by.

Suspended

At this point the possibility of betrayal became a factor in Schilder's situation. At an ecclesiastical meeting near the end of 1943, at which the tensions in the church situation dominated people's feelings, Mr. Groeneveld came to the discovery that certain people who were not friends of "KS" seemed to know where he was hiding. Therefore Schilder would very quickly have to find a different address. Through the intervention of Rev. F. de Vries of The Hague, he was brought to the home of Dr. Jasperse, who was a physician in Leiden.

While he was at the Jasperse home, Schilder was able to play a role in the case being brought against him at the synod. It was there that he wrote his famous letter of December 13, 1943, which he addressed to "The General Synod of the Reformed Churches in the Netherlands, coming together in Utrecht in the middle of December, 1943." During this period he also had a few opportunities for personal contact with members of the committee dealing with the case against him.

When I went to visit Prof. Schilder at the home of Dr. Jasperse, shortly after the suspension, he told me that the rumor to the effect that he refused personal contact with the synod was slander. It was obvious that he could not appear at the synodical meeting itself, but he did have contact on certain occasions with the members of the synod's committee. Such contact took place in 1944 at a secret address near Wassenaar.

Prof. Schilder would ride a bicycle along the Witte Singel (a road) to the Vliet River and then take back roads to get to the location for the meeting. But when the days grew longer and it was impossible to make the journey in the darkness, this possibility was no longer open. We should remember that Schilder was running a risk not only for himself but also for his host. At that time Leiden was teeming with Dutch Nazi "policemen," and other professors in this university town had already been arrested. The same thing could easily happen to Schilder.

And so it was not a question of not *wanting* to meet with synodical representatives, but simply of *not being able*. Even so, the synod went ahead with its proceedings. This was not only unchristian, it was inhuman. Simply put, it was horrible that a brother should be treated in this way — even if the synod had been completely correct in its charges against him. The "cement of love" was lacking, to borrow some terminology from Dr. Praamsma. It was the lack of love that led to such practices.

On one occasion during the time Prof. Schilder was staying with his friend Jasperse in Leiden, there was a rumor that all homes were about to be raided in a search for able-bodied men. (Such raids took place in a number of Dutch cities.) Therefore it was regarded as necessary that he disappear for a while to a different hideout. He spent a week at the home of Mr. G. Steinman in Kethel (between Schiedam and Vlaardingen). This man later wrote as follows about the time he spent with Schilder the diver:

> All of a sudden he stood before us. And perhaps it is a good thing for our people to find out the way things were. In those days before his suspension, I formed — and still treasure — an unforgettable recollection of this man, whom at that time I continued to view as our ward pastor from Delfshaven, the minister who taught me when I went to catechism.
>
> On the evening of a day on which I again mailed letters for him in various surrounding places (people were not supposed to know where he was), we took a walk together in the darkness. How he could then talk about God's nature — when he saw the play of the clouds, the moon, and in the background the outlines of a quiet village! Afterwards we sat in the house and reminisced about the old days in Delfshaven and Vlaardingen. How he appreciated our efforts to divert his attention for a while from the difficulties he had to endure! This restless spirit was forced to be calm.
>
> We were supposed to call him "Uncle Gerrit," and on his identity papers his name was "Gerrit Leydekker." The

first few times we called him by this name it felt awkward, but after a while it became easier.

The next morning we brought him water to shave, but my mother forgot to supply him with a mirror. In his great modesty he did not ask for one either, but by the time we realized what we had forgotten, he had already finished shaving, using the back side of his pocket watch as a mirror.

In this "butterless" time we were accustomed to making butter ourselves; to do so, we had to start early in the morning and churn about twenty liters of sour milk. This was a very heavy job that often took about an hour. "Uncle Gerrit" observed this process when he was first with us, and one morning we found him standing with an apron on in the front part of the kitchen churning milk, just as if he had never done anything else in his life. That day he stole the hearts of all of us — from the youngest to the oldest. He was one of us, and nothing was then too much for us to do for him.

As Mr. Steinman continued his narrative about the time of the suspension, with Schilder remaining in Kethel, he turned his attention to the developments in Utrecht, where the synod was meeting:

> Schilder's brother in The Hague had come to see him a number of times, and we came to the realization that there was a strong possibility that an insane decision to suspend him might be made that very week. We did not believe they would dare do it; I don't think Schilder believed it either. Yet we were receiving very somber reports. In those days he lived in a tension that was almost unbearable.
>
> And then the twenty-third of March, 1944, arrived. Early that morning his brother had already stopped by, and together they composed the well-known telegram to the synod.[55] Unfortunately, it did no good. We shared his anguish and went out to try to find out what was happening, but no one could help us. I don't think we ever really realized what he suffered and struggled through during those hours.

---

[55] The text of this telegram is printed on pp. 290-291 below. —TRANS.

Finally, late in the afternoon, Candidate Herman J. Schilder, who was his nephew,[56] came by with the unbelievable but nevertheless true report that Schilder had been suspended as both a minister and a professor. Then we did not know what we could do for him, and in a frenzied desire to do *something,* we called Rev. Hermanus Knoop and cautiously let him know what had happened. Within an hour Rev. Knoop was in Kethel. KS was busy talking to someone else just then, and I can still see Rev. Knoop sitting there as he waited in the living room. When the door opened he heard the voice of KS. "His master's voice," said Rev. Knoop, and there, for the first time since Knoop's return from Dachau, these two friends encountered each other again, just in this hour when they needed each other so much.

Some men had come together at exactly this time in order to support this wounded yet great man on a day that was so bitter for him — Rev. Knoop, Candidate H. J. Schilder, and Mr. Arnold Schilder. Rev. C. Vonk of Schiedam also came by. And together they talked about the unity of the church of the Lord.

The next day Schilder would leave again. Despite his great difficulties, he had found opportunity to show us, in a way that was detailed and thorough, yet simple, the path that must now be followed. And then he left. We waved good-bye with tears in our eyes. He left with many words of thanks for what we had been able to do for him — thanks that we did not need, for he had done much more for us than we would ever be able to repay.

---

[56] H. J. Schilder (1916-84) became a candidate for the ministry in 1943 and accepted a call to the church in Noordeloos, but he was not approved by Classis Gorcum because he could not accept the decisions made by the Synod in 1942 in relation to the covenant and presumptive regeneration. His case went before the Synod in 1944, and the decision of Classis Gorcum was upheld in June — which was after that Synod had suspended "KS" but before it deposed him. "KS" himself maintained that this case was of prime importance in terms of demonstrating concretely what the synodical decisions of 1942 really meant. Information regarding this case can be found in a book of some 580 pages entitled *Op de grens van Kerk en secte* (Rotterdam, no date), which is made up of documents accompanied by commentary by H. J. Schilder. His statement to Classis Gorcum can be found on pp. 43-47, and the letter sent to him informing him of the Synod's decision is on p. 194. H. J. Schilder was ordained as a minister in the liberated Reformed churches in 1944, and in 1953 he succeeded B. Holwerda as professor of Old Testament studies at the seminary in Kampen. —TRANS.

I have quoted these lengthy passages[57] here because they acquaint us so well with Schilder *as a person:* they show us Schilder during the time when he was most in need. Dr. Jasperse also talks about Schilder *as a person* when he tells us how things went when he was finally deposed on August 5, 1944. He describes the events as follows:

> On March 23, 1944, there came his suspension as a professor at the Theological Seminary and as an emeritus minister of the Rotterdam-Delfshaven congregation. The latter suspension made Schilder especially angry and upset, for the synod made this decision without so much as consulting his former consistory. This was unheard of — it was hierarchy through and through. It offended him greatly that the sheep who had formerly been entrusted to his pastoral labors were disregarded. He talked about this much more than about his own interests.
>
> Later, on August 5, 1944, his deposition followed. As on so many other occasions, he sat in the easy chair by the piano. It was already late in the afternoon. Suddenly the telephone rang: it was his brother, who lived in The Hague. "Say, Piet, I have to give you the sad news that they have just deposed Klaas." He overheard it, and the color drained from his face. At once he came to the telephone. His brother repeated the somber report with its scandalous content. All he could bring himself to say back to his brother was: "So." Then he sat down again, and all he said was: "Did they really *dare* do that?"
>
> All evening he was deeply under the impression of what had happened — who would not have been? He, the *faithful son of the church,* who had battled ceaselessly, day and night, year in and year out, to defend the church against the attacks of the Evil One — he had now been faithlessly kicked out by his own brothers.[58]

Trying his best right to the end

He was "kicked out," wrote Dr. Jasperse. Was he saying too much here?

---

[57] See *Gedenkt uw voorgangeren,* pp. 59-60. —TRANS.
[58] See *Gedenkt uw voorgangeren,* p. 61. —TRANS.

How Prof. Schilder labored and struggled to prevent this sorry outcome — right up to the day of his suspension! On the morning of March 23, the day he was suspended, Mr. A. Schilder sent a telegram to the synod on behalf of his brother the diver. When you read through the text of this telegram carefully, you will see that it sheds a certain light on the situation, a light that is necessary if we are to come to a correct judgment regarding the synodical sentence. The telegram reads as follows in English translation:[59]

> I have been authorized by my brother to bring the following to your attention.
>
> *First,* in part to respond to the urgings of many people and also with reference to the communications and statements of your committee of discussion, he reminds you of the difficulty of understanding one another fully, which is a point your committee has denied but one which he continues to regard as valid.
>
> *Second,* he rejects the statement of this committee to the effect that his standpoint, in all its parts, is transparent to the synod. This opinion is in conflict with the text of his response, which had to limit itself to the questions that were posed, and which, as far as further details were concerned, had to refer to the coming refutation of the report and conclusions which he would regard as necessary.
>
> *Third,* for the sake of truth and justice and for the sake of the Church of Christ as she watches, and also for the relief of both your and his conscience, he invites you as yet to give him an opportunity to defend himself in writing against the tentatively negative answer of your committee, and asks that his written defense be included in the published Acts of Synod and be added at this time as an item on your Agenda.
>
> *Fourth,* he would feel compelled to protest against any effort to continue dealing with this matter while ignoring his rightful request that you wait for his written defense,

---

[59] The Dutch text is somewhat more dense and compact in both terminology and sentence structure than my English translation, which is what one would expect in a telegram. I have made no effort to duplicate its texture, and so I ask readers to bear in mind that what they are reading is not the actual (Dutch) wording. —TRANS.

without which his views and attitude, as regards both the account in the Reports, which he disputes, and his standpoint on questions of doctrine and church order, cannot be genuinely transparent.

Fifth, he is still of the view that the unity of the churches will be positively served by awaiting the possibility of regular and unhindered interaction, which means that action on this and related cases should be suspended for the present.

We can regard this telegram as a last urgent appeal to the conscience of the members of the synod not to judge and condemn him without hearing him; rather, Schilder urged that they give the man they were about to sentence a chance to defend himself. Yet people like Dr. Praamsma maintain that the synod, even after the suspension, tried its best to hang on to Prof. Schilder.[60]

To the very end, Schilder continued to plead with the synod to wait until the enemy was driven from Dutch soil so that the people involved in this dispute could talk together in a free and open way that befits brothers. He was not granted this request.

No, I do not believe Dr. Jasperse was going too far when he declared that Schilder had been "kicked out." Schilder "tried his best" — but not the synod.

Not put to shame

Schilder had to suffer a great deal of personal pain. But he bore it in faith, and that was why he was able to emerge from his ordeal undefeated.[61]

---

[60] He makes this comment on p. 383 of his book *The Foolishness of God.*

[61] At this point in the story Schilder's character and personality become important for understanding what followed, for he did not retire from the church scene in disgrace. His opponents may well have underestimated him. Prof. H. Evan Runner, who was one of his students in Kampen before the war, comments on the curious mixture of simplicity and genius we find in Schilder: "He was a very friendly, kindly man of the people, I would say, who had a gigantic intellect, and therefore most of the people couldn't get close enough even to realize that he was a very simple man." Schilder's colleague D. K. Wielenga speaks of him in similar terms: "Prof. Schilder was a tremendous fellow — also as a person. It was not easy to get to know him well. I was not a friend of his, but I liked him very much. The feeling was mutual, and I believe the reason for this was that I said precisely what I thought about things, and that was not always done. Schilder was simplicity itself, a simple child of God, a tremendous fellow, a pious chap, an enormously clever man, an unusually talented person. It is not without reason that he became a professor without being placed on a dual nomination. He was

He thought he was standing alone in those frightening days. In faith he took his stand, confirming in his own life the words he had so often held before others:

> *Dare to be a Daniel,*
> *Dare to stand alone!*

And he was not put to shame. A synod had cast him out, cut him off as a rotten member of the Church. And since he was faithful to the ecclesiastical regulations to which he had agreed by affixing his signature, he had to take its action seriously. But *the Church* had *not* kicked him out. It would only be a matter of weeks before he preached his first sermon in a liberated Reformed church.

That first service took place in Bergschenhoek. I attended it along with my wife. What joy beamed forth from his whole being when he shook my hand after the service and said: "You both followed me in the past — and now you follow me in my humiliation?"

We did not experience that service as a humiliation at all. Schilder was preaching again! He even administered the sacrament of baptism, in which the parents presenting the baby could respond with a calm, joyful, and heartfelt "Yes," because "the aforesaid doctrine" as presented in Scripture and the confessions was again being taught in their church.[62] For the closing song we sang the following familiar words from Psalm 56:

> *For this I know, that God is at my side.*
> *In Him, whose word I praise, I do confide;*
> *He heard my voice when in my fears I cried.*
> *The L*ORD *is my Defender.*

---

sometimes as naive as a dove, and was unbelievably disappointed in certain people. He was as open and honest as gold, an Israelite in whom there is no guile — absolutely none. He was on fire for the church and for his students — always. That's why I am so tremendously indignant at the treatment he was given. I can't find a good word to say about the insolent, unchristian way he was dealt with during the war and the years just before it. May God forgive them, but it is almost unforgivable! I have no words to describe it: it was villainous — that's all there is to it. But I did not go along with the liberation because Schilder was such a nice fellow. The issue was the Lord's cause. I am not a partisan person — I am Reformed" (see *Vrede door recht*, by Peter Bergwerff and Tjerk S. de Vries [Groningen: De Vuurbaak, 1980], p. 37). —TRANS.

[62] The form traditionally used for baptism in Reformed churches asks the parents whether they accept "the doctrine which is contained in the Old and the New Testament, and in the articles of the Christian faith, and which is taught here in this Christian church, to be the true and complete doctrine of salvation." It then goes on to ask the parents whether they "promise and intend to instruct these children in *the aforesaid doctrine* . . ." —TRANS.

> *In God I trust, to Him my praise I render.*
> *I do not fear, I trust His mercies tender.*
> *My foes shall flee when He appears in splendour.*
> *Why fear then human pride?*

Schilder took his text from I Corinthians 4:6-7. Nowadays people sometimes say there is too much preaching about *the church*. I believe we have learned from Schilder not to talk about the Church too much, but to assign to the Church the place in preaching which Scripture gives her. Who can preach about the Bridegroom without at the same time also talking about the Bride? When a minister confesses the Church to be our Mother, can he remain silent about that Mother?

For Schilder the answer was no. His first sermon after the liberation of the Church was a testimony about the apostolic refusal to give way to extra-scriptural restrictions and decrees. Such a refusal was present in the *laying* of the foundation of the Church, and it is also necessary to *preserve* that foundation. Finally, we must refuse to be bound by such restrictions because of the *character* of the foundation of the Church.

Freedom restored

A great deal of fuss has been made about the fact that the man who was persecuted so much until just before the well-known liberation meeting of August 11, 1944, and had been in hiding, could now suddenly appear in public. But for those who are properly acquainted with the facts of the matter, this is easily explained. At the beginning of June, 1944, there was a change in our circumstances: because of initiatives on the part of the Germans, the situation became much better for us.

I can testify that I was a witness to these developments in a special way. After Prof. Schilder's suspension, I spoke in various places (within limited circles) about what was taking place at the synod. I regarded this as necessary because I was a free man: since I was not an office-bearer, I was not bound in any way. It was not until the liberation was upon us that our ministers, once they had made their choice on August 11, would be able to enlighten our people as to what was going on. But I could tell people about it before then — and I did. My activities in this regard became an occasion for the consistory in Goes to censure me (along with wife), although this particular episode in my life makes no real difference to the bigger story. There were all sorts of censure and suspension cases being undertaken at the time!

One of my speaking trips took me to Pijnacker, where some brothers and sisters told me that a certain A. Kapteyn wanted to talk with me about an important matter having to do with Prof. Schilder. I looked this man up at the address I was given on the Juliana van Stolberglaan. He presented himself to me as someone who had fairly recently transferred membership from the Christian Reformed churches to the Reformed *(Gereformeerd)* churches. He held an influential position in one of the departments in The Hague and could see to it that Prof. Schilder would no longer be regarded by the Germans as a problem: Schilder would even be able to get permission to publish again.

It should not surprise anyone that I was suspicious of this strange and laconic communication. When I asked Kapteyn what guarantees he could give that these facts were genuine, he told me that he could get written authorization to that effect from Prof. Nelis, the man to whom ecclesiastical affairs in the Netherlands were entrusted by the Germans. Nelis was an S.S. officer (a *Sturmbannführer*) connected with the office of the commander of the security police in the occupied territory of the Netherlands. Thus he was not just anybody. He told me that Rauter[63] would also be prepared to provide papers to show that no one was to disturb Prof. Schilder.

What was I to do with these givens? This man Kapteyn sounded very sure of himself. That he had important connections in The Hague was obvious from the information he possessed. Moreover, he was on good terms with J. J. C. van Dijk, a pre-war cabinet minister, and also with Prof. V. Rutgers, and he invited me to check with Rutgers on the truth of his claim that he had performed many "services" for the Reformed churches in his function in The Hague. He had made it possible for *The Watchman* to continue to publish and had also seen to it that the synod of the Reformed *(Gereformeerd)* churches had enough paper to keep publishing its magazine for the young people. When it came to the facts concerning Prof. Schilder, he had been urged to take up contact with Dr. J. Hoek, who at that time was the first clerk of the synod, but he thought it would be better that Prof. Schilder himself be informed first about changes in the situation.

I let Prof. Schilder's brother know about the conversation I had with Kapteyn. From correspondence that was published later, it is

---

[63] Walter Rauter was the SS commander for all of the Netherlands. He was later killed by the underground resistance forces. —TRANS.

Chapter 3 — Occupied Possession

apparent that Mr. Arnold Schilder had been contacted by this Prof. Nelis at about the same time (June 5, 1944), and that it was Nelis who had taken the initiative in passing on this information about the position in which Prof. Schilder now found himself vis-à-vis the occupying forces.[64]

And so we have various indications to the effect that the initiative to restore freedom to Prof. Schilder came from the Germans. The upshot is that the standing order for his arrest was withdrawn in June of 1944. There had been a change in the position the Germans took toward Prof. Schilder.

We will probably never find out about all the factors operating in the background. Prof. Schilder himself has written as follows about this matter:

> What official occasion was there for the Germans to think about the possibility of changing my position in June of 1944? According to communications that were received from Mr. Nelis of the security police, the attention of the Germans had been drawn to certain publications of the well-known committee meeting in Voorburg, which, after the shameless suspension of the undersigned on March 23, 1944, performed the service of publishing some highly needed reading material by way of explanation.
>
> Through these publications it became apparent [to the Germans] how disgracefully the synod proceeded against a man who could not defend himself when attacked, and whose freedom of movement was hindered by German persecution as well as by a decree that he was not allowed to publish anything. Now, this was not saying too much regarding the synod: the professors in Kampen were acquainted with the text of the decree forbidding me to publish, at least as far as its cardinal formula was concerned, and the curators also knew all about it, and thus the synod as well. Moreover, all three of these groups had been informed in writing by me. Via the curators, the synod also had access to the information that my absence from my teaching duties in Kampen had been permitted.
>
> But the Germans found this whole matter unpleasant in relation to their own ends insofar as it was now being

---

[64] One can read about this matter in the supplement to the yearbook of the liberated Reformed churches for 1946.

made known to the people that an ecclesiastical figure caught up in an ecclesiastical struggle was being hindered in his freedom of movement by the Germans. The Germans were only too happy to persecute the church, but they did not want to be *seen* as doing any such thing. And so, by way of Mr. Nelis, they sought contact with my brother.

Thus the facts of the matter are clear enough. Until July of 1944, Prof. Schilder operated on the assumption that he was being sought by the German occupying forces, and so he stayed in hiding. When the Germans took the initiative to change his situation for the better in July of 1944, he no longer regarded himself as obliged to remain in hiding: the very same day on which he got the word (July 22), he let the synod know that his circumstances had changed. Shortly before his deposition in August of 1944, he had a discussion with some representatives of the synod in The Hague. Thus no one who was acquainted with the facts needed to be surprised that he appeared in public on August 11, 1944.

A question of "church order" — not "doctrine"

That such slander about Schilder's person and character had to be added to the other things to which he had already been subjected is sad beyond words. The things that happened in our church life in that dark year 1944 are greatly to be regretted. We are reminded of what we read in the book of Isaiah: "And justice is turned back, and righteousness stands far away; for truth has stumbled in the street, and uprightness cannot enter" (59:14).

The facts have been established by now and do not all need to be reviewed here. Much has already been written about these matters.[65] Yet I want to make a few observations that shed a special light on the

---

[65] The author is referring to books and brochures written in Dutch. The most important of them is a brochure entitled *The Truth Is a Tricky Business* (Dutch: *De waarheid luistert nauw*), which he published under his real name (K. C. van Spronsen), rather than his pen name (Rudolf van Reest). It was actually written by Schilder himself but could not be published with his name on it because he had been forbidden to publish anything. Other publications about the case include the brochure *De Schorsing van Prof. Dr. K. Schilder,* by Prof. Greijdanus, and the book *The Facts of the Case* (Dutch: *De feitelijke toedracht*), by Rev. Geert Janssen. There is also an account of the liberation and the events surrounding it that has been prepared especially for the use of schoolchildren: *Bewaard bevel: De Vrijmaking in kort bestek,* by H. van Tongeren (Enschede: J. Boersma, fourth edition published in 1962; partial English translation by Janette Veenema under the title "Mandate Maintained: The 'Vrijmaking' in a Nutshell" [1965]). For the standpoint of the synodocratic churches regarding these matters, see Dr. C. N. Impeta, *Waar het om ging* (Kampen: Kok, 1956). —TRANS.

facts surrounding the suspension and deposition of Prof. Schilder. We will then see how far the decline had gone by this point, and how fully the Solomonic pattern of life had displaced the Scriptural Davidic pattern.

Prof. Schilder had asked to be heard when the notorious five questions were put to him, questions to which he was to respond with no more than a categorical "yes" or "no." The reporter for this concluding drama in the Schilder case was Prof. Doede Nauta. He ended his report (which was accepted by the synod) by saying that there were not sufficient grounds to grant the request of Prof. Schilder that he be heard. He also wrote: "Especially because the points at issue here are not so much concerned with greatly differing views as with maintaining good order in the Churches and upholding the authority of the Synod, we do not regard it as necessary that consideration be given to the possibility mentioned by Prof. Schilder."

The confessions tell us not to condemn anyone without a hearing (see Lord's Day 43 of the Heidelberg Catechism). For the sake of maintaining "the authority of the Synod," this fundamental rule of all proper conduct was trampled underfoot.

The greatest evildoer gets every opportunity to defend himself in the courts, as we saw again when Adolf Eichmann was tried for his war crimes. But from Prof. Schilder this fundamental right was withheld — and not by a worldly court, but by a circle of his *ecclesiastical* peers, who, at the end of this drama, proceeded to call upon the Name of the Lord. The "prayer letter," which was a sort of "pastoral" statement sent by the synod to all the Reformed *(Gereformeerd)* churches in the Netherlands, ended with this request: "Bow before Him in deep humility and beg Him to crown this act of discipline directed against Prof. Schilder with His blessing."

There is nothing more horrible than to see deeply sinful actions undertaken in the Church being accompanied by the most pious gestures. The High Priest tore his mantle during the case being made against the Savior. The "heretics" were turned over to Rome in the midst of pious declarations by their accusers: the worldly judge was then to burn them. The victims, in their burning pain, would have the cross of the Savior held before them devoutly.

Luther was also hit with a papal ban that was accompanied by the most pious declarations. But he did not allow himself to be deterred, for he said of the decretals: "They look like a body that has a face, gentle and tender as that of a young maiden, with tremendous limbs like those of a lion, and with a tail full of cunning like that of a serpent."

A classical committee that was involved in the case of Rev. Hendrik de Cock ended its report with the following declaration: "May the work of this committee be of assistance in settling this difference in the spirit of the Lord and for the good of His Church." This was the same horrible style used in 1944. And that's not all: in these "ecclesiastical procedures" in which faithful prophets of the Lord were cast out, "doctrinal questions" were turned into "questions of church order."

This was also true in the case of our Savior. His accusers said the following about Him before Pilate: "We have found that this man turns the people aside; He forbids them to pay tribute to the emperor, saying that He is Himself Christ the King." The complaint against Paul and Silas in Philippi was: "The men are stirring up the city." In Thessalonica the very same thing happened when Jason and some brothers were dragged before the rulers of the city: "Those men who are stirring up the whole world have also come here."

The issue in all such cases is *power*, but this motive is camouflaged by raising the question of "order." During the time of the case against Schilder, Rev. C. Veenhof reminded people of this in an article dated January 21, 1944, and published in *Church and Youth*. In this article, entitled "Christ in Conflict with Hardened Israel," he observed: "When there is talk of order and preserving the peace, in most cases the motive operative in false rulers of the church is to neutralize those who are faithful witnesses to Christ." He also wrote: "The central question as to the *truth* of the preaching of the apostles was not raised. The *power question* was more important for the gentlemen of the Sanhedrin." Also: "They all think in terms of the maintenance of their own position, power, and influence, and so they expunge Christ from their life." Finally: "In this situation there was only one thing left for the councilors of Israel to do. There was only one weapon available to them, the weapon of half-heartedness, of calculating diplomacy — *intimidation*."

What, then, was the real motivation for the ecclesiastical assassination of a faithful prophet in Christ's Church? In a letter dated February 25, 1944, which the synod sent to the consistories, no mention was made of Schilder's "departure from doctrine"; instead the synod talked about "mutiny in the churches." Schilder was undermining "the authority of major assemblies."

In his letter of January 14, 1944, Schilder had sent the following statement to the consistories: "I cannot bind myself to those decisions because I regard them as internally contradictory and in part incorrect." He also wrote: "In my judgment, because those decisions are internally contradictory, no office-bearer will be able to avoid coming into conflict with them once he goes into the question more deeply." Schilder's enemies maintained that he had no right to make such a declaration.

Yet, rather than *rebelling* against the church order in giving such a response, he was really holding to it strictly. The synod had dealt with the matter definitively, and ruled that it was not open for further discussion. The chairman of the synod had made his concluding address, and so the matter was settled for the next three years.[66] Candidates for the ministry would be asked whether they agreed with the decisions of the synod concerning this matter, for when they became office-bearers, they were not to teach anything that was not in full agreement with the decisions that had been made about this matter.

Now, was it not Schilder's duty to make the churches aware of his views on this question? In addition to being a confessing member, he was also a professor of dogmatics, and thus someone who dealt with these matters daily and had to instruct students concerning them. Thus it was his duty to communicate his dissent to the consistories, which represent the source of the synod's mandate. Moreover, Reformed church order stipulates that it is the duty of the consistories to read and study the decisions of synods, to test them to see whether they are in accordance with Scripture and the confessions, and if they are, to ratify them. If there is any confessing member who finds that he cannot agree with what has been decided, he is under an obligation to make this known.

Now, the synod denied that the consistories had the right and responsibility to ratify those synodical decisions; it even declared that this was a foreign and unreformed practice in our ecclesiastical life. But in a discussion of "First- and Second-Hand Authority," Prof. P. Deddens later showed how badly the synod erred, even though the professors advising the synod included three men whose teaching field

---

[66] A general synod is supposed to be held only every third year — not for three years off and on, as one might suppose from what happened after the Synod of 1939 convened. The churches sent delegates to meet as a classis four times a year, whereas regional or particular synods are held once per year. —TRANS.

was church order. Deddens wrote: "Those who are familiar with the facts of the matter do not know what is more amazing — the audacity of the reporter, moderamen, and synod as manifested in what they said, or the gross ignorance from which they spoke." He then went on to explain what the real Reformed practice in regard to these matters is.

In the meantime, the synod proceeded. The basis of the accusation against Schilder had to do with a question of "order," namely, that he was guilty of "public schism" *(scheurmaking),* which was a "gross sin" under Article 80 of the Church Order.[67] Schilder, it was charged, did not conform to the synodical decisions, for he had told his consistory in Kampen, in accordance with Article 31 of the Church Order, that he did not regard those decisions as settled and binding.[68] It was said that he openly attacked the doctrinal decisions without submitting a gravamen,[69] and that he incited the churches not to consider themselves bound by them.

Nauta admitted that these actions of Schilder, taken individually, were not of the sort that would call for disciplinary measures, but when added together they did justify discipline! One wonders how he reached this conclusion: no matter how many times we add zero to zero, the total is still zero.

Did the gentlemen at the synod *really* find the things Schilder had done so terrible? If the answer is yes, there is another question to be asked: Why didn't they proceed to take action against some other people as well? Since 1944 there have been scores of ministers and church papers that declared openly: We do not regard those doctrinal decisions as settled and binding. Yet such statements on their part gave rise to no ecclesiastical proceedings. And no classis now asks candidates for the ministry whether they agree with those decisions.

---

[67] This article reads as follows: "Furthermore among the gross sins which are worthy of being punished with suspension or deposition from office, these are the principal ones; false doctrine or heresy, public schism, public blasphemy, simony, faithless desertion of office or intrusion upon that of another, perjury, adultery, fornication, theft, acts of violence, habitual drunkenness, brawling, filthy lucre; in short, all sins and gross offenses, which render the perpetrators infamous before the world, and which in any private member of the Church would be considered worthy of excommunication." —TRANS.

[68] Article 31 reads as follows: "If any one complains that he has been wronged by the decision of a minor assembly, he shall have the right to appeal to a major ecclesiastical assembly, and whatever may be agreed upon by a majority vote shall be considered settled and binding, unless it be proved to conflict with the Word of God or with the Articles of the Church Order, as long as they are not changed by a General Synod." —TRANS.

[69] A gravamen is an appeal to an ecclesiastical assembly in which it is argued that a given decision is in conflict with the Word of God or the Church Order. —TRANS.

Chapter 3 — Occupied Possession

It appears that the men of the synod did not really care about those decisions after all.

A strong indication of how completely useless the synodocrats themselves regarded their so-called decisions concerning doctrine is apparent from the challenge which Prof. C. Veenhof issued to them in a pair of articles published in *The Reformation* on January 24 and 31, 1948. In those articles, которые were later reprinted in great quantities, he declared:

> In these days something has happened which, to all appearances, will prove to be of church-historical importance. To the series of facts which have determined the history of the Reformed *(Gereformeerd)* Churches, a new one has been added. Within the framework of this series of articles — but interrupting its regular course for a moment — I want to focus some attention on it and try to place that event in the proper light.
>
> Those who are acquainted with ecclesiastical events in "our dear fatherland," especially with the developments in Reformed circles, know that some amazing things have taken place. One of them is that the decisions of the general synods of 1942-46 are being sabotaged and scorned — and that in a most shameless and unspiritual way.
>
> We hear about ministers who, when they regard it as useful, declare outright that they pay no attention whatsoever to the decisions concerning doctrine which were so solemnly sworn and by which their consciences are supposed to be bound. We hear about consistories that explicitly seek and call "protesting" ministers, that is, ministers who despise the "synodical" decisions concerning doctrine.
>
> If you draw attention to these facts, people answer you by saying: "Yes, such things are possible, but who can prove them? Moreover, are the churches to be held responsible for the immoral deeds of one or more of their members or office-bearers? Have there not always been people in Christ's church who covertly proclaimed deviant doctrines?" Indeed, there is something to be said for such reasoning. Yet we have to add immediately that if a faithful church hears such reports, it is *called* to under-

take a thorough investigation of such signs of contempt for her doctrine.

At this moment, the fact of the matter is that someone functioning as an *office-bearer* in one of the "*Reformed (Gereformeerd) Churches*" is *ignoring, sabotaging, disqualifying, and rejecting* the decisions concerning doctrine, and is doing so in the most *clear and public form* conceivable, *explicitly and with great emphasis*. What has happened is this: a few days ago, the second edition of the well-known book *Our Confession of Faith* appeared. Its author, Rev. J. G. Feenstra, takes great liberties, in the manner indicated above, with the truths of faith confessed by the bound churches,[70] and does so in full view of all the people of the church . . .

What fascinates and preoccupies me here is the fact that a minister, an office-bearer in the bound Reformed churches, *consciously and openly denies* a part of the confession of those churches — and then a part that those churches have recently confirmed in such a deeply earnest way as belonging to the doctrine of the church, that any refusal to accept it was taken as grounds to suspend and depose office-bearers, or to keep people from holding office; moreover, the part he denies has, at the most recent general synod of those churches, been promulgated as a set of binding "doctrinal statements," in virtue of "the doctrinal authority of Christ's church."

Prof. Veenhof then reviewed what Rev. Feenstra wrote in his book about the questions at issue and drew the irrefutable conclusion that it is in complete contradiction with what was demanded by the synods that had bound the churches. And on the basis of those same synodical demands, they had cast out some faithful servants. Veenhof concluded:

Yes, through the challenging book of Rev. Feenstra, the bound Reformed churches have been cast into a serious crisis! And because we always *seek their good* and do not combat them except *for their own sake* and in *their* and

---

[70] This term is sometimes used by people in the liberated Reformed churches to refer to the synodocratic churches, which had bound themselves to the synodical decisions concerning doctrine. —TRANS.

our own interest, we wish to point to the seriousness and unavoidability of this crisis.

We cannot do much about the crisis, but what is possible for us will indeed be done. Therefore we are sending a copy of this issue of *The Reformation,* and also the previous issue, to the consistory of Scheveningen, where Rev. Feenstra is a member. We will also have a copy of this issue sent to Classis The Hague, to which the Scheveningen church belongs. And we will send copies to a number of the most important church papers on "the other side." Then we will wait to see what must happen and does happen, praying that God will yet bring those churches to reflection and repentance, if it is not too late!

We do not doubt that there has been prayer and will be prayer. But there has *not* been "reflection" and "repentance." What is being taught, said, and written in the bound churches today is ten times worse than what was going on in 1948 — or must at least seem ten times worse in the eyes of those who persecuted and cast out faithful office-bearers. In all of this, we see how the falling away that was already manifest in the 1930s was carried through consistently and became a hardening.

In this sad and sorry process there was something even worse going on: it was taken very ill of Prof. Schilder that he informed the churches that he would not be able to bind himself to the synodical decisions, and also that he advised the consistories not to bind themselves either. Was this really a bad thing for him to have done?

In the first place, we should realize that it fit within the framework of the traditional Reformed *(Gereformeerd)* church order, with which Schilder was thoroughly familiar. Thus he was following established ecclesiastical channels. In the second place, he foresaw the inconsistency which was discussed above and about which Veenhof wrote. But in the third place — and this was the most important consideration for him — he was thinking of his students, whom he loved and wished to protect against corruption in their ecclesiastical lives. That was also why he wrote his letter of December 13, 1943, to the general synod, asking that no binding decisions be made that would call for stated agreement on the part of the students when they took their classical examinations as candidates for ordination to the ministry.

In his reminiscences about Schilder's period in hiding, Dr. Jasperse puts it in a way that lays bare Schilder's thinking on this matter:[71] "He foresaw that his *students* would be subjected to great temptations. This he found to be terrible. 'In that case I may no longer keep silent,' was the end of almost every conversation in those days. The students had to be assured that they had their teacher behind them when they declared honestly that they could not agree to those declarations."

This highly learned man, who was more learned than many of the other professors, did not want to leave his students in the lurch — indeed, he *could* not do so. He wanted to support them as they were taking their first wavering steps in their ministerial career, for he realized the significance of the kinds of difficulties that were being laid in their path.

He saw what consequences there would be *especially for the Church* if such assurances of agreement with the synodical declarations were to be required. Jasperse writes: "There would be two routes into the pulpit. But he also saw the meanness and the temptation in the new requirement, for he was equally well aware of the weakness of the human heart, including the hearts of his students. Therefore he himself, as the stronger one, stood in front of them; he stepped into the breach on their behalf. One time, indignant at the action of the synod, he said to me, literally: 'Let them attack *me* instead.' " That was *faithfulness* — also toward the students.

This should help us see why Schilder could not do anything other than what he did do. Such a man, who in every respect and in every area, takes the truth so seriously and insists on strictly observing what he has promised when he gives his word, could hardly stand idly by when games were being played with people who gave their word in the Church of the Lord.

To him, the corruption that was underway was horrible. Not only was it destroying the character of people, it also was in flagrant conflict with the holiness of the Lord, the holiness that was to be treasured in His House.

A double standard

At this juncture there is another consideration to be raised. People had reproached Schilder for not submitting to the synodical decisions and for advising the churches not to do so either. This was ultimately the "sin" for which he was thrown out of the church and cut adrift

---

[71] Published in *Gedenkt uw voorgangeren*, pp. 58-63. —TRANS.

from his life's work. Was this really regarded as such a serious matter?

I have already indicated that when Schilder took this step, he was only doing his duty. According to Reformed *(Gereformeerd)* church order, the synod is not some sort of "supreme college" of church leaders but a gathering of *delegated* representatives of the consistories. In the nature of the case, the delegating bodies must stand above those whom they have delegated. The delegates are responsible to the consistories that have issued them their credentials. And so the consistories would have to *ratify* what was done.

But even apart from such considerations, were his accusers and judges in any position to make a fuss over what he had done? What had they done themselves in comparable circumstances? I will point to two instances.

There was a synodical decision regarding membership in the Dutch Christian Student Union. (I dealt with this matter earlier in the book.) It had been determined that the organization represented a danger to our young theologians because it was infected with Ethical-Irenic tendencies at first and later with dialectical theology. The rotten fruit resulting from the mentality of the Dutch Christian Student Union was evident from the Netelenbos case first of all, and later from the Geelkerken case as well. Thus it represented a very acute danger to our churches. The Synod of 1920 decided: "All who are called to give leadership to our Reformed students are urged to make the students aware of these objections and to advise them most strongly against membership."

What effect did this "synodical decision" have? A professor at the Free University immediately responded by declaring that it could be "incalculably useful" to be a member of the Dutch Christian Student Union. Thus he denied the synodical decision.[72]

And he was not the only one. Prof. F. W. Grosheide, one of the fiercest opponents of Schilder, wrote nine years later that the Synod of 1920 had never forbidden membership in the Dutch Christian Student Union but had only said that there were some difficulties connected with membership. His conclusion was that opposition to the Dutch Christian Student Union should therefore cease, and that a student should not be suspect simply because he was a member of this organization.

---

[72] The person in question was Prof. A. Anema in his brochure *Our Time and Our Calling*.

And Buskes, in his book *Hurray for Life,* wrote: "The decision of the general synod did not bring about any real change in the situation. The chapter of the Dutch Christian Student Union at the Free University continued to exist, and no professor there ever advised me against membership. People like Profs. Herman Bavinck and C. van Gelderen continued to support the Dutch Christian Student Union. After a short time this entire matter was relegated to the past . . ." That was how seriously people took the decisions of a general synod!

The second example is even more disturbing. In 1936, the synod made some decisions regarding membership in the Dutch Nazi movement. By then it was evident that this movement and organization represented a very acute spiritual danger. The number of members of this movement who were also members of our Reformed *(Gereformeerd)* churches was estimated at about eight thousand.

Now, the very same two professors who were fiercest in attacking Schilder on the grounds that he did not conform to a certain synodical decision and that he advised the consistories not to ratify that decision (those were the only weapons they seemed to be able to rely on in their attack) — those two professors did the very same thing, formally speaking, that Schilder later did: they did not accept the decision regarding the Dutch Nazi movement, even though it was a godless organization. Prof. Hepp declared that he did not regard the synodical decision of 1936 against the Dutch Nazi movement as settled and binding. Prof. H. H. Kuyper did the same thing.

It is well worth taking the trouble to look at the personal advice which Prof. Kuyper gave to the consistory at Goes when it consulted him regarding a concrete case. As we do so, we should bear in mind what was done to Schilder when he followed such a route in an instance that was completely parallel to it in formal respects.

The situation in Goes was that the consistory there, shortly after the Germans took control in our country, had to deal with a leading member of the congregation who joined the Dutch Nazis and then proceeded to play a very important role in the movement. In the light of the synodical decision of 1936, the consistory sought the advice of H. H. Kuyper, as an expert in church law. He gave them his advice in a written communication of October 23, 1940, in which he stated:

> Although I have always stood up for the authority of synods in opposition to Independentism, as your consistory will be aware, there are cases when the decisions of a

synod are of such a nature that the consistories, whether because they have objections of conscience against them, or whether because those decisions involve serious dangers for the congregation, cannot carry them out. Our synods do not have infallible authority, and blind obedience cannot be demanded of the churches.

As the Synod of Sneek has been informed from more than one side, many churches were not able or willing to carry out the decisions of Amsterdam (1936). This was also known to me personally. A renewed declaration by the Synod did not bring about a change in this situation.

The exercise of censure is not an ecclesiastical measure but an exercise of the power of the keys which Christ has assigned to the office-bearers, which power they are to exercise on His authority and in His name. Therefore a consistory can never transfer the responsibility for the exercise of such censure to the Synod if it is convinced that the censure is not in agreement with what God's Word prescribes.

The consistory may only bind if it is convinced that what it binds on earth will also be bound in heaven by Christ. To exclude someone from the kingdom of heaven even though he is in other respects an upright Christian in his walk of life and is attached to our confessions in a heartfelt way, simply on the basis of a political error, is to impose a sentence which, according to my deepest convictions, would not be ratified by Christ. After all, among His own disciples He tolerated the false political idea that He would be an earthly messiah delivering Israel from Roman rule.

For this reason alone, when people have asked me for advice, I have never told them to go ahead and exercise discipline against members of the [Dutch] National Socialist movement or the Christian Democratic Union, provided that the people in question showed themselves in other respects to be upright Christians in their confession and their walk of life. And at the Synod of Amsterdam I openly declared that, despite the decisions of Synod, I would not be able to give any other advice than this if people should ask me about this matter.

Now that serious dangers are threatening our churches, it is being realized in ever broader circles that the decisions of the Synods of Amsterdam and Sneek went too far, and that they will lead our churches into the greatest difficulties since we are now under the rule of National Socialists who will not permit us to censure members of our churches simply because they are National Socialists. In your own circles you have already learned from experience that the occupation authorities do not shrink from drastic measures when something is done that is an affront to their authority. And I will now tell you something in confidence: I have been warned through the Ministry of Justice that if censure is exercised against members of our churches because they are members of the Dutch Nazi movement, catastrophic consequences will follow for our churches.

Apart from my personal difficulties with such an exercise of discipline, I can give no other advice to your consistory than this: refrain from exercising such censure — although I am well aware from information acquired from other sources that the brother involved in the case you have in mind has given great offense in your congregation.

Your consistory bears a doubly heavy responsibility. Now that ecclesiastical gatherings are permitted only on the condition that no political matters are dealt with, leaving open the possibility that a complaint from a member of the congregation to the effect that censure is being exercised against him because of his political standpoint might come to be regarded as a political matter . . .

"Our synods do not have infallible authority, and blind obedience cannot be demanded of the churches," said H. H. Kuyper. That was precisely what Schilder maintained. Kuyper had also affirmed: "A consistory can never transfer the responsibility for the exercise of such censure to the Synod if it is convinced that the censure is not in agreement with what God's Word prescribes. The consistory may only bind if it is convinced that what it binds on earth will also be bound in heaven by Christ."

That was how H. H. Kuyper was talking back in 1940, when the campaign against Schilder was already underway. Yet, when many consistories in 1944 did precisely what he was talking about (in formal respects), they were placed outside the federation of the synodical churches and attacked as "schismatic churches."

Perhaps someone would wish to argue that H. H. Kuyper was speaking with one eye on the restrictions imposed by the German occupying authorities. In my judgment there is no validity in such an argument, for at stake here are *principles,* whose value or worth is not dependent on the changing political situation; rather, they derive their normative character and validity from Scripture and the confessions.

A devastating judgment about this *Realpolitik* on the part of H. H. Kuyper was pronounced — unknowingly — by Prof. G. M. den Hartogh, who was professor of church order at Kampen. (The consistory at Goes had sought his advice on the same matter.) The answer he gave was in effect a repudiation of his Free University colleague:

> I can sum up my answer to your written request for advice by referring you to the form for the ordination of elders, in which we find a prayer for "grace, that they may persevere in their faithful labors, and never become weary by reason of any trouble, pain, or persecution by the world." That was how the prophets and apostles and evangelists, the reformers and the heroes of faith in greater or smaller circles in all ages, including the previous century (especially during the Secession) viewed and understood their calling from the Lord.
>
> This is also the obligation resting upon all the members of our churches, and especially the office-bearers, who are "watchmen over the house and city of God" and "examples for the flock." No "persecution," no threat of sharp measures that can have all sorts of painful consequences, releases those office-bearers from their promise to discharge their office in accordance with the Word, "faithfully" and according to their "ability."
>
> Discipline *can* still be exercised, also in relation to the decisions of 1936 and 1939 to which you refer. But if you so decide, then it *must* indeed be done. The *principles*

that were condemned by the general synods of 1936 and 1939 certainly have not disappeared or become more innocent than they were taken to be back in those years! Quite the contrary!

Therefore, speaking generally, we can say that with regard to members who are more or less infected by the principles mentioned, there is certainly no less need than before to exercise discipline, a discipline flowing from the condemnation of those principles, so that those who have wandered away can be brought back. This will also be to the benefit of the congregation, which now stands exposed to some special spiritual dangers.

The members of the congregation who are standing firm must not be allowed to be grieved or offended because of a weakening of discipline, which would be a desecration of the covenant with God, a desecration which could in essence provoke the wrath of God against the congregation. How the Name of the Lord would be dishonored in the sight of those who are outside the church if the Reformed Churches, which have such exalted pretensions, should shrink from the consequences of certain principial decisions they once made with an eye to honoring the King of the church!

Let there be no false fear of worldly powers. Let there be a reverent fear of Him who has all power in heaven and on earth, and who in particular is the King of the Church He has bought with such a high price. Let us cling to the words found in our confession: "This holy church is preserved by God against the fury of the whole world, although for a while it may look very small and as extinct in the eyes of man" (Belgic Confession, Article 27).

In the Lord's providence, the president of your consistory presented a well-documented report about this matter at the last synod and defended the conclusions flowing from that report. The way which the Lord has indicated for you to follow is that you are to act in accordance with the decision, which no one has refuted on Scriptural grounds or would be able to refute on such grounds.

Chapter 3 — Occupied Possession

> I cannot answer your question whether it is true that most Reformed churches are doing nothing to carry out the decisions of 1936 and 1939. But it is clear to me that you may not follow any possible examples of unfaithfulness.
>
> And it is indeed necessary to speak of *unfaithfulness* here — unfaithfulness to a fundamental principle of Reformed ecclesiastical polity, as it is expressed in Article 31 of our church order: that which is approved by a majority vote at our major assemblies will be regarded as settled and binding unless it is shown to be in conflict with the Word of God, and so forth. The churches that are not carrying out the decisions of 1936 and 1939, and the advisors who are telling them to go easy on this matter, are acting in good measure in an independentistic spirit.
>
> Their action is also a slap in the face for those who, courageously and faithfully, even if it meant imprisonment, continued to issue warnings in the spirit of the measured and wise prescriptions and of the gradual exercise of discipline called for by the synods of 1936 and 1939. And they are hurting the tens of thousands who daily remember those faithful ones, thinking of them as people who have shown a willingness to surrender everything for the Name and cause of the supreme Pioneer and Perfecter of our faith (see Hebrews 12:2). There is a glorious reward of grace which is reserved not for those who give up right at the start but for those who persevere to the end.

Certain people, Prof. den Hartogh had written, were "acting in good measure in an independentistic spirit." That was his judgment about the advice which H. H. Kuyper was giving to the churches.

The difference between what Kuyper and Hepp did, on the one hand, and what Schilder later did, on the other, is striking. Schilder asked the consistories to reflect on what a synod had done and pointed to a course of action open to them, through which they could ask for a revision of the decision at the next synod. In giving this advice he was completely in line with Reformed church order. Kuyper and Hepp simply cut themselves off from synodical decisions and advised the churches to disregard them. In Kuyper's case there was no intention to ask for a revision at the following synod by having consistories bring the matter up again. He was simply giving the consistories a tip: don't act in accordance with the decisions of the synods of 1936 and 1939.

Schilder acted *in accordance* with the church order — yet he was condemned and cast out! Kuyper acted *contrary* to the church order, but his conduct did not even come up for discussion. A double standard was being used.

Schilder was attacked for what he did and was called "publicly schismatic." He was deposed from his office as professor and even from his office as an emeritus pastor of the Reformed church of Rotterdam-Delfshaven, which was the last congregation he served before becoming a professor. The latter deposition was in complete conflict with the church order, which does not give a general synod the competence to do any such thing.[73] His accusers were also his judges in this matter. The proceedings could hardly have been any more crooked than they were. But I will not write any more about this here. The facts are well enough known, and a great deal has been written on the subject.

People may wonder how all of this could happen in a time of war, when people were being carried away to concentration camps, martyred in prisons, and deported to Germany as slaves. Our country was being plundered, and the Nazis were poisoning our national spirit with their pagan theories and persecuting the church. If we ask how such an offensive against Schilder could be mounted in a time when all of this was going on, there is only one answer possible: the church was in a deep decline. It no longer lived by the Word of the Lord. Instead it acted on the basis of its own ideas and illusions of power.

---

[73] Under Reformed church order, the general synod plays no role in such a matter. The church order of the Canadian Reformed Churches reflects the historic Reformed practice in stipulating: "When ministers, elders or deacons have committed a public or otherwise gross sin, or refuse to heed the admonitions by the consistory with the deacons, they shall be suspended from office by the judgment of their own consistory with the deacons and of the consistory with the deacons of the neighbouring Church. When they harden themselves in their sin or when the sin committed is of such a nature that they cannot continue in office, the elders and deacons shall be deposed by the judgment of the above-mentioned consistories with the deacons. Classis, with the concurring advice of the deputies of regional synod, shall judge whether the ministers are to be deposed" (Article 71). See also the note on p. 315 below. —TRANS.

And in its blindness, it took its own dogmatic contrivances to be the binding truth of God.

Those were symptoms of Solomonic "decline," of which I wrote earlier. They were symptoms of the sort that must in time lead to a "rupture of the kingdom." For once Solomon was finished, Rehoboam would follow.

It was indeed a dark day when, on March 23, 1944, the decision to suspend Schilder was made. The whole world was on fire, antichristian powers had the believers by the throat, our families were being torn apart, our organizations were being banned, the press was being muzzled, fright and terror were paralyzing people — yet while all of this was going on, an ecclesiastical body fanatically continued to proceed against a brother who was more faithful than any of the others, even though this brother was not even able to attend the proceedings or defend himself!

I began this chapter with the story of the devastation of Jerusalem, which happened at the same time that the Jewish people were murdering one another. Those events were paralleled by the developments in our own country in the year 1944. What happened among us was no more an incidental episode than was the Jewish civil war; rather, it was a drama with a background, the result of a process that had been underway for years, stirring and churning in our ecclesiastical life. What happened to Schilder was not, then, something that fell unexpectedly from the sky. Developments in the spiritual world, like other events in our experience, happen in accord with laws of cause and effect.

The 1920s and 1930s give us the material that renders the developments of 1944 somewhat comprehensible. We are reminded of what Seerp Anema had said in the brochure quoted earlier: "May God preserve us from the triumph of Solomonic practices. If they win out, we will perish just as the kingship in Israel perished."

Chapter 4

That They May All Be One

August 11, 1944

For many people, August 11, 1944, was a revelation. How clearly we still remember that day! Word had been passed from person to person, all through our country, that there was to be a meeting in some building in The Hague. The purpose of the meeting was to reflect on the situation now that Prof. Schilder had been deposed.

Who would have supposed that so many people would turn up for that meeting? When we arrived at the designated building, we were greeted by brothers who gave us the surprising news that the number of people who had come was so great that it had been decided to seek the use of one of the biggest churches in The Hague. The meeting was to be held instead in the big Lutheran church.

On to the Lutheran church we went. What a stream of people! Although trains were being attacked from the air and food was scarce and the Germans were to be feared, there was no keeping the people away. They had come from as far as Friesland and Zeeland, Limburg and Groningen. The big Lutheran church was full to overflowing.

And what a swell of excitement when the tall figure of Prof. Schilder was suddenly spotted among the many familiar faces. Who would have expected him here?

For Schilder himself, this encounter was equally surprising. Not for a moment did he suspect that the appeal to come to The Hague would be heeded by so many people — or indeed, *could* be heeded. It was an unforgettable day!

And then there was the elderly, stately figure of Prof. Greijdanus, who spoke in a moving way at this meeting and declared: "People do not need to feel sorry for me." This learned, intensely pious, gray-haired man, who was so scrupulous and serious about all ethical matters, had also been suspended. The disgraceful verdict pronounced against him had been based on Articles 79 and 80 of the church order, and also on claims that he had sinned repeatedly against the fifth and

Chapter 4 — That They May All Be One 315

ninth commandments.[1] It had happened only eleven days before, and it was written in black and white in the Acts of that shameful synod. Yet this man said: "People do not need to feel sorry for me." Indeed, the people should really feel sorry for the men of the synod, who had voted in favor of that deeply sinful proposal.

There was also Rev. Hermanus Knoop, the short but brave man in charge of the meeting. Less than a year before, he had been released, as though through a miracle, from the prospect of a horrible death in Dachau's hell, where his friends Revs. J. Kapteyn and J. W. Tunderman had both died in agony. At one point, when Schilder and Knoop stood next to each other in the high pulpit, the contrast in their physical appearance led to chuckles on the part of the crowd, leading Knoop to say in a tone of voice that penetrated to every corner of the building: "In every respect I stand behind Schilder!"

When Dr. Praamsma, in his history of the Dutch Reformed churches, deals with this liberation meeting of August 11, 1944, he does not find much good to say about it. He writes: "Viewed historically, this Act and the 'liberation' bound up with it was a *caricature* of what was written, and what happened, in 1834 and 1886." But for us, the events of 1944 are completely in the line of 1834 and 1886. In all three of these church reformations, the issue was extra-Scriptural decrees and demands to the effect that people were to bow before an ecclesiastical hierarchy. Those demands resulted in the persecution of faithful office-bearers who wanted nothing other than to live and act in accordance with God's Word and the confessions. There was no principial difference between the events in these three cases.

But I do agree with Dr. Praamsma when he writes: "The Reformed *(Gereformeerd)* churches were damaged by this event, and their power was sadly diminished. It could no longer be said of them: 'The people held them in high esteem' (Acts 5:13). They had to admit

---

[1] Article 80 is quoted in a note on p. 300. Article 79 reads as follows: "When ministers of the Divine Word, Elders or Deacons, have committed any public, gross sin, which is a disgrace to the Church, or worthy of punishment by the Authorities, the Elders and Deacons shall immediately by preceding sentence of their Consistory and that of the nearest Church, be suspended or expelled from their office, but the Ministers shall only be suspended. Whether these shall be entirely deposed from office, shall be subject to the judgment of the Classis, with the advice of the deputies of the Regional Synod mentioned in Article 11." As for the matter of the fifth commandment, it was charged that Prof. Greijdanus had attacked the authority of synods (the church is our mother!). As for the violation of the ninth commandment, it was claimed that he had borne false witness in declaring that the synod was guilty of hierarchy. —TRANS.

— to their shame — that although their confession was pure, love had grown cold among them."

In fact we could go further and say that love had not just grown cold but had disappeared altogether. This comment applies not just to 1944 but to quite a few of the years that preceded it, as I have shown earlier in the book.

What 1944 really represented was the catastrophic capstone of a process than had gone on for a couple of decades. Only a church that lived in the sin of forsaking the Word could have fallen into such practices as the ones that came into play in 1944 and thereafter. Despite the fact that the war situation grew in intensity and claimed ever more victims, also among the civilian population (think of all the people who died of starvation during the hunger winter that began at the end of 1944), those practices were maintained, including suspensions, depositions, and disciplinary actions. In the review of the preceding year which Prof. Schilder wrote for the first yearbook of the liberated Reformed churches, he observed that ecclesiastical life had been disturbed by a "revolution" which came "from the top, where it was prepared, and which, under the most extreme wartime pressure, was defiantly carried forward to its uttermost consequences."

The liberation

The meeting of August 11 was a revelation for all of us — not least for Prof. Schilder. Given the horrible circumstances in which our country and people found themselves, how did so many people who were one in heart and soul manage to come together so spontaneously?

There was no organization in place that could make this possible. Information that was passed from person to person proved sufficient to bring about this meeting. More than 1100 men and women assembled, driven by a single thought — to be together at a time when the Church of the Lord was in such great need. Anyone who maintains that hundreds of people came together that day in order to bring about a "schism" in the church, after considering the matter in an organized and deliberate way, is sadly mistaken. There was no organization: there was only a mystical unity and spiritual bond and love for the Church, and thus also a love for her faithful servants, who were being persecuted — that much the people knew. The people wanted to manifest their own faithfulness and devotion to the Church.

Therefore they defied the physical dangers posed by the occupying powers and the deadly dangers of a war that raged over their heads.

The liberation, which had its beginning in this meeting, cannot be viewed otherwise than as a deed of the LORD. In his review of the year's events, Prof. Schilder wrote about the meeting as follows: it was "a meeting which appears more and more to have been most timely and of which we may testify gratefully that, under God's guidance, it renewed the countenance of our national life. I believe that without this meeting, the liberation would not have attained the surprising and wonderful blessings which it now sees allotted to it. Even after only a year, those blessings, in terms of their extent and significance, go far beyond anything that the Secession or the Doleantie was granted in the same period of time, or even a longer period, in terms of real gain for the life of faith."

By the time the first yearbook was ready to be published (1946), there were 216 liberated churches in our country, and they were served by some 152 ministers. The total membership (including baptized members) stood at 77,303.

Rev. Knoop sketches the situation

Rev. Knoop, who presided over the meeting of August 11, gave an introductory address which can be summarized as follows: The Synod that met in 1943 and 1944 has shown by its words and deeds that it wants a split in our churches. What are we to do now? In Reformed *(Gereformeerd)* life in general, and in our ecclesiastical life in particular, degeneration has become evident. All down the line there is deformation to be seen, and we are *all* guilty of it. In the past there was a great blossoming and an expansion in all directions, especially in public life. No longer did our countrymen look down on us as narrow-minded people who take religion too seriously.

There are a number of manifestations of deformation that can be pointed to. We believed we had "arrived" and we no longer regarded the present dispensation as a time for work; we thought we had entered into our rest. We placed *ourselves* in the foreground. There was an exaggerated self-consciousness, and we began to think in terms of power relationships in the church, in politics and in social life. Secondary matters became primary for us. We came to place *ourselves* first, instead of assigning primacy to *Christ,* the Lord of the Church. Our Chinese lanterns and flags served to adorn *our* life, as we talked about *our* church, *our* school, *our* Free University, *our* Antirevolutionary Party. But as Sikkel already pointed out in a sermon, God may choose to break down *our* church, as long as *His* Church is built.

We became absorbed in a successful battle in our national life. We became wealthy and enriched. We were so intent on success that we became shamefully lacking in eschatological awareness, and so we no longer lived each day in the expectation of Christ's return. We had it too good here; we no longer thought in terms of bearing our cross for Christ's sake.

At our ecclesiastical gatherings, the spiritual welfare of the congregations was no longer our leading concern; the financial situation was of greater interest to us. There was a yearning for power and influence. This gave rise to ecclesiastical diplomacy, which meant that we no longer dealt honestly with each other. The spiritual antithesis in relation to those outside the Church was no more. And so our churches were well on the way to becoming a sect.

There was a widening gap between those who had received a higher education and the ordinary people. We wanted to save our life as it is — also our church life — which is why we were in the process of losing it. And at the same time we were losing each other. In and through all of this, the church has sabotaged its primary calling in its major assemblies. Consider the decisions made in 1936 in relation to the Dutch Nazi movement. The main question we came to ask was: How can we ministers make sure we do not lose our freedom of movement? We began to "shorten our defensive lines,"[2] as the Germans said they were doing when assailed by their enemies. We began to deal with the so-called "differences in opinion," and thereby needlessly made the church into a quarreling church. This led to the imposition of the synodical yoke, which represented a binding of our conscience, and was thus a yoke which Christ has *not* asked of us.

Our major assemblies were infected with the spirit of the times. The exercise of discipline at those assemblies was a violation of the rights of the local churches. The result was that Christ's own authority was attacked, and faithful office-bearers were persecuted. The synod has been leading us to follow the path of a sect. The way to unity has been sabotaged.

---

[2] When the German armies on the eastern front were pushed back by the Soviet armies, the news of the retreat would be announced from Berlin as "shortening our defensive lines." Rev. Knoop was suggesting that similar duplicity was present in what Reformed people claimed to be doing. —TRANS.

O God of the covenant, have mercy on us! What is our task now? There must be no compromise with sin in the church, and we must not postpone action. Christ asks obedience of us; He asks us to subject ourselves to His Word. May the Almighty God and Father help us to that end.

I have reproduced the heart of Rev. Knoop's address because his comments help us get at the main point of this book. We must regard the process that took place in 1944 as the sad and sorry consequence of what had been unfolding in the preceding decades and manifesting itself ever more openly in our church life.

"Return"

The meeting of August 11 took place shortly before the frightening division between the northern part of the Netherlands and the southern part.[3] On August 12, Dr. M. B. van 't Veer, who was a solid supporter of the liberation, conducted an information meeting in The Hague. Shortly after that he was suddenly taken away from us. His funeral took place just before the division between the north and the south, and so I was able to attend it. At his graveside, the pastoral labors he had performed in Amsterdam were highly praised by a colleague, for Van 't Veer was faithful in everything. Yet if he had not died, Van 't Veer would have been suspended by his consistory, and this same colleague would have agreed with the suspension. That was typical of the ethical situation in those days. Literally everything was subjected to diplomacy.

Shortly after that we had "Mad Tuesday,"[4] which was followed by the division of our land into north and south. At that point I lost all contact with Prof. Schilder. What we got to hear in the south were reports and rumors that we could not check out. The Germans did a good job of it when they hermetically sealed off the northern part of the country using the Moerdijk as border.

---

[3] By the fall of 1944, the Allied advance after D-Day came to a halt just south of the Meuse River that cuts through the Netherlands as it flows toward the ocean. Thus contact was lost between the north and the south until the following spring, when the Allied advance resumed. —TRANS.

[4] This was a day on which the land was ablaze with reports that the Germans were about to withdraw from the country or be swept out. Freedom was at hand! But the rumors were not well founded, and most of the country had to endure the better part of a year of additional German occupation. —TRANS.

In the south we were freed in October of 1944. We then began preparing to come to the assistance of the people in the north just as soon as the Germans were pushed out. We knew that the needs in the north were very great.

At the request of the military authorities that took control of the south, I served as an officer assigned to purge the press. Once the northern provinces were liberated in May of 1945, I assumed responsibility for the province of Utrecht. Part of my task was to ensure that the underground press which had done so much good work had paper so that it could continue to publish.

I was given a list of papers that had gone wrong during the occupation years, and also a list of papers published underground, and of papers that had remained loyal to our country by resisting the Germans. (Papers in the latter category had of course been banned.) But the people operating the Dutch government-in-exile in London had overlooked *The Reformation* when they drew up these lists, and so I put it on the list myself. If there was any periodical that deserved to appear just as soon as the Germans were chased out, surely it was *The Reformation.*

It happened that there was paper enough in Utrecht. When I visited the printing shop where *Folk and Fatherland* (the paper of the Dutch Nazi movement) had been printed, I was amazed at the enormous quantities of paper in its storerooms waiting to be used. The people running this paper had provided amply for themselves. They did not realize or intend it at the time, but they had also provided for *The Reformation!*

Was it a "coincidence" that the military authorities assigned me to Utrecht, and that I wound up in the office that controlled the allocation of paper? And was it mere chance that in Utrecht the presses were still turning, and that there was plenty of paper on hand? Was it mere chance that there was a man in charge there named Van Boetselaer who gave me a free mandate and approved my decisions without question? We don't believe in "chance."

An automobile was placed at my disposal, and one of my first trips was to Kampen. I did not go to Vloeddijk 101, which was Schilder's old address, but to Vloeddijk 14, where he now lived. The Germans had requisitioned his former home and made a shambles of his impressive library; they had even taken away materials which he needed to defend himself before the synod. And the synod was aware of this!

In any event, I found myself standing at the front door of Vloeddijk 14. I will never forget the look on the face of "KS" when he suddenly saw me before him. I told him that I had plenty of paper at my disposal, and that *The Reformation* could now be published again. "When?" he asked, amazed. "Just as soon as you have copy ready, Professor," I answered. "I'll have it ready this week," he replied spontaneously. And within a week I had enough copy to publish the first issue in Utrecht. The lead article was entitled "Return."

Because it was not possible to print the paper in Goes at that time, a printer in Utrecht helped us, and we were quickly back in business. Schilder's first article started as follows: "When with the help of treason on the part of Dutch Nazis, including a former Reformed *(Gereformeerd)* minister in The Hague who has not been suspended, a German hand halted the printing press that produced *The Reformation* after the publication of the issue of August 16, 1940, and took away from the publisher his list of subscribers, which had swelled amazingly quickly after May 10, 1940, and locked up the editor behind a cell door with a 'P' on it, presumably to mark him as someone in transit (a 'passant'), probably on his way to a concentration camp, that editor did not have the opportunity to inform his readers as to the reason for the paper's disappearance or to express his conviction that it would appear again at some time and in some form or other. The time of its reappearance proved farther away than we thought. But by the great grace of God it has finally arrived. And for this we give Him our heartfelt thanks."

There were some readers of our paper who found this first article a bit disappointing. They would love to have seen the first articles in *The Reformation* filled with recitals of all the things that had happened personally to the editor-in-chief. What had he gone through during the occupation years at the hands of the Dutch Nazis and of the Germans and of the synod that had cast him out? There was not a word about these things. There was only this small communication contained in a typically Schilderian sentence. But from that sentence we recognized that "KS" was indeed back.

He took up the thread where it had been broken off on August 16, 1940. What mattered to him was God's cause and the Church he loved — not his personal circumstances. Schilder saw himself as a servant — nothing more. Consider the prayerful words with which he concluded his lead article: "With the prayer that our re-won freedom may be used for our work, which is weak and may now be hindered by others even more than it was before, and to make possible the consistent working out of the principles that have our undivided attention, an attention that has been deepened because it was tested by fire, we now lay the needs of this paper before Him, knowing that He rules the ages and propels the peoples of the world forward toward the culmination but always 'loves' the 'peoples' of Israel (Deuteronomy 33:3)."

The upshot was that we should continue as usual. It was his wish that because the last number of the paper published before it was shut down was Volume 20, Number 45, the first issue published again after the five-year gap should be Volume 20, Number 46. And it was done!

The bush was not consumed . . .

Then followed a period of hard work — almost inhumanly hard work. I was living temporarily in Utrecht, in a house confiscated from a Dutch Nazi who had been arrested. "KS" showed up often at my place. It was there — and usually in haste — that he got copy ready for his paper. Sometimes he came late in the evening and began correcting copy, which we had to wait for so that we could proceed with printing. Then he would ask for permission to sleep at our place. Now, we had only one bed at our disposal, but that was no problem for Prof. Schilder, for there was also a couch. When I would object that we had no blankets for the couch, he would dismiss this concern by saying: "That makes no difference. I'll just cover myself with my coat."

He had only one desire, and that was to be able to work — day and night, if need be. Sometimes he even worked when he was ill. On one occasion when he was not feeling well, he had to go back to the station from our house. Naturally, he had a heavy suitcase along. I had no way to bring him in an automobile. A man who was helping me at the time, who later emigrated to Canada, offered to walk along with him to the station. Prof. Schilder declined this offer, pulled me aside, and said, "I would rather go alone, because I have a sore throat; if someone comes with me, I have to talk with him, and I'd rather not talk just now." I gave faithful brother Postema the proper signal, and he went with Schilder, not saying a word.

Schilder was not as strong in those days as he had been before the war. Yet he kept on toiling and working day and night, sometimes in impossible places and very difficult circumstances.

One day he asked me to accompany him the following Saturday to Zutphen, where he was to hold an information meeting concerning the liberation. I had a hard time refusing him anything, and I did then have a car at my disposal, which was unusual in those days. It was an old Ford which had spent four years in hiding under a haystack. "We have to be there early," Prof. Schilder told me. "I believe the meeting starts early."

I was a bit late that day and first had to remove some stuff from this little vehicle. My wife came along with us, and Schilder's younger daughter also joined our party. Along the way I asked, "At what time does the meeting actually begin, Professor?" He responded by shrugging his shoulders and saying, "That I don't know precisely." My next question was: "Where will the meeting be held?" He didn't know that either, he grumbled in response. Neither did he have an answer when I asked him where we were to report when we got to Zutphen. At that point I gave up trying to get information.

We finally drove into Zutphen, afraid that we were late for the meeting. Fortunately, I had with me the address of a young man who helped us with the distribution of *The Reformation* in the local area. He knew about the meeting and said: "But you are far too early! The meeting does not begin until six o'clock this evening." When "KS" heard this, he looked a bit glum. "What am I supposed to do with all that time?" he asked. "Is there a room here somewhere where I can work?" The young man offered his own room, and that was where Prof. Schilder ensconced himself. We then went into the woods for a walk, where we could recover somewhat from our hasty journey.

I will never forget that information evening in Zutphen. The place was packed. It was known that many members of the synodocratic churches planned to attend; therefore the local pastor could not very well stay away. After all, he had to make sure that his sheep would not be misled. Thus he attended and also joined in the debate.

At one point Schilder got to hear the following line of argument: Now, Professor, surely one does not just walk away from one's Mother when she is ill! You have written much about that sick Mother. And that she is indeed sick we freely admit. But what properly disposed child would run away from that sickbed and then go out into the street to say all sorts of bad things about that Mother? Surely you can see that it's just not done! Think of all the things which that Mother has given you! You have yourself written beautiful and glorious things about her in your brochure *Our Mother*. Remember all that she has done for you. She has made you a professor — indeed, a professor of dogmatics. Must you not then show your gratitude for all those good things? And what are you doing now?

The expression that began to form on the countenance of "KS" was well worth studying. In his response he left the pastor's comments to the very end. Then he dealt with them in a short and powerful way. He said: "If you have carefully read my brochure *Our Mother,* you will know *what* that Mother is. It was indeed a gift *(gave)* that I became a professor, but it was at the same time a task, an assignment *(opgave).* I believe that through the grace of the LORD I have been faithful in that assignment, and my responsibility is first of all to the LORD, who gave me the assignment. This awareness has led me in all that I have done. If you suppose that it is characteristic of a Mother to be giving gifts, then you have never properly understood the function of a mother. Gift-giving can be done by any neighbor lady or an aunt or a nurse — one need not be a mother for that. The task of a mother is to bear children. And that is the task of the Church; it is what makes her our Mother. And in that mother-task the Church was being hindered by the unscriptural restrictions which an erring synod began to lay on office-bearers and candidates for the holy Service of the Word. That Mother was not 'ill'; she was being hindered in her mother-function, and therefore she had to be liberated from the bonds that were hindering her in her most essential function. If you do not understand the situation in these terms, then you have understood nothing of the real meaning of the Church." The local pastor opposing Schilder seemed to shrink under the powerful blows of this argumentation. He did not say another word.

And so we saw "KS" busy again writing and speaking. He telephoned us from many different places, including very small villages in Groningen and Friesland. And then one day he would stand before us unexpectedly again in our temporary dwelling, or he would show up at the Kemink printing shop in Utrecht, where the paper was temporarily being produced. There, too, he was a welcome guest because of his winning ways, his friendliness, and especially his simplicity.

I also remember an occasion when he suddenly stood before me at my office on the Maliebaan in Utrecht, which was in the very building that had once served as headquarters of the Dutch Nazi leadership, including Anton Mussert. It was a pleasant moment for him when he was given a publication drawn from the enormous library of the Dutch Nazis (made up of all sorts of stolen books): it was a copy of his own brochure directed against the Dutch Nazis and the Christian Democratic Union, entitled *Not One Square Inch*. The brochure was stamped "Dutch Nazi Headquarters, Press Library, Utrecht." This brochure was one of the very first publications to be banned when the Germans took control in our country. It was remarkable that in the former office of the Dutch Nazis he could now personally be handed a copy of his own banned brochure! To have people listen to you is better than to receive the fat of rams, as Samuel had already announced (see I Samuel 15:22).

How hard Prof. Schilder worked once he had the freedom to spread his wings again. When *The Reformation* commemorated the tenth anniversary of his death in its issue of March 23, 1962, it published a picture of a piece of cardboard found at the home of brother Jasperse, which dated back to the time just after the liberation meeting of August 11, 1944. This piece of cardboard was part of the personal appointment calendar which "KS" had used to keep track of his speaking engagements. He was out almost every day, every evening. From this calendar we learn what sort of schedule he kept between August 19 and September 22 of that year, including speaking engagements in the following places: The Hague, Bergschenhoek, Delft, Bilthoven, Rotterdam-South, Rotterdam, The Hague, Voorburg, Delft, [one name illegible here], Amsterdam, Rotterdam-South, Enschede, Groningen, Deventer, The Hague, Delfshaven, Leiden, Charlois, Rozenburg.

After this first period — and we should remember that this was still the time of the German occupation — Prof. Schilder spent weeks traveling through the province of Groningen, usually by bicycle. He undertook unbelievably long journeys on his bicycle, sometimes even through bad weather. He traveled repeatedly from Kampen to the city of Groningen, which is a distance of 115 kilometers. How he labored and toiled to make our Reformed people everywhere see again the old Reformed *(Gereformeerd)* principle of "Church *covenant*" and "Church *federation*," which, as his successor at the helm of *The Reformation* rightly remarked, represented his anti-hierarchy struggle in a nutshell.

After the war Schilder was involved in an automobile accident: a car in which he was a passenger ran into a tree, and the result was a painful shoulder fracture for him. I heard him preach in IJmuiden while he was suffering this pain, and I could see that it hampered him considerably. But the work went ahead, relentlessly and unhindered.

Prof. Holwerda once said: "The liberation cost the ministers among us ten years of their life." We may take it that it cost Schilder and Holwerda even more years than that. But because of their conviction rooted in faith and their willingness to be of service, they both recognized and accepted the saying "Terar dum prosim" (the image of the candle: I am willing to be consumed, as long as I am useful).

Not only did our people need to be informed about the recent ecclesiastical events, there was also the need to reorganize church life after such a sizable liberation. This, too, involved a lot of work. Ecclesiastical congresses were held in Rotterdam, Enschede, Groningen, and Amsterdam, at which there were discussions about mission work, the union of all Christ-believers on the basis of the Word and the confessions, the ongoing reformation of our church life, and the training of servants of the Word, which was now undertaken by Revs. D. K. Wielenga, C. Vonk, P. Deddens, and Prof. K. Schilder. There was also a widespread desire to call together a general synod, which was already held in 1945 in Enschede.

When Schilder, in later years, spoke about this synod, his eyes shone. There he felt he was a brother among brothers. One of the most beautiful things he found was that people could again talk with each other freely and without reserve. They did not have to fear ecclesiastical diplomacy or secret conversations in which decisions on the matters at hand were cooked up in advance by a certain group, with the result that they came up for discussion only in a formal sense at the public meeting, so that if one made an eloquent case and presented elaborate arguments, it made no difference whatsoever to the outcome. An ecclesiastical propriety was evident in the meetings of this synod because people were bound to one another insofar as they had subjected themselves to the Word and to the one good confession of the church, the confession to which they all subscribed.

The most important matters to which this synod gave its attention were the filling out of the number of professors at the reconstituted seminary in Kampen and the ending of the old battle about giving doctoral degrees.[5] Synod simply gave its approval, and Prof. Schilder wrote: "Here, at one stroke, the recognition we sought was attained. It was one of the most beautiful moments in the history of this synod."

---

[5] Before the liberation, the Free University's faculty of theology was opposed to Kampen's proposal to institute doctoral programs and degrees. Supporters of the two institutions clashed over this matter at synods. —TRANS.

If we were to sum up the history of the Church under the heading "Of Struggle and Victory," the Synod of Enschede would surely have to be reckoned as a victory. Here the liberation was consolidated. At the conclusion of his review of the first year of existence of the liberated Reformed churches, Prof. Schilder wrote: "There is a story that goes back to the days of J. J. van Oosterzee:[6] the theological school in Kampen, which was then still very weak, received a telegram from him at one of its very first meetings, in which he expressed his best wishes by using a statement from the Bible: 'Yet the bush was not consumed' (see Exodus 3:2). I am not raising an exegetical question here: what he meant is clear enough. And this *meaning* I want to make my own, not by way of congratulation but as public thanksgiving to the King of the church, using Van Oosterzee's statement to close this review."

Sisyphean labors of toiling synods

How is it possible that the bush was not consumed? If it was nothing more than a fire that was started and tended by human beings, it would certainly have been consumed. The fires that had been lit beneath the liberation burned fiercely.

When people began to realize that Prof. Schilder was not about to be isolated from his people, that is to say, from the members of the Reformed *(Gereformeerd)* churches, more scheming was undertaken. I still remember clearly the general synod of 1945 of the bound churches in Utrecht, the one at which Rev. C. Veenhof read his "declaration." At the outset Rev. Veenhof had had some difficulties with the liberation. In his declaration, which he had first made before his consistory, he said that he wanted to free himself from the "declaration of sentiments" *(verklaring van gevoelen)* which the Utrecht consistory had accepted.[7] This declaration had led to an "unclear situation," he admitted later on. Veenhof now maintained that "all that activity of making interpretations and declarations would lead ultimately to the corruption of the church." He complained that "a simple statement concerning doctrine has been made into a piece of rubber that could be stretched in all directions." He also said: "While the *words* of the

---

[6] Van Oosterzee (1817-82) was an Ethical-Irenic theologian who taught at the University of Utrecht from 1863 through 1882. —TRANS.

[7] At first Rev. Veenhof had tried to interpret and explain the decisions of the Synod in such a way as to render them more or less acceptable. —TRANS.

formula are being maintained, the content is actually being hollowed out." The result was that "words spoken in the church could no longer be taken seriously." Because of this declaration, Rev. Veenhof and twenty office-bearers with him were suspended.

That week I wrote an article for *The Reformation* in which I gave my impressions of this synod, making it clear that the synodical leaders, who realized by this point that they had made a miscalculation during the occupation years, had sunk below zero in terms of their approach. Rev. Veenhof had made his declaration and had thereby freed himself from the Utrecht Declaration. For the synod, therefore, it made no sense to deal further with this declaration, which they had only introduced in order to hang on to the protesters who were still in their churches.

The spirits of the men at the synod were also very low. You could see it in their faces, and in the slack way they talked. They had run completely stuck with all their ecclesiastical scheming, but there was no way out for them. And so they did what they could to save face for themselves and to try to keep within their church federation those protesting members whom they had initially suspended, deposed, censured, and cast out so freely. Everything the synod did was geared toward this end, and the upshot was that the Utrecht Declaration was adopted, which meant that the synod was denying its own standpoint and declarations and acting against the advice of its own pre-advisors.

G. C. Berkouwer sat there in the president's chair, a sunken heap of a man. J. H. Bavinck told the synod that he had talked a great deal with protesting members and for their sake wanted to place more emphasis on the "demand" of the covenant. S. J. Popma spoke as a broken man who had finally run stuck in all his diplomacy. Even Hepp still spoke: he was the one who did not regard the synodical decisions of 1936 against the Dutch Nazi movement as settled and binding — but he was never suspended for it. He tried to save something by saying that he, from his side, "was now willing to give in somewhat." And so the sorry parade went on. There was no sign anymore of the style of the church: it was like the haggling and tinkering of boys who have broken an expensive vase in their rowdiness and are trying to fit the pieces together again.

Over all the proceedings lay the somber shadow of the liberation, which had taken along thousands of the children of 1834 and 1886. This shadow over the synod dominated the discussions, the mood, and the feelings of the delegates; not even exquisite prewar cigars made by the Schuppen company could bring about a change for the better.

The schemers had imagined a much different outcome: "KS" would be put out at a time when he could not defend himself or even stir from hiding. They would not have to fear his pen or his strong arguments or his irrefutable logic. Nor would they have to take notice of his unshakable bond to the Word as they dealt with the people of the church, who had begun to listen to him more and more.

But who would have expected things to turn out as they did? A church reformation, a secession, a Doleantie — it was a reformation that went far beyond 1834 and 1886 in terms of numbers. Dark, somber and hopeless was the outlook and attitude on the Maliebaan when the synod met there in the year 1945.

A second impression I would like to pass on is that of Rev. C. Veenhof preaching after he had baptized two children. His theme was the rediscovery of the law by King Josiah after it had been lost for many years (see II Chronicles 34). After his own liberation, which was a very memorable week for him, he had said to me: "Now I can *preach* again!" It was a cry of triumph issuing from a liberated heart. And his whole sermon, the entire beautiful service, was a celebration. There was no somber shadow, no sadness or hopelessness. Despite the pain about the rupture which the synod had caused, there was a mood of elevated gratitude and deep joy over the liberation from human restrictions. And the joy could be read on the faces of the people. *They* were the real church people — "little people" *(kleyne luyden),* most of them drawn from the middle class, the laborers, the clerks. Among them were old people, very old people, but also young people and children. The church was so full that they sat on the steps going up to the pulpit; they even wound up filling the platform behind the minister.

Never have I heard such singing as in this church filled with liberated Christians on that Sunday, August 19, 1945, when the joyous sound first went up from the organ, and then from hundreds of throats: "God has done something wonderful among us." It was the same mood to which our fathers testified in connection with the church reformation of 1886. And the joy was so great that there was no trace of bitterness or even of sharp reproach against those who had pronounced the ban that drove them out. On the contrary, along with the joyful thanksgiving there was the intense prayer: "Lord, bring *all* Your captives back. Make the people in the bound churches just as happy as we are."

Why have I included these impressions in the book? Because they help acquaint us with the spiritual attitude that became manifest all over our country in those days. People knew in their hearts that what was happening was in essence and origin not human work but the work of the LORD, the King of the Church, who had delivered His people anew. Therefore the bush could burn without being consumed.

As for the people who had split the church, they sat with the broken pieces in their hands. At their synod of 1945, there were no fewer than sixty submissions that had to do with the decisions taken at the previous synods. Apparently the official "Elucidation" of the decisions of 1942 had had a negative effect, and the "Pre-advice" of the synod's own committee instructed to study the submissions in advance did not help matters either, for no fewer than sixteen points were proclaimed anew in an effort to clarify what previous synods had meant to say.[8] Yet this time there was a certain moderation in speaking and acting. One could sense that it was all in vain, because the synod refused to follow the simple path — that of repentance and love. Instead the synod labored to justify itself and its actions.

In 1946 it was deemed necessary to hold another general synod. This was an extra synod that would not ordinarily have met — a so-called "revision synod." No fewer than nine particular synods had sent in submissions in an effort to restore what was broken and to heal the rupture, which was becoming deeper and wider. Seven classes made similar requests, as did some forty-five consistories, to say nothing of the many individual requests made to this synod.

---

[8] The "Elucidation" referred to here was a document of some 32 typeset pages prepared by G. C. Aalders, G. C. Berkouwer, S. J. Popma, and Jan Ridderbos. That Popma's name stood under this document surprised Schilder: in letters written while he was in hiding, he speculated that it was done without Popma's consent (see W. G. de Vries, *K. Schilder als gevangene en onderduiker*, pp. 50, 52, and 93). The document was entitled "Toelichting op de uitspraken van de Generale Synode van de Gereformeerde Kerken in Nederland inzake eenige punten der leer, in opdracht der Synode opgesteld." It is not to be confused with another official "Elucidation," the one having to do with Schilder's suspension. The latter "Elucidation" is a document of some 52 typeset pages signed by the officers of Synod, including Berkouwer as President. The pre-advice document of the 1945 Synod's "Committee I" was considerably longer — 78 typeset pages. It was signed by A. D. R. Polman (the Chairman of the Committee) and Jan Ridderbos (the Reporter). Its title was "Praeadvies van Commissie I inzake de bezwaarschriften tegen een zinsnede uit de Verklaring van Utrecht 1905 of (C. Q. en) tegen de Uitspraken van Sneek-Utrecht 1942 en tegen de daarop verschenen Toelichting." The "Toelichting" referred to in this title is of course the 32-page "Elucidation." —TRANS.

This information should help us answer the question whether the decisions taken at the previous synods "lived" in the bosom of the churches! There were seventy objections to the dogmatic decisions, and forty objections to the decisions concerning church order. And out of all of this emerged the "Replacement Formula."[9] The report of the committee took up thirty pages of small print in the *Acts*. Mr. Scheps, in reporting on this synod, observed that the reading of the report drove some members of the synod into the arms of Morpheus (i.e. they fell asleep). But nothing was really "replaced." What it amounted to instead was camouflage, and it was once again stated expressly that the actions taken against Profs. Greijdanus and Schilder were just.

Although this "revision synod" met in January of 1946, in August there was yet another one — this time the "regular" synod. Again there were objections on the table. Among the thirty submissions was the well-known "Testimony and Gravamen" submitted by Dr. J. Schelhaas and twenty other ministers in Friesland. But once again the dogmatic decisions and the so-called "new church law" were upheld. The church as institute does not have an easy time repenting!

Three "revision synods" had to deal with the upheaval which the synodocratic churches encountered among their own members: the objections voiced by their own congregations had to be dealt with. Yet the outcome was to uphold the original decisions!

No one was really satisfied with this outcome. Things were no longer being done in the style of the church; instead there was haggling and tinkering and a vain effort to patch things up — diplomacy all the way. In *The Facts of the Case,* a book containing extensive quotations from the documents generated during ten years of battle in the church, Rev. Geert Janssen writes: "Although the screw [by which the churches and office-bearers were bound] was first turned until it was very tight, it was *in practice* made much looser after the liberation of thousands became a fact, so that no one would be bothered by the synodical restrictions, even if he were to protest ten times more vehemently against the synodical decisions and pressures than those who were disciplined for their objections during the war years. What the so-called Frisian ministers did in this regard is an eloquent

---

[9] The Replacement Formula was in substance the same as the decision of 1942, which was in turn a reaffirmation only of *the first part* of the 1905 decision regarding regeneration. The reaffirmation (without the rest of the 1905 decision) was then made binding. —TRANS.

and satisfactory proof of this. Further proof is the silence of many who 'hypocritically' subject themselves but quietly go their own way."

By 1959 the screw was made much looser still when the Synod of Utrecht decided to set aside all those doctrinal pronouncements over which there had been so much strife. In some circles there was great rejoicing. But the Synod carefully qualified its decision in the following terms: "Although the Synod does not accept the claims to the effect that these doctrinal statements are in conflict with God's Word and the confessions of the church and therefore clings to their legitimacy, it has nevertheless decided, in order to strengthen the unity in our churches and to further the local and national approaches being made to the liberated churches, and also to get out of the sphere where misunderstanding is possible, to set those statements aside without putting any other statements in their place, yet when it comes to the rule of faith in regard to the doctrine of the church concerning the covenant of grace and baptism, to hold to what the Three Forms of Unity themselves say about these matters." Amazing! The Synod clings to the legitimacy of the doctrinal pronouncements and does not regard them as conflicting with God's Word or the confessions — yet it drops them![10]

Second American journey

The liberation gave people room to live and breathe again. Who can say just how much of a burden on people's souls the human restrictions, ecclesiastical disciplinary actions and expulsions had become?

Prof. Schilder also experienced the liberation as a deliverance. It was not that he had *sought* this development, as some have maintained. We know of Luther that right up to the moment of Church reformation (his excommunication), he did not seek or want any liberation. He himself said: "I was like a blind horse that does not know where it is going." But *God* had the reins in His hands, and He is the one we must thank and praise every year on October 31 when we commemorate the reformation of the Church.

It was the same way with Prof. Schilder. In every situation in which he found himself, he asked: What do Scripture and the confessions of the Church say? It was the Lord who led him toward a liberation from human restrictions. And thousands came along.

---

[10] See *De braambos,* Vol. 2, pp. 9-10.

And so there was joy for Schilder after much disappointment. On the Seminary Days, when thousands of people streamed into Kampen from the area of the Dollard (in the northeast) and from the territory beyond the Schelde River (in the southwest) and from numerous places in between, I have observed him walking along the Ebbingestraat and across the Vloeddijk. How he loved those Seminary Days, which brought masses of people together in Kampen as never before![11] There he felt that he had *not* been driven into isolation and did not stand alone, as he had feared during darker hours. There was faithfulness among the "little people" *(kleyne luyden),* the church people. They were faithful to him because they were faithful to the Reformed confessions.

There was also great joy for Schilder in his second American journey, which he undertook in 1947. My wife and I had just been in the United States for the second time: we were there from October of 1946 to October of 1947. When we were finally ready to go back to the Netherlands on the boat, a pair of friends brought us to Newport News, Virginia, where we were to embark. After dropping us off, they went straight on to New York to pick up Prof. Schilder, who was arriving there.

The doors of the Christian Reformed Church were completely closed to him. In 1939 he had been welcome there, as we saw earlier. On that occasion, the Reformed people in the United States had ascertained that he was properly Reformed. But slander and fear had done their work subsequently — especially fear! Many ministers in the Christian Reformed Church were one with Prof. Schilder in their hearts when it came to his views on dogmatics and church order; indeed, a number of them assured me of this personally.

When I was in Chicago, where I discussed the Dutch ecclesiastical situation with Rev. William Kok, a Christian Reformed minister there, I expressed my disappointment about the fact that the Chicago churches had also closed their doors to Prof. Schilder. His answer was: "I also find it regrettable, but you must bear in mind that the Christian Reformed churches in the United States have twins in their womb. We have the very same situation here that you have — Kuyperian views contra Kampen views. If the apple of discord should

---

[11] A "Seminary Day" *(Schooldag)* came once a year — and still does. The supporters of the Seminary traveled to Kampen from far and wide to enjoy fellowship and listen to speeches. —TRANS.

get rolling here, our churches would also be split, and this we want to prevent." Such was the prevailing sentiment. Yet many members of Christian Reformed churches were able to hear Prof. Schilder's speeches and sermons in 1947, for in the Protestant Reformed churches the doors and hearts stood wide open to receive him.

That Prof. Schilder undertook this journey in a joyous and liberated mood was evident from the travel reports he sent back to his paper, *The Reformation.* In one of the very first letters we read: "Soon I will step ashore. Many people believe I am lonely. I certainly was lonely for a while in 1944. But now it is 1947. Now I see who the lonely ones are — Ridderbos and Grosheide and all those other pre-advisors. Many have shaken their hands to congratulate them for their 'successful' campaign. But no one thanks the Lord for their blessed work. They stand alone: people do not sing 'Hallelujah' at what they had the nerve to do. Yet if they had worked under the leading of the Spirit in their assembly, they should indeed have been hailed with a 'Hallelujah.' "

On the boat trip he became aware that bad weather signals had already gone up in anticipation of his arrival. He was shown an announcement in *The Banner,* a paper published by the Christian Reformed Church, in which the churches were told that he was not to be allowed to speak or preach in the pulpits of the Christian Reformed Church. The heading over the announcement was "Consistories, Attention!" The announcement itself read as follows: "Reliable sources of information state that Prof. Dr. K. Schilder and Rev. D. van Dijk expect to arrive in our country some time in the month of August to engage in preaching and in speaking engagements to provide information as to the schism which occurred in the 'Gereformeerde Kerken of the Netherlands' and led to the organization of a new denomination known as the 'Gereformeerde Kerken maintaining Article 31.' We beg to inform our consistories and churches that we do not maintain church correspondence with the denomination to which Prof. Dr. K. Schilder and Rev. D. van Dijk are affiliated, and therefore do not recognize this new denomination as one of our sister churches, and *consequently cannot invite their ministers to speak or preach in our pulpits.*" This decree went out "by order of the Synodical Committee," and it was signed by R. J. Danhof.[12]

---

[12] The "Synodical Committee," which was under the impression that Rev. Douwe van Dijk would be coming with Schilder, consisted of Dr. Danhof, who was also Stated Clerk of the

Talk about hierarchy! That was how far the Christian Reformed Church had already moved down this path by 1947. It had a permanent synodical committee with a permanent secretary (the Stated Clerk), and also an official church paper. And now this weapon was used against Schilder.

Although the doors of the Christian Reformed churches were closed, those of the Protestant Reformed churches swung wide open. Moreover, Prof. Schilder had plenty of opportunity to address officebearers and members of the Christian Reformed churches during this journey, for they did want to listen to him.

While he was on the boat, he also had a chance to preach a "Reformed" sermon. The text he chose was Romans 2:11: "For there is no partiality with God." In a travel report for *The Reformation* he wrote as follows about this sermon: "It was an unusual experience to give such a 'sermon' on board a ship like the *Veendam*. The audience was mixed, in national, and especially confessional, respects. That's exactly why I chose this text. If you ask why this text came immediately to mind for me, then I can give you no other answer than to say that it is one of the statements in the Bible that forces the homilete to touch on central points of Reformed doctrine and expound them — and then in such a way that they approach the non-Reformed hearer from an angle from which he was not expecting any opposition."

Although Prof. Schilder was not allowed to speak in church buildings of the Christian Reformed Church (not even to give a lecture, which is a most unamerican restriction), he did have a great deal of contact with the ministers of this denomination. They sought him out. He wrote: "Within twenty-four hours after arriving we had, among other things, 'gone over' the developments in the Netherlands with two ministers of the Christian Reformed Church." In both cases the conversation was refreshing. Schilder observed: "We should not have illusions about what the synodical side managed to accomplish. Doubt-

---

Christian Reformed Church, Dr. Y. P. De Jong (Grand Rapids), Rev. Watson Groen (Seattle), and Rev. Emo W. F. Van Halsema (Passaic, New Jersey). This "Synodical Committee" had earlier declined an invitation to send representatives to the synod of the liberated Reformed churches scheduled to begin meeting in Groningen in April of 1946, having sent the following message in response to this request: "Inasmuch as the Christian Reformed Church does not at the present time maintain church correspondence with the Reformed Church of the Netherlands maintaining Art. 31 of the Church Order, we as a synodical committee are not authorized to send delegates to your meeting of Synod." The Christian Reformed Synod of 1946, meeting in June, approved the action of the "Synodical Committee" in this matter. —TRANS.

less it has succeeded in finding *helpers,* but a *disciple* you will not find here anywhere."

When he lodged in Hudsonville (near Grand Rapids) at the home of Rev. B. Kok, the first thing he noticed was a copy of *The Reformation,* and two houses further it was again the first thing he saw. He would come upon this paper in more places in the United States.

In the Christian Reformed Church there were many people who were in complete agreement with the liberated believers in the Netherlands. Prof. Schilder wrote about this in one of his letters: "Yesterday a member of the Christian Reformed Church said: 'They are afraid because they know that if Schilder tells what he believes and what he maintained over against the synod in the Netherlands, the people in the Christian Reformed Church will say in great numbers: *But we believe that too.*' "

During this second journey to the United States, Schilder was again very busy. He spoke in many places, often before a mixed audience, and he took up all kinds of subjects.

In the United States there is a great deal to be seen in the way of natural beauty. Although he saw everything and noted it in his mind, we hear very little about natural beauty in the travel reports he sent back. At the beginning of one of his reports we are given the impression that he means to talk about something other than ecclesiastical affairs. The report begins as follows: "October 2, 1947. I'm still on the way to California. Cacti! Too bad that the most beautiful part of this journey is made at night. But the moon became merciful at about 1:30 in the morning, and then I saw utterly beautiful things — at least, as long as I could keep my eyes open."

But about those beautiful things the reader, whose interest is surely awakened by this point, does not get to find out any more, for the very next sentence is: "Now we have to talk about 'Heyns.' " And then we get a substantial chunk of covenantal dogmatics. The moon may be shedding a silvery light over a romantic, blossoming, exotic, landscape dominated by cacti, but the reader sees Schilder pursuing a path through the thorny cacti of Heynsian covenant theology, and he now has to familiarize himself with such terminology as "preparatory grace" *(gratia praeparans)* — some four columns of it in *The Reformation.*

Yet with his receptive and reproductive mind, Schilder could have offered his readers some of the very finest journalistic prose, if he had only set himself to the task. Consider, for example, the beginning of another of his travel reports, in which he describes how he took leave of the mighty Pacific Ocean with its imposing rocky coast. He was traveling in an automobile with an American minister.

> A good chauffeur must be a beautiful sight for an artist. See how easily he leans backwards, and watch the play of his hands. The right hand gently caresses the steering wheel, while he leaves the left hand free to move around as it holds a cigar, or to do something else that occupies his attention. Sometimes he lets the left hand drift out the window casually. It is as though he is bored, or perhaps he wishes to point out something to a drowsy colleague seated in the back. And then he lets the right hand exercise a little influence on the steering wheel again, and it obeys, but soon he lets it go and it returns to its former position. And meanwhile the driver has managed to negotiate a bend in the road in order to stay on his route.
>
> I am not an artist myself, but even *I* sensed something of the significance of the casual gesture with which, late one Saturday afternoon, October 4, Rev. Doezema of Bellflower, who is the son-in-law of Rev. Herman Hoeksema, steered the car in which we rode away from the road that runs along the coast of the Pacific Ocean. When that bend was taken for the second time that afternoon, I knew: *now* KS is going back, back, back . . .

"I am not an artist myself," Schilder tells us here. I do not believe he was just being modest; he actually believed it. He could sometimes think too little of himself. But that he really was an artist is clear from these few lines of prose. He could have been one of the best correspondents of one of the greatest newspapers in the world. Yet he was the editor-in-chief of *The Reformation,* which had no more than some thousands of subscribers. That's how things sometimes go in God's kingdom.

I want to pass along another beautiful sentence from the same article. This one is about the poor handwriting in which he is composing copy for *The Reformation* as he rides along in a swaying train: "And if I again make excuses in public for my poor handwriting in this swaying train of the Northern Pacific Railway, I hope the typesetter will not be so irritated that he winds up sneering: when you are home, your handwriting is not so wonderful either. I would like to stay on friendly terms with the typesetter, for up to now I have found Dutch typesetters to be more decent than American ones. In the United States the typesetter is the boss — not the editor. If I produce copy here for American periodicals, the editor has so much respect for the typesetter that he neatly retypes the whole thing. Otherwise the typesetter would say, 'No, thank you . . .' " When he qualified his statement about the Dutch typesetter with "up to now," Schilder was being very careful, for in the Netherlands typesetting has been thoroughly americanized.

Rev. John D. de Jong, a Protestant Reformed minister who happens to be of Frisian origin, sent me a letter about Prof. Schilder's visit to the United States. He wrote:

> What struck our people in particular in the speeches and sermons of Prof. Schilder was the purely Reformed and Biblical line and foundation. Personally I would want to put it this way: *his proclamation of Christ is powerful.* He sees the Christ in all of the Scriptures, also in the Old Testament, where many people are hardly able to find a Christ at all. His vision is prophetic, and in his own unique manner he preaches the riches of the Word of God. There is curse and blessing, comfort and admonition. Strong emphasis is placed on responsibility. In his preaching we also find a progressing eschatological element, which is so necessary for our time. Yes, brother, our people who could understand him have really enjoyed Prof. Schilder's sermons and addresses. Whether he talked in his lectures and sermons about the antithesis or the Antichrist or "common grace" or the covenant or Christ in the Old Testament, God's people were excited, drawn along, edified, stimulated, and built up.
>
> I also saw people from the Christian Reformed Church who kept coming back to hear him. One time, right after the service, as people were walking out of church, I heard one brother say to another: "And *this* is the man who is not allowed to preach in our churches? What a shame!" Another member of the Christian Reformed Church said to me personally: "This is the man they don't want in our churches now, but I call it a great scandal."

> Now Prof. Schilder is far away again; the "danger" has passed, and "peace" has been preserved in the church, at least on the level of appearance. We also have to do something for the "peace" of Jerusalem; one often forgets that the "thrones set for judgment" (see Psalm 122) are within!
>
> I have often asked myself: Was there no place for this man of God in the Reformed Church in the Netherlands, the churches I loved and in which I was born and raised? I must speak from the heart here: if such men are thrown out for such "sins," then the church is cutting off her own life-blood; she makes herself into a sect as she alienates such faithful sons from herself.

This was a sharp but true judgment. But we should note that it also applies to the North American churches that closed their doors to Prof. Schilder. Those churches may have had twins in their womb, yet the time of birth will surely come for both of them — unless they perish in their mother's womb, in which case churches become sects.

The church has never managed to maintain peace at the expense of Truth — it always turns out that Truth must pay the price. People at Calvin College and Seminary found this out when the battle broke out among the professors there.[13] And what was the eventual result?

A battle on all fronts

In the meantime, "KS" carried on a battle on all fronts back in the Netherlands. One might have thought that because he was involved so frontally and intensively in a church struggle, he would no longer have time for the sorts of issues on other fronts that used to draw his attention before the war and would not be vitally interested in them. But right after *The Reformation* began to be published again in 1945, national affairs drew his prophetic interest, just as they had before.

In his "Letters to a Younger Contemporary," a series of articles in *The Reformation,* he began to point out some of the dangers con-

---

[13] The struggle among professors to which the author refers took place in the seminary (which was in effect the theological faculty), and in 1952 it led the Synod of the Christian Reformed Church, which exercises ultimate authority over Calvin College and Seminary, to dismiss or refuse to reappoint four professors, two from each side, namely, Harry R. Boer, William Hendriksen, William H. Rutgers, and George Stob. They were not deposed as ministers. —TRANS.

fronting the younger generation from the side of the "spirit of London."[14] He wrote: "The Germans — or better: the Nazi locusts — had scarcely landed in great swarms on our fields, in our houses and silos, our palaces, offices, and temples, before we began to hear the assurance from both right and left: *naturally we will have to throw a lot of ballast overboard later* . . . And what is the situation now, right after the war? The air is filled with anti-ballast slogans. We have all heard them: No more antithesis, but the 'breakthrough' instead. A new unity will be ours. The Social Democratic Workers Party led the way by changing its name to the Labor Party" *(Partij van de Arbeid).* He also observed: "We have to understand our times. There is a 'commandment of the hour' *(Gebot der Stunde).* It is this, that the clock which plays a little tune to mark the hour, a tune to tell us that every hour is an 'hour of commandment' *(Stunde des Gebots),* has to be silenced for a little while. My grandfather had a very fine standing clock. But the old man died in a concentration camp or somewhere like that. Then suddenly the clock stopped ticking (or did someone stop it?), and it never ran again. It stopped when the old man died . . . Mercy, how touching . . ."

How well Schilder, using just a few sentences, typified the spirit of the age dominant in the time just after the war! He saw right through the dangers that now began to threaten us, especially the young people of the church. If they were taken in by the new conception of national unity, the antithesis would be rendered irrelevant.

Here Schilder was the same man he had been during the 1920s and 1930s: he was the prophet who knew his time. Animated by a charisma, he penetrated to the heart of the spirit of the age, stripping away every covering. In prophetic faithfulness he held the Word high in its application to every area of life.

As we look around us now some twenty years later, we see how accurate his reading of the situation was. The old Frank Buchman slogan from the 1930s got a new content after 1945: Let the new Netherlands be launched![15] What this meant concretely was that we should return to the way things were before Kuyper's arrival on the

---

[14] The mentality and outlook that developed among Dutchmen who spent most of the wartime period in England, where the government-in-exile operated. —TRANS.

[15] Frank Buchman (1878-1961) was the leader and spokesman of the Moral Re-armament movement. This movement was originally intended to appeal to Christians on a non-denominational basis. Eventually it broadened its basis so as to draw in people of the non-Christian religious traditions. —TRANS.

scene — no antithesis, but a unity in which *one* ideology would have the decisive say.

Just as before, he used the various columns within his paper to combat the new corruption that was spoiling our national life now that the Germans had been pushed out and no longer represented a threat. I think of an unforgettable meditation which he based on Jeremiah 32 and 34 and entitled "Betrayer of the Country? Betrayer of the Church!" Here he made the Old Testament message relevant to the situation of our people in 1945 and showed that the betrayal of the Church must lead to the betrayal of the country. He wrote: "The Reformed and Antirevolutionary people in the Netherlands also, in large measure, misunderstand the distinction between betrayal of the country and betrayal of the Church. They take great joy and delight in the imprisonment of those who betrayed *the country* during the years 1940-45. But they barter away, and thus betray, the *church* treasures — at least in part. They are willing to make deals when it comes to their *political* confession, forgetting all too often that it has grown out of their confession of *faith*. They give up the antithesis; that is to say, they wipe away the last boundaries . . . Remember, therefore, you Antirevolutionaries, you Reformed people, that the disaster for our nation, and also for our 'social policy,' begins when we betray *the church* and ignore *the church*. When the church *devalues* its words — and under foolish synodocratic leadership, that's just what it's working at vigorously — then the church becomes a disaster for *the nation* . . ."[16]

Here we are presented with one of the key points in the struggle Schilder was engaged in: our political confession has grown out of our confession of faith. We have learned from experience not to create sovereign little law-spheres with their own so-called normative authority. We confess that the Three Forms of Unity, in giving faithful expression to what the Scriptures teach, are the foundation for all of life in all its variety and contexts. It was out of this conviction that the Congress of Amersfoort was born in 1948.[17]

---

[16] In the Dutch text, the author points to what happened in New Guinea in the early 1960s as bearing out the truth of what Schilder was saying. —TRANS.

[17] People of the liberated Reformed churches came together in Amersfoort to discuss the consequences of the liberation in relation to prospects for genuine cooperation in political and social matters. It was shortly after this Congress that the Reformed Political Alliance *(Gereformeerd Politiek Verbond)*, or GPV for short, was established as a political party of and for members of the liberated Reformed churches. The author has more to say about these matters in *De braambos,* Vol. 2, pp. 173-178. —TRANS.

The philosophy of the law-idea

Not everyone shared Schilder's convictions on this point. Even today there are some people among the intelligentsia who are blind to the role the confessions play in all of life. They fail to see that the confessions are *not* exclusively ecclesiastical in character.

Schilder's stand on this issue was also determinative for the position he took with reference to the philosophy of the law-idea.[18] Thus he eventually took up a position against men like Profs. Herman Dooyeweerd and D. H. T. Vollenhoven. At the time of Schilder's death, Vollenhoven stressed that Schilder was first and foremost a theologian — and a man of the church. Vollenhoven went on to say: "Therefore few in our circles were surprised that when many of his friends could not follow him in the action he had taken in the ecclesiastical area in 1944, he terminated his membership."[19]

Vollenhoven also explained an important difference between the philosophy of the law-idea and the thinking of Schilder: the former "characterized faith as a function which is present in all men and which, since the fall into sin, is directed in a wrong way by unbelieving man; but in the Christian who has been made alive again, that function is directed in the right way. Schilder, on the other hand, regarded faith as a 'capacity' *(vermogen)* which is made 'active' again through the calling of the preached Word."[20]

Schilder did not polemicize much against the men of the philosophy of the law-idea. The tragedy of the matter is that although they recognized the injustice done to him through ecclesiastical diplomacy and politicking and largely stood on his side, their philosophical thinking kept them from drawing the conclusions, in terms of ecclesiastical obedience, which the LORD required of them too.

---

[18] This phrase is both the name for the overall philosophical position held by Dooyeweerd and Vollenhoven and the original name (in a Dutch equivalent) of the first edition of Dooyeweerd's major philosophical work. This work was later republished in a second edition in English under the title *A New Critique of Theoretical Thought*. —TRANS.

[19] Vollenhoven was referring here to Schilder's membership in the Association for Calvinistic Philosophy. It should be borne in mind that Schilder held a doctoral degree in philosophy. —TRANS.

[20] "In Memoriam K. Schilder," *Philosophia Reformata*. Vol. 17, No. 4 (1952), pp. 149-150. For a more recent statement that sheds light on Schilder's disagreement with the philosophy of the law-idea, see J. Douma, *Another Look at Dooyeweerd: Some Critical Notes Regarding the Philosophy of the Cosmonomic Idea* (Winnipeg: Premier Publishing, no date [1978]). —TRANS.

Yet right from the beginning, Schilder had recognized that there were dangers and objectionable elements bound up with the Association for Calvinistic Philosophy. A letter Schilder wrote me dated September 29, 1949, demonstrates how careful he was in ensuring that sympathizers of the philosophy of the law-idea who were also members of the liberated Reformed churches did not set their stamp on *The Reformation* after 1945.[21]

There was indeed a significant difference between Prof. Vollenhoven, who established a "school" or following of his own at the Free University, where many people got excited about the philosophy of the law-idea, and Prof. Schilder, with his following at Kampen. However much these two professors sympathized with one another at the outset, they parted company in working their ideas out, especially when a choice had to be made in relation to the liberation of the churches. "KS" was never a follower of the philosophy of the law-idea. On the contrary, he combatted this philosophy. One can read about the position he took in his commentary on the Heidelberg Catechism, where he rejected the so-called "pistical function" as a separate law-sphere, and thereby cut the ground out from under the entire philosophy of the law-idea.[22] Moreover, what this philosophy adds up to in practice is something we found out during the time of the liberation.[23]

Perhaps no one saw more clearly than Prof. Benne Holwerda that it would be a mistake to remain joined with the men of the philosophy of the law-idea in the Association for Calvinistic Philosophy after it was no longer possible to be one with them in the church. He wrote:

> Even when I thought I could still sign Article 2 of the Statutes [of the Association for Calvinistic Philosophy], I no longer saw any possibility of working together by means of the Association. The same people who continued to accuse and condemn us in the church, on the ground that we were departing from the confessions and creating schism, wanted to accept us in the *Association* as people who take their stand on the foundation of those same confessions. Therefore I wrote in my official letter

---

[21] See *De braambos*, Vol. 1, pp. 101-102. —TRANS.

[22] See *Heidelbergsche Catechismus*, Vol. 1 (Goes: Oosterbaan & Le Cointre, 1947), p. 355; Vol. 2 (1949), pp. 410-416, 421-434, 443-444, 451-456. —TRANS.

[23] See *De braambos*, Vol. 1, p. 127.

of resignation: "That people try to hold on to us in the philosophical setting *at the same time* that they *continue* to cast us out ecclesiastically is only in *appearance* an act of *rapprochement*. In *essence* it is a new act of *repudiation*. What it indicates is that people are *playing games* with us. The *yes* to our expulsion on Sunday turns into a *no* for Monday through Saturday, only to turn into a *yes* again the following Sunday . . . Such people believe that if we continue to work together in Christian organizations, the fire of schism will be restricted to the church. But what it means in reality is that the fire of *insincerity* is carried over from the church to Christian organizations. Through that fire, the foundation for the Association's edifice will also be consumed."

Prof. Schilder said in this context:

I would rather not restrict Prof. Holwerda's warning to *ecclesiastical* consequences; instead I see them as affecting the entire *ethical* domain. If you confess something on Sunday, confess it also on Monday, and vice versa. Do not make something into a problem of the greatest magnitude on Sunday if you are planning to regard it as secondary on Monday. Do not say on Sunday: "This is revolution," and on Monday: "What constitutes revolution in one sphere of life may have nothing to do with revolution in some other sphere."

The "ethical question" which "KS" here posed as primary still applies to our situation today. Prof. Holwerda viewed the situation in the very same light. He wrote:

Everyone knows that our confessions do not represent a complete or perfect expression of the Word. What I believe is that no one is able to found a political or social or academic confession *directly* on the Word; catechism instruction, preaching, and ecclesiastical formularies will have influenced the entire confession of his faith in essential respects right from his earliest years. And even if it were possible to separate one of these, his academic confession could *never be in conflict* with his ecclesiastical confession, for *the Word is one*. In this context I find appeals to "sphere sovereignty" dangerous; it is as though people are suggesting that the Word has a certain content for the "sphere" of scholarship and science, a separate content *alongside* its content confessed by the church, and that the former could even be in conflict with the latter. What we actually get then is not just sovereign spheres of life but also sovereign confessions in the very same number and sovereign little bibles for each of those spheres. When this is done, the Word has been broken, even if one claims to want to uphold the authority of the Word. We may never suggest that the Three Forms of Unity are "ecclesiastical" in the sense that they apply only to the church and not to the [political] party, the [Calvinistic] association for philosophy, etc. To do so would be to withdraw the party and the association from the authority of the Word, the authority which the church confesses to be complete and full.

In this polemical context, the liberation bumped up against certain consequences of what had happened in 1944. Back in the 1930s we had begun to see again the importance of the church's confessions for *church life,* and now we came to understand that the church's confessions have authoritative importance for *all of life.* This would not only cause controversies with people and associations outside the liberated Reformed churches, but even *within* liberated circles. And those controversies continue to this day.

People like Profs. Schilder and Holwerda took a very clear position on this matter — first of all with reference to the Association for Calvinistic Philosophy. But initially the choice made there seemed of less consequence than the choice made in some other sectors of life, for the work of this circle of Calvinistic philosophers did not live among our people. In 1928, Prof. Dooyeweerd said: "If I am not comprehensible to a simple shoemaker, then my philosophical work is useless." That was at the beginning of his career. When he came to the end of it, the shoemakers (and it is sometimes said that *they* are the most philosophical people among the simple folks) did not appear to have much interest in the philosophy of the law-idea. Thus Dooyeweerd's own test did not give us much reason to be encouraged about the "usefulness" of his philosophical work.

The reason for this lack of acceptance did not lie only in Dooyeweerd's difficult style and choice of words, for others have popularized his ideas for him — or at least *tried* to do so. The system itself did not speak to our people. It was as though their Reformed intuition sent out danger signals as soon as they came into contact with this philosophy in some way or other. And the eventual outcome showed that their intuition was correct.

One would have expected that the proponents of the philosophy of the law-idea, who accepted the "ecclesiastical papers" (this is how the confessions are referred to in their circles) as valid for the church alone, would at least have judged ecclesiastical matters and developments in terms of them and would therefore have concluded in 1944 that the expulsion of Schilder and company was in conflict with Scripture and the confessions and the church order. They should then have refused to accept this expulsion and liberated themselves from the synodocracy. Yet they did not do so.

Prof. Holwerda comments as follows:

> At that moment they came forward with a philosophical distinction and said: "Those sentences [meted out to Schilder and company] are not so serious, for they only concern the church as a temporal societal relationship *(tijdelijke samenlevingsverband).*" In other words, the position these men took on this church question was not determined by ecclesiastical formulae alone but also by *philosophical* formulae. This I regard as disastrous. Philosophy now becomes completely dominant in the church: the ecclesiastical formulae have no authority in the church until they have been diluted and hollowed out by philosophy. These men should say openly: "The norm for our ecclesiastical action is the philosophy of the law-idea." And so we were first thrown out because of the theological insights of Prof. Ridderbos and company; after that we were left in the lurch by you [i.e. the men of the philosophy of the law-idea] on the basis of your philosophical distinctions.

Schilder was fully in agreement with what Holwerda had written here. The philosophy of the law-idea was not accepted by our people in the 1930s. And in the 1940s we saw that they were right not to accept it.

The confessions of the Church are not to be limited in their application to the domain of the church. They govern *all* of our life — wherever we may live and move in the family, the school, politics, social life, science, and scholarship, and so forth. It was one of the fine fruits of the liberation that we came to recognize this again.

Yet this insight was not some new invention on the part of "KS"; it was not that he was the first one to suggest that we should accept the confessions as our foundation for political and social life, and for Christian education as well. When our fathers drew up our confessions, this was exactly what they had in mind. And so one of the consequences of our ecclesiastical liberation was a liberation in other areas of life — in other words, an extension of reformation to all of life's contexts and settings.

An internal battle

The same issue also gave rise to some internal strife. Not everyone who liberated himself from the synodocracy understood and accepted the place of the confessions in all of our life.

Disagreements about this matter created some difficulties for Prof. Schilder after the liberation. In his articles in *The Reformation,* he had to devote more and more attention to enlightening people within his own circles concerning this matter. The difficulties came up especially because for some of them, the liberation had been the building of a tower whose cost they had not calculated in advance.

This sort of thing should not surprise anyone. Every time there is a reformation, people of all sorts come along. This was already the case when the Hebrews made their exodus from Egypt. This pattern continued all through church history: the church reformations of 1834 and 1886 show us the same phenomenon. In this regard there was nothing new under the sun.

The "Bos action" and "Oosterbeek" should not have surprised anyone. But who can say how utterly wearying this internal strife must have been for Prof. Schilder? I think of the "Open Letter" he wrote to Rev. B. A. Bos,[24] in which he tried to hold this man to the "simplicity of the liberation," beginning with these words: "For some weeks I have walked around asking myself what I could do to make the simple things of God's church simple again."

When he wrote his third (and last) letter to Rev. Bos, he concluded with these words: "I have not been angry at you; it's just that

---

[24] Rev. B. A. Bos, who as a member of the synod that deposed him in 1944, originally had defended Schilder and went along with the liberation but later returned to the synodocratic churches as a minister. Still later he served as a minister in the Christian Reformed churches of the Netherlands. For more on this man, see Van Reest, *De braambos,* Vol. I, pp. 34-36. —TRANS.

I think you are jumping to conclusions. You say that your brochure was written during a night in which you remembered standing before a possible firing squad six years before. I also had a night when I had to answer five questions put to me by a synod. Then I did not see KS but the CHURCHES which, if KS gave the wrong answers in an effort to escape an ecclesiastical firing squad, would be delivered over to FALSE LAWS. And Rev. Bos, I still see those QUESTIONS because I still see the CHURCHES. And may it not happen to you that in this matter you wind up giving new encouragement to that which is lacking in spiritual discernment."

The numbers that returned to the synodocratic churches were never very large. In his review of the year 1950, Prof. Schilder could write: "The Oosterbeek conferences[25] have run stuck; they have been denied (in their results) by more than one of their members." The statistics in the yearbook show only a slight decline in membership, which was soon made up again.

We should bear in mind that these were also the years of emigration. In the liberated Reformed churches there were a great many people, some of them with large families, who left the Netherlands. Schilder concluded his review of the year with the words: "We are still always amazed, just as in 1944, at what God allows us to see in the way of concrete treasures of community and of strength, despite our own sin and that of others."

If the Oosterbeek conferences of 1950 led anyone to suppose that there had been changes for the better in the synodocratic churches, what happened later showed that he was sadly mistaken. Nowhere did this become more obvious than at a meeting in Amersfoort. It was supposed to be made clear at this meeting that there had indeed been changes (even though not a single disciplinary measure of 1944 had been rescinded).

Rev. E. T. van den Born, a liberated minister, was given an opportunity for a fifteen-minute address at this meeting. He used the brief period of time allotted to him to make the situation clear, and he concluded with these words: "I appeal to your heart and conscience at this moment, which may be a truly church-historical moment, to tear up your deposition decrees before the eyes of God and men and to extend a brotherly hand to us again and to trust us as brothers who are of the same household as you are. Remember that the eyes of the

---

[25] At these conferences, Rev. B. A. Bos and others tried to find a compromise between the liberated Reformed churches and the synodocratic churches. —TRANS.

Lord Christ are also upon this meeting. He also sees the disciplinary measures between you and us. Here I place before you your deposition decree. You are to say either YES or NO. If you say *yes* and get rid of the decree, there will be rejoicing in heaven over injustice that has been corrected. If you say *no,* there will nevertheless be joy in heaven over a church that came to reformation. Isn't it true, Dr. Bos?[26] Didn't you also say this once? I thank you for giving me this quarter of an hour."

If something had indeed changed in the synodocratic churches, steps would have been taken at this meeting to retract the decrees of suspension and deposition. But there was a deathly silence: no one raised a finger to do what Rev. van den Born called for. For in fact there had been no change. All that happened was that a smoke-screen had been laid down.

The people of the synodocratic churches continued further down the path they had chosen. There was one liberated minister (Rev. J. van der Schaft) who was suspended *twice.* When he wrote about his suspension, he declared that he had come to the conclusion that the "hierarchical yoke" had not yet been broken — "not by these consistories, not by the delegates to the Synod of The Hague, and not by this Synod itself." After he published this opinion, this minister received his second letter of suspension from the "synodical" consistory — and so did elder J. Turkstra, who was suspended along with him. (It was also Turkstra's second suspension.) The second one was "worse than the first one," according to Rev. van der Schaft.

In addition to the action undertaken by Rev. Bos, which Schilder, to his great disappointment, felt constrained to fight, there were other battles to be waged against people within liberated circles. That this was necessary should not surprise us. Church reformation often demands sacrifices — sometimes very personal ones. The divisions run right through families, as Christ Himself said they would.

When I visited North America, Rev. Herman Hoeksema of the Protestant Reformed Churches warned me about what he called the "150 percenters." He meant people who are more than 100 percent committed to the cause, people who show off and let their own tongue carry them away and soon find that they have to eat their bold words, people who make no bones about pronouncing black what they used to call white.

---

[26] The reference to "Dr. Bos" appears to be an error. The chairman of the consistory of the Amersfoort church at that time was Dr. N. H. *Bos;* he was presumably the person being addressed here. —TRANS.

We had such people in our liberated circles, people who had maintained at the outset that joining with people from the synodocratic churches for prayer, no matter what the setting or meeting, was an impossibility because of the "ethical conflict" between us, but who eventually cleared out and submitted themselves to the Caudine yoke again.[27] Perhaps we could say here that the most eloquent statement one could make about these developments is to remain silent. Fortunately, there were not many people of this sort: although they consumed themselves, they did not consume the liberation.

But there were two other directions in our liberated churches against which Prof. Schilder had to fight during the last years of his life. No one will ever know how painful and difficult this was for him. He conducted this battle as the man with "gentle eyes" and a wise heart, and in the process he left us with some written material which continues to be worthy of careful study today.

In the first place, there were those who opposed the so-called "continuing reformation." They were people whose concerns in 1944 had been largely restricted to questions of church order. They did not realize that after the liberation we would also have to organize education on our own and go our own way in social and political matters. The background to their outlook was their failure to see the general decline and degeneration in Reformed *(Gereformeerd)* circles which I sketched earlier and which dates all the way back to the 1920s. They regarded the battle of 1944 as incidental and not as symptomatic; they failed to recognize that it was the inevitable and necessary culmination of a process that had been underway for many years. They did not understand that corruption in the church means that there is also corruption in politics and education and social life as organized on a "Christian" basis.

They thought that the church battle should be no more than a battle in the church and should not affect Christian action and organization in other spheres of life. They did not ask themselves whether everything would now go downhill, for they did not realize how completely things were already amiss in Reformed *(Gereformeerd)* circles. And so they took offense at the conclusions drawn at the Congress of Amersfoort in 1948. It was at this conference that our people began to talk about the "ethical conflict" and to consider the consequences

---

[27] Caudium was a city in Italy where a Roman army surrendered in 321 B.C. and underwent the humiliation of being placed "under the yoke." —TRANS.

of the depositions and the extra-Scriptural bindings and decrees. Was it still possible, after all that had happened, to "cooperate" in social and political matters?

For Prof. Schilder, such questions were not difficult to answer. In his review of the year 1947, he already pointed to deformation in the Christian political parties and in the Christian National Labor Federation. He wrote: "We shall have to face the question how confessional faithfulness can be combined with all sorts of political and social symbioses." For him "confessional faithfulness" was not a narrow ecclesiastical concept but something that extended to all areas of life and all organizations. But there were some who did not wish to extend such faithfulness to the political and social spheres.

Yet "KS" wanted to be very careful in dealing with brothers who had manifested their ecclesiastical faithfulness to the confessions but did not see the implications clearly for other areas of life. In his review of the year 1950 he wrote: "In and through all of this there is one ray of light that continues to excite us: up to now our Churches have been able to withstand the crisis. The debate about 'continuing reformation' will not lead to fragmentation for those in whose life the continuing concrete *rejection* of the concrete *deformation* has corrupted the oneness between the Lord's Supper table and the pulpit. Patience and caution will be combined in the communal bond which has been under systematic attack for six years, and which, to the great amazement of many, still continues to draw us together."

That was how "KS" approached the question of the the proper relationship to those who still did not realize that church *deformation* must always have a deforming effect on every area of life, and that church *reformation,* like a salting salt, will likewise penetrate all of life and affect every relationship. He therefore talked about "gentle eyes."

This is not to say that he declined to make his own standpoint known faithfully and honestly and to give instruction where it was needed — clear, unequivocal instruction that was not open to two or more interpretations. In 1948, he wrote openly and directly:

> There are some among us — and we understand this fully — who believe that the Antirevolutionary Party is being forsaken by liberated people, which is something they regard as a loss that will have a harmful effect on church life. But it is a good thing for them to discover that the

politics of the Antirevolutionary Party, in both incidental points of program and principial matters, is being denied by many leading people, both appointed and salaried, from the "Reformed churches" (synodocratic). Finally, over against such spirits we must know how to set out our own position. For although ecumenical endeavor must not be foreign to us, we must be like Paul, who was willing to travel all the way to Spain, provided it was with *the* gospel message, which dares to say: "Even though we, or an angel from heaven, should preach to you a gospel contrary to that which we have preached to you, let him be accursed" (Galatians 1:8).

Reactionary phenomenain the wake of the liberation

Right to the very end — indeed, to the week before his death — Prof. Schilder had to do battle with brothers who, in certain respects, could not go along with the course of events arising out of the liberation. Those brothers were indeed properly faithful and liberated, but they were too preoccupied with possible problems arising from the church federation; they lived too much on the basis of negative reaction. During the years 1942 through 1944, they had undergone so much pain, misery, and schism because of all the church meetings that they were blinded to the fact that the misery was not the consequence of the church meetings as such but of an all-corrupting spirit that had dominated those meetings. The misery stemmed from the spirit of deformation which had affected the federation of Reformed *(Gereformeerd)* churches, with the "new church law" as its necessary consequence, leading in turn to hierarchicalism and the setting aside of the old Reformed church law.

Prof. Schilder opposed this spirit of reaction very strongly, for in the long run it would lead to ecclesiastical nihilism. Because he could see so clearly the spiritual dangers in phenomena manifesting themselves in every area of life, he also realized what disastrous consequences would result if this spirit of reaction came to dominate our churches. It is deeply tragic that during the last years of his life, he had to fight against this sort of thing within the circles of his own brothers.

The Synod of Kampen (1951) represented the low point in terms of the spirit of reaction, for such a spirit seemed to triumph there. No standing committees, no pre-advisors, no reports to be printed in the acts of synod — just get the business over with as quickly as possible and go home. It was as though people supposed a synod could produce nothing but evil.[28] And there were consequences, also in terms of relationships between people. It is not pleasant to think you have a task at synod as a pre-advisor only to find that the members of the synod scarcely tolerate your presence there — and also let you feel it. Ultimately, only Prof. Schilder and his colleague Prof. P. Deddens managed to stick it out to the end of the synod.

That this should happen to Schilder in the last year of his life was very painful. In a letter to me dated January 26, 1952, he observed: "This past year I have given ten weeks as a present to the synod, because I believed it was very necessary that the brakes be put on here and there." And there was indeed a good deal that had to be slowed down or halted if the cause of the liberated Reformed churches was to be kept from running off in the wrong direction altogether.

In his review of the year, Prof. Schilder did not have much to say about this synod. Those who know the art of reading between the lines written by Schilder will find the same attitude reflected there as he had expressed to me when passing on his opinion of this synod. The last sentence he wrote about the synod speaks clearly enough: "Moreover, there is a fixed law of the embankment, which gives us reason to think this ship will turn around." Indeed, that embankment was there in the form of some later synods. Unfortunately, "KS" did not live to see the needed reversal.

"Christ also shed His blood for the church *federation.*" This little sentence by "KS" has offended some people; it has been suggested that he wrote it in a "thoughtless moment." Now, when "KS" sat behind his typewriter, he never had "thoughtless moments." I cannot recall a single occasion on which he had to take back something he had written because it had been effectively criticized.

He was not being "thoughtless" either when, in his last article for *The Reformation,* entitled "Needy Churches," he argued and documented from the Scriptures the following position: "Thus also the *church federation,* for which the Lord Christ bled in order to give it back to us as liberated . . . The federation is much stronger now . . .

---

[28] The thinking that was prevalent at this synod came to further expression in the 1960s among those members of the liberated Reformed churches who wound up in the unaffiliated churches outside the federation, sometimes called the "Buiten-Verband" churches and now known officially as the Dutch Reformed Churches (see p. 17) above. —TRANS.

its strength lies in the firmness of the Kurios [Lord] position of the glorified Head of the Church."

That was not "thoughtless" language on his part but a confession — one that was grounded in Scripture. There are a number of passages in which we read not of churches (plural) but of the church (singular), even though it is clear that more than one congregation is meant. I think of Acts 9:31: "So the church throughout all Judea and Galilee and Samaria enjoyed peace . . ." And don't all local churches together form the one Church of our Lord Jesus Christ, of which He alone is Head and Lord?

It is most regrettable that Prof. Schilder's last days were darkened by the very tiring struggle to get erring brothers to see their mistakes. He had to warn so often against reactionary phenomena that appeared in the wake of the liberation. He did so in his paper, in speeches, at the Seminary Days, and in personal encounters.

Frequently he would say: "I have no desire to be anything other than what I have always been — *Reformed.*" The fact of the liberation did not change anything for him in terms of what he believed: the Scriptures, the confessions, and the church order were still precious to him. For him, continuing reformation did not mean breaking off what was good and Reformed but reforming what had become deformed.

He saw the danger not only of synodocracy but also of an autocracy of ministers or of the local consistory. He saw the falling away that had taken place in the churches and outside them — not just in procedures and organizations but also in the hearts of the people making use of those procedures. The springs of life flow from the heart (Proverbs 4:23) — also from the heart of the ecclesiastical organization. And when that heart does not bow before the discipline of the Word, there is just as much danger of an autocracy of the ministers or consistories as of a synodocracy. All autocracies are equally devastating for the church and for the souls of men.

At the end of his life, "KS" left the following testament, which is still worth pondering today: "Independence" is something different than "standing alone." All the local churches are independent — they are complete and form a "body *(corpus)* of Christ." But no single church may keep to itself. Even in its independence, each church must seek federation with other churches and must hate "standing alone." The church federation is not a matter of our own preference: it is what Christ prefers, and through it we "taste" of Him and sample

Him. Hence the same confession that teaches the independence of the local churches (plural) also speaks straightforwardly of "the church" (singular).

Here the confession is simply following the pattern we find in Scripture itself. In Revelation 1:4 we read: "John to the seven churches [plural] that are in Asia." But in Acts 9:31, as we saw, we read about "the church [singular] throughout all Judea and Galilee and Samaria." Ultimately the churches (plural) will disappear. They belong to this dispensation, which is bound to time and place. But the *one* Church, the *one* Body of Christ, will abide for all eternity. In this dispensation we must already learn to understand something of this — otherwise we will have no sense of what true ecumenism is. We are and remain "needy churches" — churches that need one another. Therefore there should always be fresh joy in encountering each other at classical and synodical meetings.

Prof. Schilder came to the end of his life while he was engaged in this Scriptural instruction. His last polemic was devoted to it, and the last sentence he wrote in this context was: "No more space — the rest follows next week . . ."

But "the rest" never did come from his pen. God had decided that this child of His, utterly weary from the battle, had done enough, and He took him away.

Working right to the end

Anyone who observed Schilder closely during the last years of his life can testify that he was consumed in the service of his Savior. Disappointments of various sorts did not pass him by. A very great loss for him personally was the death of his faithful and pious fellow battler Prof. Seakle Greijdanus. In the church yearbook for 1949, Schilder wrote about him as follows: "Our Greijdanus is no longer with us. If there is anyone able to testify how much loneliness his departure can cause, it is the undersigned who, without a question ever being posed or an agreement being made, was able to enjoy Greijdanus as a friend and brother during the critical days in which ecclesiastical cruelty triumphed — but at a distance (for it was wartime)."

That was how his "In Memoriam" began. This opening was followed by a substantial disquisition regarding Prof. Greijdanus as a man of scholarship and was concluded with these sentences: "We have seen him die. And we have seen him live. And now we know most assuredly that the grave of Greijdanus continues to lie between Dr. J. Ridderbos and company and the congregation of God's first-born. They cannot pass by that grave unless they speak of the open injustice done to this man of God and call it by its name."[29]

"KS" suffered a great deal — not just because of what was done to him personally but also because of what his friends and brothers underwent in the way of grievous injustice, vilification and disdain. Indeed, he suffered more than many could have imagined.

But in and through all of this, he also worked very, very hard — harder than many would have thought possible. When I go through the letters I received from Prof. Schilder during the last years of his life, which touched on the work he did for *The Reformation* and the commentary he was writing on the Heidelberg Catechism, I am struck by the enormous amount of energy he put into his labors and by his ambitious hopes for his Catechism commentary, in particular.

It was one of his cherished hopes that this commentary would be translated into English or German. In connection with the prospect of a German translation, he wrote to me: "I have thought of the Zollikon Verlag in Zurich, in the German-speaking part of Switzerland, but this is the company that publishes Barth's *Church Dogmatics,* and I have the impression that they have no desire to bring out an anti-Barthian production." He also thought of having an English version published in North America, and in this connection he wrote to me: "The work is written in such a way that the scholarly questions are buried in the footnotes, making the text generally readable for those who are interested, even if they have no academic education. I plan to write twelve volumes; perhaps there will be even more. Three have already appeared. Volume 1 deals with Lord's Days 1 through 4, Volume 2 with Lord's Days 5 through 7, and Volume 3 with Lord's Days 8 and 9. Don't laugh — even if there is reason to laugh. People could say that if I continue in this fashion we will wind up with 24 volumes rather than 12. This may seem about right, but in the later expositions I will be able to refer to explanations given earlier."

Right to the end of his life he was full of plans and the desire to work. He was driven by the fear that Barthianism would wash over our ecclesiastical life. In various letters he pointed to this great danger: "I believe my books can be of help to the ministers, especially the

---

[29] Dr. J. Ridderbos, as an Old Testament professor, was a close colleague of Prof. Greijdanus, who was a New Testament professor; yet he played a major role in his suspension from office. —TRANS.

ones who are suffocating in heresies and Barthianism." Here he was thinking especially of North America and Germany.

Yet he also had some wonderful days at the end of his life. I think of the special anniversary issue of *The Reformation* published to celebrate its first twenty-five years of operation. When he found the printed final version of this special issue in his mailbox, he immediately sent off a telegram to Goes: "All of you strongly complimented and heartily thanked. It's a thumping success. —Schilder."

And what a beautiful afternoon it was when he celebrated his sixtieth birthday in the Aula (auditorium) of the Theological School in Kampen and received countless tokens of love and devotion from our Reformed people and also from his colleagues, his students, and the curators of the School. When he spoke a brief word of thanks that day, he concluded by saying: "To live in the fear of God in accordance with His law remains the end of all things."

Did Schilder anticipate the possibility that his days on earth might soon be over? It is noteworthy that a few days before his sixtieth birthday, he wrote an article on the changeover to the new year. In this article, entitled "In the Cemetery," he devoted some attention to "moving on to the cemetery" and showed us how a believing Christian should think about death and burial. The cemetery is not our resting place, he maintained: we know rest in this life. Therefore he ended the article with these words:

> As for those beautiful names and inscriptions we use ("resting place" and "here rests . . . "), let's cut such nonsense out. Let Chrysostom no longer lull us to sleep with his eloquence. When you go to church, sing: "This is the place where rest is given."[30] Call church the resting place. Perhaps it will soon turn out to be your last resting place — and then "outside the city" in a little diver's hideaway *(onderduikershokje)*. And inscribe on your workbench: "Here rests So-and-so." In good time, ask your family to promise that they will not allow the stone carvers and maker of memorials, to whom Chrysostom had given such an honorable place, to carve "Here rests So-and-so" on your gravestone. And bear in mind that we can very quickly be done with beautiful gravestones if we carve on our church doors: "Resting Place." The stone carvers

---

[30] Here Schilder was quoting from Psalm 36, stanza 2 (1773 rhymed version). —TRANS.

guild took quite a tumble during the years 1940 through 1945.

And in that issue he also published his open letter entitled "To a Younger Contemporary," in which the same theme seemed to occupy his attention. We read: "But old year's eve[31] continues to excite us: we are moving on . . . to the grave. It is appointed to man that he must die one day, and then comes the judgment (Hebrews 9:27)."

These are remarkable thoughts, which were united in Schilder with an undiminished desire to work and an amazing energy. Perhaps such elements, which might seem contradictory in the eyes of some people, could be combined in "KS" because he inscribed on his work bench: "Here rests KS." And so he sought rest not in the grave but in his work.

He continued his intensive labors right through the last years of his life. In Goes we accumulated abundant evidence of this. He deeply regretted that his presence at the Synod of Kampen (1951) cost him ten precious weeks he would love to have spent on his Heidelberg Catechism commentary. In February of 1952 he wrote: "I regret it so much that I was held back by the synod last year. If I did not believe that I *had* to be there, I would have chosen my study over the meeting room."

In November of 1951 he spoke on the radio and delivered a sermon in the Lutheran church in The Hague (the one that is so important for the liberation because the meeting of August 11, 1944, was held there). The program was introduced and concluded with organ music by Feike Asma.[32] When I asked him for permission to publish that sermon, I got a few scribbled lines in response. "Can't oblige you, not on paper — had no time." When I asked him whether Feike Asma's music had been included in the broadcast at his (Schilder's) request, he wrote back: "No, that was something they thought of themselves. Perhaps it was because I once stood up for F. Asma with the National Christian Radio Association. But I think it was probably happenstance."

On February 22, 1952, he first sent me a disturbing warning about his health: "I hope to be able to continue working regularly on my Catechism commentary; I have just been visited by the doctor, and

---

[31] In English we speak of "new year's eve." All that is meant is the last evening of the (old) year, which, in Reformed churches, is usually marked with a special service. —TRANS.

[32] Feike Asma (1912-84) was one of the best-known Dutch organists and served as organist of the Lutheran church in The Hague from 1943 to 1965. —TRANS.

Chapter 4 — That They May All Be One 359

that visit has certain consequences about which I don't want to talk at this time."

At that point he was still deeply involved in composing his last review of the year for the church handbook, promising to "mail it Sunday evening at the latest." Who would have supposed that this would be his last such review? He wrote with an ailing heart, but it still became one of his longest reviews — sixty-two pages of small print.

There was nothing that escaped his intense scrutiny. He talked about the prayer service that inaugurated the Synod of Kampen, and about the business transacted at that synod. He commented on the outcome of the court cases involving church property,[33] and on relationships with other churches in the Netherlands, and on the effects of false ecumenism. When he turned to the student organization, he included a warning: "We will have to reckon with the fact that our students — indeed, all our young people — will be exposed more and more to intensive propaganda of and for the 'breakthrough mentality,' which found such a strong theoretical foundation in Barthianism."

He also talked about the "social message" of the Ecumenical Council of Churches, a Dutch organization. His comments make it clear that his heart was filled with concern for the youth of his own church: "We would be deceiving ourselves greatly if we became persuaded that we as churches can or may ignore it, that is to say, walk by it thoughtlessly without *self-consciously taking a position.*" A little later he came back to this matter: "It will remain a bitter necessity to arm our young people and our laborers in the social, economic, and political domains against such large-scale action aimed at leveling and the 'breakthrough.' "

He pointed to the dangers posed by the appearance of people with the "breakthrough" mentality even in the leadership training school of the Christian National Labor Association. He commented on the work done by the societies within the liberated churches, including societies for young people, students, women, and men. He went on to talk about elementary and secondary education, which also needed to be liberated, for "what are we to think of an attempt at the secondary schools to make the children of our liberated churches read the book

---

[33] The liberation led to some disputes about the ownership of church buildings, some of which took years to be settled in the courts. —TRANS.

by Mr. K. Norel, which creates a completely false impression of our churches?"[34]

Among the other topics he touched on were the Reformed Teachers College at Enschede, established by people of the liberated Reformed churches; the conferences arranged for ministers, elders, and deacons; the Seminary Day (Kampen); the library fund of the Seminary; missions; contact with churches in other countries; relations with the Christian Reformed churches of the Netherlands; Bible translations; a new metrical version of the psalms for use in worship; and the efforts to find new buildings for worship. His final conclusion about the year that had passed was: "This past year presents us with a picture of steady work. All kinds of questions may come up, but the work goes steadily forward . . . As we catch our breath — for in such a time as this we get no more than *pauses* for rest — may we use the opportunity, in fear and trembling, to consolidate and to establish some principial boundaries. We have a task in the Netherlands, and thereby also in the world."

And then his thoughts turned again to the false ecumenism of the World Council of Churches and to the dangers of the great "breakthrough." These were ultimately the greatest dangers for Western Christianity, and in this regard he viewed the "Voice of America" radio broadcasts as being no less dangerous than what was going on behind the Iron Curtain.

But we could be assured of "rest." In the final sentence of his review he wrote: "Not 'God' *is* the way, but God in Christ. And His truth corresponds with *His* peace — a peace that still goes beyond

---

[34] In this book, entitled *Een vaste burcht* (Kampen: Kok, 1951), Norel commented as follows on the conduct of Schilder: "There was a striking difference between the attitude of Prof. Schilder and that of Hendrik de Cock [during the time of the Secession of 1834]. De Cock put up with all manner of injustice — not from his lawful synod but from the unlawful synodical executive. After he was not only suspended but also deposed, losing his salary in the process, he still hesitated for a long time before breaking the bond with the [church] fellowship." Norel went on to argue that 1944 differed from the events of 1834 and 1886 in *substance* as well as in *procedure:* "In the case of both Kuyper and De Cock, the issue was whether the church, with the Reformed confessions as its foundation, would tolerate *unbelief* and even award it priority over Reformed preaching. But what was at issue in the conflict of 1944 was only a *misunderstanding* to the effect that a certain conception of the covenant was the only one allowed in the church." The blame for the resulting division was assigned to Schilder: "Prof. Schilder regarded it as necessary to break with the church federation immediately; through his action, church after church was split during that horrible winter of 1944-45, when the enemy oppressed us more fiercely than ever before and thousands of our men . . . were caught up in a life-and-death struggle at sea and behind enemy lines at home" (pp. 180-181).

our 'understanding.' For Christ is the Christ of the *Scriptures.*" He wrote these words about a month before he died.

He was never trapped within a little circle of his own or in the mentality that tends to turn the church into a sect. To the very end he continued to think ecumenically in the true sense of the term. He took the whole world — for it is *God's* world — into the broad vision of his thinking and labors.

And so his review of the year remains most relevant and could be reprinted and read with profit today, even though it was originally written for a church handbook. Various matters that drew his visionary attention were only germinating as he wrote but have developed, in the ten years that have passed since then, into realities we can now see and are forced to deal with.

I think first of the course of events in the synodocratic churches. Earlier we saw that in the 1930s there were three streams in the churches, which at that point were still Reformed *(Gereformeerd)* churches, and that each one was seeking to carve out a channel for itself. The first stream was an aging Kuyperianism which was becoming silted and choked in dogmatic constructions as its proponents began, more and more, to deny the Kuyper of the antithesis and to exploit the Kuyper of common grace: they were entering a period of "Solomonic glory" in facing the outside world, even though they were decaying from within. Secondly, there was the stream of the "younger generation," which was oriented more toward the left and was under both Ethical and Barthian influence as it grew stronger. Finally, there was the reformational stream under the leadership of Prof. Schilder, which went back to Scripture and the confessions.

The first two streams cooperated to block the third — and there was enough paradoxical homogeneity between them for this strategy to succeed. But after the events of 1944, these two streams began to do battle with each other again, and the "younger generation" oriented toward the left won more and more influence and power. Once the reformational stream had been thrown out, there was not much left to stand in the way of the "younger generation."

In this last review of the year, "KS" took time to point to some of the symptoms manifesting themselves in synodocratic circles. In the process he quoted Rev. H. H. Binnema, who, writing in *Truth and Unity,* commented as follows on the suspensions and other events of 1944: "It is painful for our leaders that those disciplinary measures have done so little good for the churches. The church-dissolving action which people believed Prof. Schilder was engaged in is to be found among many of the younger men in a different form and in a much greater measure. What Thijs Booy stands for represents an undermining of all of church life in its elimination of the boundaries *(uitwissing der grenzen).*[35] And if such a development were limited to one person, it would not be so dangerous. But among our younger men there are many in whose minds such destructive views find acceptance, and in our church press we judge these matters in relatively gentle terms. *Among many younger and older members of the congregation, church awareness has declined.* In this regard the younger people in the liberated churches are ahead of ours, for among them one still finds a fire and zeal for church affairs."

That was ten years ago. We all know what sorts of changes for the worse have taken place in synodocratic circles since then. Among the aging leaders who had joined with the "younger generation" oriented to the left in the effort to cast out those who faithfully adhered to the Reformed confessions was Prof. K. Dijk, who had been opposed to extending Prof. Schilder's suspension by even one month. (He wanted to proceed with immediate deposition instead.) Men like Dijk now entered a sad evening phase of their lives, as they watched the degeneration spreading all around them.

People who had managed much more ecclesiastical harm than Prof. Dijk had ever tried to attribute to Schilder now took the leadership in his churches as they promoted the denial and undoing of 1834 and 1886, for they desired nothing more than to get back together with the National Reformed *(Hervormd)* churches. Prof. Dijk recognized what they were up to, but he was powerless. In *The Trumpet* he wrote that he saw "a shift, usually far away from the Reformed *(Gereformeerd)* line," and he added that "the sad thing is that many rejoice in it or observe this 'deterioration' without uttering a word of criticism." He made known his feelings regarding the World Council of Churches and said that he was very disappointed that the young people's organization Youth and Gospel, to which he had been very sympathetic himself, had traded in its Reformed *(Gereformeerd)* basis for a more broadly Christian basis formula. When he spoke in Zeeland at an elders' conference, he complained about these shifts and awakened the elders to their duty to understand these developments and to oppose ministers who propagate this leftward direction.

---

[35] Thijs Booy is the author of such works as *Gereformeerden, waarheen?* (1951), which he wrote jointly with A. Bouman, and *Kerk en jeugd* (1950). —TRANS.

But Prof. Dijk was too late. He and the few who stand with him are lonely. The "breakthrough" has already come. The dam that was still in place in 1944 has been dynamited, and Prof. Dijk was one of the people who had helped light the fuse. Now there is nothing to hold back the new stream in the churches. The stream that had begun to dig a channel for itself in the Reformed *(Gereformeerd)* churches during the 1920s and was spiritually akin to Netelenbos and Geelkerken was given free rein through the expulsions that took place in 1944. There was nothing that could be done about it anymore.

The protesters who remained in the synodocratic churches and did not liberate themselves but thought they would still be able to save the situation by working along "medical" lines did not get far either. We know from church history how Da Costa and others tried to use the "medical" approach in the National Reformed *(Hervormd)* churches and how little was actually accomplished.[36] Those who continued to protest after the events of 1944 were no more successful: they represented a voice crying in the wilderness.[37]

There are protesting ministers in the synodocratic churches who boast that they are free to preach along liberated lines in their own pulpits — and indeed they are. Yet they should consider what will happen when they leave their congregation — and that time will surely come one day. At that point the sheep whom the Savior has entrusted to their care will, in all likelihood, be delivered over to a type of preaching and "pastoral" care that they themselves would regard as disastrous.

Such protesting ministers are like the pastors who were concerned during the time of the Reformation but nevertheless remained Roman Catholic. When they passed on, that was the end of Biblically faithful pastoral care for their flock, and today the congregations they served are just as Roman Catholic as the rest of them. A "medical" approach might look like a pious sacrifice, but what the Lord wants of us is obedience: to obey is better than to sacrifice, and to listen is better than offering the fat of rams (see I Samuel 15:22).

---

[36] See Harry Van Dyke, *Groen Van Prinsterer's Lectures on Unbelief and Revolution,* pp. 29-33 and 68-72. —TRANS.

[37] Such protesters, of which there were many, including Rev. Maarten Vreugdenhil and Dr. Evert Masselink, who were editors of *Truth and Unity,* maintained that Schilder should not have been disciplined. Masselink argued this point in a brochure entitled *Onverantwoord en onnodig: De schorsing en afzetting van Prof. Schilder onhoudbaar* (Groningen: J. Niemeijer, 1952). The Synod of Rotterdam (1952-53) considered Masselink's plea but decided not to lift the deposition. —TRANS.

Growing degeneration

Before he died, Schilder observed some of the symptoms of the growing degeneration that could not help but end in apostasy. He pointed to those symptoms with great concern.

Earlier I quoted some sentences in which his concern came to expression. In a time of growing wickedness and apostasy, we do not live on an isolated island. Schilder was well aware of this, and he also knew how appealing the new developments might seem to the young people of the church. In the last years of his life, such matters occupied a great deal of his attention. At the Young Women's Society League Day in Rotterdam in 1951, he gave a speech entitled "Your Ecumenical Task" in which he warned the young people of the church against false ecumenism and instructed them in true ecumenism.[38] He was deeply concerned, for the temptations were many and various.

I think of something he wrote in his review of the year 1950: "Repeatedly we stand amazed at the power of our church life. This is a power we do not owe to any kind of 'leadership' (in fact, leadership is missing 'among us,' *and deliberately so),* but we know it is the fruit of a renewed warmth and depth in *the preaching.*" In my judgment, this is the reason for the power of the liberation, and it also explains the peace it has given us. If the preaching remains faithful, that is, faithful to Scripture and the confessions, the Holy Spirit can continue to work. After all, we confess that He works through the Word — and through the Word of preaching.

"KS" found his own peace and comfort in this awareness, and he bore it in mind when he contemplated the future of our churches and our young people. And it was because the preaching was faithful to Scripture again that he was able, in God's grace, to have such an enormous impact. Not only did he preach in faithfulness to the Scriptures himself, always drawing on the Word, he also taught this way of preaching to his students and to many others who came under the sway of the reformational work in which he was engaged.

Some of the people who stayed in the synodocratic churches and continued to be "concerned" about the course of events in their own church circles, especially when it came to such matters as the young people falling away and the trend toward worldly amusements and the elimination of the antithesis, have said to us: "Things are indeed bad among us, and we realize that it is better in your churches, but in

---

[38] This speech is reproduced below as Appendix III. —TRANS.

ten years you people will be just as far as we are." I do not believe such defeatist talk is justified. We must remember how much depends on preaching that is faithful to Scripture. If the pure proclamation of the Word continues, we can rest assured that the promises of the gospel also apply to the young people of the church. This realization is one of the priceless treasures of the liberation — provided we bear in mind that this gift *(gave)* is also a task *(opgave),* as "KS" taught us.

A "torso"?

Earlier I mentioned that I received a letter from Schilder on February 22, 1952, in which he passed on the following disturbing message: "I have just been visited by the doctor, and that visit has certain consequences about which I don't want to talk at this time." Although "KS" had always seemed so strong, he now needed the doctor's attention!

But who would have thought the worst? Surely he himself did not suspect it! Not many years before, he had said to one of his colleagues: "I have been reading and learning for fifty years, and now I begin to see a bit of light here and there. Perhaps the Lord will give me another fifteen years at most to continue my work. Then my time here below will be over — short, but what an inducement to use the time."

The Lord did *not* give him those additional fifteen years. In God's providence Schilder's work was already finished, and so he could go to his heavenly Father, about whom he had proclaimed such glorious things, drawing on the Scriptures.

People may speak of a "torso" in connection with his work. After all, he was far from finished in terms of what he had planned to do. In his commentary on the Heidelberg Catechism, only ten Lord's Days had been covered, and we certainly needed his treatment of the Lord's Days dealing with the covenant, the sacraments, the church, the Ten Commandments, and the Lord's Prayer. People were looking forward eagerly to the rest of his commentary.

It has also been written that "KS" offered only fragmentary work. He did not give us a circumscribed and finished dogmatics; rather, his ideas in dogmatics are scattered throughout his works and have to be garnered from here and there.

I believe we must look at the importance of the life and work of Prof. Schilder from a different angle. In this context I think of a sermon he preached during the 1930s under the title "The Vocative to

Reformation." This sermon was based on Micah 6:8, where we read: "He has told you, O man, what is good; and what does the LORD require of you but to do justice, to love kindness, and to walk humbly with your God?" Micah did not present us with a circumscribed and finished dogmatics either; rather, he prophesied against the apostasy and self-willed religion of his time, which was prepared to carry piety so far that people would even sacrifice their own children to Moloch in order to be freed of their sins. But when it came to the one sacrifice offered by God, who was willing to give up His own Son, they dismissed it in their vain pride.

"What does the LORD require of you but to do justice, to love kindness, and to walk humbly with your God?" These words from Micah can also be used to express the theme of Prof. Schilder's life. His successor at the helm of *The Reformation* reflected on this theme when he marked the tenth anniversary of Schilder's death and observed that in "KS" we see a concentration on the major issues, the really important things. Because he lived in a time when people were falling away and the Word was being forsaken, a time of self-willed religion and foolish human thought constructions to which the sheep of Christ's flock were being bound, this prophet of the twentieth century offered people the message of Micah: "He has told you, O man, what is good; and what does the LORD require of you . . . ?"

That was the message he brought, and for that message he was cast out. But he continued to bring the message to the liberated churches, until finally the LORD said: Now it is enough. Now they can see it for themselves — the young and the old, the intelligentsia and the simple ones, the obedient ones and the disobedient ones. They have all heard it, and now there are others who can carry the message further. As for you, My faithful child, it is enough: enter into My rest.

Schilder could also accept his death as a *deed*. In this regard, too, he was prophetically faithful. He had uttered some "loaded" words about death. Earlier he had spoken "loaded" words about faithfulness to one's people and fatherland and was subsequently called upon to be faithful to those words during the time of the occupation. Now he had to live up to what he had said about death.

On one occasion he explained it as follows: "If we are still to complain, let each one complain about his own sin (Lamentations 3:39), but let him not complain about the point in time at which he is to die, since we are now allowed to view death as abnormal insofar as it contains an element of the curse but normal insofar as it concerns the abandonment of our present mode of life. It would be abnormal if we did not die. Therefore, as soon as the curse has been paid, the fear of death also disappears. Anyone who views the matter in these terms can understand that in all dying — including the dying that goes on today — there is a certain deed to be performed. The deep center of our existence gives itself up in death; that's why this point in time is allotted to us. Death is never simply something that comes over us."[39]

Prof. Schilder then had to apply this awareness in his own life: *his* death was also a deed. Very shortly before he died, he was visited by his colleague Prof. P. Deddens. Schilder said to him: "Even if it should turn out that the world would say, 'Things are not well with him,' things would still be going well. Between the Lord and myself things are in order. If I die now, I go to Christ."

The last time he sent copy to Goes for publication in *The Reformation,* he included the following words for the information of the readers: "To my regret, I will not be able to finish the remaining articles in this series. For a while I will have to cease all work for the paper. I take this step on medical advice: the doctor's conclusion is that I must take a period of complete rest, doing nothing special. For me this will be an uncommon trial, but one which I must receive thankfully from the hand of God. The gift of joyful rest is also in God's hand when He opens it. How others will manage to take over my work should soon be evident to you as readers. As far as the Catechism is concerned, Lord's Day 10 is as good as finished; some details will follow later. It is a Fatherly hand that opens itself here and reaches out to me . . . KS." And that was the very last time those familiar initials appeared in *The Reformation.*

The end

During the night that ended in the early morning of Sunday, March 23, 1952, he was suddenly called home. Schilder had entered his eternal sabbath rest. The date was striking, for his *suspension* also fell on March 23.

No one had expected such a sudden end. During the last week his life had been busy, as usual, with all sorts of jobs. He had conferred with the executive committee of the Young Men's and Young Women's Leagues, had written copy for *The Reformation,* and had, in his usual humorous manner, composed an appeal for money to

---

[39] Taken from a lecture on death, as printed on p. 8 of *Gedenkt uw voorgangeren.*

place an organ in the Aula (auditorium) of the Seminary. As he made his weekly appeal in support of the "organ offering," he announced at the end that on his doctor's advice he would have to stop writing these chatty columns. He concluded with the following moving sentence: "Remember: if you take good care of my successor in the art of begging, I will regard it as a small flower on my table."

From this comment it is evident that he was thinking in terms of a sickbed. But God had decided otherwise, and His will was better, for "KS" was not a man to be sick. The Lord knew that, and so He took him directly from the bench and table at which he worked to heavenly glory and eternal sabbath rest.

His death was like his life, for he was transferred from the activity of wearying, painful work here below to the activity of blissful, joyous work in heaven. The awareness that there was work and struggle in heaven was real for him. Hence he did not accept the distinction between the church militant and the church triumphant. Both parts of the Church are still engaged in a struggle aimed at the consummation of all times — the parousia, the return of the Lord. In heaven there is also the prayer "How long, O Lord?" And hadn't he told us that prayer is the mightiest weapon in this battle?

To be transferred from one part of the Church to the other when the two parts are so closely bound together — that fit in well with the way Schilder lived. And so we may regard his death, during the night that led from Saturday, March 22, to Sunday, March 23, as a continuation of the style which God, in His grace, had given him.

A child of the King

Schilder's burial was that of a king's child. In a letter written twenty years earlier, he had told one of his intimate friends how he would like to be buried when the time came, namely, in a very sober manner. At the grave itself there should be no more than the reading of a chapter from God's Word. The chapter he chose was John 17, which is the well-known passage in which the Savior prays for the unity of His Church.

Thousands of people lined the streets of Kampen (the police estimate was four thousand in all) to follow the procession to the grave. Before the burial took place, there was a gathering for mourners in the Aula of the Seminary, and then another in the New Church. The coffin was decorated only with the corps ribbon which Schilder had worn as an honorary member of the Student Corps known as "Fides

Quadrat Intellectum."[40] The presence of this ribbon was a symbolic expression of the close bond between this professor and his students.

Once the crowd of mourners had gathered around the grave, John 17 was read aloud, in accordance with Schilder's wishes. In this chapter we find the words that were later engraved in his tombstone: "That they may all be one."

A few days after the death of Prof. Schilder, I visited Prof. Benne Holwerda to ask him to join with several others in carrying on the work of "KS" in *The Reformation*. Holwerda was surely the man best qualified among Schilder's colleagues to take over. He agreed to my request, but with much hesitation. He said to me: "I suppose it has to be done, but I dread the task."

In the article which he then proceeded to write, which was broken off in the middle of a sentence when the Lord called him home suddenly and unexpectedly,[41] Holwerda discussed the reactions which the death of Schilder had evoked among the leaders of the synodocratic churches. His title alone spoke volumes: "From Suspension to Beatification." Those who had taken part in Schilder's suspension, deposition and expulsion suddenly turned him into a saint. Holwerda thought it was abominable.

Now they had words of extravagant praise for Schilder. Mr. W. C. F. Scheps wrote: "Entered into eternal rest . . . , death reconciles oppositions." Rev. F. C. Meyster: "Those who are in Christ can never be separated from His love — not even through their own doing, fortunately." Dr. A. de Bondt: "What a wonderful thing it will be in eternity to enjoy opportunities for fellowship with the purified spirit of this sparkling, gifted person." Prof. Herman Ridderbos: "Called to a higher order of life to which his spirit and his pen here on earth were repeatedly driven in such a remarkable way."

In the face of all this praise, Holwerda asked the all-important question: "Was the suspension justified — yes or no? These gentlemen will surely remember the charges: public sins of schism, as defined in Articles 79 and 80 of the Church Order — desiring to stir up mutiny and to bring about sects in the churches. Such language also draws on the form for the celebration of the Lord's supper, where we find the declaration that the person guilty of these sins has no part in the kingdom of Christ if he does not repent!"

---

[40] On the meaning of this name, see the note on pp. 140. —TRANS.
[41] He died on April 30, 1952, when he was only 42 years old. His unfinished article has been included in *Gedenkt uw voorgangeren,* pp. 74-76. —TRANS.

Holwerda's question needs to be answered — and it could still have been answered, even at the open grave of a brother who had been cast out. But no answer was given. Today, ten years after Schilder's death, it still has not been given.[42]

Thus we must ask whether it was appropriate to read John 17 at this open grave. Was Schilder guilty of public schism? Or was he one who joined the Savior in praying "that they may all be one"?

We can be completely comforted and assured on this score. Prof. Schilder worked and struggled for the unity of the Church. No sin was further from him than the sin of desiring schism or stirring up mutiny.

Schilder did not establish a new church. What he did was to help protect and strengthen the foundations of the one catholic Church which we confess every Sunday. The reading of John 17 fit in very well with what he actually tried to do.

In our time, this beautiful chapter of the Bible is misused in a horrible way. Various winds of doctrine, numerous sects, different types of movements, false ecumenists, the World Council of Churches — all of these take this prayer of the Savior on their lips and then press for the greatest possible organizational unity involving all of Christendom. Such false unity is the great temptation Satan places before us in our time. He even dares to approach us with the treacherous question "Is it not written . . .?" What danger we face when Satan starts quoting the Bible!

Schilder once wrote that many Christians believe in eleven of the articles of the Apostles' Creed rather than the full twelve. The article

---

[42] In 1988, the General Synod of the churches that deposed Schilder did officially express the following misgivings and regret about the events of 1944: "Looking back to the events of 1944 and the years thereafter, we first want to express our sadness about the part our churches played in the schism that came about in our churches. We acknowledge that at that time, our churches, out of a concern for the purity of doctrine, placed too much of a stumbling block before certain brothers and sisters. Our churches could have gotten along without those doctrinal statements concerning the covenant and baptism, as is apparent from the fact that they were set aside in 1959; and therefore, when those doctrinal statements did not bring about the rest for which the people hoped but led, on the contrary, to opposition, they should not have been maintained as binding in character. Our churches did not pay enough attention to the needs of the conscience of certain brothers and sisters, and thereby they themselves became the occasion for the schism brought about by those brothers and sisters. And even if the things that have happened can no longer be changed, we regret to the uttermost that our churches themselves became the occasion for brothers and sisters to have to bear the burden of being condemned as schismatic — a burden they continue to bear to this day. We ask the church to join us in praying that the Spirit will heal us and make us whole." —TRANS.

"I believe a holy universal [catholic] Christian church"[43] is not part of their body of convictions grounded in faith. They believe in God the Father — although they do not see Him. Likewise they believe in God the Son and God the Holy Spirit although they do not see Them either. But that's where their belief stops. Because they do not see the unity of the Church become manifest, their confession breaks off at that point. In effect they do not believe that the unity of the Church is something real. For them the "holy universal Christian church" is not a matter of faith.

Faith is the key here. For just as God the Father, God the Son and God the Holy Spirit are real, so truly does the Church exist in her unbreakable unity, universality, and catholicity. The existence of the Church is an article of *faith* on our part: even if we *see* nothing of this unity, we still believe it. We believe it because God instructs us accordingly in His Word.

In John 17 Christ prays to the Father and says: "Father, the hour has come; glorify Thy Son" (vs. 1). This is the starting point and summary of what follows in this chapter. Jesus is aware that His time has come. He is about to earn the deliverance of the Church through His suffering, and He asks that He may be glorified in this too. It is a prayer between the Son and the Father: the Son here asks for His rights, and He *knows* that His request will be granted. Among those rights is His Church, along with the revelation of the unity of that Church. That unity is to be earned on Golgotha, and so He comes before the Father to ask for His own glorification, which He is about to earn through the completion of His suffering.

As for us, we must keep our sinful hands off this holy prayer. The people of false ecumenism act as though *we* — who are no more than poor wretches, puny creatures, foolish people cleaving to the dust (Psalm 119:25) — must now see to it that this prayer of the Son is heard by the Father. We will go to work to make sure that this "unity" for which the Son asks is actually achieved! Therefore we organize conferences, establish a World Council of Churches, and even involve the Soviet Union in our efforts[44] — all of this to make sure that the

---

[43] Both the Dutch and German editions of the Apostles' Creed contain the word "Christian," which was inserted in the sixteenth century. Many translations of the Creed in use today do not include this word. —TRANS.

[44] The World Council of Churches included representation from churches in the Soviet Union, despite the fact that such delegates were virtual government appointees placed in office by a Communist regime! —TRANS.

prayer of Christ can be heard on the basis of *our* efforts. What foolishness!

The Son's prayer for the unity of the church was already heard long ago, and therefore we confess every Sunday: "I believe a holy universal [catholic] Christian church, the communion of saints . . ." If the promoters of false ecumenism were correct in what they assumed, we would be better off eliminating that article from our confession of faith, for it is impossible for *us* to bring about this unity: it is the work of the Father, the Son, and the Holy Spirit.

Who are the people spoken of here as "one"? John gives us a clear answer to this question: they are the people who keep His Word. "Sanctify them in the truth; Thy Word is truth," Christ prays (vs. 17). Whoever does not keep that Word is not included in the unity of the Church. Christ does not even pray for those who do not keep the Word.

And then follows the passage from which I have drawn the title of this chapter: "I do not ask in behalf of these alone, but for those who also believe in Me through their word; *that they may all be one*" (vs. 20-21). Church reformers are not people who fight for *unity* but people who fight for *truth*. The *unity* that follows is the *fruit* of their struggle.

The Bible text read at Schilder's burial and engraved in his black marble tombstone corresponds to his life and work, to the battle he went through. Prof. Schilder struggled to keep the Word. In prophetic, priestly, and kingly respects, he executed his office faithfully. Thus he was among the ones of whom Christ prayed to the Father "that they may all be one."

Schilder was a tool in God's hand to lead us to the liberation. What was at stake for us in the events of 1944 culminating in the liberation was keeping the Word. Because of the foolish extra-Scriptural restrictions and the dogmatic constructions imposed upon the Bible, the Reformed people could no longer keep God's Word; the Word was being darkened, garbled, rendered powerless.

The liberation was a work of God in the history of His Church. And it was another proof that the prayer of Christ in John 17 has been heard. Therefore we must be sure not to downgrade this deed of God to merely human work. And we must never manifest the slightest willingness to see this work undone. If we ever find ourselves drifting away from what God has given us in the liberation, we will have to ask ourselves whether we are interfering with our Savior's high-priestly prayer in John 17.

The unity of the Church does not depend upon *us* — it already exists. Thanks be to God, the unity of the Church stands above every threat, firmly anchored in heaven, because of Christ's high-priestly prayer. What we are called to do — even to the point of allowing our own blood to be shed — is to *keep the Word*. And this is where our brother Schilder has set an example for us.

Let us, then, remember those who have gone before us. I make this appeal especially to the young people in our churches.

Who are those witnesses?

Every year, when we have our Seminary Day *(Schooldag)* in Kampen, there are many young people present. Some of them are there for the first time. They shuffle through the crowded rooms of our seminary building and look with interest at the portraits of former professors who are no longer on earth and ask: "Who are those men?" Such a question is also asked when they come upon the portrait of "KS." Let the older generation not be found without an answer when this question is asked.

The Old Testament points very clearly to the importance of instructing the younger ones. Deuteronomy 6:20 tells the Israelites to have an answer ready when their sons ask them: "What do the testimonies and the statutes and the judgments mean which the LORD has commanded you?" The answer which the LORD laid in the mouths of the fathers of those questioning sons is nothing other than a piece of *church* history — the liberation from slavery in Egypt. For the youth of today, the church history of the new dispensation has to be added to this answer, for that history, too, was written by God's hand.

Another story from the Old Testament that comes to mind here: the one we read in Joshua 22. The two and a half tribes occupying the land east of the Jordan after the land of Canaan was conquered had built an altar by the Jordan, "on the side belonging to the sons of Israel" (vs. 11). This deed almost touched off a large-scale civil war because of a misunderstanding with grave consequences. But then came the moving declaration in which the two and a half tribes beyond the Jordan made it clear why they had built the altar: it had been done for the sake of coming generations, as a witness to them, so that their children could say to the generation that followed them in turn:

"See the copy of the altar of the LORD which our fathers made, not for burnt offering or for sacrifice; rather it is a witness between us and you" (vs. 28).

There is a third passage in the Old Testament to which I could appeal here. Consider what we read in the well-known fourth verse of Psalm 78: "We will not conceal them [i.e. the things our fathers have told us] from their children, but tell to the generations to come the praises of the LORD, and His strength and His wondrous works that He has done."

When the seed of the covenant, the young people of the Church, ask, "Who is that?" they must hear a proper answer from the mouth of the older generation. And that younger generation must in turn be able to say, when called upon to assume leadership: "This man was a battler for the *truth* and for the *unity* of the Church."

"That they may all be one." These words from our Savior's high-priestly prayer have been engraved in brother Schilder's black tombstone. There is no more characteristic or pure or correct way to sum up the meaning of his life.

Appendix I:

North American Developments

by Theodore Plantinga

Van Reest's account of Schilder's work and his role in the church struggles in the Netherlands was written for people on the other side of the ocean. It does not take up the question what became of the liberated Reformed people who left the old country to take up a new life in North America. Where were those emigrants to seek a church home? In answering this question I do not propose to either approve or criticize their actions; I am simply trying to present the situation as it must have looked to them so that we may have some understanding of their motives and reasons.

There were three major possibilities. One was to join Christian Reformed congregations. A second was to join (or establish) Protestant Reformed congregations. A third was to establish congregations of their own maintaining correspondence (or a sister church relationship) with the liberated Reformed churches in the Netherlands. The third was the route eventually chosen. But how that choice was made is a matter that calls for some explanation and comment.

Although Van Reest has left this matter out of his Schilder book, he did discuss it at some length in two other books, which he also wrote in Dutch. Since they were about the North American scene, they have been read with interest on this side of the ocean. The first of them, entitled *Van kust tot kust* (From Coast to Coast), came out in 1948 and stems from the same period as Schilder's second American journey. In this book we find quaint travel observations about the United States (especially California and Michigan), Canada, and even Mexico, interspersed with information about the Protestant Reformed Churches.[1] During this journey, Van Reest spent his time largely with Protestant Reformed people, and he later urged — as did Schilder — that immigrants from the liberated Reformed churches in the Netherlands affiliate with these churches. The book is even dedicated to Rev. Herman Hoeksema!

The second book, entitled *Terugzien na vijfentwintig jaren* (Another Look After Twenty-Five Years), came out in 1972, almost a quarter of a

---

[1] For Van Reest's discussion of Protestant Reformed matters, see pp. 32-34, 153-155, 179-181, 187-190, 196-212, and 238.

century later, and was based on another leisurely journey through North America. In this book Van Reest still spoke very favorably of the Protestant Reformed churches and people, but he devoted more attention to Christian Reformed developments; indeed, large sections of the book are comprised of penetrating observations on developments within the Christian Reformed churches. The things that have come to pass in the nineteen years since that journey have shown that Van Reest was a man with sound Reformed instincts. He expressed considerable appreciation for the strengths of the Christian Reformed churches, but he could also point nicely to where things were drifting away from Reformed moorings. In this context he also focused substantial attention on the movement that used to be known as the Association for the Advancement of Christian Scholarship (AACS), expressing agreement with many of its objectives while pointing to dangers in its Kuyperian intellectual constructs, especially as they have to do with the church.[2]

Van Reest dedicated the second book to Andrew Petter and his family. Now, Petter was a Protestant Reformed minister serving in Orange City, Iowa, during Van Reest's 1947 trip, and he reports that the Petters "spoiled him shamefully" while he was a guest in their home.[3] The Petters also played host to Schilder in 1947. But by the time Van Reest returned to North America a quarter of a century later, Petter was no longer Protestant Reformed but Christian Reformed. Many others in the Protestant Reformed Churches (i.e. the Hubert De Wolf group) had also gone over to the Christian Reformed Church; in 1953 they broke away from the Protestant Reformed Churches — which continued under the leadership of Herman Hoeksema (who died in 1965) — and reconsidered the events of 1924.

The story of those friends of Van Reest who were no longer Protestant Reformed is actually part of the story which he had begun to tell in his Schilder book. Had things developed the way Van Reest would have liked, Petter would still be Protestant Reformed, and the immigrants from the liberated Reformed churches in the Netherlands would be as well. And so we must ask: what happened?

In the Schilder book, Van Reest does discuss the initial Christian Reformed decision on Schilder and the liberation as that decision came to expression in the notice in *The Banner* in 1947, instructing Christian Reformed consistories that Schilder was not eligible to conduct worship services in Christian Reformed churches (see p. 334 above). Although Christian Reformed people now tend to downplay the significance of that event, Van Reest makes much of it in his 1972 book, as do Canadian Reformed commentators on these developments. The Christian Reformed Church, Van Reest

---

[2] For his comments on the Christian Reformed scene, see pp. 45, 60-79, and 105-129. For his comments on the AACS, which is now known by the name of the school it operates in Toronto, i.e. the Institute for Christian Studies (ICS), see pp. 73-74 and 144-164. For his 1972 treatment of the Protestant Reformed Churches, see pp. 24-31.

[3] See *Van kust tot kust*, p. 189.

laments, had chosen for the side of the synodical churches in the Netherlands "without hesitation."[4]

Prof. Doede Nauta, who participated in the proceedings against Schilder on the synodical side, paints a similar picture of how the Christian Reformed Church arrived at its decision: "It goes without saying that the course of events in connection with the schism and the relations between the parties could not be closely followed in North America. When the CRC finally took note of the schism as an actual fact, it could only be with deep regret. There was no hesitation, however, in displaying an attitude of the greatest loyalty toward its sister church in the Netherlands. An invitation which had been received early in 1946, to be present at the synod of the 'Vrijgemaakten,' as that group was then called (in accordance with Article 31 of the Church Order) was rejected without any reservation . . ."[5]

Was the signal sent out via *The Banner* in 1947 misread? What is significant in relation to this episode is not just what happened but also what did *not* happen. A generation that came to maturity after these events took place might well expect to find in the historical record evidence of fact-finding and deliberation on the part of Christian Reformed leaders and synods — in other words, thoughtful reflection that undergirded the decision of the "Synodical Committee" and the announcement in *The Banner.* But in the official record such evidence of deliberation is lacking. Virtually no official attention was ever devoted to the question: what are we to make of the deposition of Schilder and the division that came about in the Reformed churches of the Netherlands in 1944?

What happened was that the "Synodical Committee" declined to send official representatives to the synod of the liberated Reformed churches planned for April of 1946 on the ground that the Christian Reformed Church did not have a correspondence relationship with these churches. The general synod that met in June of 1946 then approved this action of the "Synodical Committee," but it did not undertake any investigation of the 1944 events in terms of either the doctrinal issues or the fairness of the proceedings as judged by the church order. Many Christian Reformed people consider this to have been a very serious and consequential error, and there were a num-

---

[4] Dutch: *zonder aarzeling* (see *Terugzien,* pp. 121-122).

[5] "The Gereformeerde Kerken in Nederland and the Christian Reformed Church," in *Perspectives on the Christian Reformed Church,* ed. De Klerk and De Ridder, p. 313. What seemed simple and straightforward to Nauta when he wrote this essay for a book published in 1983 had earlier been rather mysterious. In an interview of July 6, 1966, he said: "But all and all I must admit, especially in retrospect, that we faced some mysterious matters." One of those matters was what is involved in suspending and deposing an office-bearer for the sins listed in Article 80 of the church order (see the note on p. 300). In that interview he declared: "Their *office* was taken away — I acknowledge fully that *this was already bad enough!* — but they were not thereby placed outside the church, even though some of their followers felt that this is what it amounted to and suggested as much" (see Puchinger, *Is de gereformeerde wereld veranderd?,* p. 276). How Nauta (who even writes on church order matters) and other synodical leaders could understand the deposition of Schilder and some other office-bearers in these terms is one of the continuing mysteries that still stands in the way of Reformed unity. Berkouwer seems to have had

ber of requests brought forward to have the rights and wrongs of 1944 investigated carefully, but the fact of the matter is that the synod of the Christian Reformed Church, despite its love of study committees, did not accede to them.[6]

In the 1972 book, Van Reest takes a somewhat different approach to the 1947 announcement in *The Banner* and argues that the choice against Schilder should not simply be read as expressing the will or sentiments of the ordinary church members. The liberated Reformed people have a responsibility with regard to those members of the Christian Reformed churches who are in disagreement with the more recent developments. Van Reest writes:

> The trust is gone, and at every synod held in Grand Rapids, motions expressing distrust are made. In the press the distrust also comes to expression. And I was struck by the fact that here and there people begin to raise the question whether the liberation in the 1940s really should have been condemned, and whether the leadership in the Christian Reformed Church in those days did not let itself be hoodwinked. This course of events places a question before the liberated Reformed believers in the Netherlands, namely, whether we do not have a task with regard to the many Christian Reformed people in the United States and Canada who are protesting. We cannot simply say: "They made the wrong choice back in 1945, and that's the end of the matter *(daarmee is ook deze kous af)*." The fact is that the *leadership* made the wrong choice, and it is quite well possible that the leadership is also making the wrong choice today . . . (p. 61).

Yet the significance of the official decision and its consequences cannot be minimized, according to Van Reest:

> The Christian Reformed Church had chosen its path, a path which must lead inevitably in 1947 to the closing of all doors in this denomination to this man of peace [Schilder]. The ties

---

a similar difficulty. J. J. Buskes (a theological opponent of Schilder!) once said of him: "Berkouwer understands everything — except what it means to be suspended" (see Puchinger, "Kerkelijke momenten en personen," in J. de Bruijn, ed., *Een land nog niet in kaart gebracht: Aspecten van het protestants-christelijk leven in Nederland in de jaren 1880-1940* [Amsterdam: Passage, 1987], p. 292). The elderly Berkouwer, however, is still preoccupied with the events of 1944. In a book published some four and a half decades after he presided over the synod that deposed Schilder, he devotes extensive attention to Schilder and the 1944 conflict (see *Zoeken en vinden: Herinneringen en ervaringen* [Kampen: Kok, 1989], pp. 235-366). In the same book he discusses Hepp (pp. 71-91) and the Geelkerken case (pp. 107-135).

[6] For a survey of official Christian Reformed actions on this matter, see Appendix I in W. W. J. Van Oene's *Inheritance Preserved: The Canadian Reformed Churches in Historical Perspective* (Winnipeg: Premier Printing, 1975), pp. 229-260.

> with the synodical community in the Netherlands were still too strong in those days to permit any risks to be taken . . .
>
> The church doors, which in 1939 had stood wide open [for Schilder] were now completely closed, just as though he were a heretic of the first order. From the communiqué [the announcement in *The Banner*] it is apparent just how hierarchically things were organized in the Christian Reformed Church of North America. For that matter, this is already evident from the official name, where we find not the plural (churches) but the singular (the Christian Reformed *Church*.) And that the announcement was made "by order of the Synodical Committee" also tells us quite a bit about the hierarchical character of this organization (pp. 58, 59; see also p. 77).

Now we are in a position to see why many of the immigrants who were members of the liberated Reformed churches in the Netherlands did not simply join Christian Reformed churches, and why some others who did join ran into difficulties. First of all, these churches were hierarchical: although they still professed to operate by the traditional Reformed church order of Dort, they were introducing the same hierarchical tendency that had played a key role in the 1944 struggle in the Netherlands. The way Schilder's visit to North America in 1947 was handled illustrated the hierarchical tendency. To have joined the Christian Reformed Church would in effect have meant casting aside lessons in church order and procedure which had been learned in the Netherlands at great cost during the years 1936 through 1944.

In addition, there was a doctrinal difficulty, and it was also related to the events of 1944. The Christian Reformed churches had, in effect chosen against Schilder and in favor of his theological opponents in the synodical Reformed churches in the Netherlands. They did so through the position they took in 1946 at the preparatory meeting of the Reformed Ecumenical Synod held in Grand Rapids, where the manner in which the synodical churches in the Netherlands had interpreted the 1905 Conclusions of Utrecht was upheld.

One might wonder whether the initial ecumenical synod of the Reformed churches was wise in attempting to pass judgment on a body of churches that claimed to be Reformed but were not represented at the meeting. One of the Christian Reformed delegates, Dr. Herman Kuiper, had strong misgivings on this score and dissented from the synod's decision to investigate the ecclesiastical quarrel in the Netherlands. He had the following declaration recorded in the minutes: "The undersigned wishes to have it recorded in the minutes of the Ecumenical Synod that he has refrained from taking part in the discussions and decisions re the ecclesiastical difficulties in the Netherlands since he was persuaded that the Christian Reformed Synod of 1946 did not desire its delegates to the Ecumenical Synod to take part in this matter" (see Art. 99 of the *Acts).

It is also worth noting that the delegation from the synodical churches in the Netherlands included Dr. G. C. Berkouwer, the president of the General Synod that suspended and deposed Schilder. Another member of its four-man delegation had also been played a role in the proceedings against Schilder — Dr. G. C. Aalders. In fact, the four-man group that composed the official "Elucidation" *(Toelichting)* of the synodical doctrinal decision which led to Schilder's deposition (see the note on p. 330 above) included both Berkouwer and Aalders, who clearly carried the day in the discussions in Grand Rapids.

The synodical churches had asked to have their position evaluated at this ecumenical synod. The response of the synod (made up of representatives from only three churches — the synodical group from the Netherlands, the Christian Reformed Church, and the Reformed *(Gereformeerd)* Church in South Africa — was that the position presented by the synodical churches for evaluation was "in conformity with the Scripture and the Creeds."[7]

Some years later, at the repeated urging of Canadian congregations and classes, the Christian Reformed decision of 1908 to take over the Conclusions of Utrecht of 1905 was nullified by the Synod of 1968 (see the note on p. 101), and so an obstacle to closer relations between Christian Reformed and Canadian Reformed churches was taken away at that point, which was some two decades after immigrants had begun arriving in North America in substantial numbers. By then the earlier adherence to the "Conclusions of Utrecht" had already had its effect on immigrants arriving in Canada. The theological emphases which the 1942 synodical declarations in the Netherlands expressed have been disavowed by a great many Christian Reformed ministers; whether the mentality behind those declarations has functioned significantly in Christian Reformed circles is still a matter of disagreement among those who are in a good position to know.

The Christian Reformed loyalty to the synodical side in the Netherlands also came to expression in the question of sermons to be used in reading services. Mr. John De Haas, a liberated immigrant who settled in Alberta after World War II, was part of a Christian Reformed house congregation in Lethbridge, Alberta, which met under the supervision of the consistory of the Christian Reformed Church in Nobleford. He proposed to have sermons prepared by liberated Reformed ministers in the Netherlands read on a regular basis (alternating with sermons by ministers from the synodical churches), but it was not permitted. De Haas appealed the decision of the consistory to Classis Pacific early in 1949 and lost, and then to the Christian Reformed Synod of 1949, where he also lost. He concluded that there was no place for him in the Christian Reformed Church, and in 1950 he became one of the founding members of the Canadian Reformed Church of Lethbridge. Later

---

[7] See Art. 89 of the *Acts;* for a formulation of the synodical position as discussed at this synod, see Supplement IV on pp. 87-90.

that year the Lethbridge congregation joined with some others for a meeting of "Classis Canada."[8]

Such arguments about reading sermons came up in other Christian Reformed congregations as well. Moreover, the doctrinal differences between liberated Reformed immigrants and the Christian Reformed Church also came to expression in the difficulties encountered by Mr. J. J. Knegt, an elder in the Christian Reformed Church in St. Catharines, Ontario, in January of 1949. This man was suspended from office because he could not agree with the Three Points on Common Grace adopted in 1924 (and set aside in 1962). He then became a member of the Canadian Reformed congregation in nearby Hamilton. And there are more such episodes that could be mentioned. The upshot is that the liberated immigrants did run into opposition, but the situation was by no means uniform from congregation to congregation. Naturally, the stories of opposition and conflict were the ones that became known.

After 1968, when the "Conclusions of Utrecht" ceased to function as an obstacle between Christian Reformed and Canadian Reformed churches,[9] the official talks between these two federations of churches ran aground on a substantive issue, namely, the desire on the part of the Christian Reformed Church to maintain a sister church relationship with the synodical Reformed churches which had deposed Schilder and so many other office-bearers in the Netherlands. The Canadian Reformed Churches wanted the Christian Reformed Church to cease recognizing the synodical churches in the Netherlands as "faithful Reformed churches" (see 1974 *Acts*, p. 95).

The issue was not first or foremost that the synodical churches had done an ecclesiastical injustice to Schilder and other office-bearers thirty years before: *current* trends in the Netherlands were pointed out as reason for concern. Such trends had already been mentioned in the discussions in the 1960s and had been reported to the Christian Reformed Synod of 1969, where the following (Canadian Reformed) concerns about the synodical churches in the Netherlands are listed: the decision of Assen (Geelkerken, 1926) in defence of Scripture has been set aside; it has been decided in principle that there are no objections to membership in the World Council of Churches; women are admitted to special offices in the church; a new church order giving hierarchical power to synods was adopted; professors in official, ecclesiastical positions openly attack the infallibility of the Bible without being disciplined; and the Reformed foundation of the Free University has been removed (see 1969 *Acts*, p. 351).

In short, the liberalizing trends in both theology and church polity that had begun to manifest themselves ever more openly in the synodical churches in the Netherlands represented a concrete obstacle to fruitful contact in North

---

[8] DeHaas tells his story in an autobiographical work entitled *And Replenish the Earth* (New Westminster: Covenant Publishing, 1987), see pp. 62-70.

[9] The contacts underway in that era did not only consist of talks between committees reporting to their respective synods; there were also contacts on a consistorial level.

America as long as the Christian Reformed Church continued to recognize those churches as their sister churches in the Netherlands. What happened at this point is that the Christian Reformed Church's committee for contact with the Canadian Reformed Churches asked the Synod of 1972 for permission to discontinue the contacts, and it was granted.

The contacts between the churches were also dealt with when the Synod of the Canadian Reformed Churches next met in 1974 and was informed by its committee that the Christian Reformed Synod had decided to discontinue the contacts.[10] At the next Canadian Reformed Synod, meeting in 1977, it was decided to issue an appeal to be addressed to the Christian Reformed Synod, all consistories, and also the members. This Appeal was a lengthy document which included an informative review of the relationship between these two church bodies.[11]

By now, some of the trends in the synodical churches to which the Canadian Reformed Churches object are evident in the Christian Reformed Church as well, and so the gap between Christian Reformed and Canadian Reformed has been widening. Nevertheless, some years after the original talks broke down, the Council of Christian Reformed Churches in Canada,[12] which had been entrusted by the Christian Reformed Synod with the matter of remaining in some sort of contact with the Canadian Reformed Churches, tried to take up the contact again, but its efforts did not get far. In recent years, cooperation and joint ventures involving both Christian Reformed and Canadian Reformed people have been relatively rare; the translation and publication of this book represents a notable exception.[13]

It is worth noting that Van Reest himself raises a third objection to the possibility of closer relationships between liberated Reformed churches and the Christian Reformed Church, namely, the events of 1924, which he refers to in his 1948 book as "the liberation of the Churches in 1924."[14] He argues:

> ... even if the Christian Reformed Church wanted to establish a correspondence relationship with our churches in the Netherlands, we wouldn't be able to agree to it, for 1924 stands between us and them. We would be obliged to first awaken these brothers to the need to liberate themselves from the Kalamazoo decisions.[15] We cannot and may not ignore what has happened,

---

[10] See Art. 146 of the *Acts* and Appendix IV (pp. 92-99).

[11] See Art. 77 of the *Acts* and Appendix VII (pp. 102-115).

[12] This body may look like a regional or particular synod, but it is not. One reason for its lack of success in strictly ecclesiastical business is its disputed status in terms of church order.

[13] It has been a source of joy to me that I have been able to work with Canadian Reformed and Christian Reformed people alike in bringing across the story of Schilder and 1944, even though the material in the book is of such a nature that it could be expected to touch off many an argument.

[14] Dutch: "de vrijmaking der Kerken in 1924" (see *Van kust tot kust,* p. 189).

[15] The reference here is to the famous Three Points on Common Grace, which were adopted at the Christian Reformed synod of 1924, meeting in Kalamazoo. Rev. Herman Hoeksema and some others were not able to assent to these points. The result was the deposition of Hoeksema. In these events the Protestant Reformed Churches have their origin.

for the Reformed line runs through the Protestant Reformed Church *(Kust,* p. 209).

It was Van Reest's contention that 1924 was just like 1944, and the Hoeksema case was just like the Schilder case. The parallels also extend to the prelude to the major battle: in the Netherlands it was the Geelkerken case, and in North America in was the case of Prof. Ralph Janssen, whom he compares to H. M. Kuitert. Janssen, he explained in the 1972 book, was trying to bring the teachings of the Bible into agreement with what were regarded as the results of modern science (see *Terugzien,* p. 105). In the 1948 book, he explained the parallels between 1924 and 1944 as follows:

> We cannot go into the Kalamazoo decisions in any great depth here. One would have to write a separate book on the subject in order to show exactly what happened. But there are a few things that need to be indicated, mainly to point out the striking parallels between the battle waged by Rev. Hoeksema and his followers against the hierarchy of the Christian Reformed Church, on the one hand, and the battle of the "protesters" against the hierarchy of the Churches in the Netherlands, on the other. Even in the background we find sharp features of agreement.
>
> Just as we had the so-called "Geelkerken question" in the 1920s, there was a similar sort of question in the form of the Dr. Janssen case in North America. This professor taught Old Testament studies at Calvin Seminary in Grand Rapids,[16] where students for the ministry in the Christian Reformed Church receive their training. It became apparent to Rev. Hoeksema and some others that this professor was passing on to his students modernistic views regarding the Bible, e.g. when it came to the miracles in the Old Testament, and that he even sought a synthesis between the people of Israel and the surrounding pagan nations.
>
> The official objection raised against Dr. Janssen was signed by — among others — such ministers as Hoeksema, William Heyns, F. M. Ten Hoor, Louis Berkhof, Henry Danhof, Y. P. De Jong, Henry J. Kuiper, and Samuel Volbeda. Dr. Janssen was deposed by the synod of the Christian Reformed Church.[17]

---

[16] The Dutch text says Calvin *College,* but Janssen in fact taught in the Seminary. It also has him teaching "dogmatics," which was the responsibility of Foppe M. Ten Hoor at that time.

[17] The Synod dismissed him from his office as professor of theology. There has been considerable criticism of the way the proceedings against Janssen were conducted. On this matter, see Edward Heerema, *R.B.: Prophet in the Land* (Jordan Station: Paideia Press, 1986), pp. 62-70, and the 1924 *Acts of Synod,* pp. 161-191. The Janssen case is an indication that a deposition or dismissal of a professor by a synod is not a simple matter from the standpoint of church polity.

But at once there were complaints made against Rev. Hoeksema, even from the side of Dr. Janssen, who maintained that Rev. Hoeksema denied Kuyper's doctrine of common grace and thus was not Reformed! It was not long before Rev. Hoeksema was suspended and cast out.[18]

Reluctantly the church let go of Dr. Janssen: in the face of the overwhelming abundance of evidence assembled by Rev. Hoeksema, it simply *had* to be done. But the doctrine of common grace was beautifully suited to get rid of Rev. Hoeksema as well. "He must be put out," wrote a well-known minister in those days, "but how are we going to accomplish it?" Kuyper's construction regarding common grace could be of service here.

You see the parallels. When Dr. Geelkerken was put out in 1926, most of those who thought as he did left him in the lurch. Their little group was too small for them to want to be part of it. Today [i.e. 1947] one can still point to those men in our churches — the ones who held back at that time when they saw which way the wind was blowing.

But they never forgot what had been done in the case of Dr. Geelkerken. The so-called "younger generation" in the Reformed *(Gereformeerd)* churches were heard from later on, and the campaign they waged against Schilder when the synodical procedures were underway is proof of this. Prof. Schilder, who saw the dangers in this "younger generation" in the Reformed churches . . . and warned against it prophetically, made these people into his permanent enemies. And it went the very same way in the Hoeksema case.

Another parallel is the influence of the Free University of Amsterdam. When the case was being made against Rev. Hoeksema, Prof. Hepp was in North America and was giving his advice from behind the scenes. I do not need to mention what sort of role was played by the Free University in the Schilder case in the Netherlands.

Another strong parallel is that nowhere in the entire Hoeksema case do we find any indication that he was accused of departing from the Word of God or from the Reformed confessions.

---

[18] When Van Reest makes much of the parallels between 1924 and 1944, he does not sufficiently acknowledge that 1944 had a much longer build-up: think of the events at the synod of 1936. Hoeksema himself maintained that the aftermath of the Janssen case largely determined the timing of his own expulsion: "Eliminate the Janssen controversy and you are at a loss to explain why the separation of 1924 occurred at that early date. The reformation that gave rise to the Protestant Reformed Churches would have had a later date and a different setting. But when due allowance is made for the influence of the Janssen controversy upon the history of 1924, the fact remains that the former cannot be regarded as the *cause* of the latter" *(The Protestant Reformed Churches in America: Their Origin, Early History, and Doctrine,* second edition, 1947, p. 23).

(Read through the *Acts* for yourself.) On the contrary, it had to be admitted at Synod that he was "Reformed in respect to the fundamental truths as they are formulated in the Confessions even though it be with an inclination toward one-sidedness."

Why, then, were Rev. Hoeksema and some others with him finally deposed and cast out? It was because they did not bow before the hierarchical-synodical government of the Christian Reformed Church — just as among us. When you read the grounds on which Prof. Schilder was suspended, you find no suggestion that he was departing from the Word or the Confessions. His only sin was that he would not bow before the yoke of a hierarchical synod seeking to bind his conscience.

There are more parallels. When Classis Grand Rapids East began taking steps toward suspending Rev. Hoeksema and casting him out with his congregation, events were played out behind closed doors. A classical committee was appointed, and it took counsel from the theological faculty (the seminary professors) in secret . . . Finally Rev. Hoeksema was asked to do nothing more than to answer some categorical questions with either a "yes" or a "no."[19] He was not allowed to defend himself. Both at the Synod of Kalamazoo and in the meeting of Classis Grand Rapids East, the decision about him was made without his involvement — just as with us! *(Kust,* pp. 205-207)

In his treatment of Schilder, Van Reest makes much of how the Christian Reformed brothers refused to receive him or hear him out in 1947. He accuses the soundly Reformed believers in the Netherlands of a similar insensitivity to the situation of Rev. Hoeksema after he had been illegitimately cast out of the Christian Reformed Church in 1924:[20] "When Rev. Hoeksema, in 1929, five years after he had been cast out of the Christian Reformed Church, visited his fatherland, he knocked on our doors in vain. We left him standing in his isolation — this man who so much desired communion with us" (p. 205). He quotes Hoeksema's own explanation of why the break came[21] and then adds: "Every liberated person in the Netherlands will understand what he means. In 1920 and the years following upon it, we went through the very same spiritual struggle with the same spiritual values at stake, and it led to 1944. It's all exactly the same *(Het is alles precies hetzelfde).*"

---

[19] Schilder also had to answer a series of questions with either a "yes" or a "no" at one point in the proceedings against him. On the five questions put to him and the context in which they were posed, see *Het vuur blijft branden: Geschiedenis van de Gereformeerde Kerken (vrijgemaakt) in Nederland, 1944-1979,* by P. Jongeling *et al.* (Kampen: Kok, 1979), pp. 35-36.

[20] Hoeksema was not deposed by a general synod, as Schilder was, but by a classis. Hoeksema deals at length with the depositions of 1924 in *The Protestant Reformed Churches* (see pp. 202-290).

[21] The same passage that is printed on pp. 52-53 above.

Some Reformed people look back at these developments and wonder why there was never a union between the Hoeksema group and the Schilder group. In considering whether such a union would have made sense, we must first ask whether there was substantial theological agreement.[22] That Hoeksema and Schilder had a great deal in common in terms of what they had experienced at the hands of the churches that ordained them is clear, and this was no doubt part of the reason for the kinship they felt. But Van Reest's writings presuppose more theological similarity than actually existed.

There is an interesting chapter in these developments which Van Reest largely ignores in the two books in which he comments on the North American church scene. His silence did not stem from a lack of awareness: not only did he know what was happening, he also participated in the discussions by writing some articles in Protestant Reformed papers. What Van Reest fails to tell us is that Schilder apparently played a role (without intending to do so) in the split that took place in the Protestant Reformed Churches in 1953.

A related matter of historical relevance which Van Reest does not mention is that Hoeksema's health was seriously impaired when Schilder came to Grand Rapids in 1947. In a biography of Herman Hoeksema written by his daughter-in-law, we read:

> Dr. Schilder came in the summer of 1947 for his second visit. He found Rev. Hoeksema an invalid, convalescing in the sunshine of his backyard two months after he was laid low [with a stroke] in Sioux Falls. Rev. Hoeksema had neither the desire nor the stamina to converse on theological issues.[23] Their contact, at first, was limited to a simple backyard picnic or two.
>
> In the early fall a conference with Dr. Schilder and the ministers of the denomination who were able to attend was proposed. In October they met in the consistory room of First Church. With an effort that almost exceeded his physical abilities, Rev. Hoeksema prepared several brief propositions and made his way to the church next door to read them in person. He was too exhausted to stay, and had to rely on his son Homer's report of Dr. Schilder's reply to his propositions, and the reaction of his fellow ministers.

---

[22] There was confessional agreement, of course, in terms of the Three Forms of Unity. But not all churches that accept these Forms understand and interpret them in the same way; hence theological emphases come into the picture. This distinction between theological and confessional differences was used by Schilder himself, who wrote: "Between you [the Protestant Reformed] and us there are probably theological differences, but no confessional differences" (see Hoeksema's article "Criticism and Its Answer," in *The Standard Bearer*, Vol. 27, No. 4 [Nov. 1, 1950], p. 53).

[23] Hoeksema never fully recovered from his stroke, although he was eventually able to return to a demanding work schedule. Schilder's visit happened to fall in the period when he was still very weak.

Now, there was a further conference (November 4-6), in which Hoeksema was able to play a more active role. (The first conference was held on October 16.) But the fact remains that when Schilder came to the United States, he had free access to the minds of some of the Protestant Reformed ministers. Hoeksema did not agree with Schilder on the covenant and had made this known even before Schilder arrived. But when the Protestant Reformed discussion with Schilder began, Hoeksema was not there to confront Schilder on the points that divided them. The result, in the words of the Hoeksema biography, was that "not all the ministers in the denomination agreed with Rev. Hoeksema and his evaluation of Dr. Schilder. Some were quite sympathetic to the views of Dr. Schilder and they let their views be known."[24]

At the very least, then, it can be said that Schilder's coming to the United States touched off some theological debate within the Protestant Reformed Churches. But the differences between the two camps could not be confined to an academic discussion, for liberated Reformed immigrants were starting to arrive in North America (mainly Canada) and would have to be dealt with in some manner. Could they find a church home in the Protestant Reformed fellowship?

Back in the Netherlands there were two strains of advice being given to those who were planning to emigrate. Schilder and some others told them they should join Protestant Reformed Churches; it was assumed, of course, that that these churches would be somewhat receptive to the understanding of the covenant that was accepted in liberated circles. The other approach was taken by Rev. Douwe van Dijk of Groningen, who was quite influential in liberated circles, and Rev. J. Hettinga, who was active in the work of advising and helping immigrants and who spent a good deal of time in Canada, and some others as well. Such men urged the immigrants to form congregations of their own, congregations which would presumably maintain close ties with the liberated Reformed churches in the Netherlands.

Both approaches were followed in Ontario, at least, and in 1949 a Protestant Reformed congregation was established in Hamilton (with Rev. Herman Veldman, a nephew of Hoeksema, as its first pastor), and another in Chatham, organized in 1950 (with Rev. Andrew Petter as pastor). Hamilton also had a liberated congregation, organized in 1951, and a little later (1952) the two immigrant groups (which for a while had worshiped separately in the same building and at the same time) came together as a Canadian Reformed church.[25] Late in 1951, the congregation in Chatham broke with the Protestant Reformed Churches and, after some discussion, entered the fel-

---

[24] Gertrude Hoeksema, *Therefore Have I Spoken: A Biography of Herman Hoeksema* (Grand Rapids: Reformed Free Publishing Association, 1969), pp. 308, 310.

[25] In 1959 this congregation in Hamilton divided, with one part continuing as Canadian Reformed (Cornerstone Church) and the other part seeking entrance into the Christian Reformed Church (Immanuel Church). The portion of the congregation that became Christian Reformed was awarded the building (on Mohawk Road) after a court case.

lowship of the Canadian Reformed Churches, with Rev. L. Selles arriving in 1952 to serve as pastor. In both these congregations fierce battles were fought, having to do in part with the differences between Protestant Reformed thinking and the thinking of the liberated Reformed churches in the Netherlands, especially in relation to the covenant. The details of those battles need not concern us. The general tenor of what went on has been summarized by Hoeksema as follows:

> . . . the leaders in the Liberated churches have done untold harm to their own immigrants, especially in Canada, and to the cause of our laboring among them . . . Let me inform the brethren that we have as Protestant Reformed Churches faithfully labored among the immigrants in Canada; that we have literally taken them into our bosom; that we have loved them; that we have spent thousands and thousands of dollars for their benefit; that we have faithfully instructed them; and that we have tried to organize them into Protestant Reformed Churches. But it was always the influence exerted upon them from the old country that made our labor very difficult and practically impossible. Their leaders from the old country stirred them up against us, both by public articles in their papers and by private correspondence. Their purpose apparently was to create in America an extension of the Liberated Churches, or even to persuade the Protestant Reformed Churches to assume the same stand as they. I assure the brethren that this will prove to be impossible for more than one reason. I have advised the immigrants more than once, both in Hamilton and in Chatham, that they must not be incited against us by the old country, but that they must learn to stand on their own feet. They may judge for themselves what is the purest manifestation of the body of Christ in America. And I am confident that if they do so, and if they are really Reformed at heart, and understand the Reformed truth, they will certainly join the Protestant Reformed Churches.[26]

The upshot is that affiliating with the federation of churches dominated by Hoeksema did not work, however friendly Schilder and Hoeksema may have been as persons. It should be understood that Schilder's reason for favoring this approach for so long even though others in his circle had come to oppose it was grounded in his insistence that it is wrong to multiply churches needlessly. Kamphuis writes that Schilder — after 1944 — never wearied of reminding his students that "anyone who wants to serve the cause of the

---

[26] "Criticism and Its Answer," pp. 55-56. Other articles in *The Standard Bearer* go into the specifics of the difficulties in great detail.

reformation of the church and of Christian life must *never* imagine that he can *build something new;* rather, he is to accept the inheritance of previous generations and remain standing in the communion of the *church,* and must *never* isolate himself in a circle of like-minded people who enjoy a glowing sense of unity in the latest discoveries. Instead he is to accept the entire communion of the saints and in this way return to the Scriptures and to obedience to them. Reformation does mean cutting off *sin,* but it does not mean *cutting* the bond with the past. How Prof. Schilder could hammer it home that *the others* were the ones who had changed, whereas we had remained what we were — Reformed."[27]

Yet Schilder was willing to grant that in given historical circumstances, a measure of isolation might be unavoidable. He also used to say: "Whoever desires isolation is sick. But whoever shrinks away from it when it is forced upon him is even more sick."[28] And so he could finally bring himself to declare that the effort to be one with the Protestant Reformed Churches would not work. He drew this conclusion not because of Hoeksema's theology but because of a new "extra-scriptural binding" which people of his convictions could not accept. The binding in question was the so-called "Declaration of Principles," which was intended to be nothing more than an explicit statement of what the Protestant Reformed Churches had always stood for but which served at the same time as an extra document to which one had to assent as a Protestant Reformed office-bearer.[29]

There were two reasons why such a declaration was deemed necessary. The first is that liberated Reformed immigrants in Canada who had shown interest in the Protestant Reformed Churches had to be taught exactly what they would be committed to if they joined. The second is that some Protestant Reformed ministers, especially in the western part of the continent, where they published a paper of their own called *Concordia,* were drifting away from earlier Protestant Reformed emphases, partly in the wake of Schilder's visit. In addition, two of the ministers (Revs. John D. De Jong and Bernard Kok, both of whom are mentioned by Van Reest in connection with Schilder's visit of 1947), made a trip to the Netherlands a few years later during which they were alleged to have made statements that compromised the doctrinal position of the Protestant Reformed Churches and to have accommodated themselves somewhat to the theological direction taken

---

[27] *De braambos,* Vol. 2, p. 57.

[28] *De braambos,* Vol. 2, p. 139.

[29] The Declaration itself, passed provisionally at the Protestant Reformed Synod of 1950, and then adopted officially at the Synod of 1951, is too lengthy to be reproduced here. It is made up in good measure of quotations from the Three Forms of Unity and the form for baptism and has been summarized by W. W. J. Van Oene as follows: "(1) The Protestant Reformed Churches reject the errors of the Three Points of Kalamazoo and maintain that the grace of God is only for the elect. (2) They teach that the promise of God is unconditionally [valid] only for the elect. (3) They reject the doctrine that the promise of the covenant is for all who are baptized" (In *Inheritance Preserved: The Canadian Reformed Churches in Historical Perspective,* p. 65).

by the liberated Reformed churches.[30] It was maintained that they had been influenced by Profs. Holwerda, Schilder, and Veenhof.

The Declaration of Principles was supposed to restore unity in doctrinal matters, but the actual result was that quite a number of ministers and lay members of the Protestant Reformed Churches could not accept it. In 1953, a good portion of this small denomination broke away and formed another group also calling itself Protestant Reformed. The latter churches are often referred to unofficially as the De Wolf group, since Rev. Hubert De Wolf was the dominant minister among them. De Wolf was one of the pastors of the First Protestant Reformed Church of Grand Rapids, the largest congregation of all, of which Hoeksema was also a minister. Most of this congregation left with De Wolf, who retained the building for a few years and then was ordered by the courts to surrender it to the group that stayed with Hoeksema.

The De Wolf churches carried on for some years as an independent group. They entered into official talks with the Christian Reformed Church in 1957 and were received into the Christian Reformed Church in 1962, after the binding character of the Three Points on common grace adopted at the Synod of 1924 had been substantially loosened. That was why Andrew Petter and many of Van Reest's other Protestant Reformed friends of 1947 were in the Christian Reformed Church when Van Reest came back to the United States in the early 1970s.

But even before the split in the Protestant Reformed Churches took place in 1953 (more than a year after Schilder's death), Hoeksema and Schilder said farewell to one another. It was Schilder — rather than Hoeksema — who finally announced that a close relationship with the Protestant Reformed would not work. In an article published in *The Reformation* in November of 1951 (a mere matter of months before his death), he declared that the effort on the part of the liberated Reformed people to enter into full ecclesiastical union with the Protestant Reformed Churches was over. Hoeksema quickly responded to Schilder's article and accepted his decision. (Schilder's article and Hoeksema's response are reproduced below in abridged form as Appendix II.)

In a statement included in a book published in 1970, Dr. Jelle Faber summed up the developments to this point in the following words:

> When the emigration got underway after the second world war, Dr. Schilder emphasized that the work of God in another country was not to be ignored. Thus he did not say: "Establish churches wherever you go." On the contrary, his advice always was: "If it is at all possible, begin by taking into account

---

[30] Homer C. Hoeksema maintained that these two ministers "attempted to sell our churches down the river" (see "Persistent Distortion," in *The Standard Bearer,* Vol. 61, No. 16 [May 15, 1985], p. 365).

what is already to be found in a particular country." But in 1946, the Reformed Ecumenical Synod meeting in Grand Rapids had already approved the statement made that year by the Synod of the [synodical] Reformed Churches in the Netherlands as being in harmony with Scripture and the confessions. When Schilder went to the United States in 1947 to give some information to Reformed people there, he found the door of the Christian Reformed Church closed to him. Moreover, Dr. Danhof, the secretary of the "Synodical Committee," wrote in *The Banner* that Schilder was not to be received and was not to be allowed to preach, for he belonged to a new church formation that had been established in the Netherlands, which meant that the door had to be closed to him. And this decision did not only apply to him: all liberated Reformed people were regarded as bringers of a new light *(nieuwlichters)*. That action also played a role in determining the attitude that was taken. Then Dr. Schilder said: "The Protestant Reformed Churches," but after those churches had chosen in an official declaration for an extra-scriptural binding along approximately the same dogmatic lines as a fatalism grounded in election (if I may used my own words here), just as the Reformed Churches in the Netherlands had imposed binding declarations during the years 1942 through 1944, Schilder finally said: "Yes, it's certainly too bad, but the stocking is finished.[31] Now there is nothing else we can do."[32]

The adoption of the Declaration of Principles meant that there was now a confessional disparity between the liberated Reformed and the Protestant Reformed churches. But another factor in the picture is that there were theological differences between Hoeksema and Schilder all along.[33] Although both were critical of the notion of common grace, they did not approach this problem in the same way: when H. Evan Runner was one of Schilder's students at Kampen just before the war (after Schilder's first journey to the United States), he made this point to him.[34] Another important difference is the way these two theologians viewed the doctrine of the covenant. Hoeksema was convinced that the view Schilder held was essentially the same as that

---

[31] This Dutch expression means simply that the matter is finished. Schilder featured the expression in the article in which he announced this conclusion (see Appendix II below).

[32] In N. Scheps, *Interviews over 25 jaar vrijmaking* (Kampen: Kok, 1970), p. 52.

[33] On the similarities and differences between these two theologians, see A. C. De Jong, *The Well-Meant Gospel Offer: The Views of H. Hoeksema and K. Schilder* (Franeker: T. Wever, 1954).

[34] On Schilder's approach to common grace, see his brochure *Is de term "algemeene genade" wetenschappelijk verantwoord?* (Kampen: Zalsman, 1947).

of Heyns, which was the view Hoeksema had left behind in 1924.[35] Hoeksema basically identified covenant and election. Anthony A. Hoekema formulates the Heynsian objection to such thinking as follows: "If one thinks of the covenant of grace as established only with the elect, the character of the covenant of grace is totally changed, for then there can be no possibility of covenant breaking. Further, the covenant of grace is then deprived of its objectivity, since one cannot know whether one's children are covenant members or not."[36] The notion of a "sufficient grace" made available to all children of believers was also foreign to Schilder's thinking.[37]

In spelling out the problem as he understood it on the basis of his reading and also his contact with people influenced by Schilder and company, Hoeksema wrote:

> ... to put the matter in its simplest form: they do not agree with the Protestant Reformed truth of the covenant and of the promise of God. They insist upon maintaining their own view, which is Heynsian. And Heynsianism is in our conviction Arminianism, — common grace applied to the covenant. That this is true is plain from all that is written in the papers of the Netherlands, from the very first numbers of *The Reformation* which we received after the war.
>
> This conception of the covenant the Liberated mean to maintain.
>
> On the basis of that conception they maintain that they are the true church. We are not.
>
> They want to throw the church doors wide open, well aware of the fact that only Liberated immigrants will enter through that wide open door ... If we allow this, the result will be that in a few years our churches will be swamped by thousands of Liberated immigrants and the Heynsian view of the covenant.[38]

The question that remains to be asked is why the De Wolf churches did not unite with the Canadian Reformed churches that were being organized in Canada at that time. (There was not a congregation in the United States

---

[35] William W. Heyns had been Hoeksema's teacher for practical theology during his student days at Calvin Seminary. Hoeksema maintained that his former teacher's view was in effect Arminian — "pure Arminianism and Pelagianism applied to the covenant" (see *Systematic Theology* [Grand Rapids: Reformed Free Publishing Association, 1966], p. 698). Hoeksema also discussed Heyns in Chs. 1 and 2 of *Believers and Their Seed* (Grand Rapids: Reformed Free Publishing Association, 1971).

[36] "The Christian Reformed Church and the Covenant," in *Perspectives on the Christian Reformed Church*, p. 191.

[37] See J. Geertsema, "Can the Covenant Be Broken?" in *Clarion*, issue of May 19, 1979, p. 218.

[38] "Binding or Not Binding?" in *The Standard Bearer*, Vol. 27, No. 6 (Dec. 15, 1950), pp. 124-125.

Appendix I: North American Developments 393

until 1955, when the church in Grand Rapids was founded.) After all, some of their ministers had begun to drift away from Hoeksema after listening to Schilder in 1947.

There is no single answer to this question, but the following considerations will help us understand what had actually happened — and didn't happen. First of all, there were indeed a number of meetings between ministers of the Canadian Reformed Churches and ministers of the De Wolf group in 1954 and 1955. From the Canadian Reformed side, those meetings, held in Chatham, were unofficial: the ministers involved were not carrying out a synodical mandate.

When we consider why the meetings did not lead to union, we should bear in mind that both groups were small. The churches in Canada had the dynamic of growth behind them because of all the immigrants continuing to enter the country from the Netherlands, but the De Wolf congregations had struggled along as a small group for many years. In some of the De Wolf people there lived the desire to be part of a much larger fellowship, which the Canadian Reformed Churches could not offer. Closely related to this factor is the geographical situation. The De Wolf churches were located in the United States, whereas all the Canadian Reformed churches were in Canada. The fellowship and affiliation that was being considered was thus a distant one at best. To be in full ecclesiastical communion with some sound Reformed churches in another country would not have solved all that many problems for the De Wolf churches.

But the most important factor is that there was not as much theological affinity between the De Wolf ministers and the Canadian Reformed churches as one might originally have supposed. It may well be that an encounter with Schilder had led the ministers in the De Wolf group to think some new thoughts, after many years in which their personal exposure to theologians others than Hoeksema was minimal. But to be stimulated by Schilder's theology is not the same as to become thoroughly familiar with it and to be influenced by it at a deep level. From the subsequent history of the De Wolf ministers and congregations,[39] it is evident that there was not the degree of oneness in thinking that would have made it possible to consider such a step as becoming liberated Reformed churches in the United States.

From the Canadian Reformed side there were expressions of interest in establishing a correspondence relationship with the De Wolf churches. The matter came up for discussion at the first Synod of the Canadian Reformed Churches, which was held in 1954 (see Art. 95-99 of the *Acts),* and it was

---

[39] The terms of the reunion with the Christian Reformed Church allowed for some of the De Wolf churches to enter intact as congregations, while churches made up of people scattered over a large geographical area would be allowed to disband, with their people joining whichever Christian Reformed congregation was nearby. De Wolf's sizable congregation in Grand Rapids (whose members, before 1953, had been part of Hoeksema's own congregation) was among those that disbanded.

decided to make contact with these churches with an eye to being represented at their next synod. The Canadian Reformed Churches did not hold another synod until 1958, and by then the De Wolf churches were engaged in talks with the Christian Reformed Church aimed at reunion.[40]

Many years have passed since that time, and there have been various Calvinistic churches in North America that have entered into contact of one sort or another with the Canadian Reformed churches, including the congregations known as Free Reformed, which have even asked some of their men studying for the ministry to attend the Theological College of the Canadian Reformed Churches in Hamilton for the academic part of their preparation. (The Free Reformed churches have no seminary of their own.) The Reformed Church in the United States (sometimes called German Reformed) has taken up official contact with the liberated Reformed Churches in the Netherlands and also hopes to establish close ties with the Canadian Reformed Churches.

While no church union has taken place in North America, at least two U.S. congregations have been received into the fellowship of the Canadian Reformed churches. (In the United States, such churches are called American Reformed.) One is a formerly Orthodox Presbyterian congregation in Blue Bell, Pennsylvania (near Philadelphia), and there is another such congregation in Laurel, Maryland (between Baltimore and Washington). Various individuals who disagree with developments in the Christian Reformed Church have become Canadian Reformed, but no congregation has made such a switch.

But Schilder as theologian and exegete continues to be a force on the scene in North America, in various circles. Some of his writings are available in English. Moreover, there are still ministers, professors and even lay people who continue to read study material in Dutch, and some of them draw gratefully on Schilder. But his Dutch is far from easy (when compared, for example, with that of Herman Bavinck), and so even people with some knowledge of this language do not make as much use of Schilder's writings as one would wish. Perhaps this book will give rise to renewed theological interest in Schilder.

---

[40] Rev. W. Pouwelse maintains that the De Wolf churches were closer to the Christian Reformed Church, doctrinally speaking, than to the Canadian Reformed Churches: see his discussion of the doctrinal differences in a series of three articles entitled "Covenant and Election," published in *Clarion,* Vol. 34, Nos. 2-4 (Jan. 25 and Feb. 8 & 22, 1985), pp. 29-30, 58-59, 75, and 77.

Appendix II:

The Stocking Is Finished

by Klaas Schilder

From the United States and Canada I have received reports, some public and some private, that compel me to write this article. Those reports have to do with the Protestant Reformed Churches. What has happened there in recent weeks leads me to make the following statements.

(i) I have never regretted what I wrote about the Protestant Reformed Churches in the past, or what I have done and pleaded for, and I still believe I was doing the right thing then.

(ii) But now that they have changed course over there, contrary to all fraternal advice and theological argumentation, I accept the consequences of their change of course, and I do not regard it as responsible to keep silent any longer. What remains to be said is this: The stocking is finished,[41] and so we must call it a day *(we zetten er een streep onder)* and say goodbye — with a feeling of regret, but in full awareness of what we are doing.

As for statement (i), readers of *The Reformation* know that for years, beginning long before the liberation took place, I have said: "Let's make sure we don't forget about those Protestant Reformed Churches, and do what you can to set right what was done wrong in relation to them." I believed then — and still believe today — that the Christian Reformed Church in North America, following poor leadership and incited by some preposterous argumentation (à Mastricht!) here and there at its Synod of Kalamazoo (1924), perpetrated an abominable injustice toward — to mention only one name — one of her most capable ministers and theologians, Rev. Herman Hoeksema. You will recall that the battle had to do with so-called common grace. Now, as for all the things that Hoeksema wrote about this matter, there is no person who will subscribe to all of it, from A to Z. But the ammunition which the Synod used against him did not hit its target at all; the Synod was too rash. The upshot was that he was suspended anyway, and then came all the rest of it. The result was a situation of miserable misunder-

---

[41] Throughout this article and in some prior articles as well, Schilder uses a Dutch saying that means simply that some matter is finished or settled. Because it comes up at various points, I have retained it literally in the translation. The article (Dutch title: "De kous is af") was published in *The Reformation* on November 17, 1951, pp. 61-63. Two paragraphs near the end of the original Dutch article have been omitted in this translation. —T. PLANTINGA

standing, like the one that celebrated its orgiastic triumph in the Netherlands in 1944.

When I made my first visit to the United States in 1939, the damage that had been done already made a deep impression upon me. And when there was a conference of ministers at which Hoeksema appeared fully prepared for the battle whereas the others had virtually nothing to say in response to him, with some of them even taking refuge behind a newspaper, without making any attempt to understand him (now that was a conference [*samenspreking*] based on a one-sided written preparation!),[42] I understood that this injustice would never be made right. I also understood that Hoeksema is of concern to us in the Netherlands, for we should not allow ourselves to become accountable in relation to the injustice done to him by the Christian Reformed Church, with which we were in correspondence. Naturally, part of the Free University was angry (you should come and see today what they have made of common grace over there), but that didn't matter. I am convinced that to some extent, the wrath of the Free University as it rained down upon us in 1944 was also a consequence of the dark cloud that has hung there since my trip to the United States. I know enough about the correspondence that was carried on behind my back. The Protestant Reformed Churches may remember it, or perhaps forget it; it doesn't matter to me, for I have never taken pride in saying that we here in the Netherlands have taken upon ourselves *some of the scorn aimed at them.* That was not something of merit on our part; it was simply the consequence of the propagation of certain misunderstandings in which some Free University people dared to engage.

Now, I believed then — and I still believe it today — that it was our task first of all to keep the number of churches in God's wide world as small as possible, at least within regional bounds. It is necessary to recognize some geographical church boundaries; as for other church boundaries, they must be eliminated or prevented from arising *insofar as it is within our power.* We expected that the *stream* of immigrants, whom we were sorry to see departing from our churches as they moved especially to Canada, would not be part of our church federation in the Netherlands, and this indeed turned out to be the case (although for a long time the churches in Indonesia did remain part of our federation here, and still are today). Instead those immigrants would organize themselves within a geographically based federation in their new "fatherland." When they were crossing the ocean, I thought that if it was at all possible, we should keep them and the Protestant Reformed Churches, toward which we had some obligations in virtue of past history, from *needlessly* increasing the number of institutes. Taking account of the fact that the Protestant Reformed Churches were special to

---

[42] Schilder is referring here to Hoeksema's address at that conference, published by the Reformed Free Publishing Association as a separate booklet under the title "The Reunion of the Christian Reformed and Protestant Reformed Churches: Is It Demanded, Possible, desired?" —TRANS.

us from a *historical* point of view (as having been isolated unjustly by the Christian Reformed Church, and then having rightly liberated themselves), we sought help for our immigrants at the right time (at first they were overwhelmed with friendliness on the part of people with which they could better not establish ties); and we were happy that at first the help we sought was given. We were *also* happy about this for the sake of the Protestant Reformed Churches themselves. Whoever is sensible and obedient does not take a self-satisfied delight *(binnenvetters-pleizier)* in being needlessly isolated. Such isolation must *always* be the fault of the *others,* e.g. of people who refuse, permanently, to give a clear answer to clear and necessary questions.

When colleague Hoeksema and I were involved together in an extensive and patient final conference and he himself proposed to bring our theological discussions to an end, declaring (after hearing my reply), "That is Reformed," I went back to the Netherlands a cheerful man.[43] I thought to myself, "Well then, there are still people who respect the divine command not to take pleasure in expanding the number of 'denominations.' "

I do not regret all that I did in those days. I will say again, this *had* to happen, and that *was permissible* — in those circumstances.

As to statement (ii), the spirits are still not at rest. To my considerable amazement, colleague Hoeksema, who knows from his own painful experience what misery can result from foolish bindings, did not step into the breach when the inclination also arose in his own circles to begin "binding" again. He helped to draw up a "Declaration" and recommended it to the church — a "Declaration" which I dealt with at great length (you will soon be able to buy my what I have written about this matter in the form of a separate publication)[44] arguing that it is not necessary, that it does not represent a good interpretation of the Confessions, and that, insofar as it proposes to sharpen or clarify the Confessions through new formulations, it labors under certain delusions which, if the "Declaration" is once accepted, will create a little church with a narrow basis. The basis would be so narrow that, note well, because of what has *"ecclesiastical validity"* for this small group (I can already hear the jeers from the Dutch synodocracy in The Hague!), this small church would have to start "dealing with" people, people who simply want to affirm what our revered fathers affirmed before us and placed in the preface to the Statenvertaling's New Testament.[45]

---

[43] Hoeksema claimed he did not say, or mean to say, that Schilder's reply was Reformed: see his response below. —TRANS.

[44] The publication Schilder is referring to here is a brochure entitled *Bovenschriftuurlijke binding — Een nieuw gevaar* (Goes: Comité tot verspreiding van goodkope Geref. lectuur, no date). —TRANS.

[45] What Schilder is referring to here is the fact that the term "condition" was used in the preface to the Statenvertaling. —TRANS.

And it has come to pass. The Declaration has been definitively accepted. The able theologian Hoeksema allowed himself to become entangled in a system in which contra-Kalamazoo manipulations (rather than anti-Kalamazoo achievements) could be produced — and those manipulations became unavoidable. Alas, we are already hearing about discipline exercised against people who dared to continue speaking the language of the Statenvertaling and have not a drop of Arminian blood in their veins. I do not propose to pass judgment on all the possible stories of which the ins and outs are not known to us here in the Netherlands. I am passing judgment only on the consequences of accepting the Declaration.

I will not even make a judgment regarding the correctness of the following letter that was received by our office:

Grand Rapids, 10-23-1951

Gentlemen:

For some time there has been a rupture in church life here in Grand Rapids between brothers of the same household, who ought to be one because they stand on the same basis, namely, Scripture and the confessions. The rupture came about because in the church in which there had not yet been any acts of unscriptural censure or suspension, the church to which we felt the closest affinity, there were certain phenomena of ecclesiastical dissolution and binding which were making it extremely difficult for some of us, and impossible for others of us, to join ourselves to this church, and so we waited for an official decision from the Synod. There were others, however, who regarded it as their calling to let their reformational voice be heard in the churches in order to force them into a crisis in which it would become apparent which way they were going — whether back to the Word, or farther along the downward path.

It is now clear to all of us who have constituted ourselves as the Orthodox Reformed Church that it would be sinful to live in the federation of the Protestant Reformed Churches, given that its Synod of 1951 has officially accepted the Declaration of Principles and has excluded, by public announcement, all those who could not agree with the content of that declaration, regarding them as mutineers and heretics. That this is in fact what happened is evident from the censuring of brothers H. R. De Bolster and H. De Raad.[46] These brothers had objections to

---

[46] Both were immigrants who had belonged to the liberated Reformed churches in the Netherlands and were then students at the Protestant Reformed Seminary. Henry De Raad did not enter the ministry but became a Christian school teacher and recently retired from his position as principal of the John Calvin School in Abbotsford, B.C. Henry De Bolster later became a minister in the Christian Reformed Church and served as the first president of Redeemer College. —TRANS.

the Declaration of Principles and demonstrated on scriptural grounds what was false about this Declaration. But the consistory decided that the protest was in conflict with the Protestant Reformed truth and also that these brothers were not to speak up in the congregation regarding this matter. Naturally, these brothers refused to obey the command of the consistory because they would then no longer be able to exercise the office which Christ has given us. Next came censure because of agitation. One of the grounds for this decision was that the covenant idea which they propounded really contained the notion of a universal atonement and a denial of the total depravity of man and the vicarious suffering of Christ.

For these reasons, those who were unable to agree with the Declaration of Principles liberated themselves from the Protestant Reformed Church and joined with others who did not regard it as justifiable to join with these churches, and together they lawfully continued the church of our Lord Jesus Christ in America, which church came to be called the Orthodox Reformed Church.

Will you be so kind as to place this in the next issue of *The Reformation*? Thanking you in advance for taking the trouble to be of assistance, we remain yours, with cordial fraternal greetings. In the name of the consistory,
J. LAND
706 Alexander SE
Grand Rapids (Mich.), USA

We reckon with the possibility that there were some factors at work in these events which were not known to us here and are not included in this discussion. This could well be the case in good faith — we are accusing no one.

Neither is it necessary to sift through the details of this letter. *The Standard Bearer* should not regard our publication of this letter — under the qualifications mentioned above — as an unfriendly deed.

We have enough in *this* fact, that if *I* were to live in Grand Rapids, *I* would also refuse to accept the Declaration of Principles. I would also refuse to remain silent. *In the name of this order* — an order which I call disorder and which I abhor — I would also have to be censured. The die is cast, and the Evil One has again managed to spoil something beautiful. Yet another little church has been established, and it was not necessary, not necessary, not necessary. For I know what the Arminian position is, and I also know that one can set the entire Declaration aside without falling into Arminianism. On the contrary, in order to hang on to sound, fundamental Reformed ideas, we affirm that the promise of God is not prediction[47] and is not realized without involving our responsibility. And faith is never a condition in the Arminian sense, any more than the condition of which the preface to the Statenvertaling speaks is an Arminian notion.

And so, the stocking is finished. All there is left for us to do is to continue to prophesy. We will ask, but we will not beg. We will help, but we will not haggle. We do not wish to take upon ourselves the blame for establishing yet another church — number such-and-such. However, when we reject a foolish binding, we will not regard the consequences of such *obedience* as the sin spoken of in Articles 79 and 80 of the Church Order. We will say: "Keep your heads high, for God is the Leader of history." The one who is isolating *himself* this time — for the first time, alas, in his beautiful life — is our friend Hoeksema. And so we say farewell to him — not as a good friend but as "angel" of the receiving church, the church that receives immigrants with arms that are both gentle and carefully controlled in their embrace. K.S.

Postscript. Perhaps there are some readers who are now thinking, "The title of this article is not quite correct. This is not a matter of a stocking being finished; rather, the unfinished parts are just lying there." But I maintain that the title *is* a good one. The article is not about other people or about the possibility of cooperation with them, but about *our task*. We were responsible. If we had done nothing (insofar as the possibility of action rests with us) in terms of seeking affiliation with *what was already there* ecclesiastically, then we would have been guilty right from the outset. But our people and churches *have* sought contact and *have* made it clear in good time what our position is and what views we do *not* hold, and we *have* patiently looked over the whole Declaration on this side of the ocean, and if after all of this the people in the United States — even while we were discussing steps toward a correspondence relationship! — succumbed to the temptation of requiring more in the church federation than is good, then *our* stocking is finished. We should not talk about the matter any more but simply go our way . . .

To make people responsible, to press them to make a decision — that is much more often the knitting the church must do. —K.S.

---

[47] On this disputed point, see Hoeksema's series of articles entitled "Promise and Prediction," in *The Standard Bearer,* Vol. 28, Nos. 10-13 (Feb. 15 through April 1, 1952), pp. 223-228, 244-247, 268-273, and 292-294. To the last of these articles Hoeksema appended a brief note that his friend Schilder had just passed away. In a small "In Memoriam" elsewhere in the same issue, Hoeksema wrote: ". . . although I certainly did not agree with him in regard to the question of the covenant and the promise, I nevertheless esteemed him for his work's sake, esteemed him, too, as a highly gifted scholar, and, above all, as a brother in Christ." —TRANS.

Response by Herman Hoeksema[48]

Dr. Schilder writes that the stocking is finished. But I would say that the knitting of the stocking was a complete failure, and that the failure must be blamed not on our churches, but on the churches in the Netherlands. Instead of knitting a stocking, we tangled up the whole business. And the best that can be done is to unravel that tangle and start from the beginning, that is, if the Liberated Churches in the Netherlands still desire correspondence with us. And in spite of the history we made in the last couple of years, I think that a certain form of correspondence between our churches is desirable . . .

Now Dr. Schilder . . . once more states that at the close of his reply I must have said: "That is Reformed." I have called his attention to this error before, and now I will repeat it emphatically, and hope that Dr. Schilder will take note of it that I did not say: "That is Reformed," but that I said: "He is Reformed." (The difference is plain to all that can read.) If I said, "That is Reformed," I would have subscribed emphatically to all that friend Schilder said at the conference, and that meant that I would have subscribed to the Heynsian view of the covenant, which in my conviction is far from Reformed. But we must remember, in the first place, that we had a very friendly discussion with Dr. Schilder, although we agreed to differ. In the second place, we were undoubtedly all somewhat under the influence of Schilder's charming personality, and in his entire talk he emphasized repeatedly that our differences were no differences of principle, but rather of terminology . . .

And therefore, friend Schilder must never write again that I said at the end of his reply: "That is Reformed." For I never did. But I do remember that I said, "He is Reformed," understanding that statement in a general sense, and certainly not in the specific sense in which we as Protestant Reformed Churches, since 1924, are Reformed. That I do not regard the Liberated conception of the covenant as Reformed, Dr. Schilder knows very well. And he was aware of that even before he came to this country in 1947.

How then could Dr. Schilder, when he returned to the Netherlands, advise his people everywhere, when they immigrated to this country or to Canada, to join the Protestant Reformed Churches? Surely, we desired correspondence. But correspondence does not necessarily mean an organic union. The differences between us were rather fundamental, although Dr. Schilder called them differences in terminology. Of this we were not convinced. But, as I said, Dr. Schilder advised his people to join the Protestant Reformed Churches when they came to America, although we stood in no relation as sister churches as yet, and therefore could not receive attestations from them,

---

[48] In an editorial published in *The Standard Bearer,* Vol. 28, No. 7 (Jan. 1, 1952), pp. 148-153, Hoeksema responded to Schilder's article. Some excerpts are reproduced here. —T. PLANTINGA

or they from us. The result was that when we labored in Canada among the immigrants, we did not at once organize them into Protestant Reformed Churches, but first thoroughly instructed them, so that they knew the differences in doctrine between their churches and ours. Only when they were sufficiently indoctrinated and understood our position, and agreed with our truth, did we organize them into churches in our communion. And even after those churches were organized, like Hamilton and Chatham [two Ontario cities], we did not receive membership papers from any Reformed Church of the Netherlands and did not receive prospective members into the communion of our churches until they had first been instructed with regard to the truth as taught in our Protestant Reformed Churches. Naturally, this caused trouble. For evidently in the Old Country the people had received the impression that when they came to America, they would be received without question and without condition as members of the Protestant Reformed Churches. That they labored under such an impression certainly was not our fault, but was the fault of Dr. Schilder, who, according to reports, had advised all the people of the Liberated Churches to join the Protestant Reformed Churches in America. But once more the differences in regard to the doctrine of the covenant and of the promise were too great and too fundamental to permit members from the Liberated Churches into our communion. Hence we demanded that they promise to submit to our instruction, and in the meantime not to agitate against our doctrine. That was honest and fair to all concerned. We did not excommunicate any brethren and sisters in our Lord Jesus Christ and bar them from the table of communion. But we wanted to preserve the Reformed truth in its purest form, the truth as we have always maintained it in our Protestant Reformed Churches. The result is, first, the sad history of Hamilton, and now the even worse history of Chatham. Certainly, that the stocking was not knitted and properly finished was not our fault.

. . . the letter written by Prof. Holwerda to the immigrants in Canada . . . revealed [among other things] . . . (3) That the impression was created that no definite interpretation of the Confessions was maintained and binding in the Protestant Reformed Churches. (4) That the impression was made that there was ample room for the covenant view of the Liberated in our Protestant Reformed Churches, and that therefore the immigrants could make free propaganda for the Liberated view in our churches. (5) That only on that basis were the immigrants advised to join the Protestant Reformed Churches, but at the same time that, if the conception of such men as the Revs. Hoeksema and Ophoff were maintained in the Protestant Reformed Churches, they should never join.

This was not knitting a stocking, surely not the stocking of ecclesiastical correspondence, but was working on a tangled and hopeless mess.

On our part, in the light of all this history, and especially in the light of our experience with the Liberated in Canada, the Mission Committee felt

Appendix II: The Stocking Is Finished

the need of a definite statement which might be used by them and by our missionaries as the basis for the organization of our churches. That need was filled by the Declaration [of Principles]. And that Declaration was passed by our last Synod.

Let not Dr. Schilder therefore say that the stocking is finished. It must be entirely unravelled, until we come to the first false stitch, and then start knitting anew.

In conclusion, I want to emphasize once more that the stocking is not finished. And if Dr. Schilder feels that because of the stand of our churches as revealed in the Declaration of Principles he does not want to unravel the tangle and start knitting anew, it suits me. Nevertheless, I want to state that in that case I am disappointed in him, and for the rest say, "Vale, Amice Schilder."

Appendix III:

Your Ecumenical Task

by Klaas Schilder

As you know, the speech I am about to deliver is entitled "Your Ecumenical Task."[49] In this title you have a strange word — ecumenical. Don't blame me if you think it is too learned: the topic has been given to your servant in those very words.

However, you should not let the word "ecumenical" frighten you. All of you speak "ecumenical language" every Sunday, when you confess with the church of all places: I believe a holy, catholic, Christian church. And "catholic" has the same meaning as "ecumenical." The "ecumene" means "the entire inhabited world"; therefore "ecumenical" means "pertaining to the entire cultural world" or "concerning the entire human race." In your Book of Praise you can find an ecumenical heirloom, the Nicene Creed, which dates back to the so-called First Ecumenical Council of 325. There the Arians were condemned, and also the Cathari (or Novatians), who, so it says, could not join the ecumenical church if they did not agree with the dogmas — that's what it says — of the universal and catholic church. Stipulations were also made concerning the so-called baptism of heretics.

All of this sounds rather strict, and dogmatic, and precise. Well, it is indeed strict, and dogmatic, and precise, because it is the Church that is speaking here, and she is standing on guard for the benefit of the whole world. For exactly that orthodox Church has the oldest papers of the ecumenical movement; she is like a lioness as she fights her attackers on the ecumenical hunting ground.

The church that is strict and orthodox and takes a firm stand against heresy has never been a sect. She has understood from the beginning that God's truth has been set as the norm for the whole world; and that therefore everyone who wants to render a service to the "ecumene," the wide, wide world, must preach the truth only according to the command of Christ; and that the first service, the first ecumenical security service that can be ren-

---

[49] This speech was given at a Young Women's Society League Day in Rotterdam on "Pentecost Monday," 1951, and was published in *The Reformation,* Vol. 26, No. 33 (May 19, 1951) and reprinted in Schilder's "Verzamelde werken," in the third volume on *De Kerk* (Goes: Oosterbaan & Le Cointre, 1965), pp. 467-479. It was published in English translation in Australia in 1975 by a group calling itself the Launceston Committee, which has given permission for its republication here. Some changes have been made in word order, punctuation, and diction. —T. PLANTINGA

dered to the world is to fight against heresies such as the one propounded by Arius, and to call them by their name. Using an image from Isaiah: if the church dogs, i.e. the watchdogs of the Good Ecumenical Shepherd Jesus Christ, bark loudly against the wolves, they are performing their ecumenical service, fulfilling their ecumenical task. Whoever readmits or flirts with a heresy that has been condemned by the ecumenical church at any one time removes himself from the first and oldest ecumenical movement, willed by God.

This movement has, in fact, been underway since the moment God spoke to His first created people as His covenant partners: go, dwell on the earth, as My "watchers" over this My ecumenical heritage, and cultivate her to My honor. When Adam put the first spade into the ground, he performed an ecumenical service. When he, as head of the family and as "church father," gave his "woman" the divine covenant law as the fundamental law for all times and places, that was the first "ecumenical message." When Eve bore her first son, that was the first move of the "ecumenical movement." When they sinned, that was the first "ecumenical misdeed." When God gave the mother promise, that was the first "ecumenical restoration."

When Cain killed his brother, in the first church persecution, that was the first thrust toward a contra-ecumenical organization, the first sectarian deed, the principial deviation from ecumenical paths. Cain was the first sectarian, and exactly as a sectarian, he eventually gathered the most votes and had the largest number of followers. Then that great fool thought he was ecumenically minded and worked ecumenically (he was as dumb as sin can make a man); he thought that in order to be able to work ecumenically, you had to have the greatest number. But God said no: to be active ecumenically in the ecumenical apostolate means to fulfill the mission mandate, the mandate which makes you take the Word of God, received in a certain place, out to the whole world, saying: "I have now passed on to you what I have received from the Lord."

In his conversion, Adam remained faithful to that oldest and legitimate ecumenical movement, and Abel and Seth followed him in this respect — but Cain chose the sect. He separated himself. As forerunner of the antichrist, he wanted to win the entire world for his revolution against the truth "received" from God. And he thought that numbers will determine who wins the battle. But God says: the ecumenical movement started from Me, and it will also be brought to a proper end by Me. Therefore, the question "Who is serving the ecumenical apostolate?" can only be answered well if it is preceded by the question "Who keeps the 'received' Word of God unchanged and goes out to the wide world with it?"

The oldest, the original, the "genuine" ecumenical movement is not winning the world numbers for your deviating message, but winning as many people as possible for God's judgment-laden, directive message. Heresy is always a denial of the ecumenical apostolate. To become an ally of hers is to disturb the original ecumenical movement, thrust forth from the old paradise. The flood was an ecumenical judgment, albeit to preserve the ecumenical church, and the ecumenical apostolate. The sectarians as well as the isolationists were drowned, but the church was preserved. The way of the ecumenical movement of the apostolate invariably goes through the ark. And if therefore our form for baptism — in the prayer — speaks about that flood, then I dare say: your baptism, which found its prototype in the flood, meant that your foot was placed on the ecumenical path. Therefore, whoever says: "Baptize all who are brought into the baptismal house, even if they take their stand over against the ecumenical divine message," may win large numbers (for a while, at least . . .), but he only opposes the ecumenical apostolate. He opposes the church, which has wanted to be ecumenical all through her life, and supports the sect, the schism.

Sin always produces the separation of Cain; the separatists are usually in the majority, while those who stand for the right ecumenism are usually in the minority. Your own confession says as much when it states: this Holy Church, i.e. the ecumenical community, sometimes appears very small for a while, and in the eyes of men to be reduced to nothing. And then it points to Ahab's "wicked era." Ahab was king of Israel; therefore his task was to preserve the church in its purity. He was supposed to see to it that Israel's course was not altered, so that the pure water of God's word of grace and of the messianic blessing could, one day, at Pentecost, flow into the "ecumene," that wide world life.

If Ahab had preserved Israel's life purely, he would have worked with Elijah, that great ecumenical figure. Preservation of the Church is the first social deed, the primary ecumenical act. But Ahab married a Tyrenian princess, Jezebel, who was up to her neck in synthesis, and in world trade and world politics, and in the ecumenical largest-common-denominator-religion, that message of-and-to-and-for-oneself. So Jezebel played the role of ecumenical figure in apostolic robes and cap, upon which, in the Esperanto of those days, were embroidered the initials S.o.N. (Shepherdess of Nations).

But Elijah knew that the S.o.N., the Shepherd of Nations, the Pastor Ecumenicus, was Christ, the Messiah according to the promise. Therefore, he turned Mt. Carmel into an Ecumenical Union Square. Carmel became the Place de la Concorde of his Reformation: he banned the syncretists. That's why the Revelation of John mentions both Jezebel and Elijah. There Jezebel is banned by the Shepherd of Nations, and the power, the authority of Elijah is given to the two witnesses in Chapter 11. They are prophesying on the Place de la Concorde of the Revolution: the wide streets of the great city which spiritually is called Sodom and Egypt and which is built where Christ's cross once stood. So she is also called Jerusalem, but then the Jerusalem, relieved of the ecumenical mandate since Pentecost, forsaken of God. On this Place de la Concorde, the witnesses read the Formula of the True Concord — the Biblical testimony. Unadulterated. And they have made their witness in the orthodox way (Revelation 11:7 states: they have "finished"

Appendix III: Your Ecumenical Task

their testimony). Over against that forsaken Jerusalem, on the last page of Scripture stands the accepted, the fulfilled, the Eternal Ecumenical Jerusalem — the City of the Great King, built square, with its gates open to all sides.

Of course, you understand that much more can be said about this subject. But this small amount is enough to remind you that our Pentecost is the Ecumenical Feast of the church — and thus the obligatory Ecumenical Feast of the World. Whoever does not let himself be gathered to the true church at Pentecost, which, according to Acts 2, can be quite easily distinguished from the false church, and who thus takes something away from the Gospel-according-to-the-Scriptures as it is inseparable from Christ as God's Son and our Guarantor, has forfeited the right to speak of and for the ecumenical apostolate. Even if he shouts until he is hoarse for the Ecumenical Message and for the Ecumenical Movement and for the Ecumenical Apostolate, it won't make any difference. The "messages" must be true to the Message; and if they are not, the ecumenical dawn will not appear. The ecumenical feasts of God are the feasts of His *"extremists"* and thus of *His* "extremists." There are other extremists too. But whoever finds "extremists" an abusive term suited only for sectarians has thereby sent the ecumenical apostolate down a dead end street. That dead end is exactly where the devil wants us: he wants the Place de la Concorde reserved for the heralds of the revolution, not for the heralds of God's Reformation in Revelation 11.

No wonder the Bible is full of the ecumenical proclamation of the Great Ecumenical Drama. "Ecumenical" is not a new term but a very old one. The Jews had already transcribed the Greek word "oikoumene" into Hebrew letters in the rabbinical scriptures and left it untranslated. Luke starts the Christmas message with the ecumene: Caesar Augustus wants the ecumene registered for the Roman Empire (the Beast of Daniel, and of Revelation). But from a stable in Bethlehem, the Great Son of David began at that very moment to "register" the ecumene for Himself, and for the God of David.

Ecumene is then the inhabited world, viewed as the operative area of world politics. The Beast grasps at the latter — but the Spirit has been ahead of him for centuries, when He had David anointed as king of the birthplace of theocracy, i.e. as king of Israel's ecumenically directed community, keeping the ecumenical seas of the world pure. Jesse's living room, where David was anointed, and the stable of Bethlehem, the starting point for the world rule of the Son of David, are the stages of God's Ecumenical Movement, a movement as old as the world ruled by God's Covenant. Emperor Nero, who in the Revelation of John is an image of the ecumenical anti-christ, is called Ecumenical Daemon in Greek emperor's titles, just as Emperor Claudius is called Ecumenical Benefactor, or Savior.

"Ecumenical" has here become a matter of world politics and world culture. Therefore Scripture commands that there be ecumenical preaching (Matthew 24:14). Over against the Satanic temptation of ecumenical world power, Christ places the "It is written"; He wants to become the Ecumenical

Savior-Judge only through obedience (Luke 4:5). Christ predicts an ecumenical temptation in the last days (Revelation 3:10), and also catastrophe (Luke 21:26); and thus the prophet Agabus predicts an ecumenical famine (Acts 11:28). In this regard he is an ally of John on Patmos who, at the opening of the third seal, sees the black horse of famine dash across the world (Revelation 8:5-6). All this is the beginning of the ecumenical judgment (Acts 17:31).

In short, the Bible, from Genesis to Revelation, speaks continually about the one great ecumenical Drama. On the one side is the ecumenical preaching (Romans 10:18; see also Psalm 19:4); on the other side is the ecumenical error, the ecumenical temptation under the leadership of the Antichrist, God's great adversary, with his "catholic," i.e. universal, propaganda service, with his ecumenical contra-speech against the Speech of God and against all His Sayings.

Today, many people want to argue away the "antithesis." With their principial denial of a principial antithesis, they try to force a "breakthrough" between the existing parties.[50] Several years ago Adolf Hitler with his "paranymphs" did just that; Rosenberg was his prophet. Many proselytes will always be found for this breakthrough theory, in whatever form it appears. But when the separate-from-the-antithesis movement, with the help of this theory, has gathered the crowds of dissidents against the antithesis-positing-gospel, then the Antichrist will take up the antithesis-preaching again. He will refer back to Genesis 3:15, but only to set over against it his word, his "contra-gospel." The text is old: I shall put enmity between the serpent and the seed of the Church-woman. But the explanation is new. For the serpent, even in the days of early Christianity, was the symbol of paganism, e.g. in Pergamus, with its Asclepius-worship. Asclepius was the god of light and life. The Christians, however, had their God of Light and Life. That was the God of whom John speaks in the first chapter of his Gospel, when he says: in the beginning was the Word, and the Word was with God and the Word was God. In that Word was Life, and the life was the Light of men. And that Word has now become flesh. It has come to bruise the head of the old serpent.

But this Bible language is cast aside as worthless by the antichristians. So when united heathendom goes so far as to proclaim the serpent, the Asclepius-symbol of an "autonomous" light and "autonomous" life, as the ecumenical symbol, then the antichrist will affirm: I will put enmity between this my serpent and you, O woman of the Church; between your seed and her seed. That seed of the serpent will bruise your head, and you will not

---

[50] Here Schilder is referring to the political situation in the Netherlands after World War II. Many prominent Christians denied the relevance of the "antithesis" in the political sphere and in other spheres, advocating a "breakthrough" that would be a departure from the existing party formation on the basis of creeds. The new political parties would have secular bases, as did the Labor Party. —TRANS.

Appendix III: Your Ecumenical Task

even get the chance to bruise the heel of that other seed. Then the ecumenical antithesis will have been proclaimed again. God's Word is always right in the end.

That's why the first task of the church will always be the proclamation of that centuries-old antithesis. She does not tolerate a breakthrough on the basis of false slogans proclaiming unity. What she desires is a breakthrough with the sharp weapon of that Biblical antithesis — over against all groups and all movements that have denied and ridiculed the Biblical idea of the antithesis and have cursed it as the greatest folly and a fragmenting force, including, therefore, the ecumenical church movement which has no confession, and also the youth movement that has allowed itself to become part of this "ecumenism."

Girls, it looks like an endless job, if not a jaunty bluff, to speak to you about "your ecumenical task" in this context and in the face of so much dramatic force. What can you do, with your small numbers, and in such a small country, a country which is steadily losing its own characteristic power in ecumenical world politics? I can already hear you asking the question.

But you should not hold up the Pentecost Spirit any longer with such questions, nor bore each other with them any more. Don't you think that in Moscow they tell each other that the boys and girls have an ecumenical task?

Yes, but — you may object — they have those large numbers to boast of. That may well be — but could the Pentecost congregation of Acts 1 and 2 boast of large numbers when it received the mandate to go out into the world preaching and baptizing? Yes, you say, but the Pentecost congregation saw powers and signs, and the white rider on the white horse went out to conquer. Whereas we today, living in the atmosphere at the end of the age, now see more readily the gray, the red, the black horse, of death-and-Hades, of war-and-blood, of hunger-and-famine, than the white horse of the triumphant gospel — so what can we yet do? It's a bit disappointing. Sometimes we think it appropriate to quote the French poet who once said: I was born too late into a world which is already too old.

So, catholic girls, are all these things somewhat disappointing? But then you should be quite ashamed before God. Has the Bible foretold anything different from what you see today? Indeed not: it has calmly prepared you for a future like the present — a future of decreasing church numbers, of undermined authority, of the lumping together of classes, and after that of races, and of political groups in a so-called democracy whose authority steadily dwindles to the degree that it becomes more infatuated with that one man, who mesmerizes her with his slogans, and with his suggestions that he is bone of her bone, flesh of her flesh. It has been foretold us.

If our numbers do not shrink over the whole world, we should ask ourselves whether we have ever really comprehended Christ's eschatological discourses and properly understood the Revelation of John. If you, girls, have remembered even one percent of what was in all those sermons by the ministers and the books by the professors of your own church, then you know: we must not choose isolation ourselves, and we must not apathetically shrug our shoulders at the decrease in numbers, and say: "Those who left knew no better" — because we ourselves are also guilty if they leave good-naturedly, instead of with a hearty curse that would show, at least, that they are shocked at the atmosphere of the latter days.

But now the other side of this coin: you must never complain about an isolation into which you are pushed by others, as though it were some misfortune, or grumble about dwindling numbers, like a child who watches his playmates go someplace more interesting. All of this has been foretold us, and what it means, in simple terms, is that God does not give you permission to use this decline as an argument to say that your ecumenical task stops as soon as we go below a certain number. For the ecumenical task of the church is not bound to any place or any time, and consequently not to any number either.

Therefore, your first ecumenical task is witnessing. People sometimes say, a bit scornfully: Well, that's easy enough. You'd better give us something more manly. And especially: if you talk about an "ecumenical task," give us a work program immediately, and a program of guidelines. Otherwise we cannot do a thing.

Have those people forgotten what Kuyper wrote in 1878? An election platform should, in his opinion, be as short as possible. The best platform is a single word which everyone remembers and quotes — a shibboleth. If necessary, a sentence or a slogan or a few words. But there is no question of a political confession of faith in such a platform. And concerning the program of guidelines Kuyper wrote: "Of your principles you can only give a program if the principles of the others are set over against yours." And if you, in general, are in the opposition, then you cannot, according to Kuyper, put up a program of principles at the outset, "because in the beginning you do not know where you are." You will find these words in Kuyper's introductory article in *Our Program*.

I ask: what else is said here than that if you do not witness — and that as sharply as possible — then the program of guidelines and the principially dominated election platform will fail completely? Some people say to you: we should not start without a well-formulated program, for witnessing is too easy for us. Kuyper said: without witnessing you will never come to a good program, because your principles will only be formulated when the others state theirs. To conduct opposition in general is something that can only be done after a while. You must start by witnessing. That is certainly our ABC today: conduct opposition in a general way. We have no alternative when those who deny the antithesis try their wholesale breakthrough. Moreover, Kuyper says, the case is as follows: if (and that is also our ABC today) the point is the purging of what used to go together without belonging together, then a signal flag must be raised — a signal flag of very distinct colors which can arouse the real friends to enthusiasm again but which will make the half-hearted hybrid hangers-on leave as soon as possible, shaking their heads. Thus Kuyper in 1878. And then that tremendous effort followed, for decades.[51]

I am sometimes afraid that nowadays you are being taught to deny the great value of a faithful testimony. For a while we have been accustomed to cabinet ministers at our conferences, and to a few friends in Parliament. But now that we see our numbers decreasing — and I refer not only to our little circle but to the entire Christian, confessional sector of the nation — many are saying: Let ecumenical matters take their course. If we can no longer perform "great deeds," like Piet Hein,[52] we will leave the witnessing to Maranatha brethren. Witnessing is too old-fashioned for us, at least in the context of world politics. It may be done in the church, but not outside of it.

However, I tell you that your ecumenical task, your primary mandate, is faithful witnessing. If witnessing does not turn into a pseudo-religious self-characterization but remains the quiet, level-headed passing on of the content of Scripture as we confess it, then it represents the beginning of all Christian efforts in the ecumenical sphere. Did you think witnessing is easy? It is the most difficult thing there is, because it means coming not with stories, nor with pictures, or haloes or heroes, but with the Word, which says: To the Jews I am a stumbling-block, and to the Greeks foolishness. When in Revelation 11 the two witnesses, i.e. the two office-bearers, have their backs against the wall, on the Place de la Concorde of the Revolution, they have to "complete" their witnessing, to get out of it whatever they can. Not just repeating old slogans, but speaking pointedly about the carefully disclosed consequences of what God has told us for today, tomorrow, and the day after tomorrow. And do you think this is a cosy affair? You'd better not — it will cost you your life. Pawns are tolerated in a chessboard counter-offensive; but sounding trumpets that spurn ensemble-playing are smashed in anger.

To be a witness of Jesus Christ's Name and Word means doing justice to the Holy Spirit. It was He who came to explain Christ's work in the world at Pentecost. Thus He is the Ecumenical Perfecter in God's Triune Universal work.

This witnessing is necessary for the others, you say? Yes, sure, but — you'd better not blow your trumpet too much. You yourself need it in the

---

[51] Schilder is referring to to a wide range of activities in all spheres of life, such as had been stimulated by Kuyper, the captain of the "little people" *(kleyne luyden)*. The confession of Christ as King produced a self-conscious Reformed testimony in science, the arts, education, industry, and so forth. —TRANS.

[52] Admiral Pieter Pieterszoon Heyn captured the Spanish "Silver Fleet" in the Caribbean (1628) during the war waged by the Dutch for their independence from Spain. A nineteenth-century folk song glorified his "great deeds," perhaps to a degree out of proportion to their strategic value. —TRANS.

first place. Just ask people who really study, and who do not repeat a string of pious essays and slogans throughout their lifetime. Just ask them how they fared. They will tell you: I have learned most on my own. And I myself needed that study as much as I needed bread, because I knew that if I did not do that, I'd become either a Niagara of words or a silent timid person — but not a witness.

Do you know why you need witnessing, in this sense, so badly? Well, for this simple reason: on today's ecumenical market you can buy so many pigs in an equal number of pokes. The word "church" is constantly being devalued. In a painfully suppressed conflict with the confession, it is simply being denied that we could tell you that belief in the existence of an obviously true church is what turns Reformed girls into "catholic" girls. They play for so long with the foolish concept of "revelation of Christ's body" that they begrudge the true church a true revelation. And then, nevertheless, the Ecumenical Drama will be brought to its final act this way.

And then the word "democracy," although it contains the concept of "people," is watered down to "people's democracy" — but who still knows what that is? Nevertheless, it leads the ecumenical drama to its last act. And then the teaching of the Scriptures is abandoned more and more in the fundamental doctrine about the relationship between authority and freedom. The result is that, even with the approval of statesmen who were brought up in the church, the sovereignty of God-given authority in the state is surrendered, first in part, but eventually in toto.

And then nothing is left to remind us of a royal house, except an administrative apparatus, with dear memories of the past, as part of the federal world-state-to-be. The king in the state then becomes the governor of a constituent part of the federation.[53] And concerning authority in the church, the basis is not sought in Christ's kingship, as known from His own Word, but in religious autarchy and ecclesiastical pretentiousness. What this means, basically, is a transfer of the idea of people's sovereignty to the sphere of what pretends to be "church." Nevertheless, in this manner also, the ecumenical drama is accelerated into its final act. The name of Christ is mentioned, but any further confessional examination of the name of Christ or of the name Christian is forbidden.

The present federalism in world politics, also in church *y* and the church *ics,* means a rapid revolution under the pretext of a thoughtful reformation. We are in the thick of it already. It boils down to this, that states and churches allow themselves to be put on a par and incorporated into one great Corpus Humanum, a Body of humanistically conceived World State and World

---

[53] Around 1950, the debate on federalism revealed that there were distressingly deep rifts in the Dutch nation. Frequently the debate centered on the vestigial powers that would be left to the Sovereign of the Netherlands in a federal Europe. It was conceivable that the House of Orange, with its rich and glorious history of over 400 years, would be left without any authority. —TRANS.

Appendix III: Your Ecumenical Task

Church. That world church is something different from a world-wide confederation of churches. The one is already inclined to the other; soon the one will support the other and will associate with the other. And the so-called natural law will exploit the doctrine of the two states from Augustine's badly managed inheritance in order to reach the final goal — the identification of the heavenly state with the secular state. The misapprehension of Augustine's final intent will make them say: self-love will cause people to despise a transcendent God. Humanity will become a God unto itself. And love towards this "God" would place the individual over against his self-made God. Thus the individual will eventually submit freely and "religiously" to the exponent of World-State-and-World-Church — the antichristian "*Führer*," the "First Brother" of all people. And at that, the Ecumenical Movement, which has completely freed itself from the confession of God, the transcendent one, and of Jesus Christ, the Mediator and Guarantor of the Covenant of Grace, has reached its goal: the Beast will have seduced all the nations, and the ecumenical Pentecost movement will be completely contradicted in an ecumenical Counter-Movement.

Therefore your second ecumenical task is to preserve the Ecumenical Pentecostal Movement, guided by a clearly understood Word of God in a maintained confession of the Christian church on the basis of apostles and prophets. Your task is to calmly allow yourself to be known by, and in, a burning love for your church, with her firmly bound and confessionally prefaced membership book, which, nevertheless, always has room for new pages to be inserted. In that church you have to oppose the present Humanistic Ecumenical Movement to its face. In other words, you must love your church as God's visible, legitimate congregation, and allow, and then also command, the expansion only to the pure church.

Seek expansion for the Word of God. That is: never run away from your place. Do not hanker after a place different from the one where God has placed you — a helper in your circle, a girlfriend to your boyfriend, a wife to your husband, a mother to your child, and above all, a member of your church. Do not be enticed away by the mere magic formula "ecumenical," and never believe the story that the dividing line runs between ecumenical conviction, on the one hand, and partisan conviction, on the other. For this is not the dividing line; and you should never venture into conviction ethics. The dividing line lies elsewhere. It lies between ecumenical love for God and ecumenical infatuation with man; between an ecumenical *r*oad to the right, and the ecumenical *g*oad to the left; between military service in the Ecumenical Army of the Christ-King assigned to us by the Spirit of Pentecost, and puppet service in the Ecumenical Legion of the Beast disguised as God.

Perhaps — let me end with this — perhaps some people think, in or outside this hall, that my speech today had a new sound, that it represents a retaliatory response to happenings of late.[54] But they are mistaken. For your

---

[54] Schilder is referring here to the liberation and its aftermath. —TRANS.

League (under your selfsame president), this speaker, as early as 1934, delivered an address about "Two Priscillas (known from Church History)." Allow me to close by reading a few literal quotations from it, for then you will know I am only giving you an old story: "The first Priscilla waits for Christ, and prepares for the day of days, yes, prepares for that day, for her part, by serving Christ, by doing, 'here and now,' i.e. in the time and in the place God has appointed for her, what the law of love asks of her. However, Priscilla II calls ever more nervously: Maranatha, maranatha. She goes to the place where the Lord is supposed to appear, but does not see Him, as He gathers His sheep, in His office, in the church ... Priscilla II ... tears the church away from the place which God has reserved for her ... Priscilla I, however, knows all about going into the desert, with the persecuted church, because of the Name of Christ ... And whereas Priscilla II projects the church into the sky, and makes the believers peer into the sky for a new cloud chariot for Christ Triumphant, Priscilla I is the woman who has both feet on the ground of reality, and therein waits on the salvation of the Lord ... Priscilla II turns the clock back ... But Priscilla I spends her hours well on simple womanly chores every day ... And thus she, who served the saints and God's missionary Paul, allowed the clock to continue quietly, the clock of revelation history and of missionary history."

Let us close here. A few years ago we heard a lot about a "movement" (the Dutch Nazi Movement, or N.S.B. in Dutch). It passed around passwords but not the Word, paroles but no confession. Remember that the Kingdom of heaven comes with power, but only in the unity of confession. Join yourselves, as catholic girls of the Netherlands, under your Ecumenical Shepherd. He comes, He comes to judge the people, in righteousness and equity. His Spirit has already been working for nineteen centuries, ripening the grapes in the vineyards of the "ecumene." As His laborers, "black but lovely," hoe the paths of His vineyard and catch for Him the foxes which ruin the vineyard.

Appendix IV:

Church Polity in 1886 and 1944

by C. Veenhof [55]

In the following summary statements, Veenhof spells out the position which he and his fellow office-bearers took with regard to questions of church order.

Freely and fully we embrace the principles of church order which were indeed accepted, self-consciously and rightfully, during the Doleantie.

We maintain that the authority of the Consistory is of a *higher* sort than that of the major assemblies because it is given directly by Christ Himself; it is thus an *original, full*, and *abiding* authority, whereas the authority of major assemblies flows from Christ by way of the churches and is therefore *derived, limited*, and *temporary*.

Article 31 of the Church Order states that the decisions of a major assembly shall be considered settled and binding unless they are shown to conflict with the Word of God or with the articles [of the church order] decided on in this General Synod, and so forth. We maintain that what is meant by "are shown to conflict with . . ." is "to conclude for oneself that it has been proven that God's Word forbids the observance of that which has been found good" [by the synod or a major assembly]. In case one reaches such a conclusion, one is of course obliged to try to show the ecclesiastical assembly why God's Word forbids [what has been decided] — otherwise, according to the judgment of Prof. F. L. Rutgers, Article 31 would be *nonsense*.

And we maintain that it is in conflict with the Church Order to suspend an office-bearer while completely *ignoring* the Consistory that is in the first place affected by this suspension.

---

[55] The material in this appendix grew out of a statement which consistory members of the Reformed Church of Utrecht, under the leadership of Rev. Veenhof, made in response to the events of 1944. The position they articulated was not accepted: Veenhof, a minister named M. de Goede, and many elders were suspended. They then joined the liberated Reformed churches. The statement of their position was eventually published in the form of a brochure by Veenhof entitled *In den chaos: Een woord over de huidige crisis in de Gereformeerde Kerken* (Utrecht: J. Wristers, no date). The excerpts published here are drawn from pp. 60-78. The Dutch version abounds in emphasized text; some of the emphasized words and phrases are presented here in roman type. —T. PLANTINGA

In explaining and defending his overall position on church order, Veenhof offers some general observations about the principles underlying Reformed thinking on this matter.

Reformed church law and the system of Reformed church governance is very, very simple in its structure — so simple that even a child can understand it and see how it works . . .

In Reformed church law and the Reformed system of church governance, the exclusive aim is to create a *situation* and call forth a type of *order* which will make it possible for Jesus Christ to exercise an effective kingship over His Church. Kuyper once said: "All church law really serves to allow the ecclesiastical offices to work in conformity with the will of Christ" *(De Heraut,* No. 1192, November 4, 1900).

The great danger that lives in the heart of every office-bearer and looms before us in every ecclesiastical assembly is the tendency, which is usually not recognized by those who fall victim to it, to *undertake the rule of the church oneself.* This is naturally done on the excuse — usually offered in good faith — that what one wants is what Christ has commanded. This inclination is the root of all hierarchy. Prof. Rutgers often declared in his writings: "Everyone, by nature, has a small pope in his heart" (see *De Rechtsbevoegdheid onzer Plaatselijke Kerken* [Utrecht: Kemink & Zoon, second printing 1887; originally published in 1886], p. 30). Dr. Kuyper used to maintain that clericalism, i.e. the tendency of office-bearers to take care of things apart from the congregation, is the great danger . . .

In recent years it has become very fashionable to defend an ecclesiastical action that has been taken by way of an appeal to history. When a classis or a synod makes a decision and then is criticized for it, the defence almost always consists of pointing to similar decisions made by previous synods, or of showing that earlier scholars had argued that we should act in just such a way when a situation of this sort arose.

We cannot warn strongly enough against this way of reasoning! What has been done or been said or has happened *in the past* can never be a *norm* for what ought to happen or be done or be maintained *today.* What we face here is historicism, an absolutizing of what has happened and what has been said, and its influence is disastrous. The norm for our action is not what has happened but what God has said, from which then flow the pure principles of church order.

Veenhof maintains that the consistory, acting in Christ's name, exercises the highest authority in the church. He draws extensively on Kuyper for support.

Appendix IV: Church Polity in 1886 and 1944

Kuyper once wrote that a reformation is only possible when the congregation has a clear insight into the truth and into the law that governs the churches. . . . , In 1879 he wrote: "The authority of a synod is limited to its service character. That is to say, its authority does not derive from God as a directive to govern the Churches but is entrusted to the Synod by the Churches themselves. Thus the Synod does not stand above the Churches; rather, the Churches stand above the Synod. And over both is God's Word" *(De Heraut,* No. 68, March 30, 1879).

In 1882 he wrote: "The higher (never *est)* authority over a synodical meeting rests with the meeting of the *provincial* [i.e. regional or particular] synod, and the authority over the provincial meeting rests with the *classical* meeting, and the authority over the classical meetings rests with the *consistories;* whereas the consistories are the only assemblies which owe their origin directly to the office. When this order is reversed, the foundation of the church is turned upside down, the office is misunderstood, and one has in principle accepted the Roman Catholic conception of church law rather than the Reformed one" *(De Heraut,* No. 232, June 4, 1882).

That same year Kuyper also wrote: "The assemblies of these churches which have come together on a footing of equality, as bound by God's Word, have no authority on earth above them, except the consistories that have delegated their members. The churches are not bound to broader assembles (synods) any further than they have bound themselves" *(De Heraut,* No. 235, June 25, 1882).

We read that in 1883 some people maintained that the Reformed position always was that classis and synod are clothed with authority. But how, asks Kuyper — *how?* "In such a way that Christ has given the Synod or classis direct authority over the churches? No, no, no — three times no. That's the *episcopal* system. It's just the other way around: the classis receives its authority from the *consistories,* and the Synod receives its authority from the *classis.* It's not the case that the classis stands under the Synod, and the consistory under the classis. On the contrary, the Synod stands under the *classis,* and the classis under the *consistories.* The authority does not flow from the Synod to the classis, and from the classis to the consistories; that's the episcopal system. On the contrary, the authority flows from Christ to the consistories, from the consistories to the classis, and from the classis to the Synod. This — and this alone — is the Reformed system" *(De Heraut,* No. 287, June 24, 1883) . . .

In 1887 Kuyper wrote: "According to our Confession, the governance of the local church comes about through the various office-bearers gathering and working together to form a council or college. In this way — and in no other — the consistory originates, and this consistory is the only independent college of governance in the church ... In a Synod of Reformed churches there is no competence to make regulations or to order matters unless the members of the Synod bring proposals forward from the consistories, in which consistories those proposals were first brought up in the name of King Jesus" *(De Heraut,* No. 517, November 20, 1887) ...

In 1893, one year after the union of the Secession churches and the Doleantie churches, J. C. Sikkel wrote: "Let us give up any idea of a ruling synod, for this idea is really ... a papal notion. The *consistories* rule the churches. And they do so only *in accordance with God's Word.* It is for the sake of the Word that they maintain the confessions and exercise discipline ...

"The *consistories* constitute the classes and synods — not the other way around. Classes and synods derive their competence from the *consistories* — not the other way around. And when classes and synods meet, they are bound to the church order, which in Article 84 forbids any church to lord it over any other church. If a synod were to make laws or rules for consistories or for cases of discipline or for elections or for observing the sabbath or for the right to vote in the churches, it would be making unlawful decisions and moving in a papal direction.

"A synod is only a temporary gathering as a manifestation of the church federation, and it has not the slightest authority over the churches, but is only a gathering of the churches, to allow the meaning of the church federation for the welfare of the churches and for the honor of the Lord to be worked out and to bring to outward expression the calling which the churches have together.

"And when the meeting is over, *there is no more synod, and there is no more classis;* there are only *churches,* and in every church there is a *consistory* when the supervisors come together. And the consistory itself rules the congregation in accordance with the Word of God, while being bound to the confessions and the church order, but without implementing any other regulations than those which it has itself made" *(De Heraut,* No. 794, March 10, 1893).

> *In his discussion of Article 31 ("settled and binding unless ..."), Veenhof again appeals to* De Rechtsbevoegdheid onzer Plaatselijke Kerken, *which he calls the Doleantie's Bible for church order. The conduct of the leaders in the Reformation era cannot be properly understood apart from the principle that comes to expression in Article 31. He also argues that if discipline is needed in relation to office-bearers, it must be undertaken by the local consistory, which, at certain junctures spelled out in the church order, seeks the advice or concurrence*

Appendix IV: Church Polity in 1886 and 1944

> *of another consistory or a major assembly. The woes of the churches in the 1940s are due in good measure to the neglect of these principles of church order.*

In the practical actions taken by the churches it became evident that there had been some very consequential changes in thinking regarding the rule of Christ's church. The results in terms of the course of events that has unfolded among us could have been foreseen; indeed, they have manifested themselves ever more clearly.

First of all there was chaos in the confessional life of the churches, a chaos which — in a single word — is perplexing. The confessional life of the churches has become diseased and untrue. Who now knows exactly where we stand?

Consequently there has been a schism in the churches, a schism which is gradually continuing and becoming broader. An important nuance of the Reformed outlook — one which I believe is both Scriptural and reformational, and up to now was at least *tolerated* — has been ruled out as having no place whatsoever in the Reformed Churches. The proceedings against Candidate H. J. Schilder, in particular [see the note on p. 288 above], speak clear language regarding this matter and have had very serious consequences. With those proceedings, the break had already come, in principle.

Index

AACS 376
Aalders, G.C. .. 134, 135, 202, 330, 380
Aalders, J.C. 134
Afscheiding 29, 86
Algra, Hendrik 153, 168, 191, 224
Amersfoort Church Messenger 193
Amersfoort Congress 341, 342, 348-350
Anema, Anne 19, 30, 31, 218, 244, 305
Anema, Seerp 19, 74, 76-79, 81-84, 93, 154, 313
Anselm 140
Antirevolutionary Party . 55, 60, 66, 73, 75, 95, 97, 244, 318, 351, 352
antithesis: see common grace
application: see preaching
Asma, Feike 358
Assen: see Synod of 1926
Banner and "synodical committee," 202, 203, 208, 211, 334, 376-378, 391
baptism and regeneration 42ff, 101, 143, 145, 148, 207, 241, 288, 292, 331, 332, 370
Barkey Wolf, A.G. 96-98, 103, 168, 229, 230
Barnouw, A.J., 219
Barth & Barthianism 28, 34, 36-38, 139, 151, 166, 168, 172, 174, 190, 192, 198, 199, 234, 356, 357, 359
Bavinck, C.B. 152
Bavinck, Herman 26, 27, 29, 32, 33, 83, 89, 128, 195, 198, 202, 306, 394
Bavinck, J.H. 328
Beets, Henry 207
Berkhof, Louis 383
Berkouwer, G.C. 328, 330, 377, 380
Bilderdijk, Willem .. 13, 49, 75, 77, 90, 91, 166, 181
Binnema, H.H. 361
Boeijinga, A.M. 168, 169, 191
Boerkoel, J.D. 109, 119, 130, 160, 181, 185-189, 193
Boersma, O. 31
Booy, Thijs 362
Bos, B.A. 347-349
Both, H.L. 168
Bouma, A.J. 221, 222
Bouma, C. 152
Bouwman, O. 167, 202
"breakthrough" 261, 359, 360, 363
Brillenburg Wurth, Gerrit 35, 39, 40, 48, 222
Brunner, Emil 174, 192, 198
Brussaard, J.C. 29, 35, 135
Buskes, J.J. ... 32-38, 97, 131, 171, 232, 306, 377
Buytendijk, F.J.J. 35, 135
Calvin, John 45, 195, 218, 224f
Calvin Theological Seminary, .. 339, 383
Calvinist Congress 168, 172, 192
Calvinist Weekly 151, 162, 169, 170, 175, 176, 189, 191, 222, 265
Canadian Reformed Churches 7, 17, 18, 33, 101, 312, 378, 380- 382, 388, 389, 392-394
Chatham congregation ... 387, 389, 393, 402
Christian Democratic Union .. 168, 174, 175, 197, 198, 307, 325
Christian Reformed Church (North America) 52, 53, 101, 163, 184, 203-205, 208, 211, 273, 333-336, 338, 339, 375-383, 385, 387, 390-398
Christian Reformed Churches (Netherlands) 146, 234, 294, 347, 360
church order 49, 164, 166, 175, 190, 199, 200, 252, 266, 267, 291, 296, 298-300, 303, 305, 309, 311, 312, 314, 331, 333, 334, 346, 350, 354, 369, 377, 379, 381, 382, 400, 415, 416, 418, 419
Church and Youth (periodical) 298
Colijn, Hendrik . 74, 75, 84, 85, 88, 89, 91, 92, 95, 97, 165, 166, 172, 177, 182, 228, 267-269
common grace and antithesis 51-54, 60-62, 66, 67, 82, 83, 93-96, 139, 145, 148, 165, 166, 169, 184, 203, 204, 221, ... 318, 338, 340, 341, 361, 364, 381, 382, 384, 390-392, 395, 396, 408-410
Elout 81
Ethical-Irenic theology ... 21, 23, 34, 39, 40, 48, 58, 59, 63, 65, 68, 93, 126, 131, 151, 166, 169, 170, 176, 180, 305, 314, 319, 327, 344, 350, 361

Index

Eykman, J. 97
Faber, Jelle 7, 9, 140, 390
Fabius, D.P.D. ... 31, 48, 67-74, 89, 156
Federation of Calvinists .. 93, 139, 150, 153, 182
Feenstra, J.G. 168, 192, 302, 303
Ferwerda, T. 100, 101
Fides .... (Kampen student organization) 140, 368
Franeker Church Messenger 178, 190
Free Reformed Church (N.A.) 234, 394
Free University of Amsterdam ... 28, 32, 34, 35, 38, 61, 66, 71, 72, 79, 84-86, 89, 101, 117, 134, 151-154, 163, 165, 167, 171, 177, 197, 200, 217, 250, 256, 259, 266, 267, 305, 306, 309, 318, 343, 381, 384, 396
Frisian Church Messenger 222, 255, 256, 260
Frisian Daily 224-226
Geelkerken, J.G. 29, 32, 33, 35, 36, 41, 49, 83, 134-136, 150, 235, 305, 363, 377, 381, 383, 384
Gospel and Folk 252, 256, 266-271
Greijdanus, Seakle 49, 54, 140, 148, 162, 164, 176, 200, 202, 203, 267, 281, 296, 314, 315, 331, 355, 356
Groen, J. Jr. 188
Groen, Watson 334
Groen van Prinsterer, Guillaume 52, 68, 72, 74-77, 79, 95, 156, 157, 166, 181, 247, 363
Groeneveld 282, 283, 285
Grosheide, F.W. ... 54, 56, 57, 134, 135, 265, 305, 334
Gunning, J.H. (contemporary of "KS") 121, 123, 126
Gunning, J.H. (1829-1905) 71, 89
Haitjema, T.L. 97, 139, 168, 190
Hamilton congregation 381, 387
Hepp, Valentijn 61, 112, 135, 136, 139, 144, 151, 154, 155, 181, 189, 200, 202, 203, 210, 211, 221, 222, 307, 311, 328, 377, 384
Herald. 19-21, 41, 48, 69, 96, 110, 117, 134, 145, 153, 158, 159, 161, 162, 166, 189, 202, 203, 217, 218, 221-223, 226, 228-231, 234-236, 265
Hervormd (Church) .. 28, 29, 35-37, 68, 69, 71, 73, 91, 94, 95, 104, 112, 122, 142, 144, 150, 165, 210, 362, 363
Hettinga, J. 387

Heyns, William 337, 383, 392
Hoedemaker, P. 79, 89
Hoek, J. 294
Hoekema, Anthony 392
Hoeksema, Gertrude 387
Hoeksema, Herman .. 8, 13, 52-54, 184, 203-205, 208, 211, 337, 349, 375, 376, 382-393, 395-398, 400-402
Hoeksema, Homer C. 386, 390
Hoekstra, T. 134, 135, 152
Hofstede 95
Holwerda, Benne 104-106, 188, 288, 326, 343-346, 369, 390, 402
Honig, A.G. 15, 152
Huygens, Constantyn 46, 75
Idenburg, A.W.F. 89, 95
Ingwersen, A. 85-90, 92, 93, 99
Janse, A. 44, 145, 168, 169, 176
Janssen, Geert .... 273, 296 , 331
Janssen, Ralph 383, 384
Jasperse, P. 107, 278-280, 285, 286, 289, 291, 304, 325
Jones, Stanley 96, 97, 102
Jongeling, B. 67
Jongeling, P. 385
Kaajan, H. 162, 172, 192, 215
Kagawa, Toyohiko 96, 97
Kampen . 10, 14-16, 21, 32, 38, 44, 47, 61, 74, 98, 109, 128, 140, 144, 151-153, 159, 160, 163, 167, 180, 182, 185, 186, 190, 194, 196, 200, 205, 210, 237, 262, 263, 267, 275, 278, 279, 281, 282, 288, 292, 295, 296, 300, 309, 320, 325-327, 333, 343, 352, 357-360, 368, 373, 385, 391
Kamphuis, J. 11, 279, 389
Kappeyne van de Copello, Johannes 26
Kapteyn, A. 294
Kapteyn, Johannes 188, 255, 315
Kierkegaard, S. 15, 131, 174
Klaarhamer, P.J.W. 31, 57
Knegt, J.J. 381
Knoop, Hermanus ... 216, 217, 253-256, 277, 288, 315, 317, 318
Kok, Bernard, ... 336, 389
Kok, William, ... 333
Koopmans, J. 269
Kraemer, Hendrik 34
Kranenburg 282
Kruiswijk, Gerrit 171
Kuiper, A. 166
Kuiper, Henry J. 202, 379

Kuiper, Herman 383
Kuitert, H.M. 383
Kuyper, Abraham . 19-22, 26-29, 32, 33,
  41, 42, 46, 47, 53, 54, 57, 60, 61, 66,
  67, 74, 77, 79-83, 85, 87, 89, 90, 93-
  95, 97- 101, 103-105, 108, 117, 126,
  132, 145, 148, 149, 154, 161, 165,
  166, 171, 176, 190, 195, 197 -199,
  201, 202, 217, 222, 228, 229, 231,
  234, 235, 247, 259, 274, 360, 361,
  410, 411, 416, 417
Kuyper, Abraham Jr. 161, 162
Kuyper Herman H. . 117, 153, 154, 158,
  161, 166, 171, 176, 187, 190, 191,
  195-199, 202-203, 218, 219, 227-
  229, 231, 232, 247, 260-262, 265,
  307- 309, 311, 312
Kuyper-Van Oordt, Hendrika .. 145, 176,
  189
Kuyperianism 28, 38, 41, 98, 145, 151,
  154, 361
Labor Party (of the Netherlands) 33, 34,
  92, 261, 340, 408
Land, J. 399
Landwehr, J.H. 51
Leeuwarden Church Messenger 191
Leiden Church Messenger 242
Lindeboom, C. 134, 135
Lindeboom, Chris G. 129
Lindeboom, Lucas 31
Lohman, A.F. de Savornin 73, 89, 99
Los, S.O. 203
Luther, Martin ... 17, 45, 103, 104, 108,
  109, 184, 297, 332
Maccovius, Johannes 46
Marnix van St. Aldegonde .. 75, 78, 219
Masselink, Evert 363
"medical" approach to church
  reformation 105, 106, 363, 367
Meynen, W.W. 265
Meyster, F.C. 134, 135, 276, 369
Militant Church 37
Miskotte, K.H. 97
Mussert, Anton 171, 249, 324
mysticism 27, 47, 96, 136, 205, 240,
  271
National Reformed: see (*Hervormd*)
Nauta, Doede 297, 300, 377
Nazi movement in the Netherlands . 86,
  131, 153, 171, 174, 175, 187, 190,
  197, 198, 216-218, 225, 227, 231,
  241, 245, 247, 248, 263, 307, 308,
  318, 320, 328, 414
Nelis 294-296
Netelenbos, J.B. . 28-30, 32, 41, 68, 69,
  305, 363
Niemöller, Martin 229-231, 255
Noordmans, O. 97
Norel, K. 360
Noteboom, J.W. 244
Oosterbaan, P. 134
Oosterbeek conferences 348
Orange, House of 75, 76, 78, 86, 88,
  214, 218-220, 238, 248, 256, 261,
  271, 376, 412
Oxford Movement 96, 168
Petter, Andrew 376, 387, 390
philosophy of the law-idea 115, 342,
  343, 345, 346
Polman, A.D.R. 190-192, 330
Popma, S.J. 193, 328, 330
Pos, H.J. 35
Pos, Mary 170
Post, J.S. 199
Pouwelse, W. 394
Praamsma, Louis ... 280, 281, 286, 291,
  315
preaching 16, 17, 31, 45-48, 58, 70, 93,
  99, 101, 102, 115-117, 119, 120, 122,
  124-126, 128, 152, 158, 159, 165,
  180, 184, 188, 197, 204-207, 240,
  268, 292, 293, 298, 329, 334, 338,
  344, 360, 363-365, 407-409
Pro Ecclesia 196, 265, 266
Protestant Reformed Churches 8, 53,
  205, 208, 334, 335, 349, 375, 376,
  382, 384-391, 395-398, 401, 402
Reformed Church in U.S. (German
  Reformed) 394
regeneration . 26, 42, 43, 101, 143, 145,
  288, 331
"Restored Federation" Churches 35-37,
  39, 136, 150
Réveil 77, 166
Ridderbos, Herman 369
Ridderbos, Jan 201, 260, 330, 334, 346,
  356
Ridderbos, N.H. 349
Rietberg 168
Rispens, J.A. 127
Rullmann, J.C. 97, 134
Runner, H. Evan 292, 391

Index

Rutgers, F.L. 89, 99, 294, 415, 416
Rutgers, V. 294
Schelhaas, J. 331
Scheps, N. 191, 233, 279, 331, 391
Scheps, W.C.F. 369
Schilder, Arnold (brother of "KS") . 288, 295
Schilder, Herman J. (nephew of "KS") 288, 419
Schippers, R. 266
scholasticism   41-43, 46, 47, 55, 57, 60, 93, 98, 140, 149
Schouten, J.L. 215
Schuurman, Barend 34, 35, 38, 39
Secession *(Afscheiding)*   10, 17, 29, 32, 35, 38, 60, 61, 77, 86, 95, 97, 102, 103, 106, 136, 143, 159, 166, 190, 194, 199, 211, 234, 309, 317, 329, 360, 418
self-examination ... 43-45, 47, 161, 162, 197
Selles, Lubbertus 9, 388
Severijn, J. 95
Sietsma, K. 255
Sikkel, D. 192,
Sikkel, J.C. .. 31, 48, 51, 57, 61, 73, 85, 89, 93, 157, 162, 318, 418
Smilde, E. 44, 73
Smit, L., 129
Snoep, J. 63
Söderblom, Nathan 96, 97
Spier, J.M. 155, 166
Standard 19, 20, 41, 43, 68, 81, 86, 177, 217, 225, 226
Standard Bearer 207, 208, 386, 389, 390, 392, 399-401
Steen, H. 176, 198
Steinman, G. 286, 287
Storm 266-269
Stufkens, N. 34
Synod of 1905 (Utrecht)   101, 330, 331, 379, 380
Synod of 1908 (Chr. Ref., N.A.)101, 380
Synod of 1914 (The Hague) 53
Synod of 1917 (Rotterdam) 51
Synod of 1920 (Leeuwarden) 29-31, 305
Synod of 1924 (Kalamazoo, Chr. Ref. N.A.) 204, 381ff, 390
Synod of 1926 (Assen) .. 35, 36, 49, 50, 64, 93, 139, 144, 150, 235, 381, 384
Synod of 1933 (Middelburg) 169
Synod of 1936 (Amsterdam) .. 175, 181, 190, 193, 215, 217, 227, 255, 267, 307, 309-312, 318, 328, 384
Synod of 1939-43 (Sneek & Utrecht) 101, 201, 215, 260, 262, 307, 308, 330, 380
Synod of 1943-45 (Utrecht) 285, 287, 327, 328, 330
Synod of 1945 (Enschede, lib. churches) 326
Synod of 1946 (syn. churches) 330ff
Synod of 1946 (Chr. Ref., N.A.) 334, 377
Synod of 1946 (lib. churches) 409
Synod of 1946 (Ref. Ecumenical) ... 379, 380, 391
Synod of 1949 (Chr. Ref., N.A.) 380
Synod of 1950 (Prot. Ref.) 389
Synod of 1951 (Kampen, lib. churches) 352f, 358ff
Synod of 1951 (Prot. Ref.) 389, 398
Synod of 1954 (Can. Ref.) 393
Synod of 1958 (Can. Ref.) 394
Synod of 1959 (Utrecht, syn. churches) 332
Synod of 1962 (Chr. Ref., N.A.) 101, 380, 381
Synod of 1968 (Chr. Ref., N.A.) 108, 381
Synod of 1969 (Chr. Ref., N.A.) 381
Synod of 1972 (Chr. Ref., N.A.) 382
Synod of 1974 (Can. Ref.) 381
Synod of 1977 (Can. Ref.) 382
Synod of 1988 (syn. churches) .. 18, 370
Tazelaar, C. 151, 169, 176, 189
Teeuwen, C.J.W. 167
Telder, B. 47
Telkamp, J.H. 221
Ten Hoor, F.M. 383
Trumpet 50, 109, 119, 160, 181, 188, 251, 362
Truth and Unity 361, 363
Tunderman, J.W. 255, 315
Turkstra, J. 349
"Unaffiliated" *(Buiten-Verband)*
    Reformed churches 17, 353
Utrecht Church Messenger 192, 221
Van 't Veer, M.B. 188, 319
Van Dalen, Willem 171
Van den Bergh, Willem 73
Van den Born, E.T. .. 152, 188, 348, 349

Van den Brink, H.C. 35
Van der Schaft, J. 349
Van der Schuit, J.J. 234
Van der Vaart Smit, H.W.. 48, 134-136, 171, 229, 231, 232, 235, 245, 246, 249, 250, 252-256, 259, 265-271
Van der Vegt, W.H. 183, 190-192
Van der Waal, Cornelis 51, 52, 96, 169
Van der Woude, C. 172
Van Dijk, Douwe 334, 387
Van Dijk, J.J.C. 249
Van Dijk, K. ....
Van Dooren, Gijsbertus 9, 44
Van Gelderen, C. 32, 306
Van Halsema, Emo W.F. . 207, 209, 334
Van Laar, Willem 129
Van Nieuwkoop, J. 276, 277
Van Oord, J. 61
Van Oosterzee, J.J. 327
Van Randwijk, H.M. 33
Van Schelven, B. 31
Van Schelven, C.L.F. 51
Van Schelven, A.A. 217
Van Voort 95
Van Wijk, W.P. 206
Veenhof, C. . 8, 9, 29, 44, 155-157, 188, 298, 301-303, 327-329, 390, 415, 416, 418
Veldkamp, Herman 255, 256, 260
Veldman, Herman 53, 387
Vellenga, IJ.K. 192
Vink, J.A. 223, 224, 255
Visscher, Hugo 95
Visser, 't Hooft, W.A. 97
Voetius, G. 46, 49
Volbeda, Samuel 383
Vollenhoven, D.H.T. 61, 115, 120, 176, 196, 202, 266, 342, 343
Vondel 75, 76, 272
Vonk, C. 188, 288, 326
Vonkenberg, J.E. 20, 22, 23, 25, 31, 58-67, 85, 103
Vreugdenhil, Maarten 211, 363
Wachter 163, 205
Watchman (De Wachter, N.A. periodical), 205
Watchman (Dutch periodical), 155, 163, 168, 294
Watchtower (South African periodical) 178

Waterink, Jan. 145, 146, 151, 169, 176, 189, 198
Weatherhead, Leslie 96-98, 102, 168
Weidenaar, J. 205, 206
Wielenga, B. 134-136, 200
Wielenga, D.K. 292, 326
Wielenga, J.D. 190
Wiersinga 35
Wiersinga, H.A. 154, 172, 242
Winckel, W.F.A. 94
Wisse, G. 112, 143, 144
Woltjer, R.H. 35, 89
Word and Spirit 35, 36, 39, 136, 177
Zemel, D. 153, 154
Zevenbergen, Willem 35, 188
Zeydner, W.A. 37
Zijlstra, A. 263
Zwart, Jan 128
Zwier, D. 163, 206

R.B. A Prophet in the Land by Edward Heerema
A biography of Rienk Bouke Kuiper, Preacher - Theologian - Churchman.
P.Y. De Jong: This book had to appear. It is well written. It makes R.B. come alive. It reminds the reader of the tremendous impact which his life and labors have made on the Reformed community.
Subject: Biography   Age: 14-99
ISBN 0-88815-054-7   Can.$9.95 U.S.$8.90

The Church in the Twentieth Century by L. Praamsma

The Church in the world — that's the central theme of this stimulating survey of the fortunes of God's people in the twentieth century. Dr. Praamsma shows that our world is in turmoil; he highlights the warfare, upheaval, revolution, political confusion, and moral degeneration. The Church stands in the midst of this turmoil with a message of hope and redemption.
Time: 1900-1975   Age: 13-99
ISBN 0-88815-041-5   Can.$14.95 U.S.$12.90

The Church Preserved Through Fires by S.G. Hur
A History of the Presbyterian Church in Korea
Rev. G. Van Rongen wrote: This book was written by the right person. Dr. Hur became the minister of the Korean Presbyterian Church of Sumoonlo on November 14, 1962. He must have had some special interest in Church history. It was therefore not strange that in the year 1970 he was appointed as professor of Church History at the Korea Theological Seminary at Busan.
Time: 1860-2000   Age:15-99
ISBN 1-894666-78-x   Can.$17.95 U.S.$15.90

A Theatre in Dachau by Hermanus Knoop
In the concentration camp of Dachau the God of all grace did wonders of grace by His Word and Spirit every day. Oh, it was indeed a dreadful time for me that I spent there, and yet it is not at all a hollow phrase when I say that I would for no amount of money have missed this time of my life, since it was so unspeakably rich in grace. I saw God there. The LORD was in this place. It was a house of God and a gate of heaven.
Time: 1940-1943   Age: 14-99
ISBN 0-921100-20-5   Can.$14.95 U.S.$12.90

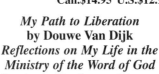

My Path to Liberation by Douwe Van Dijk
Reflections on My Life in the Ministry of the Word of God

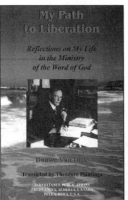

J. Bruning in *Una Sancta* of August 7, 2004: . . . In short, Rev van Dijk provides you with a realistic picture of the Church and its struggles, and encouragement to deal with current issues in a Scriptural and Church orderly manner. . . . I learned much from this book. Although written in a personal and easy style, it is a treasure for (future) office bearers and very educational for all who love the church. From time to time we hear the phrase "we have a rich Reformed heritage". This book definitely conveys some aspects of this heritage and will enrich you; it will also arm you.
Time: 1890-1960   Age: 16-99
ISBN 0-921100-26-4   Can.$19.95 U.S.$16.90

Is the Bible a Jigsaw Puzzle . . .
by T. Boersma

An Evaluation of Hal Lindsey's Writings. Is Lindsey's "jigsaw puzzle" approach the proper way to read Scripture? Was the Bible written to foretell the events of our decade?
Subject: Book of Revelation　　　　　　　　　　　　Age: 16-99
ISBN 0-88815-019-9　　　　　　　　　　　　Can.$7.95　U.S.$6.90

Annotations to the Heidelberg Catechism
by J. Van Bruggen

John A. Hawthorne in *Reformed Theological Journal*: . . . The individual Christian would find it a constructive way to employ part of the Sabbath day by working through the lesson that is set for each Lord's Day. No one can study this volume without increasing his knowledge of truth and being made to worship and adore the God of all grace. This book will help every minister in the instruction of his people, both young and not so young, every parent in the task of catechizing and is commended to every Christian for personal study.
Subject: Catechism　　　　　　　　　　　Age: 13-99
ISBN 0-921100-33-7　　　　　　Can.$15.95　U.S.$13.90

Before the Face of God
by Louis Praamsma

A Study of the Heidelberg Catechism in two workbooks for catechism students.
Subject: Catechism　　　　　　　　　　　　　　　Age: 10-99
Lords Day 1-24　ISBN 0-88815-056-3　　Can.$11.95　U.S.$9.90
Lords Day 25-52　ISBN 0-88815-057-1　　Can.$11.95　U.S.$9.90

The Church Says Amen
by J. Van Bruggen
An Exposition of the Belgic Confession

We need to stand on the shoulders of those who have gone before us, to learn how they applied God's promises in the grit and grime of life's struggles . . .
— from the *Preface* by C. Bouwman

W.L. Bredenhof in *Clarion*: This would be an excellent book for the use of study societies, for individual refreshment on the doctrines of the church, or as a textbook for preconfession or adult education.
Subject: Belgic Confession　　　　　　　　　Age: 13-99
ISBN 0-921100-17-5　　　　　　Can.$15.95　U.S.$13.90

The Belgic Confession and its Biblical Basis
by Lepusculus Vallensis

The Belgic Confession is a Reformed Confession, dating from the 16th Century, written by Guido de Brès, a preacher in the Reformed Churches of The Netherlands. The great synod of Dort in 1618-19 adopted this Confession as one of the doctrinal standards of the Reformed Churches, to which all office-bearers of the Churches were (and still are) to subscribe. This book provides and explains the Scriptural proof texts for the Belgic Confession by using the marginal notes of the Dutch *Staten Bijbel*. The *Staten Bijbel* is a Dutch translation of the Bible, by order of the States General of the United Netherlands, in accordance with a decree of the Synod of Dort. It was first published in 1637 and included 'new explanations of difficult passages and annotations to comparative texts.'

Subject: Creeds
ISBN 0-921100-41-8
Age: 15-99
Can.$17.95 U.S.$15.90

The Church: Its Unity in Confession and History
by G. Van Rongen

"The planet on which we live is becoming smaller and smaller. It seems as if it is no longer true that the East is far from the West. Distances are shrinking. At the same time, our world of interest is becoming larger and larger. What is happening on the other side of the globe can be watched as it happens.

"In the field of church life, too, this process of shrinkage and expansion is going on. These modern times have brought us into contact with other churches which we had hardly ever heard of a few decades ago. After the war, our immigrant churches went through a period in which we settled into a new country and had to build up our church life from scratch. Now, however, we are able to have closer contact with our ecclesiastical environment and have discovered some of these churches.

"This has raised the question: How are these other churches to be regarded? Must we, with a good conscience, leave them alone? Or, knowing that Christ wants His Church to be one, ought we to initiate dialogue with them? This is why our immigrant churches in various countries have been involved, sometimes for many years, in discussions with other churches."

Subject: History / Doctrine
ISBN 0-921100-90-6
Age: 13-99
Can.$14.95 U.S.$12.90

Christian Faith in Focus
by Gordon Spykman

This book is designed to serve the Christian Community as a study guide for personal enrichment and group discussions. Each of the thirty-two chapters is introduced by a pertinent Scripture passage, followed by brief explanations, leading up to questions which act as pump-primers for a free exchange of ideas.

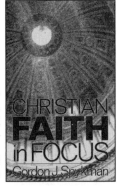

Subject: Theology / Chr. Life
ISBN 0-88815-053-9
Age: 16-99
Can.$9.95 U.S.$8.90

Books on Church History

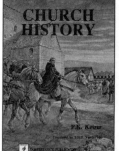

Church History by P.K. Keizer

Mary Pride in *The Big Book of Home Learning, vol. 3*: [Keizer] . . . neither overloads the student nor skips over anything important . . . The writing is interesting and pious — from a solidly Reformed Protestant viewpoint — and does the teenager the great service of distilling the lives and teachings of many important people in a form he can remember . . . An excellent resource.

Time: A.D. 33-1970   Age: 13-99
ISBN 0-921100-02-7   Can.$12.95 U.S.$11.90

The Romance of Protestantism
by Deborah Alcock

The Romance of Protestantism addresses one of the most damaging and (historically) effective slanders against the Reformed faith, which is that it is cold and doctrinaire. What a delight to find a book which documents the true warmth of the Protestant soul. I recommend this book highly.
— Douglas Wilson, editor of *Credenda/Agenda*

Time: 1300-1700   Age: 12-99
ISBN 0-921100-88-4   Can.$ 11.95 U.S.$ 9.90

Christian England by David L. Edwards
Its Story to the Reformation

Time: A.D. 360-1540   Age: 16-99
ISBN 0-19-520229-5   Can.$16.95 U.S.$12.95

John Calvin: Genius of Geneva
by Lawrence Penning
A Popular Account of the Life and Times of John Calvin

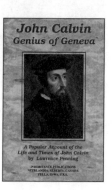

Penning shows the Life of Calvin against the turbulence, religious unrest, and intellectual ferment of the times, when Europe stormed with Reformation and Counter Reformation, and traces the incredible full life and work of the man who was not only the greatest of the of the sixteenth century Reformers, but who was the greatest man of his age. Here we see too, the man Calvin: a man of infinite tenderness as well as of great temper; one who despised money for himself, but who thought it very important when counseling a friend entertaining thoughts of marriage.

Time: 1509-1564   Age:15-99
ISBN 1-894666-77-1   Can.$19.95 U.S.$16.90

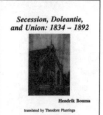

Secession, Doleantie, and Union 1834 - 1892
by Hendrik Bouma

. . . Bouma the story-teller charms us with a moving story about ecumenicity's outward, public side. . . In good Dutch Reformed style, Rev. Bouma wants things out in the open.
— From the *Introduction* by Nelson D. Kloosterman

Subject: Church History   Age: 14-99
ISBN 0-921100-36-1   Can.$15.95 U.S.$13.90

Christians in Babel by Egbert Schuurman

There was a time when people spoke of a Christian culture. That term is now meaningless. From a biblical point of view our culture can probably be identified as Babylonian. Here man worships various gods as he builds whatever his science and technology enable him to build.

Subject: Church and World   Age: 16-99
ISBN 0-88815-062-8   Can.$4.95   U.S.$3.90

A Christian Union in Labour's Wasteland
Edited by Edward Vanderkloet

Seven essays dealing with relationship of Christianity and labour in our industrial culture.

Subject: Christian Labour Association of Canada   Age: 16-99
ISBN 0-88906-101-7   Can.$4.95   U.S.$3.90

At Work and Play by Bradshaw L. Frey, William E. Ingram, Thomas E. McWhertor, & William David Romanowski
Biblical Insight for Daily Obedience

". . . seeks to show students in secular universities how to achieve an integrity that is both academically and Christianly authentic. I have not seen a better tool for the purpose." —J.I. Packer

Subject: Christian Life of Students   Age: 16-99
ISBN 0-88815-154-3   Can.$6.95   U.S.$5.90

Labour of Love - Essays on Work
by Harry Antonides and others

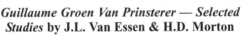

Essays dealing with relationship of Christianity and labour in our industrial culture.

Subject: Christian Labour Association of Canada   Age: 16-99
ISBN 0-88906-107-6   Can.$4.95   U.S.$3.90

Guillaume Groen Van Prinsterer — Selected Studies by J.L. Van Essen & H.D. Morton

Essays on God's Hand in History; A Christian Heroism; The Struggle for Freedom of Education; etc.

Subject: Christian Education in History   Age: 16-99
ISBN 0-88906-019-3   Can.$13.95   U.S.$11.90

Johannes C. Sikkel: A Pioneer in Social Reform by R.H. Bremmer

To use Sikkel's words, "We Christians have the calling to proceed, to explore the way, if possible to clear the way, and in love to bring to our fellowmen the witness to the way of God. We Christians must believe that God lives, and that His grace is able to triumph over the spirit of evil. And in faith and with zeal, we must prayerfully look to the victory."

Time: 1856-1920   Age: 14-99
ISBN 0-921100-89-2   Can.$6.95   U.S.$5.90

Seeking Our Brothers in the Light: A Plea for Reformed Ecumenicity - Edited by Theodore Plantinga

Al Bezuyen in *Revival*: The book should well serve office bearers and lay people interested in closer contact with the liberated Churches. The work is not exhaustive but rather functions as a spring board from which further study can find a solid beginning and seeks to clear the water that must be entered if ecumenical relations are to take place between the CRC and American / Canadian Reformed Churches.

Subject: Ecclesiastical Unity / History   Age: 15-99
ISBN 0-921100-48-5   Can.$7.95   U.S.$6.90

Books on Reformed Doctrine & Theology

Covenant and Election by Dr. J. Van Genderen

All the commands and prohibitions of the Decalogue flow out of the covenant relation: "I am the LORD your God." That is the prologue to the entire law (Calvin). God thereby declares that He is the God of the Church. In light of these words the Reformer of Geneva expounds both the Ten Commandments as well as the summary of the law. For Calvin the law is the law of the covenant of grace. It is a confirmation of the covenant made with Abraham. Even though the law serves to bring out transgressions (Galatians 3:19) it is clothed with the covenant of grace (the covenant of God's gracious acceptance).
— from the book

Subject: Covenant Theology Age: 16-99
ISBN 0-921100-60-4 Can.$11.95 U.S.$10.90

Always Obedient — Essays on the Teachings of Dr. Klaas Schilder; Edited by J. Geertsema

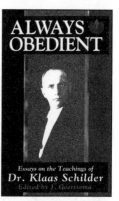

"It is a delight to be Reformed," wrote Dutch theologian Klaas Schilder (1890-1952), a man whose life and work demonstrated unwavering loyalty to biblical authority. While parting with Abraham Kuyper on some issues, Schilder shared Kuyper's conviction that "there is not an inch of human life about which Christ, who is Sovereign over all, does not proclaim, 'Mine.' "

Subject: Theology Age: 16-99
ISBN 0-87552-239-4 Can.$15.95 U.S.$10.99

American Secession Theologians on Covenant and Baptism by Jelle Faber & Extra-Scriptural Binding — A New Danger by Klaas Schilder

Jelle Tuininga in *Christian Renewal*: . . . The main purpose of Schilder was to dissuade and discourage Hoeksema (and the Prot. Ref. Churches) from adopting the so-called Brief Declaration. Schilder saw this, correctly I believe, as an "extra Scriptural binding" which would only lead to separate church federations instead of unity. . . I am happy that the publisher has made these essays available in English to a larger audience. The more so, because they deal with important issues which are now coming to the surface again. We must be informed on such salient points.

Subject: Church History / Theology Age: 16-99
ISBN 0-921100-46-9 Can.$13.95 U.S.$11.90

Essays in Reformed Doctrine by J. Faber

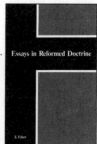

Cecil Tuininga in *Christian Renewal*: This book is easy reading as far as the English goes. It can, I judge, be read by all with great profit. . . I found the first chapter on *The Significance of Dogmatology for the Training of the Ministry* excellent. The six essays on the Church I found very informative and worthwhile. . . What makes this book so valuable is that Dr. Faber deals with all the aspects of the Reformed faith from a strictly biblical and confessional viewpoint.

Subject: Theology / History Age: 18-99
ISBN 0-921100-28-0 Can.$19.95 U.S.$17.90

A Sign of Faithfulness by H. Westerink

H. Westerink's book on Baptism is a jewel. One seldom comes across a book that simultaneously matches such simplicity to profundity, and vice versa. The author excels at clarifying the marvellous continuity (and discontinuity) between the old and new covenant with respect to the question of baptism — infant baptism in particular. — J. Mark Beach

Subject: Covenant / Baptism **Age: 12-99**
ISBN 0-921100-00-0 **Can.$9.95 U.S.$8.90**

Christian Day Schools - Why and How by D.L. Kranendonk

This book is an attempt to show that there is a Christian alternative view of life that can give us an understanding of the fundamental problems of education.

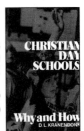

Subject: Education **Age: 18-99**
ISBN 0-88815-016-4 **Can.$6.95 U.S.$6.30**

Rationale for a Christian College by Theodore Plantinga

To discuss the idea of a Christian college is to think about both "curriculum" and "community." This short book is a down-to-earth exposition of the plan for a Christian college.

Subject: Education **Age: 18-99**
ISBN 0-88815-084-9 **Can.$5.95 U.S.$5.40**

Preaching With Confidence by James Daane
A Theological Essay on the Power of the Pulpit

Speaking the Word of God confidently is the obligation of the preacher, insists James Daane, for the Word is not merely advisory; it is efficacious. When God speaks, the world does more than listen — it changes.

Subject: Preaching **Age: 12-99**
ISBN 0-8028-1825-0 **Can.$6.95 U.S.$5.90**

Calvin: Commentaries
(Topical Selection by Joseph Haroutunian)

This volume, demonstrating the main elements of Calvin's doctrine as they appear in his many commentaries on the books of the Old and New Testaments, speaks with singular power to the ordinary reader today. Included are more than two hundred selections under headings ranging from the Bible, knowledge of God, and Jesus Christ to the Christian life, election and predestination, and the church.

Subject: Doctrines **Age: 12-99**
ISBN 0-664-24160-3 **Can.$13.90 U.S.$11.90**

Separation of Church and State by Norman De Jong & Jack Van der Silk

Since World War II Americans have increasingly come to believe in separation of church and state, yet the majority also want prayer in the public schools and a return to traditional religious values. The authors demonstrate numerous inextricable links which bound church and state together.

Subject: Christian Politics **Age: 14-99**
ISBN 0-88815-063-6 **Can.$9.95 U.S.$8.90**

Music Book & Compact Discs on the Genevan Psalms

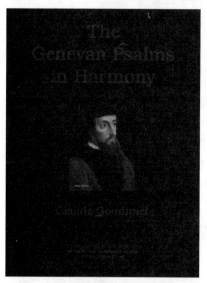

The Genevan Psalms in Harmony
by Claude Goudimel

This book is ideal for churches, organists, choirs, and Christian families. Approximately 450 4-part settings of the Psalms. The melody is both in a Soprano and a Tenor setting, and all the stanzas of the Psalms from the *Book of Praise* are included.
ISBN 1-894666-66-6   Can.$ 59.95 U.S.$ 49.90
(15% discount for 6 or more copies!)

Theresa Janssen Plays the Genevan Psalms of Claude Goudimel for you to sing along
(or play along on your favourite solo instrument)

An ideal set of 4 Compact Discs for those who want to learn to sing the Genevan Psalms by heart. Each of the 150 Psalms is played twice, once with the melody in the Soprano and once with the melody in the Tenor. The organ registrations (of the organs at West End Christian Reformed Church, Robertson-Wesley United Church, and Grace Lutheran Church in Edmonton, Alberta) used for each of the Psalms are available at http://www.telusplanet.net/public/inhpubl/Goudimel.htm which can be of great help for (young) organists.
4 Compact Discs CMR 109-112   Can.$ 40.00 U.S.$34.00

Great is the Lord! Him Greatly Laud
The Odé Ensemble Sings Anglo-Genevan Psalms of Claude Goudimel

Annelize Viljoen, soprano;
Helga Schabort & Philna Badenhorst, altos;
Antonie Fourie, tenor; Eric Kayayan, bass.
(The sheet music of this C.D. is published in *The Genevan Psalms in Harmony* by Claude Goudimel.)

Psalm 65:1 & 6; Psalm 38:1 & 10; Psalm 9:1 & 6; Psalm 28:1 & 5; Psalm 13:1 & 3; Psalm 43:1 & 5; Psalm 45:1 & 6; Psalm 37:1 & 5; Psalm 54:1 & 3; Psalm 32:1 & 5; Psalm 2:1 & 4; Psalm 40:1 & 7; Psalm 46:1 & 5; Psalm 62:1 & 6; Psalm 53:1 & 5; Psalm 17:1 & 5; Psalm 50:1 & 11; Psalm 34:1 & 7; Psalm 11:1 & 2; Psalm 41:1 & 4; Psalm 57:1 & 5; Psalm 59:1 & 8; Psalm 10:1 & 7; Psalm 26:1 & 7; Psalm 33:1 & 6; Psalm 48:1 & 4.
Compact Disc CMR 108-2   Can. $21.99 U.S.$ 18.99